Family Cookbook

Family Cookbook

Caroline Bretherton

LONDON, NEW YORK,
MUNICH, MELBOURNE, DELHI

Senior Editor Scarlett O'Hara
Senior Art Editor Sara Robin
Editor Lucy Bannell
US Senior Editor Rebecca Warren
US Editor Christy Lusiak
US Consultant Kate Curnes Ramos
Managing Editor Dawn Henderson
Managing Art Editor Christine Keilty
Senior Jacket Creative Nicola Powling
Jackets Assistant Rosie Levine
Producer, Pre-Production Sarah Isle
Senior Producer Oliver Jeffreys
Creative Technical Support Sonia Charbonnier
Art Director Peter Luff
Publishing Manager Anna Davidson
Publisher Peggy Vance

DK INDIA
Senior Editor Dorothy Kikon
Senior Art Editor Ivy Roy
Editor Arani Sinha
Art Editor Simran Kaur
Assistant Art Editors Karan Chaudhary, Gazal Roongta
Managing Editor Alicia Ingty
Managing Art Editor Navidita Thapa
Pre-Production Manager Sunil Sharma
DTP Designers Sourabh Challariya, Umesh Singh Rawat

First American Edition, 2013
Published in the United States by
DK Publishing, 4th Floor, 345 Hudson Street, New York 10014

13 14 15 16 17 10 9 8 7 6 5 4 3 2 1
192157 – Oct/2013

Contents

How to use this book

This family cookbook has six chapters of recipes: purées and food for **Babies and Toddlers**, options for healthy **Family Meals**, **Easy Entertaining** ideas for when you need to produce something special, suggestions for **Food to Go** for packed lunches or family picnics, much-loved and easy-to-achieve cookies, cakes, and breads in **Baking**, and a **Cooking with Kids** section, with step-by-step recipes children can cook for themselves. There are also useful features tackling subjects such as Kids' Parties, Picky Kids and Teenagers, and Batching and Freezing. **Recipe Choosers** give an inspiring selection of dishes from the book on themes such as Pantry Meals, Quick Breads and Desserts, and Cheap Eats.

The Chapters

Babies and Toddlers

This section has been specially compiled to provide a range of healthy recipes to take your baby from simple first tastes through to more complex meals and finger foods. All the choices here are healthy and balanced and the texture of all of them can be adjusted to suit the weaning stage of your baby.

Family Meals

This chapter is subdivided into sections including fish, poultry, meat, vegetables, pasta, rice, and eggs and cheese. Each section begins with appetizers, soups, and salads before

Delicious dishes such as Braised lamb with spring vegetables (p135) fill the Family Meals chapter, many with variations, tips on how to prepare ahead, or suggestions for making the most of leftovers.

If you're entertaining you will want to create something special. This Mediterranean chicken (p106) makes an impressive dish that tends to go over well with adults and children alike.

progressing into suggestions for main courses. The vegetable section includes main course vegetarian options, as well as soups, salads, and sides. All the meals are designed to appeal to a growing family with plenty of new twists on family favorites as well as recipes that give more economical items such as pasta, rice, eggs, and cheese a starring role.

Easy Entertaining

Entertaining another family for lunch, friends for dinner, or catering for a larger number of people at a celebration, demands a little more from your culinary skills. Catering for all ages and tastes can be demanding, but with some planning and preparation it needn't be stressful. In this chapter you will find brunch options, barbecue recipes, a mouthwatering array of desserts, and lots of inspiration for hot and cold fun snacks and treats for kids' parties, including birthday cakes.

Food to Go

Whether you are preparing a summer picnic with the family, or simply looking for inspiration for the children's lunchboxes, this chapter will help. Everyday sandwiches are turned into interesting and tasty fare to eat on the go, and there are recipes for delicious wraps, salads, side dishes, and baked goods that are all easy to transport.

Baking

Baking is probably the most family-friendly activity you can try in the kitchen, so here you will find many simple recipes that are easy to prepare. As well as the familiar cakes and cookies, there are delicious recipes for savory bakes and simple breads to extend your baking repertoire. Seasoned bakers will find some fresh and exciting ideas here with inspiration from around the world, as well as some tried-and-tested classics.

Cooking with Kids

We all want our children to grow up eating well, so it's a good idea to introduce them to cooking as soon as possible. Children who have helped to prepare a meal are far more likely to eat it, after all. All the recipes included here are ideal for children to cook and most are accompanied by helpful step-by-step photography to guide you while you supervise your young chefs. There are recipes for children to make for their own parties, healthy meals they could serve to the family, and items that they could make and give as gifts.

Feature pages

Scattered throughout the book are feature pages that include handy tips for common situations that arise in the family kitchen. So, there is a feature on coping with Picky Eaters, managing After School, and feeding Picky Kids and Teenagers. There is advice on Smart Shopping, and The Hardworking Fridge, suggestions for being Smart with Leftovers, providing Meals for a Week, and Batching and Freezing. There are also tips on feeding Vegetarian Kids, Cooking for Allergies, dealing with Unexpected Guests, and hosting Kids' Parties.

The Recipes

Information boxes A really helpful feature of this book is the extra guidance given after many recipes on how to freeze or batch cooking, with suggestions on what to prepare ahead, and tips on being clever with leftovers. There is also advice on adapting meals for fussy eaters, or highlighting meals that might appeal to them, plus notes on cooking for a crowd, as well as many other handy cook's tips.

Icons These appear at the top of every recipe and advise on preparation and cooking times, and highlight recipes that are vegetarian or freezable.

Special equipment Any special equipment you will need for a specific recipe, such as a food processor or hand-held blender, will be listed at the beginning of the recipe. Check if any items are listed so that you can gather together your equipment before you start cooking.

Nutrition boxes All recipes have a breakdown of the amounts of key nutrients, including saturated fat, contained in one serving. If the recipe says that it serves six, then the breakdown is for one sixth of the total recipe. Nutrition boxes in the Babies and Toddlers chapter give amounts of iron and calcium rather than saturated fat.

Variations Many recipes have suggestions for a variation to provide a new twist on the recipe or ideas on how to alter the ingredients to satisfy different palates.

Cook smart

Feeding a family can be challenging when you are trying to cater to different tastes and various schedules, while providing well-balanced, tasty meals. As well as offering fresh ideas for family meals alongside some tried-and-trusted favorites, this book aims to make this process more streamlined so that your time in the kitchen is spent wisely, producing, where possible, one meal for all and making good use of leftovers, as well as batching and freezing, and preparing ahead.

One meal for all

All too often home cooks end up preparing more than one meal every night—either because each family member likes different things or because they come home at various times. Cooking just one meal for everyone to share means less time spent in the kitchen and more with the family—and this ideal is not impossible to achieve. Throughout this book, there are suggestions for preparing parts of meals ahead, adapting recipes to suit different tastes (from adding spices to producing a vegetarian option), as well as recipes that are ideal for reheating as and when family members make their way through the door. Don't ditch the leftovers before reading the ideas on how to rework them into the next day's meal, and many recipes also include a variation, so that you can try a new twist on an old favorite—an easy way to change things up.

Spanish tortilla (p248) makes a nutritious meal with green beans or broccoli. Save the leftovers to eat the following day packed in lunch boxes or with a tomato salad.

Spicy sausage casserole (p147) is easy to adapt for different tastes. Adjust the spiciness or add vegetables to make the dish go further. Serve with plenty of mashed potatoes for hungry teens.

Plan ahead

To save time, trouble, and money, it makes sense to be smart about the amount of time you spend in the kitchen. Planning weekly meals, or at least weekly shopping lists, means you make the most of the food you have in the fridge and freezer, and avoid getting stuck with nothing to eat on a busy day. When you know the family's schedule for the week, you can plan around it. It's easier when everyone will be at home and eating together, but there will also be days when people will require meals at different times. Try to plan ahead by cooking extra food one day so there is more for another day, or making sure that, when schedules differ, you have an easy one-pot dish simmering away that you can reheat as needed. Don't forget your leftovers—roasted meats can be included in another dish such as a curry or pilaf, enjoyed again as part of a tasty wrap in a packed lunch, or as part of a children's party.

Batch and freeze

Multiplying the quantities of ingredients to cook twice or three times the amount of a recipe is an easy way to get ahead in the kitchen. Certain foods really lend themselves to cooking in bulk and freezing in portions; any recipe using chicken leg or thigh portions, for example, is easier to freeze than one using a whole chicken, while dishes with plenty of liquid, such as soups or stews, tend to freeze better than drier ones. All the recipes in this book that are suitable for freezing are labeled with freezer symbols, so look out for those to make planning ahead even easier.

Freezing food is a safe and easy way to preserve it for another day, but do make sure the food is properly stored in heavy-duty freezer bags or airtight, lidded, freezerproof containers. If food is badly wrapped and exposed to the air in the freezer, it can become dry and discolored due to "freezer burn" and will have to be discarded. Remember to label containers clearly, with the contents and the date on which it was frozen, to help you use frozen food in rotation and ensure it is not left in the freezer too long. Defrosting frozen food is best done slowly, overnight, in the fridge, and once defrosted the food should never be refrozen.

Store food safely

Few of us have time to go shopping every day, so it is important to think carefully about how you store food as well as how you cook it. To avoid possible contamination, check the temperatures of your fridge and freezer; the fridge should be set to between 37°F (3°C) and 41°F (5°C), and the freezer to at least 0°F (-18°C). A build-up of ice can affect the temperature of either appliance, so be sure to defrost them regularly.

Wrap well all produce that is to be stored in the fridge, especially meats, fish, dairy, and liquids, to prevent leaking or spillages. Always store raw and cooked products on separate shelves, with raw meats on the bottom shelf, to prevent cross-contamination. Don't leave cooked rice standing at room temperature for too long, serve it immediately. If you are storing leftover cooked rice or pasta, make sure it has been cooked and then cooled as quickly as possible before being placed in an airtight container in the fridge. Don't keep it for more than one day before reheating. Don't reheat it again. Eat other pre-cooked food within two days of placing it in the fridge. If you are leaving meat to marinate, always put it in a non-reactive (non-metal) dish, to avoid a chemical reaction with the food that will taint its flavor and make it inedible.

Freezing times

Although most foods can be frozen, the appearance, texture, and quality of some foods deteriorates more quickly than others, even in the freezer. Label items with the date they were frozen and stick to these simple guidelines for safe freezing.

Raw poultry, fish, and meat (in small pieces) – up to 6 months

Raw ground beef or poultry – up to 3 months

Soups – up to 3 months

Stocks – up to 6 months

Stews and casseroles – up to 3 months

Pies and pastries, uncooked – up to 3 months

Pies and pastries, cooked – up to 6 months

Fruit, raw – up to 1 year *

Fruit, cooked – up to 9 months*

Vegetables, blanched – up to 9 months*

Vegetables, cooked – up to 9 months*

Butter – up to 3 months

Cheese, grated – up to 4 months

Bread – up to 3 months

* The exact length of time for which these can be frozen depends on the fruit or vegetable itself, and how it is prepared. Those with a lower water content tend to freeze better and last longer, too.

Get the kids involved

Encouraging your children to help out in the kitchen from an early age not only gives them the skills to cook for themselves, but it also helps to expand their culinary horizons and makes it more likely that they will experiment with food and try new ingredients. Trying out the recipes here will help them learn more about what goes into a healthy balanced meal made with fresh ingredients. Get small children involved with everything from setting the table to helping with simple baking, while older children and teenagers can be let loose in the kitchen to create dinner from scratch with only a little help from their parents. If you can overlook the mess and offer plenty of praise (along with only a little constructive criticism!) you may see them return to cook again another day.

Eat well

Ensuring that each member of your family has a varied, nutritious diet is not always easy. With the different ages and stages of a family, from growing babies and toddlers to less-active adults, there are different nutritional needs to consider. Young children benefit from the calcium richness of full-fat dairy products, for example, whereas most older children and adults would be advised to consume the low-fat equivalents.

Keep it balanced

A balanced diet for the whole family should include protein, carbohydrate, and healthy fats, as well as a full array of vitamins and minerals. Protein, a nutrient needed for growth and repair, is found in meat, poultry, fish, and seafood, as well as nuts, beans, seeds, and eggs. Vegetarian sources also include tofu and quinoa. Some cuts of meat can be high in saturated fat, so you might want to vary the sources of protein in your diet.

Carbohydrates are nutrients that provide energy. They are found in many sources, from wholegrain bread to sugar and fruit, so choose the sources that are better for you. Complex carbohydrates, such as whole grains, beans, and starchy vegetables, release sugar more slowly into the bloodstream, providing energy but avoiding the highs and lows that are associated with consuming simple carbohydrates, such as refined white flour and sugar.

A balanced meal includes a lean source of protein, carbohydrate, and lots of colorful, tasty vegetables. Baked fish with cherry tomatoes (p75) is a great example of a healthy family meal.

A healthy breakfast such as Granola (p268) makes an excellent start to the day, and keeps you and your family feeling full for longer. A breakfast like this means you are less likely to reach for sugary snacks.

A healthy breakfast of homemade oatmeal, granola, or whole wheat cereal, for example, will release its energy over a longer period and leave you and your family less hungry than grabbing a slice of white toast, a sugary breakfast cereal, or a sweet drink would do.

It's sometimes easy to think that fats are the enemy but this is not the case. In fact, our bodies need a source of healthy fat to provide energy and protect the heart, among other things. Good fats, such as monosaturated or polyunsaturated fat, are found in olive oil, sunflower oil, nuts, seeds, avocados, and fatty fish such as salmon or tuna. The types of fats to be avoided are saturated fats—found in some cuts of red meat, poultry skin, and full-fat dairy products—and also trans fats, which are found in many commercially made baked goods, snack foods, and fried foods.

Make it colorful

Our bodies need a vast array of vitamins and minerals to flourish, some in tiny quantities, some in greater ones. One of the easiest ways to ensure that your family's diet is vitamin- and mineral-rich is to include vegetables in a wide variety of colors. Red, orange, and green fruits and vegetables, tend to be rich in vitamins. Vitamin C, which boosts your immune system and helps your body fight off viruses, can be found in kiwis, strawberries, and bell peppers as well as oranges. Dark green, leafy vegetables such as spinach, greens, and kale are rich in many vitamins and minerals including vitamin C, iron for the healthy function of red blood cells, and calcium for the formation of strong bones and teeth.

Different needs

Cooking for the diverse nutritional needs in a family can be tricky, but it does not have to be impossible. Buying both whole- and low-fat milk for example, is an easy way to ensure both young children and adults are catered for. Growing teenagers will often need extra energy, so stock up on whole grain muffins, breads, and bananas and allow them to snack between meals on these healthy complex carbohydrates, which will release sugars more slowly into the bloodstream and keep them fuller for longer.

If you are trying to lose weight, avoid "finishing off" the children's party food—snacking on leftovers often means you have no real idea how many calories you have consumed. The whole family will benefit from a diet rich in fruits and vegetables, so start making breakfast smoothies on the weekend and check the vegetable section of the Family Meals chapter for vegetable-based recipes that the whole family will enjoy. Too much salt is not good for anyone, so try using powdered stocks and spices instead to add flavor to a meal and use good quality sea salt sparingly at the table, where it will have the most impact.

There are a few recipes, such as Quick chocolate mousse (p360) or Hollandaise sauce for the Eggs Benedict (p254) that contain raw or undercooked eggs. For these recipes, only the freshest eggs should be used, and pregnant women, young children, and the elderly should avoid these dishes altogether.

Portion caution

From the time children first move on to solid foods, it is easy to overestimate how much they will eat. When your child is very small, be led by them, and if you are concerned that they are not eating enough, cut back on snacks between meals and make sure they are not consuming sugary fruit juices that fill them up. It is often better to offer small children a few different things on their plate than expect them to make their way through a pile of pasta, which can leave them feeling overwhelmed. Try dishing up a small serving of protein, one of carbohydrate, and a couple of vegetable choices instead. By contrast, older teenagers, especially active ones, will often need second helpings (or even thirds) as they continue to grow. Toast or cereal can often be a good filler here, but make sure that the choices available are from healthy, complex carbohydrates such as whole grains or pulses.

When serving adult portions, a good rule of thumb is to choose a medium-sized plate. Don't load up the plate and make sure that half your serving is made up of fruit or vegetables, a quarter with a low-fat source of protein, and a quarter with some complex carbohydrate.

Choose good food

Beyond the basics of making sure that your family gets a balanced diet, there is the issue of the sources of that diet to consider. If you want to use organic ingredients but are limited by the cost, choose organic meat, eggs, and milk. Factory-farmed eggs and chicken are cheaper, but may not be as nutrient-rich as free-range or organic equivalents. If you choose to shop for free range or organic products, eat either cheaper cuts of meat (chicken legs or thighs rather than breasts, for example) or eat meat less often. In this case, you may need to expand your repertoire of dishes to come up with the best recipe for that cheaper cut, cook dishes that include protein in different forms such as beans and eggs, and start thinking about how to make the most of your leftovers.

Over-fishing has led to a marked decrease in the populations of a variety of fish and seafood, and it is wise to choose to eat only sustainable varieties. Check the labels of what you buy and speak to your fishmonger. There are new varieties of fish available that make a good alternative to old favorites.

Stay healthy

Picky children or teenagers whose diets are restricted due to choice may benefit from a specially formulated multivitamin. If you are concerned that someone in your family isn't getting the full array of nutrients they need for a healthy diet, it would be wise to consult a health professional.

Recipe choosers

Pantry meals

A well-stocked pantry containing canned beans or fish can be the source of balanced, nutritious meals for the family, with the addition of only a few fresh items from the fridge or freezer.

Cheesy soufflé omelet page 248

 5 mins   5-10 mins, plus resting

Cheese croquettes page 244

25 mins, plus chilling   20 mins

Baked gnocchi with cheese sauce page 212

 10 mins   25 mins

Cheesy potato-topped tuna pie page 87

 15 mins   40 mins

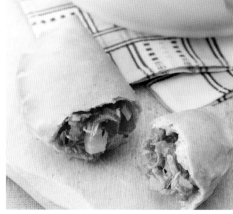

Tuna empanadas page 397

 45 mins, plus chilling   40-50 mins

Sausage and butterbean goulash page 149

 10 mins   35 mins

Cannellini bean, tuna, and red onion salad
page 390

10 mins

Tuna, tomato, and black olive pasta sauce
page 199

15 mins   1 hr 10 mins

Dan dan noodles page 214

10 mins   10 mins

Quick tomato, bacon, and garlic pasta page 205

10 mins   15 mins

Vegetable biryani
page 232

20–30 mins   40–45 mins

Mushroom and spinach curry page 184

15 mins   30 mins

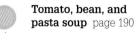

Tomato, bean, and pasta soup page 190

15 mins   45–50 mins

Quick meals

Family life can be very busy and there will often be times when you need to put together a satisfying meal quickly. Try fish and seafood dishes as well as stir fries and pasta classics.

Thai beef salad page 122

Steak glazed with mustard and brown sugar page 128

5 mins   10 mins

10 mins   10 mins

Easy carbonara page 197

10 mins   10 mins

Butternut squash soup page 156

5 mins   20 mins

Egg salad page 237

10 mins, plus cooling   10 mins

Grilled salmon and salsa verde page 72

5 mins   5 mins

Pork steaks with fried apples page 128

5 mins   15 mins

Broiled red mullet with rosemary and chile page 90

5 mins   10 mins

Thai-style stir-fried ground beef page 126

5 mins   10 mins

Sweet chile shrimp skewers page 66

15 mins, plus soaking and cooling   5 mins

Spicy chicken meatballs page 115

10 mins   10 mins

Quick rice with tomatoes, shrimp, and peas page 227

5 mins   10 mins

Quick breads and desserts

Baking shouldn't take all day. These simple breads and desserts will only take 20 minutes or less to prepare and pop in the oven. There are sweet and savory items here to have for snacks or an impromptu party.

Apricot and almond bars page 432

20 mins   35-40 mins

Blueberry muffins with streusel topping page 412

20 mins   15-20 mins

Southern-style cornbread page 448

10-15 mins   25-35 mins

Three-cheese scones page 440

5 mins   10-15 mins, plus cooling

Oat and raisin cookies page 404

10 mins   15 mins

Orange and marmalade loaf cake page 435

15 mins   45-50 mins

Strawberry shortcakes page 411

 15 mins 15-17 mins

Easy crust apple pies
page 478

 15 mins 25 mins

Buttermilk biscuits
page 271

 10 mins 10-12 mins

Savory breakfast muffins
page 442

 10 mins 25 mins

Madeleines
page 412

 15-20 mins 10 mins

Quick cheese pastries
page 442

 15 mins 10-15 mins, plus cooling

Double chocolate chip muffins page 410

 10 mins 15 mins

Cheap eats

Feeding a growing family can be expensive. Hearty stews and pasta dishes can be made with inexpensive cuts or leftovers, herbs, and spices. Omelets and soups also make economical and filling meals.

Classic buttermilk pancakes page 263

 15 mins   10-12 mins

Chicken and barley stew page 104

  10 mins   1hr 15 mins

Harvest vegetable soup page 157

15 mins 30 mins

Leftover pork chili page 146

  15 mins   1 hr

New potato, sweet potato, and tarragon salad page 160

   10 mins   10-15 mins

Spicy sausage casserole page 147

  15 mins   1 hr 15 mins

Irish stew page 136

   25 mins   3 hrs

Angel hair pasta with arugula pesto page 194

10 mins, plus resting | 10 mins

Crispy risotto cakes page 221

5 mins | 30 mins

Ham and cheese family omelet page 249

5 mins | 5-10 mins

Penne with creamy butternut squash and bacon page 204

15 mins | 30 mins

Lemon, garlic, and herb barbecued chicken page 284

10 mins, plus marinating | 30-40 mins

Pasta with peas and pancetta page 205

10 mins | 15 mins

Picky eaters

Throughout this book we have highlighted dishes that often appeal to fussy eaters or recipes that can be adapted to suit different tastes. Here are some of those, plus some tried and tested children's favorites.

Sausage and sweet potatoes page 302

10 mins   45 mins

Tomato and mascarpone pasta page 192

10 mins   10-15 mins

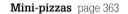

Mini-pizzas page 363

20 mins, plus rising   10 mins

Zucchini and feta loaf
page 453

20 mins   40-45 mins

Zucchini fritters
page 163

20 mins, plus draining   10 mins

Blueberry pancakes
page 265

10 mins   10 mins

Crispy southern-baked chicken page 113

10 mins, plus chilling | 45 mins – 1 hr

Spicy chicken fajitas
page 114

15 mins, plus marinating | 15 mins

Swedish sausage casserole
page 147

10 mins | 35-45 mins

"Mac and cheese"
page 210

10 mins | 15 mins

Salmon in foil page 73

10 mins | 20-25 mins

Blanquette de veau
page 138

15 mins | 1 hr 40 mins

Quick tuna pâté
page 68

10 mins | 1 min

Babies and toddlers

Babies and toddlers

Introducing a baby to solid food can seem daunting, especially for a first-time mom. However, with some simple guidelines, helping a child learn to eat and enjoy a wide variety of foods can be fairly stress free. The goal is to get to the point where a toddler can happily enjoy a nutritionally balanced meal alongside the rest of the family, providing it is not salted and is cut into manageable pieces.

What is weaning?

Weaning is really nothing more complicated than gradually introducing a baby to the tastes and textures of the kinds of foods we eat every day. To do this it makes sense to start with simple tastes and soft textures (remember that they have only had breast or formula milk up to this point) before moving on to more complex tastes and lumpier textures. It is currently recommended by the World Health Organization that a baby should start with weaning foods around six months (26 weeks). Your baby might be ready for solids earlier than this, but note that weaning should **never** occur before the age of 17 weeks.

First tastes

A baby's first tastes will be simple purées of individual fruit and vegetables and then combinations. Although store-bought baby food is quick and convenient, it can also be expensive. Making your own purée is easy; the only equipment you need is a hand-held blender, ice-cube trays, and freezer bags. Once the cubes of food are frozen, you can decant them into freezer bags, label, and store in the freezer until you need them. Babies will only eat tiny portions at first, so cooking in batches and then freezing means you can defrost one or two cubes of purée at a time to prevent waste.

Cooked peas or juicy segments of canned peaches make excellent finger foods for older babies.

Fruit and yogurt smoothies such as this Banana, mango, and yogurt smoothie (p32) can be adapted to include different fruits for your baby to try.

Your baby's milk

Breast milk remains the ideal source of nutrition for your baby and should be continued if possible during the weaning stage, as it contributes essential nutrients. Babies who aren't breastfeeding should be given formula until at least one year of age. A healthcare professional can advise you on this. Both expressed breast milk and formula can be used in recipes for your baby (referred to in this chapter as "your baby's usual milk"), for thinning purées and adding nutrients. From six months of age, you can use full-fat cow's milk for cooking for your baby, but this should not replace breast or formula as the main milk source.

Watching out for allergies

Certain foods are more likely than others to cause an allergic reaction in babies. These include cow's milk, egg, soy, wheat, nuts, and seafood. These foods add essential nutrients for normal growth and development, so do not avoid them in your baby's diet beyond six months of age, unless you have been advised to do so by a healthcare professional. Introducing new foods one at a time may not only help your baby get used to these new tastes, but also identify any possible culprits should an allergic reaction occur.

Finger foods

It is an important part of oral motor skill development and progress in self-feeding to try finger foods. Even young babies can be encouraged to pick up and try easy finger foods, such as well cooked carrots, broccoli florets, or rice cakes. It is important to remember never to leave your baby alone when he is eating in case of choking.

A balanced diet

For your baby to grow into a healthy, active toddler and child, he needs to eat a well-balanced diet. Babies need plenty of good fats, as well as a variety of fresh fruits and vegetables, good quality protein including red meat, poultry, fish, beans, egg and milk products, and some carbohydrates.

Toddlers

You should aim to introduce most food into your baby's diet when they are between six months and one year of age, as they are receptive to new tastes and textures at this age and this will ensure you don't have a toddler who is picky with food. Once your baby reaches the important milestone of his or her first birthday, they become more independent in their feeding and sometimes more specific with their likes and dislikes. Don't give up if they reject some new recipes the first time. Allow them to self-feed as much as possible, even though it might be messy. All the recipes in this chapter are suitable for toddlers as well as babies (with varying textures) but you can branch out and cook from the rest of the book as long as you are careful about the addition of salt.

Vegetable couscous (p37) is a great way to introduce lots of vitamin-rich vegetables as well as some texture into your baby's diet.

Weaning guide

Once you have decided that your baby is ready for solid food (talk to your healthcare provider if you are not sure) you can start introducing him or her to the first tastes in this chapter. Once your baby tolerates a variety of tastes and textures from the first tastes, you can move to first meals, which should be puréed, mashed, or chopped as appropriate to your child's age and oral motor skills.

First tastes

Make your baby's first tastes runny in texture, thinning out purées with your baby's usual milk or the cooking water. Start by introducing rice cereal, and single vegetable and fruit purées, then combine different flavors, making the purées less runny as he or she gets used to them.

First meals

Gradually begin making the textures thicker and lumpier until by the age of one, your child can cope with chopped up family meals. Once you have introduced vegetables, fruit, and baby rice, try out the following:

Any meat protein – beef, lamb, chicken, turkey	Well-cooked eggs
Any fish – such as well-cooked salmon, cod, tuna	Pulses – including lentils and chickpeas
Pasteurized cows' milk and its derivatives – milk for cooking, pasteurized cheese, full-fat yogurt	Gluten containing foods – such as wheat, oats, rye, and barley, and baby cereals, pasta, and bread

Drinks

While your baby is under one, he or she should continue to have his or her usual milk to drink (breast milk or formula) but may require a small amount of water in a cup with meals. Toddlers aged one year and over can drink whole milk cow's milk as their main drink. At age two, children can switch to low-fat milk (but discuss this with your healthcare provider).

Foods to avoid

You should not give your baby salt, honey, or lightly cooked or raw eggs while they are under one, nor should you give them sugary foods, which are bad for their teeth. Toddlers over one should continue to eat a diet that is low in salt and sugar.

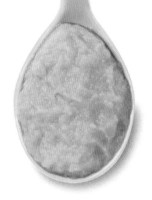

Baby rice

Your baby's first solid food should be a smooth, milky powdered rice made with their usual milk.

2 mins

MAKES 1 PORTION

1 tbsp baby rice

3 tbsp breast or baby's usual milk, cold or warm, or more to taste

1 Using a sterilized spoon, put the baby rice into a sterilized, dried plastic baby bowl.

2 Add the milk and stir well to break up any lumps until the mixture is smooth. If it seems a little thick, add more milk until the texture is right for your baby.

3 Check the temperature of the cereal if using warm milk, in case it is too warm, then serve. Use it up within 30 minutes.

MOM'S TIP

This is merely a general guide; make up your baby rice according to the package instructions. Vary the texture with more or less milk as required, and remember that older babies will have bigger appetites and need a larger portion.

CALORIES: 89kcals/376kJ	
SUGAR: 4g	
FAT: 2.6g	
saturated: 0.9g	
SALT: trace	
CALCIUM: 146mg	
IRON: 3mg	

Pea purée

This simple, sweet purée can be made in minutes as long as you have some peas in the freezer.

2–3 mins   5–6 mins

SPECIAL EQUIPMENT
hand-held blender

MAKES 8–12 ICE CUBES

7oz (200g) frozen peas

a little of baby's usual milk (optional)

1 Put the peas into a small saucepan and cover them with boiling water.

2 Return to a boil over high heat, then reduce the heat and simmer for 5–6 minutes.

3 Drain, reserving the water. Use a hand-held blender to purée the peas in the saucepan, adding enough cooking water or formula milk to make a purée. Cool. Serve, or freeze in ice-cube trays.

VARIATION

For a broccoli purée, simmer 7oz (200g) small florets for 8–10 minutes. Purée as above, with enough cooking water to make a purée. Makes 12 ice cubes.

CALORIES: 16kcals/69kJ	
SUGAR: 0.4g	
FAT: 0.4g	
saturated: 0.2g	
SALT: trace	
CALCIUM: 6mg	
IRON: 0.5mg	

Sweet potato purée

Sweet potatoes are a good source of vitamins, and add a lovely, sweet taste to other purées, too.

5 mins   10 mins

SPECIAL EQUIPMENT
hand-held blender

MAKES 8–10 ICE CUBES

7oz (200g) sweet potatoes, cut into ½in (1cm) cubes

a little of baby's usual milk (optional)

1 Put the sweet potatoes into a small saucepan and cover them with boiling water.

2 Return to a boil over high heat, then reduce the heat and simmer for 10 minutes, until tender when pierced with a sharp knife.

3 Drain and purée as for Pea purée (see left). Cool. Serve, or freeze in ice-cube trays.

VARIATION

Normal potatoes can't be puréed with a blender, as they turn gluey. For potato purée, follow the recipe above, but mash or "rice" them instead.

CALORIES: 21kcals/88kJ	
SUGAR: 1g	
FAT: 0.2g	
saturated: 0.1g	
SALT: trace	
CALCIUM: 7mg	
IRON: 0.16mg	

Butternut squash purée

A sweet purée that babies love. It's a great bright color too. Mix with other purées to add sweetness.

5 mins   15 mins

SPECIAL EQUIPMENT
hand-held blender

MAKES 8 ICE CUBES

7oz (200g) butternut squash, cut into ½in (1cm) cubes

a little of baby's usual milk (optional)

1 Put the squash into a small saucepan and cover it with boiling water.

2 Return to a boil over high heat, then reduce the heat and simmer for 15 minutes, until tender when pierced with a sharp knife.

3 Drain and purée as for Pea purée (see left). Cool. Serve, or freeze in ice-cube trays.

CALORIES: 13kcals/56kJ	
SUGAR: 1g	
FAT: 0.2g	
saturated: 0.1g	
SALT: trace	
CALCIUM: 15mg	
IRON: 0.21mg	

Carrot purée

The soft texture and sweet taste of carrots make them an ideal first food for a weaning baby.

5 mins 15 mins

SPECIAL EQUIPMENT
hand-held blender

MAKES 8 ICE CUBES

7oz (200g) carrots, cut into ½in (1cm) cubes

a little of baby's usual milk (optional)

1 Put the carrots into a small saucepan and cover them with boiling water.

2 Return to a boil over high heat, then reduce the heat and simmer for 15 minutes, until tender when pierced with a sharp knife.

3 Drain and purée as for Pea purée (see left). Cool. Serve, or freeze in ice-cube trays.

VARIATION

Parsnips have a sweet taste and are good mixed half and half with potato purée. Prepare 7oz (200g) parsnips, and cook for just 10 minutes, then purée and store as above. Makes 8 ice cubes.

CALORIES: 13kcals/53kJ

SUGAR: 1.8g

FAT: 0.3g
saturated: 0.1g

SALT: trace

CALCIUM: 10mg

IRON: 0.11mg

Apple purée

This versatile purée is great on its own, or used to sweeten stronger tasting vegetable purées.

5 mins 15 mins

SPECIAL EQUIPMENT
hand-held blender (optional)

MAKES 10 ICE CUBES

4 small apples

1 Peel, core, and chop the apples. This should give about 9oz (250g) of peeled fruit.

2 Put the apples in a small saucepan with 2 tbsp of water. Cover, bring to a boil, then reduce to a low simmer for 15 minutes, stirring occasionally, or until tender.

3 Mash, or purée with a hand-held blender. If too thick, stir in a little cooled, boiled water. Cool. Serve, or freeze in ice-cube trays.

VARIATION

For a quick canned peach purée, use a hand-held blender to purée 2 drained peach halves. If the mixture is too liquid, add a little Baby rice (see far left), 1 tsp at a time. Makes 4 ice cubes.

CALORIES: 18kcals/78kJ

SUGAR: 4g

FAT: 0g
saturated: 0g

SALT: 0.0–0.0g

CALCIUM: 2mg

IRON: 0.08mg

Pear purée

Pears are a delicious versatile fruit to use for a purée. It can be blended with other purées too.

5 mins 10–12 mins

SPECIAL EQUIPMENT
hand-held blender (optional)

MAKES 8 ICE CUBES

2 large pears, organic if possible

1 Peel, core, and chop the pears. This should give you about 7oz (200g) of peeled fruit.

2 Prepare as for Apple purée (see left) but cook for 10–12 minutes. Mash or purée as for Apple purée. If the mixture is too liquid for your baby, add a little Baby rice (see far left), 1 tsp at a time, until it reaches the desired consistency. Cool. Serve, or freeze in ice-cube trays.

VARIATION

For an avocado purée, use ½ a small, ripe avocado. (Keep the other half with the pit in, to keep it from discoloring, for later use.) Use a fork to mash the avocado before serving immediately. If it seems a little thick, stir in cooled, boiled water. Avocado can't be frozen.

CALORIES: 18kcals/74kJ

SUGAR: 4g

FAT: 0g
saturated: 0g

SALT: trace

CALCIUM: 5mg

IRON: 0mg

Mango purée

High in essential vitamins, mangoes are an excellent weaning food, although they can be expensive.

5 mins

SPECIAL EQUIPMENT
hand-held blender

MAKES 8 ICE CUBES

1 large, very ripe mango

Baby rice (optional, see far left)

1 Slice the mango through on either side of the large, flat pit, so that you are left with two discs of fruit. Take a small, sharp knife and score the flesh of each half into ½in (1cm) squares, cutting down to, but not through, the skin. Now push the skin from underneath to "flip" the mango inside out, revealing the cubed mango, which is now easy to separate from the skin.

2 Cut the flesh from the skin and purée using a hand-held blender. If the mixture is too liquid, add a little Baby rice, 1 tsp at a time, until it reaches a consistency that suits your baby. Freeze any excess mango in an ice-cube tray.

CALORIES: 12kcals/54kJ

SUGAR: 3g

FAT: 0g
saturated: 0g

SALT: trace

CALCIUM: 3mg

IRON: 0.1mg

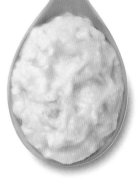

Apple and pear purée

Full of essential nutrients for your baby, apple and pear is almost always a favorite.

5 mins   10-15 mins

SPECIAL EQUIPMENT
hand-held blender (optional)

MAKES 8 ICE CUBES

2 small apples

1 ripe pear

1 Peel, core, and chop the apples and pear into ½in (1cm) pieces, keeping them separate.

2 Put the apples in a small saucepan with 1 tbsp of cooled, boiled water. Cover, bring to a boil, then reduce the heat to a low simmer for 5 minutes. Halfway through, stir and add a splash more water if the pan looks dry.

3 Add the pear and cook for 5–10 minutes, or until all the fruit is tender when pierced with a knife. Mash or purée in the pan with a hand-held blender. Cool. Serve, or freeze in ice-cube trays.

CALORIES: 19kcals/81kJ
SUGAR: 4.5g
FAT: 0g
  saturated: 0g
SALT: trace
CALCIUM: 3mg
IRON: 0mg

Banana and apricot purée

Naturally canned fruit in unsweetened juice make quick purées, here thickened with banana.

5 mins

MAKES 1 PORTION

1 apricot half, in natural unsweetened juice, drained

½ small, ripe banana

1 Chop the apricot into small pieces and place in a small bowl. Use a fork to mash it well.

2 Slice the banana into the bowl in small pieces and mash it well into the apricot. Serve immediately.

CALORIES: 45kcals/191kJ
SUGAR: 10g
FAT: 0g
  saturated: 0g
SALT: trace
CALCIUM: 7mg
IRON: 0.2mg

Avocado and banana purée

For a quick lunch on the go, pack a banana and a ripe avocado for this no-cook combination.

5 mins

MAKES 1 PORTION

½ small, ripe banana

½ small, ripe avocado

1 Peel and chop the banana into small pieces and do the same with the avocado.

2 Place in a small bowl and mash well with a fork. Serve the purée immediately.

CALORIES: 153kcals/633kJ
SUGAR: 8g
FAT: 12g
  saturated: 3g
SALT: trace
CALCIUM: 9mg
IRON: 0.36mg

Carrot and pea purée

This simple, sweet mixture is perfect for when your baby starts moving on to combination purées.

5 mins   15 mins

SPECIAL EQUIPMENT
hand-held blender (optional)

MAKES 8 ICE CUBES

3½oz (100g) carrots, cut into ½in (1cm) cubes

3½oz (100g) frozen petits pois or garden peas

a little of baby's usual milk (optional)

1 Put the carrots into a small saucepan and cover them with boiling water.

2 Return to a boil over high heat, then reduce the heat and simmer for 10 minutes. Add the peas for 5 minutes until everything is tender when pierced with a knife.

3 Drain, reserving the water. Use a hand-held blender to purée it in the pan, adding enough water or milk to make a purée. Cool. Serve, or freeze in ice-cube trays.

CALORIES: 19kcals/78kJ
SUGAR: 1.2g
FAT: 0.5g
  saturated: 0.2g
SALT: trace
CALCIUM: 9mg
IRON: 0.4mg

Cauliflower and potato purée

Cauliflower has a strong taste alone, but added to creamy mashed potato it makes a delightful purée.

5 mins   12 mins

SPECIAL EQUIPMENT
hand-held blender

MAKES 8 ICE CUBES

3½oz (100g) Russet potatoes, peeled and cut into ¾in (2cm) cubes

3½oz (100g) cauliflower, cut into small florets

a little of baby's usual milk (optional)

1 Put the potatoes into a small saucepan and cover them with boiling water.

2 Return to a boil over high heat, then reduce the heat and simmer for 7 minutes. Add the cauliflower for 5 minutes, until both are tender when pierced with a knife.

3 Drain, reserving the cooking water. Purée as for Carrot and pea purée (see left), or mash for a more textured purée. Cool. Serve, or freeze in ice-cube trays.

CALORIES: 18kcals/74kJ

SUGAR: 0.4g

FAT: 0.4g
    saturated: 0.1g

SALT: trace

CALCIUM: 6mg

IRON: 0.17mg

Carrot, parsnip, and apple purée

Parsnips and apples make a classic combination, and carrots add sweetness and color.

5-10 mins   15 mins

SPECIAL EQUIPMENT
hand-held blender

MAKES 6–8 ICE CUBES

1¾oz (50g) carrots, cut into ½in (1cm) cubes

1¾oz (50g) parsnips, cut into ½in (1cm) cubes

3½oz (100g) apples, peeled, cored, and cut into ½in (1cm) cubes

a little of baby's usual milk (optional)

1 Put the carrots into a small saucepan and cover them with boiling water.

2 Return to a boil over high heat, then reduce the heat and simmer for 5 minutes. Add the parsnips and apples for 10 minutes, until tender when pierced with a knife.

3 Drain and purée as for Carrot and pea purée (see left). Cool. Serve, or freeze in ice-cube trays.

CALORIES: 16kcals/67kJ

SUGAR: 2g

FAT: 0.3g
    saturated: 0.1g

SALT: trace

CALCIUM: 8mg

IRON: 0.11mg

Sweet potato and broccoli purée

Broccoli is high in vitamins and contains calcium and iron. Sweet potato is very high in vitamin A.

5 mins   10 mins

SPECIAL EQUIPMENT
hand-held blender

MAKES 8 ICE CUBES

3½oz (100g) sweet potatoes, cut into ½in (1cm) cubes

3½oz (100g) broccoli florets, cut into small pieces

a little of baby's usual milk (optional)

1 Put the sweet potatoes into a small saucepan and cover them with boiling water.

2 Return to a boil over high heat, then reduce the heat and simmer for 5 minutes. Add the broccoli for 5 minutes, until tender when pierced with a knife.

3 Drain and purée as for Carrot and pea purée (see left). Cool. Serve, or freeze in ice-cube trays.

CALORIES: 15kcals/64kJ

SUGAR: 0.9g

FAT: 0.1g
    saturated: 0g

SALT: trace

CALCIUM: 10mg

IRON: 0.3mg

Butternut squash and zucchini purée

Zucchini is a vegetable with a milky flavor that is readily accepted by most infants.

5 mins   10-12 mins

SPECIAL EQUIPMENT
hand-held blender

MAKES 8 ICE CUBES

3½oz (100g) butternut squash, cut into ½in (1cm) cubes

3½oz (100g) zucchini, cut into ½in (1cm) pieces

a little of baby's usual milk (optional)

1 Put the squash into a small saucepan and cover it with boiling water.

2 Return to a boil over high heat, then reduce the heat and simmer for 5–7 minutes. Add the zucchini for 5 minutes, until tender when pierced with a knife.

3 Drain and purée as for Carrot and pea purée (see left). Cool. Serve, or freeze in ice-cube trays.

CALORIES: 11kcals/45kJ

SUGAR: 0.8g

FAT: 0.3g
    saturated: 0.1g

SALT: trace

CALCIUM: 12mg

IRON: 0.22mg

Banana porridge

A great breakfast for your baby—easy to digest and healthy. It can be puréed for younger babies.

5 mins   5 mins

SPECIAL EQUIPMENT
hand-held blender (optional)

MAKES 1 PORTION

1 tbsp old-fashioned oats

¼ cup whole milk or baby's usual milk, plus extra if needed

¼ small, ripe banana

1 Put the oats and milk into a small, heavy-bottomed saucepan and bring to a boil.

2 Reduce the heat to a low simmer and cook for about 5 minutes, stirring frequently, until the porridge has thickened and the oats are soft.

3 Peel and mash the small chunk of banana into a serving bowl, then add the cooked porridge and stir together.

4 The texture can be loosened with a little more milk. The porridge can also be made smoother, if necessary, by puréeing it briefly with a hand-held blender.

VARIATION

To cook banana porridge in a microwave, put the oats and milk into a small microwave-proof bowl. Cook in a microwave on a high setting for 30 seconds, stir, and if necessary cook for another 10 seconds. Mash the banana into the bottom of the bowl, then stir together. The texture can be loosened or made smoother, if necessary, as in step 4.

MOM'S TIP

When cooking with a microwave, look out for "hot spots" in cooked or heated food. Make sure you stir the heated food thoroughly and cool slightly before giving anything to your baby.

CALORIES: 90kcals/380kJ
SUGAR: 5.8g
FAT: 2g
  saturated: 0.6g
SALT: trace
CALCIUM: 27mg
IRON: 0.65mg

Banana, mango, and yogurt smoothie

Making this thick enough to be spooned up helps a baby eat it easily, and it makes a quick, healthy breakfast.

5 mins

SPECIAL EQUIPMENT
hand-held blender

MAKES 1 PORTION

1¼oz (40g) frozen mango chunks, defrosted, or 1¼oz (40g) fresh mango chunks

½ small, ripe banana

2 tbsp thick, whole milk Greek yogurt

1 Put the mango chunks into a small bowl and purée with a hand-held blender until smooth.

2 Mash the banana into the puréed mango, then add the yogurt and mix until smooth.

VARIATION

This recipe is very adaptable and a great way of introducing your baby to the flavors of different fruits. Keeping to the same weight of fruit, and always adding the banana, replace the mango with peaches, nectarines, blueberries, raspberries, or strawberries, or a mixture of whatever soft fruits you have available. (If using berries containing seeds, push the fruit through a sieve first to remove them.)

CALORIES: 88kcals/374kJ
SUGAR: 14.6g
FAT: 2g
  saturated: 1.3g
SALT: 0.11g
CALCIUM: 52mg
IRON: 0.65mg

Peachy cottage cheese spread

This simple dish can be spoon fed or spread on fingers of toast if your baby can manage finger food.

5 mins

SPECIAL EQUIPMENT
hand-held blender (optional)

MAKES 2 PORTIONS

2 canned peach halves, in natural juice, drained

¼ cup full-fat cottage cheese

fingers of whole wheat bread, to serve (optional)

1 Depending on the age of your child, either purée the peaches with a hand-held blender until smooth, or semi-smooth, or just chop finely into small pieces.

2 Put the peaches into a serving bowl and mash the cottage cheese into them.

3 Serve on its own or spread on fingers of whole wheat bread, toasted, with the crusts removed.

VARIATION

Substitute any canned fruit for the peaches in this recipe, to get your baby used to different flavors. Try 2 apricot halves, or pear halves.

CALORIES:	53kcals/224kJ
SUGAR:	5.8g
FAT:	2.4g
	saturated: 1.7g
SALT:	trace
CALCIUM:	35mg
IRON:	0.22mg

Banana and strawberry smoothie pops

Fruit and yogurt freeze really well to make delicious popsicles for little ones.

10 mins, plus freezing

SPECIAL EQUIPMENT
blender

popsicle mold

MAKES 4–6

1 ripe banana, roughly chopped

5½oz (150g) ripe strawberries, hulled and roughly chopped

¼ cup (2oz) plain whole milk yogurt

1 Place all the ingredients in a blender and blend until completely smooth. Push through a nylon sieve to remove the seeds.

2 Pour into a popsicle mold and freeze until frozen solid. Remove from the freezer for at least 15 minutes before serving, to soften slightly.

VARIATION

Any soft fruit, when it's in season and cheap, is great to use here. You can try any berry instead of strawberries. Try blueberries for a dramatic dark color, or raspberries, or even try the same weight of pitted, chopped peaches or apricots for orange-colored popsicles. They can be frozen for up to 12 weeks.

COOK'S TIP

When making popsicles, use a silicone mold, if possible. It is much easier to extract the popsicles from these. You could also try freezing this dessert in ice-cube trays, then defrosting a little at a time to serve as a healthy dessert.

CALORIES:	30kcals/129kJ
SUGAR:	5.5g
FAT:	0.4g
	saturated: 0.2g
SALT:	trace
CALCIUM:	25mg
IRON:	0.16mg

Basic tomato sauce

Having some frozen cubes of this sauce gives an almost instant meal and adds color and flavor to other dishes.

10 mins   20 mins

SPECIAL EQUIPMENT
hand-held blender

MAKES 1½ CUPS

2 tsp olive oil

1 small onion, finely chopped

1 x 14oz (400g) can of chopped tomatoes

1 tbsp tomato paste

¼ tsp dried basil or oregano

1 Heat the oil in a small, heavy-bottomed saucepan. Add the onion and cook it over low heat for 5 minutes, until soft, but not brown.

2 Add the tomatoes, tomato paste, and dried herbs. Bring to a boil, then reduce the heat to a low simmer and cook, uncovered, for 10 minutes, stirring occasionally, until the sauce has reduced and thickened.

3 Purée the sauce in the pan using a hand-held blender before serving over pasta, or freeze in an ice-cube tray for later use.

VARIATION

This sauce is an excellent place to "hide" extra vegetables. Try adding finely diced carrot and celery to the onions before cooking. Zucchini, butternut squash, and sweet potato also work really well here.

CALORIES:	17kcals/73kJ
SUGAR:	2.2g
FAT:	0.5g
saturated:	0.1g
SALT:	Trace
CALCIUM:	9mg
IRON:	0.3mg

Easy cheesy sauce

This recipe comes in handy for many dishes. Add a cube to any dish for a smooth, creamy texture that babies love.

5 mins   10 mins

MAKES 1¼ CUPS

2 tbsp butter

2 tbsp all-purpose flour

1¼ cups whole milk

1¼oz (40g) coarsely grated mild Cheddar cheese

1 Melt the butter in a small, heavy-bottomed saucepan. Whisk in the flour over low heat. Continue to cook the flour and butter mixture over low heat for 2 minutes, whisking constantly, until the mixture bubbles and separates under the whisk.

2 Take the pan off the heat and slowly whisk in the milk, a little at a time, whisking it well between each addition until it is smooth. Return the pan to the heat and cook the sauce over medium heat, stirring constantly, until it comes to a boil and thickens.

3 Reduce the heat to low and continue to cook, stirring frequently, for 5 minutes. Be sure to whisk right into the edges of the saucepan, as this is where the sauce can burn if left undisturbed. Add the cheese and cook until it has melted and the sauce is smooth, thick, and creamy. Transfer to ice-cube trays, cool, and freeze.

CALORIES:	106kcals/440kJ
SUGAR:	2.2g
FAT:	7.8g
saturated:	4.9g
SALT:	0.24g
CALCIUM:	115mg
IRON:	0.12mg

Lentils with carrots and spinach

Lentils are a good source of protein and iron. This recipe provides both protein and vitamins and minerals.

5 mins 20–25 mins

SPECIAL EQUIPMENT
hand-held blender (optional)

MAKES 4 PORTIONS

3½oz (100g) red lentils

1 large or 2 small carrots, cut into ½in (1cm) cubes

1 tbsp butter

1¼oz (40g) baby spinach leaves, finely chopped

2 tbsp finely grated Parmesan cheese

1 Rinse the lentils well under running water and check them over for any small rocks. Put them in a pan of boiling water with the carrots and cook for 15–20 minutes until they are soft. Drain them well.

2 Put the butter into the pan and cook the spinach over medium heat for 2–3 minutes, stirring constantly, until it has completely wilted.

3 Return the lentils and carrots to the pan and add the Parmesan. Mash or purée the mixture together, depending on the age of your child. For best results after freezing, reheat the cubes in a microwave.

CALORIES:	152kcals/639kJ
SUGAR:	3g
FAT:	6g
saturated:	3.5g
SALT:	0.28g
CALCIUM:	115mg
IRON:	2.2mg

MOM'S TIP

Don't worry if your child's diapers change color after eating spinach for the first time; certain brightly colored foods such as spinach and blueberries will have this effect, but it is not harmful to the baby, only potentially alarming to the parent or caregiver!

Potato and cauliflower cheese bake

Turn cauliflower and cheese into a nutritionally complete meal with carbohydrates, protein, and vegetables.

5 mins 12–15 mins

SPECIAL EQUIPMENT
hand-held blender (optional)

MAKES 1 PORTION

3½oz (100g) Yukon Gold potato, cut into small chunks

2oz (60g) cauliflower, in small florets

2–3 cubes Easy cheesy sauce (see left), defrosted

1–2 tbsp whole milk or baby's usual milk (optional)

1 tbsp grated mild cheese, such as Cheddar

1 Put the potato and cauliflower into a small pan of boiling water. Cook for 5–8 minutes until tender. Drain. Purée with a hand-held blender, or mash, or chop the vegetables into small pieces, suitable for your child's age.

2 Place the cheesy sauce in the pan and reheat it gently, adding a little extra milk to loosen the mixture. Stir in the chopped vegetables. Preheat the broiler to its highest setting.

3 Put the cheesy vegetable mixture into a very small flame- and ovenproof dish and top with the cheese. Broil the dish for 2 minutes, or until the cheese has melted and the top is starting to brown a little. Cool before serving.

Vegetables are often more appealing in a cheese sauce. Add chunks of carrot, (cook for 10 minutes, or until tender), or replace potato with parsnip or squash, (cook for 5 minutes, or until tender).

Fussy eaters!

CALORIES:	200kcals/840kJ
SUGAR:	4.2g
FAT:	8.5g
saturated:	5g
SALT:	0.3g
CALCIUM:	133mg
IRON:	0.92mg

Sweet potato, broccoli, and rice

This mixture of purée and small pieces is a good way to introduce texture. This meal contains vitamins A and C.

5 mins   15 mins

MAKES 1 PORTION

¼oz (10g) white rice

1oz (30g) broccoli, broken into small florets

2 cubes of Sweet potato purée (see p28), defrosted

1 Cook the rice in a small pan of boiling water according to the package instructions, adding the broccoli for the last 5 minutes until the florets are quite soft.

2 Drain, return to the pan, and mash or chop the broccoli into pieces your child can manage.

3 Add the sweet potato purée to the pan and reheat it gently over low heat. Cook for 2–3 minutes, until everything is piping hot throughout. Cool before serving.

VARIATION .

Swap in the same weight of any other vegetable purée, such as squash, in place of the sweet potato used here.

MOM'S TIP

You can also add small strips of chicken to create a nutritionally complete meal. Some children may prefer a meal like this where the meat can be hidden.

CALORIES: 50kcals/210kJ

SUGAR: 210g

FAT: 0.34g
   saturated: 0.12g

SALT: trace

CALCIUM: 20.4mg

IRON: 0.63mg

Harvest vegetable bake

This is a recipe that combines vegetables rich in vitamins and protein. Select the vegetables that your baby enjoys.

5 mins   10 mins

SPECIAL EQUIPMENT
hand-held blender (optional)

MAKES 2 PORTIONS

5½oz (150g) finely diced vegetables, such as carrots, potatoes, butternut squash, parsnips, sweet potatoes, cauliflower, or green beans

2–3 cubes of Easy cheesy sauce (see p34), defrosted

1–2 tbsp whole milk or baby's usual milk (optional)

2 tbsp finely grated mild cheese, such as Cheddar

CALORIES: 215kcals/893kJ

SUGAR: 3.2g

FAT: 13.5g
   saturated: 8.4g

SALT: 0.54g

CALCIUM: 246mg

IRON: 0.42mg

1 Bring a large pan of water to a boil. Add the vegetables to the water in order of their length of cooking time. For example, for the vegetables listed, first add carrots, then a couple of minutes later add potatoes, then squash, parsnips, sweet potatoes, cauliflower, and green beans. Cook the vegetables together until they are soft, then drain well. Purée the vegetables with a hand-held blender, or mash, or chop, according to what your child can manage.

2 Gently reheat the cheesy sauce in a pan over low heat, adding a little extra milk to loosen it, if necessary, then stir in all of the vegetables. Preheat the broiler to its highest setting.

3 Put the cheesy vegetable mixture into a small, heatproof dish, or a ramekin, and top with the grated cheese. Broil the dish until the cheese has melted and the top is starting to brown a little. Cool before serving.

Vegetable couscous

An easy way to help your child get five portions of fruit and vegetables per day. Rich in vitamins and carbohydrates.

10 mins   10 mins

MAKES 2 PORTIONS

scant 1oz (25g) couscous

½ tbsp olive oil

1 small carrot, finely chopped

¾in (2cm) piece of zucchini, finely chopped

2 cubes of Butternut squash purée (see p28), defrosted

1 Put the couscous in a small bowl and rub the oil into it well, so each piece is coated in oil. Now pour enough boiling water over the couscous so that it is covered by ¼in (5mm), and cover the bowl with plastic wrap, making sure no air escapes.

2 Set aside for 5 minutes, then remove the plastic wrap. All the water should be absorbed and the couscous soft. Fluff it up with a fork to ensure the grains do not stick together.

3 Meanwhile, cook the carrot in a small pan of boiling water for 5 minutes, then add the zucchini and cook for another 3–4 minutes until all the vegetables are quite soft. Drain them well.

4 Put the Butternut squash purée in the pan and reheat it gently over low heat. Add the couscous and vegetables and mix well, adding a little extra water if necessary to get the required texture. Cool before serving. If freezing, reheat in a microwave for best results.

VARIATION

If your baby is not yet able to manage diced vegetables, purée the vegetables with a hand-held blender before mixing with the couscous.

CALORIES: 76kcals/317kJ

SUGAR: 3.25g

FAT: 3g
    saturated: 0.5g

SALT: trace

CALCIUM: 24mg

IRON: 0.35mg

Pasta with cheesy broccoli sauce

Another quick and nutritious meal for your growing child, pasta is a great food for older babies.

5 mins **5–8 mins**

SPECIAL EQUIPMENT
hand-held blender (optional)

MAKES 1 PORTION

1oz (30g) small pasta shapes

1¼oz (40g) broccoli, broken into small florets

2 cubes of Easy cheesy sauce (see p34), defrosted

1–2 tbsp whole milk or baby's usual milk (optional)

CALORIES:	243kcals/1022kJ
SUGAR:	4.7g
FAT:	10g
	saturated: 6g
SALT:	0.3g
CALCIUM:	180mg
IRON:	1.12mg

1 Place the pasta shapes and broccoli in a small pan of boiling water and cook them according to the pasta package instructions (but don't add salt).

2 Drain the pasta and broccoli, then remove the broccoli and chop it, mash it, or purée it until smooth with a hand-held blender, according to the age of your child.

3 Gently heat the Easy cheesy sauce (see p34) over low heat in the saucepan, adding a little milk if necessary. Stir in the pasta and broccoli and mix it together well before serving.

VARIATION

Any greens can be used instead of the broccoli here (but keep to the same prepared weight). Try curly kale, spring greens, or chard, or whatever is in season and available.

Pasta with quick tomato and tuna sauce

Produce a tasty and wholesome meal in minutes from the pantry and freezer.

2 mins **10 mins**

MAKES 1 PORTION

scant 1oz (25g) small pasta shapes

2–3 cubes of Basic tomato sauce (see p34), defrosted

1 x 2oz (40g) canned tuna, drained and mashed

finely grated Parmesan cheese, to serve (optional)

1 Cook the pasta in boiling water in a small saucepan according to the package instructions (but don't add salt). Drain them well.

2 Add the Basic tomato sauce (see p34) and tuna to the pan and cook together over low heat for 2–3 minutes until heated through.

3 Add the drained pasta and stir to combine before serving with a little Parmesan (if using).

VARIATION

Any canned oily fish would be good here, but stick to the same weight. Try canned mackerel.

CALORIES:	180kcals/761kJ
SUGAR:	2.7g
FAT:	4.5g
	saturated: 0.8g
SALT:	0.3g
CALCIUM:	20mg
IRON:	1.3mg

Quick macaroni cheese

All children love macaroni cheese, and babies are no exception. Add bacon bits for older children.

5 mins   20 mins

MAKES 2 PORTIONS

1¼oz (40g) small macaroni or similar pasta shapes

⅓ cup (2¼oz) full-fat cream cheese or soft cheese

2 tsp all-purpose flour

2–3 tbsp whole milk or baby's usual milk

2 tbsp grated mild cheese, such as Cheddar (do not use mold-ripened soft cheeses when feeding babies)

1 Cook the pasta in plenty of boiling water according to the package instructions, until it is soft (but don't add salt). Drain it well.

2 Preheat the broiler to its highest setting. Add the cream cheese to a saucepan and cook it over low heat until it melts. Sprinkle in the flour and whisk it in well, so that there are no lumps. Continue to cook over low heat for 2–3 minutes, then stir in enough milk to make a thick, creamy sauce. Add 1 tbsp of the cheese and stir until melted.

3 Add the cooked pasta to the sauce and stir it well. Place in a very small, flame- and ovenproof dish, sprinkle the top with the remaining cheese, and broil for 3–5 minutes, until the cheese has melted and the top is golden brown. Cool before serving.

CALORIES:	313kcals/1301kJ
SUGAR:	1g
FAT:	23g
	saturated: 14g
SALT:	0.6g
CALCIUM:	175mg
IRON:	0.5mg

VARIATION

A little canned tuna, or chopped cooked chicken can be added to the pasta before it is grilled to add extra protein, if you wish.

Orzo with creamy butternut squash

This small rice-shaped pasta is very easy for children to eat. If you can't find it, just use any tiny pasta shape.

5 mins   10 mins

MAKES 1 PORTION

scant 1oz (25g) orzo, or other small shaped pasta

2 cubes of Butternut squash purée (see p28), defrosted

1 tbsp full-fat cream cheese or other soft cheese (do not use mold-ripened soft cheeses when feeding babies)

1 Cook the pasta in boiling water in a small saucepan according to the package instructions (but don't add salt). Drain it well.

2 Mix the Butternut squash purée (see p28) and the cream cheese together in the saucepan and heat it over low heat, stirring it well, until it is heated through.

3 Add the pasta to the sauce and stir well to combine evenly before serving.

MOM'S TIP

Most babies prefer soft textures in their first foods. It is best to cook pasta for a little longer than stated on the package, until truly soft (and definitely not *al dente*), before serving.

CALORIES:	179kcals/754kJ
SUGAR:	2.5g
FAT:	8.4g
	saturated: 4.7g
SALT:	0.1g
CALCIUM:	51mg
IRON:	0.8mg

Salmon with rice and pumpkin

Salmon is a sweet, tasty fish and full of super-healthy omega-3 fatty acids—excellent food for your growing child.

10 mins   15 mins

MAKES 2–4 PORTIONS

1¾oz (50g) white rice, such as basmati

2oz (60g) pumpkin or squash, cut into
½in (1cm) cubes (prepared weight)

1 x 3oz (105g) can boneless, skinless
salmon, drained and mashed

1 tsp unsalted butter

1 tbsp finely grated Parmesan cheese

1 Cover the rice with plenty of boiling water and cook for 5 minutes. Add the pumpkin and cook for another 10 minutes, or until both the rice and the pumpkin are well cooked.

2 Drain the rice and pumpkin and put back into the pan. Add the mashed salmon, butter, and Parmesan cheese and mix it through until they are all evenly blended together.

3 Use a potato masher to mash the pumpkin gently. This will help the ingredients to bind together and make it easier to eat. Purée the mixture with an electric hand-held blender. You may need to moisten it with a splash of boiled water before serving.

VARIATION

Try making this dish with the same weight of fresh poached salmon fillet, checked carefully for bones.

MOM'S TIP

Adapt this recipe to suit older babies or toddlers by omitting the puréeing at the end of step 3.

CALORIES: 112kcals/468kJ

SUGAR: 0.3g

FAT: 4g
  saturated: 2g

SALT: 0.2g

CALCIUM: 69mg

IRON: 0.4mg

Butternut squash and pea risotto

Small children will love the mild, sweet flavors and creamy texture of this delicious, easy-to-eat risotto.

5 mins   25-30 mins

MAKES 4 PORTIONS

1 tbsp olive oil

½ onion, finely chopped

1 small garlic clove, crushed (optional)

5½oz (150g) risotto rice, such as arborio or carnaroli

3-4 cubes of Butternut squash purée (see p28), defrosted

1¾oz (50g) frozen peas

2 heaping tbsp finely grated Parmesan cheese

1 Heat ½ tbsp of the oil in a large, heavy-bottomed frying pan with deep sides. Cook the onion over low heat for 5 minutes, until it softens, but does not brown. Add the garlic (if using) and cook for another minute.

2 Keep 1½ cups of boiled water gently simmering on the stove near the risotto pan, with a ladle at the ready.

3 Add the remaining ½ tbsp of the oil to the pan with the rice. Turn the rice through the oil and onions so it is well coated.

4 When the rice begins to sizzle, add the simmering water, a ladleful at a time, stirring constantly, for 20–25 minutes (this will depend on the type of rice used), allowing the liquid to evaporate between ladlefuls. Add more boiling water if needed.

5 When the rice is cooked, but still al dente, add the Butternut squash purée and the frozen peas to the pan. Continue to cook the risotto for 5 minutes, until the peas are cooked and the rice is tender. Take the risotto off the heat and stir in the Parmesan to serve.

HOW TO FREEZE

This risotto freezes quite well, although the texture of the rice changes. Reheat it in a microwave, not in a saucepan, for the best results.

CALORIES: 219kcals/914kJ

SUGAR: 2.5g

FAT: 5.4g
saturated: 2g

SALT: 0.2g

CALCIUM: 108mg

IRON: 1mg

Picky babies and toddlers

When a child moves from breast milk or formula onto solid foods, they can often show distinct preferences for certain foods. However, it's sometimes too easy to label a small child a "fussy eater" when perhaps they aren't hungry or have not developed the palate to enjoy the same things as the rest of the family. Additionally, for many young children, texture is a challenge, and not just at the weaning stage. Toddlers are also beginning to exert their independence at mealtimes, too. When your child doesn't eat, or doesn't eat as much as you think she should, it's easy to worry that she isn't getting the nourishment she needs. These few tips and ideas should help make mealtimes easier.

New tastes and textures

As soon as your child is developmentally ready (see the Weaning Guide, p27), introduce new tastes and textures into her diet. This will help to prevent picky eating later on and make it easier to include her in family meals. Children are far more likely to try new foods if they are joining in with an adult meal. Begin by mixing new foods with tried and tested ones (such as adding new vegetables into a stir-fry or pasta sauce), and remember that some children will have to be offered new foods several times before they accept them. For children who have difficulty with texture, try blending any of the recipes in this chapter to a texture they like and gradually adjusting the texture until they get used to it.

Plate politics

Some children like to eat each item thing on the plate individually, and some go further and don't want the separate food items to touch. Serving food on toddler plates that have divided areas can help here.

child-friendly food

If a child is happy and relaxed around food he is far more likely to end up with a wide and varied diet. If your child is struggling, keep it fun, try presenting food in different ways, mix new tastes with old favorites, and involve children in the cooking process.

Mix it up Try combining old favorites with new flavors such as yogurt with mashed or grated fruit. Spreading fruity cottage cheese (p33) on toasted fingers makes an easy and nutritious finger food. You can even try presenting the ingredients in a new form, such as creating fruit pops by freezing yogurt and fruit smoothies (p33).

Get toddlers involved Young children can start to help out in the kitchen, under your careful supervision, of course. Even if they only arrange their lunch on a plate they can begin to see food as fun. Getting kids involved in the kitchen is a great way to encourage them to try new things. They are far more likely to eat something they have made themselves.

Hide it Tempt your children into eating a more varied diet by disguising vegetables in a pasta sauce such as this Hidden vegetable pasta sauce (p40). You can adjust the texture of the sauce with a blender. They will be trying different flavors here without realizing it, and you can vary the vegetables in the sauce to suit what you have available.

Fun food Children often enjoy eating from an amusingly presented plate. If children are picky around food, try making faces or shapes with their food to encourage them to try something. Create faces on the Mini-pizzas (p363), for example, or get kids to make up their own. Make up a story about the ingredients while they eat, to turn it all into a game.

Tried-and-tested ways to get your child eating

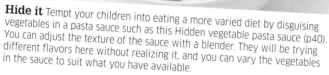

★ **Change of scenery** If the dinner table has become a battleground, try making a picnic of easy-to-eat finger foods and eating on a rug on the floor.

★ **Eat with older children** If you have older children, encourage them to eat at the table with your toddler. This can often persuade young children to eat.

★ **Offer manageable portions** Don't overwhelm your child. Offer a few small servings of different foods on a plate, so that they have the satisfaction of finishing a meal.

★ **Keep it calm** Try not to turn mealtimes into a daily struggle—it will be so unenjoyable for both you and your child. Food is one of the few things small children have any control over, so allow them a certain amount of choice, and try to make mealtimes fun. Don't let the meal drag on for more than 30 minutes if they are not eating.

★ **Don't give up** Keep offering different flavors to your child—even though they have rejected them, they may end up liking them after three or four attempts.

★ **Eat together** Set your children a good example by eating as a family as often as possible, and showing your appreciation of your food.

★ **Adjust the texture** Try grating fruits and vegetables and adding them to smoother textures such as mashed potatoes or yogurt. If your child continues to struggle with texture, seek help from a health professional.

Two spoons trick

Some babies, when confronted with solid food for the first time, want to feed themselves, but can't. Giving them one spoon to hold, while you feed them a few mouthfuls with a second spoon, is an easy way to avoid an unnecessary battle.

Mini minestrone

Pasta shapes add texture and volume to this hearty Italian-style soup. The vegetables bring lots of vitamins.

10 mins   35–40 mins

MAKES 4–6 PORTIONS

2 tbsp olive oil

½ onion, finely chopped

1 leek, finely chopped

1 carrot, finely chopped

1 celery stalk, finely chopped

1 garlic clove, crushed

1 x 14oz (400g) can of chopped tomatoes

1 tsp dried Italian herbs

1¾oz (50g) green beans, chopped into ½in (1cm) pieces

1¾oz (50g) small pasta shapes

freshly ground black pepper (optional)

finely grated Parmesan cheese, to serve

CALORIES: 87kcals/367kJ	
SUGAR: 4g	
FAT: 4g	saturated: 0.5g
SALT: Trace	
CALCIUM: 25mg	
IRON: 0.9mg	

1 Heat the oil in a heavy-bottomed saucepan and cook the onion, leek, carrot, and celery over medium heat for 8–10 minutes, until softened, but not browned. Add the garlic and cook for another minute.

2 Add the chopped tomatoes, herbs, and ⅔ cup of cold water and bring to a boil. Reduce to a simmer and cook, partially covered, for 10 minutes until the vegetables are nearly soft. Use a potato masher to crush the tomatoes lightly. Add the beans, partially cover, and cook for 5 minutes.

3 Add the pasta, with ⅓ cup of boiling water if the soup is quite thick. Stir, partially cover, and cook for 10 minutes, stirring occasionally to prevent the pasta from sticking, or until the pasta and vegetables are cooked. Taste, season lightly with pepper if you want, then serve with Parmesan.

HOW TO FREEZE

Cool the soup completely at the end of step 2, then freeze it for up to 12 weeks. Defrost and reheat, then add the pasta and cook as in step 3.

Spinach and potato soup

This soup has vitamins, carbohydrates, and protein for a growing child. Use frozen spinach if you wish.

10 mins   25 mins

SPECIAL EQUIPMENT

hand-held blender

MAKES 4 PORTIONS

1 tbsp olive oil

1 onion, finely chopped

1 garlic clove, crushed

3½oz (100g) baby spinach leaves

1 large Russet potato, chopped into small cubes

2 tbsp full-fat cream cheese or soft cheese, or more (optional)

whole wheat bread, to serve

CALORIES: 120kcals/499kJ	
SUGAR: 2g	
FAT: 7g	saturated: 2.5g
SALT: 0.15g	
CALCIUM: 60mg	
IRON: 0.9mg	

1 Heat the oil over medium heat in a small, heavy-bottomed saucepan. Cook the onion in the oil for 5 minutes, until softened, but not browned. Add the garlic and cook for another minute.

2 Add the spinach, potato, and ¾ cup of boiling water.

3 Return to a boil and add a few tablespoons of boiling water if it looks thick. Reduce the heat, cover, and simmer for 15 minutes, or until the potato is soft.

4 Use a hand-held blender to purée the soup. Stir in the cheese until it melts, adding more for a creamier consistency, and serve with whole wheat bread.

MOM'S TIP

Some children may like to float bread in their soup. This helps in two ways: it works like a sponge soaking up the soup so they eat more and there's less mess. Also, bread "boats" that float in a soup "sea" before being eaten by giant "sea monsters" (children) makes a good game!

Vegetable and barley soup

This thick, nourishing soup is a meal in one and freezes well, too, so it's excellent for batch cooking in advance.

10 mins   45 mins

SPECIAL EQUIPMENT
food processor

MAKES 4 PORTIONS

1oz (30g) pearl barley

1 onion, roughly chopped

1 celery stalk, roughly chopped

1 large carrot, roughly chopped

1¾oz (50g) butternut squash, roughly chopped

1 tbsp olive oil

freshly ground black pepper (optional)

1 Rinse the pearl barley, then put it in a small, heavy-bottomed saucepan with plenty of cold water. Bring to a boil, reduce to a simmer, and cook for 20 minutes, until partially cooked. Drain well.

2 Put the roughly chopped vegetables in a food processor and process them until they are finely chopped, but not mushy.

3 Heat the oil in a heavy-bottomed saucepan. Add the vegetables and cook over medium heat for 5 minutes, stirring occasionally, until they are soft, but not brown. Add the barley and 1¼ cups of boiling water.

4 Reduce the heat to a simmer and cook for another 20 minutes until the vegetables and barley are soft. Taste the soup and season lightly with a little pepper (if using).

VARIATION

For toddlers, add 1 tsp or ½ cube of reduced-salt vegetable stock, to give a stronger flavor to the soup.

CALORIES: 81kcals/340kJ
SUGAR: 5g
FAT: 3g
saturated: 2.5g
SALT: Trace
CALCIUM: 28mg
IRON: 0.6mg

Chicken soup and rice

A great way to utilize the goodness of a leftover chicken carcass, and loved by children.

20 mins   1¼–2¼ hrs

SERVES 4

FOR THE STOCK

1 cooked chicken carcass

a few leek tops, green part only

1 carrot, roughly chopped

1 celery stalk, roughly chopped

1 onion, quartered

½ tsp black peppercorns

1 bouquet garni

FOR THE SOUP

2 tbsp olive oil

1 onion, finely chopped

1 leek, white part only, finely chopped

2 carrots, finely chopped

1 celery stalk, finely chopped

1 garlic clove, crushed

1oz (30g) white rice

CALORIES: 224kcals/936kJ
SUGAR: 5g
FAT: 9g
saturated: 1.5g
SALT: 0.16g
CALCIUM: 34mg
IRON: 0.9mg

1 Put the chicken carcass in a large saucepan. Add the vegetables, peppercorns, and bouquet garni. Top with boiling water to cover the chicken, 5½–7 cups depending on the size of the pan.

2 Bring to a boil and simmer, uncovered, for 1–2 hours. At the end of cooking the stock should taste concentrated and delicious.

3 Strain into a bowl and cool the contents of the strainer. Once they are cool enough to handle, strip out all the chicken flesh. Chop any large pieces.

4 Meanwhile, heat the oil and cook the onion, leek, carrots, and celery over medium heat for 5 minutes, until softened, but not browned. Add the garlic and cook for another minute.

5 Add the stock and chicken to the vegetables. If there is too little liquid, add a little more from the kettle. Simmer for 15 minutes until all the vegetables are soft. Meanwhile, cook the rice according to the package instructions, then drain thoroughly. Add the rice to the soup and heat through for 2–3 minutes before serving.

Chicken and vegetable stew

This has protein and iron in the chicken and vitamins in the vegetables, especially vitamin A in the carrots.

10 mins   30 mins

MAKES 4 PORTIONS

1 tbsp sunflower or vegetable oil

½ small onion, finely chopped

½ celery stalk, finely chopped

1 small carrot, finely chopped

1 small potato, finely chopped

½ parsnip, finely chopped

1 boneless, skinless chicken breast, finely chopped

1 Heat the oil in a heavy-bottomed saucepan and cook the onion and celery over low heat for 5 minutes, until softened, but not browned.

2 Add 1 cup of boiling water. Add the carrot, reduce the heat to a simmer, and cook for 5 minutes.

3 Add the potato and parsnip to the pan and cook for another 15 minutes. Stir in the chicken, cover, and cook for a final 5 minutes, until the chicken is cooked and all the vegetables are tender.

4 Serve the stew as it is, or use a potato masher to gently crush some of the vegetables, and mix this into the stew. This will thicken the sauce and make it easier for a baby to eat.

CALORIES: 108kcals/454kJ

SUGAR: 2.5g

FAT: 3.5g
  saturated: 0.5g

SALT: trace

CALCIUM: 38mg

IRON: 1.4mg

MOM'S TIP

To cut up the vegetables small enough, use a food processor to do the job in no time and with minimum effort.

Cod with lentils and vegetables

Fish is a good source of protein for children, and along with lentils and vegetables makes a wholesome meal.

15 mins   25 mins

SPECIAL EQUIPMENT
food processor

MAKES 4–6 PORTIONS

½ onion, roughly chopped

½ celery stalk, roughly chopped

2 carrots, roughly chopped

2 tbsp sunflower or vegetable oil

1¼oz (40g) red lentils, rinsed

3½oz (100g) skinless cod fillet, or other firm white fish fillet, cut into ½in (1cm) cubes

CALORIES: 82kcals/344kJ

SUGAR: 3g

FAT: 4g
  saturated: 0.5g

SALT: trace

CALCIUM: 16mg

IRON: 0.66mg

1 Use a food processor to chop all the vegetables finely. These will be irregularly sized, but it doesn't matter. Just fish out any large pieces and cut them by hand.

2 Heat the oil in a heavy-bottomed saucepan over low heat. Add the vegetables and cook them for 5 minutes, until softened, but not browned.

3 Add the lentils to the pan, then cover with 1 cup of boiling water. Cover and cook the lentils for 15 minutes, until softened, but not browned.

4 Finally add the fish and cook for another 5 minutes, until it is well cooked and the liquid has reduced.

5 Remove the lentils from the heat and use a fork to gently break up the fish and mix it into the vegetables and lentils. The lentils can also be made creamier by mashing them gently with a potato masher before serving.

Mini pasties

These are a complete meal for your baby containing carbohydrates and protein, as well as vegetables.

15 mins, plus cooling   **20 mins,** plus resting   ❄

MAKES 6

1 tbsp sunflower or vegetable oil

1 small onion, finely chopped

1 small carrot, finely grated

3½oz (100g) good-quality ground beef or lamb

1 heaping tsp all-purpose flour, plus extra for dusting

1 x 14oz (320g) pack of good-quality ready-rolled puff pastry

1 large egg, lightly beaten

1 Heat the oil in a small, heavy-bottomed saucepan. Cook the onion and carrot over medium heat for 5 minutes, until softened, but not browned.

2 Add the meat to the pan and cook it over high heat, stirring frequently, until it is browned all over. Sprinkle in the flour and cook for another 2 minutes, stirring frequently to keep it from sticking.

3 Pour ⅓ cup of boiling water over the meat. Bring to a boil, reduce to a low simmer, and cook, uncovered, for 10 minutes until the liquid has evaporated. Let the meat cool completely.

4 Preheat the oven to 400°F (200°C). Unroll the pastry on a lightly floured work surface and cut out six 4in (10cm) circles.

5 Place 2 tsp of the cooled meat mixture on one half of each pastry circle, leaving a ½in (1.5cm) border. Brush this border with a little beaten egg, then fold the pastry over and crimp the edges to seal the filling inside. Use a sharp knife to make a small slit in the pastry to allow the steam to escape.

6 Place the pasties on a baking sheet and brush the surfaces with a little more beaten egg. Cook in the middle of the oven for 20 minutes, until puffed up and

golden brown. Let rest and cool for at least 5 minutes before serving. They can be served hot or cold.

HOW TO FREEZE

The uncooked pasties can be open-frozen, then packed into an airtight container to freeze for up to 8 weeks. Defrost as many as you need, covered, on a plate in the fridge, before baking as usual.

CALORIES:	288kcals/1201kJ
SUGAR:	2.8g
FAT:	18g
	saturated: 7.7g
SALT:	0.5g
CALCIUM:	50mg
IRON:	1mg

Banana and date mini muffins

These delicious little cakes are sweetened with banana and dates to make a healthier treat.

15 mins   12-15 mins

SPECIAL EQUIPMENT

24 mini paper liners

24-hole mini muffin pan

MAKES 20–24

⅔ cup all-purpose flour

⅓ cup whole wheat flour

½ tsp baking soda

½ tsp baking powder

½ tsp ground cinnamon

1¾oz (50g) pitted soft dates, finely chopped

¼ cup light brown sugar

1 small egg, lightly beaten

2 tbsp sunflower or vegetable oil

1 ripe banana, mashed with a fork

CALORIES: 40kcals/170kJ	
SUGAR: 4g	
FAT: 1g	
saturated: 0.2g	
SALT: 0.2g	
CALCIUM: 34mg	
IRON: 0.7mg	

1 Preheat the oven to 350°F (180°C). Place 24 mini paper paper liners into a 24-hole mini muffin pan.

2 Sift the flours, baking soda, baking powder, and cinnamon into a large mixing bowl. Add the dates and sugar and stir to mix well.

3 Stir together the egg and oil with a fork, and stir in the mashed banana. Pour the wet mixture into the dry and stir well to combine. Divide the batter evenly between the liners.

4 Bake in the center of the oven for 12–15 minutes, or until a toothpick inserted into the center of a muffin comes out clean. Transfer to a wire rack to cool.

VARIATION

Use raisins instead of dates if you prefer, or substitute half the dates with finely chopped walnuts, if your child likes them, for added protein. Note, though, that children under the age of three should not be given large nuts.

Oat and apple pancakes

Versatile for your baby's weekday or weekend healthy breakfast, dessert, or snack.

15 mins   10 mins

SPECIAL EQUIPMENT

food processor

MAKES 8

⅔ cup whole wheat flour

½ cup instant oats

1 tbsp light brown sugar

1 tsp baking powder

½ tsp ground cinnamon

1 large egg, lightly beaten

½ cup whole milk or formula

½ tsp vanilla extract

1 large apple peeled, cored, and grated, approx. 3½oz (100g) in total

butter, for cooking

1 Put the flour, oats, and sugar into a food processor and process until the oats have broken down to a fine powder. Pour them into a large mixing bowl. Add the remaining dry ingredients.

2 Whisk together the egg, milk, and vanilla extract. Make a well in the center of the dry ingredients and whisk in the liquid to make a smooth batter. Fold in the apple.

3 Melt a pat of butter in a large, non-stick frying pan. Ladle out the pancake batter in 2¾in (7cm) rounds and cook them for 2–3 minutes over medium heat, until the edges of the pancake start to set, and bubbles appear and burst on the top. Turn them over and cook for another 1–2 minutes, until slightly risen and golden brown.

CALORIES: 93kcals/390kJ	
SUGAR: 4g	
FAT: 3.7g	
saturated: 1.6g	
SALT: 0.2g	
CALCIUM: 34mg	
IRON: 0.7mg	

These are good for smuggling some fruit into your child's diet. They are also an ideal recipe for children to help prepare. Getting children involved can encourage them to try new tastes.

Fussy eaters!

Carrot cake cookies

These soft cookies will become a real favorite; they have all the goodness of carrot cake in a bite-sized snack.

15 mins   12–15 mins

SPECIAL EQUIPMENT
electric hand-held mixer

MAKES 20

7 tbsp, softened

½ cup light brown sugar

½ cup granulated sugar

1 large egg, lightly beaten

¾ cup all-purpose flour

⅔ cup whole wheat flour

½ tsp baking powder

½ tsp ground cinnamon

3½oz (100g) finely grated carrot

1¾oz (50g) raisins

CALORIES: 115kcals/485kJ
CARBOHYDRATE: 12g
FAT: 5g
  saturated: 3g
SALT: 0.1g
FIBER: 18mg
IRON: 0.33mg

1 Preheat the oven to 350°F (180°C). In a large mixing bowl, cream together the butter and sugars with an electric hand-held mixer until light and fluffy. Add the egg and beat well to combine.

2 Sift the flours, baking powder, and cinnamon into the cookie mixture, pouring in any bran that is left in the sieve. Add the carrot and raisins and stir well.

3 Put heaping teaspoons of the cookie batter, spaced well apart, onto 2 baking sheets lined with parchment paper.

4 Bake in the middle of the oven for 12–15 minutes, until golden brown and risen slightly.

5 Remove from the oven and cool for 5 minutes on the baking sheets before transferring to a wire rack to cool completely.

Fruity ice pops

Make these simple fruit pops as a way to get some vitamin-rich fruit into your child's diet.

15 mins, plus freezing

SPECIAL EQUIPMENT
blender

popsicle mold

MAKES 4–6

2½oz (75g) frozen mixed berries

¾ cup apple juice

1 Place the frozen berries and the apple juice in a blender and blend until completely smooth.

2 Press the fruit mixture through a nylon sieve to remove any seeds or small pieces of skin. Pour the fruit juice into an popsicle mold, cover, and freeze until solid (or for up to 12 weeks).

3 Remove the ice pops from the freezer at least 15 minutes before serving, to soften slightly.

CLEVER WITH LEFTOVERS

You can substitute any juice your child prefers for the apple juice here. You can use up a carton that is approaching its use-by date.

MOM'S TIP

Babies find it hard to regulate their body temperature in hot weather. These ice pops are an effective—and nutritious—way to cool them down.

CALORIES: 16kcals/69kJ
SUGAR: 4g
FAT: 0g
  saturated: 0g
SALT: 0g
CALCIUM: 4mg
IRON: 0mg

Family meals

Family meals

Finding time to eat together has become harder for many people, with long working hours and busy family timetables getting in the way. Yet time spent around the table is time well spent—it helps family relationships, communication, and can encourage healthy eating, too. Working out how to please everyone can be a dilemma, but there are plenty of recipe suggestions here that will make that decision easier. There's nothing better than pulling out a pre-prepared meal on a busy weeknight, but you don't need to buy one, as there are lots of tips on how you can get ahead on homemade meals in this chapter.

Catering for all tastes

To feed a family without fuss you need to choose a dish that everyone likes—or at least that they will all eat without requiring too much persuasion! In this chapter you will find plenty of failsafe classics, such as Ham and cheese family omelet (p249) or Chili con carne (p143), which are real weekday winners, but also exciting new dishes to try using a variety of ingredients in mouthwatering combinations, such as Lamb, apricot, and chickpea tagine (p137), Chicken and coconut curry (p99), or Smoked haddock and spinach crumble (p89). Don't be put off trying new recipes if you have a picky eater. Start with variations on favorites and work up to completely new taste and texture experiences (see Sources of inspiration, opposite).

Cooked slow and steady this Rosemary and garlic leg of lamb makes for an easy Sunday dinner (p296). It can be left to roast in the oven while you spend time with your family.

Spicy chicken meatballs (p115) are a real family favorite. Making your own meatballs means you know exactly what's gone into them. Add extra noodles if you need to fill hungry teens.

Eating for less

Rising food prices and a growing family to feed can easily stretch your weekly budget, so many of the recipes in this chapter are designed to help your cash go further either by using good value ingredients in mouthwatering ways or by leaving you with tasty leftovers that you can use for another meal. For example, replace the Friday-night take-out with cheaper, and healthier, homemade versions, such as Crispy southern-baked chicken (p113), Homemade fish and chips (p81), Indian lamb kebabs with cucumber and mango (p123), or Thai-style stir-fried ground beef (p126) with Thai coconut rice (p226). Remember you can accompany everyday meals with carbohydrate-heavy side dishes such as potatoes, rice, and pasta for economical ways to fill up your growing family, and add plenty of fresh vegetables to bulk up stews and one-pots, making the meat stretch a little further.

Sources of inspiration

There are times in the lives of most parents when they find themselves staring into the fridge with no enthusiasm for what they see there. Perhaps it seems like you've been cooking the same few dishes for your family, week in, week out, or perhaps you just lack the energy or inspiration to put together something different. If so, you'll be pleased to know that with a few changes, old classics can be given a new lease on life, try Crispy polenta fish fingers with easy tartar sauce (p80), Ricotta-stuffed chicken breasts (p110), Swedish meatballs with gravy (p127), or a Quick paella (p223). There are also great ideas to add interest to everyday ingredients such as rice, fish, or meat.

Tasty vegetable dishes such as firm favorite Creamy cauliflower cheese (p172) always goes down well, and not just with vegetarians. Serve as a main dish or a side with Roast chicken (p294).

Change things up with dishes such as Lamb, apricot, and chickpea tagine (p137) or try some new ways with familiar ingredients such as Sausage and butterbean goulash (p149).

Fuss-free family meals

Family life is hectic enough, so make your life easier with a few simple tricks. With a bit of planning, you can spend less time in the kitchen and have more fun with your family.

Kids' corner

If what you serve up has become a source of tension at every mealtime, why not ask the children to choose what the family eats one day a week? If they are old enough, get them to help you prepare it too (see Cooking with kids, p458). This will encourage them and help them feel that their opinion has been heard—and it makes one less decision for you!

Plan ahead

Time spent planning ahead will save you time later. Once a week, decide what you will cook for the next few days, then you don't have to make that decision each evening, plus you will save money and waste less by buying only the ingredients you need.

Here's one I prepared earlier...

When you cook a favorite meal, increase the quantities and freeze a few portions for another day, then you always have something on hand for that last-minute dinner. When reheating previously cooked foods that have been chilled or frozen, make sure you heat them all the way through, to kill off any potentially unhealthy bacteria. The food should reach a temperature of around 175°F (80°C) for at least two minutes before serving. All recipes marked with the freezer symbol are suitable for freezing, just make sure they are completely cool before you put them in the freezer (see Batching and freezing, p120).

Good recipes for freezing include:

Smoked fish chowder (p69)	Chinese braised beef with ginger and soy sauce (p133)
Chicken cacciatore (p108)	
Spanish chicken, chorizo, and pepper stew (p105)	Cheese and onion pie (p247)
Chili con carne (p143)	Fish cakes (p82)

Spicy coconut shrimp

These delectable little morsels are addictively good, so cook plenty, as you tend to need more than you think.

10 mins, plus resting   5 mins

SPECIAL EQUIPMENT
food processor

SERVES 4 (as an appetizer)

1¾oz (50g) unsweetened shredded coconut

3½oz (100g) panko bread crumbs or day-old bread crumbs

1 tsp chile powder

2–3 tbsp all-purpose flour

salt and freshly ground black pepper

1 large egg, beaten

14oz (400g) raw large shrimp, shelled and deveined

sunflower or vegetable oil, for frying

sweet chili sauce, to serve

CALORIES: 389kcals/1629kJ
CARBOHYDRATE: 24g
  sugar: 1.5g
FAT: 22g
  saturated: 8.5g
SALT: 1g
FIBER: 3g

1 Put the coconut, bread crumbs, and chile powder in a food processor and purée to fine crumbs. Place in a shallow bowl. Put the flour in a second bowl and season well, and the egg into a third.

2 Dust each shrimp with the flour, shaking off excess. Dip each briefly into the egg, then roll it in the bread crumbs, making sure it is well covered. Place on a plate. Repeat to coat all the shrimp. Cover and rest in the fridge for 30 minutes. This will help the coating to stick.

3 Fill a large, heavy-bottomed saucepan with a 2in (5cm) depth of oil. It is ready when a cube of bread thrown in sizzles and starts to turn golden brown. Fry the shrimp, a few at a time, in the hot oil for a minute or two until golden brown all over. Be careful not to overcrowd the pan or they will stick together. Remove them with a slotted spoon and rest on a plate lined with paper towels while you fry the rest. Serve hot, with sweet chilli sauce for dipping.

Chinese shrimp toasts

These fabulous snacks are always far better when homemade, and are a real children's favorite.

10 mins   10 mins

SPECIAL EQUIPMENT
food processor

SERVES 4 (as an appetizer)

6oz (175g) raw large shrimp, shelled, deveined, and roughly chopped

1 tsp cornstarch

2 scallions, finely chopped

½ tsp finely grated fresh ginger

1 tsp soy sauce

1 tsp sesame oil

1 large egg white

4 large slices of day-old white bread, crusts removed

sunflower or vegetable oil, for frying

1oz (30g) white sesame seeds

CALORIES: 287kcals/1200kJ
CARBOHYDRATE: 20g
  sugar: 1.5g
FAT: 17g
  saturated: 2.5g
SALT: 1g
FIBER: 1.5g

1 Put the shrimp, cornstarch, spring onions, ginger, soy sauce, sesame oil, and egg white into a food processor, and process to a fairly smooth paste.

2 Cut each piece of bread into quarters and spread with a little of the shrimp paste, being sure to go right up to the edges and mounding it up slightly so that all the paste is used up.

3 Heat a 2in (5cm) depth of oil in a large, heavy-bottomed frying pan or deep fryer. It is ready when a crust of spare bread, dropped in, sizzles and starts to turn golden brown. Spread the sesame seeds out on a plate. Press each piece of bread, shrimp-side down, into the sesame seeds, so each is topped with a thin layer.

4 Fry the shrimp toasts in small batches, sesame seed-side down, for 1–2 minutes, until becoming golden brown, then carefully turn them over and fry for another minute. Drain the cooked toasts on a plate lined with paper towels while you fry the remaining pieces. Serve hot.

Salt and pepper squid

Squid is an economical source of low-fat protein. Try this spicy Asian treatment as part of a family feast.

10 mins   6-8 mins

SERVES 4 (as an appetizer)

1 tbsp sea salt flakes

1 tbsp black peppercorns

¼ cup all-purpose flour

¼ cup cornstarch

¼–½ tsp chile flakes (optional)

4 squid tubes, cleaned, approx. 10oz (300g) in total

1¼ cups vegetable oil, for frying

lemon wedges, to serve

1 Using a mortar and pestle, crush the sea salt and peppercorns until fine. Place the flour and cornstarch in a bowl and stir in the sea salt, pepper, and the chile flakes (if using).

2 Make a slit down one edge of each squid pouch and open it out flat. Using a sharp knife, score a diamond pattern on the inside of each pouch. Cut each into eight pieces. Dust the pieces in the seasoned flour.

3 Heat the vegetable oil to 350°F (180°C) in a medium, heavy-bottomed pan. To check the temperature of the oil without a thermometer, carefully lower a cube of bread into the oil. The oil is hot enough when a piece of bread, dropped in, sizzles and starts to turn golden brown after 1 minute.

4 Cook the squid, in four batches, for 1½–2 minutes, or until golden brown, returning the oil to 350°F (180°C) between batches. Transfer to a plate lined with paper towels to drain, then place in a warm oven to keep warm. Repeat, working quickly, to cook all the squid. Serve piping hot, with lemon wedges.

Many children who profess to hate fish will eat deep-fried squid. Try the spicy version for a homemade equivalent to take-out food, but omit the chile flakes for very young children.

Fussy eaters!

CALORIES: 264kcals/1108kJ

CARBOHYDRATE: 24.5g
sugar: 0.5g

FAT: 12.5g
saturated: 2g

SALT: 3.9g

FIBER: 0.5g

Sweet chile shrimp skewers

Broil these sweet, sour, spicy skewers and serve as a delicious appetizer, or as part of a larger Asian feast.

15 mins, plus soaking and cooling   5 mins

SPECIAL EQUIPMENT
8 bamboo skewers

SERVES 4 (as an appetizer)

¼ cup granulated sugar

1 red chile, seeded and finely chopped

finely grated zest of ½ lime

½ cup rice vinegar or white wine vinegar

½ tsp salt

32 raw large shrimp, shelled and deveined

| CALORIES: 141kcals/597kJ |
| CARBOHYDRATE: 13g |
| sugar: 13g |
| FAT: 0.7g |
| saturated: 0.1g |
| SALT: 1g |
| FIBER: 0g |

1 Before you start, soak the bamboo skewers in water for at least 30 minutes. This will help keep them from burning when you broil the shrimp.

2 Meanwhile, in a small saucepan, mix together all the ingredients except the shrimp. Bring them to a boil, then reduce the heat to a low simmer and cook, uncovered, for 7–10 minutes, until the sauce has thickened to a sweet, sticky syrup. Set it aside to cool (it will thicken further as it cools).

3 Preheat the broiler to its highest setting. Thread 4 shrimp on to each skewer. Brush both sides of the shrimp with the syrup and place them on a baking sheet or broiler pan that has been lined with foil. Grill the skewers for 2–3 minutes on each side, brushing once more with syrup as you turn them.

HOW TO FREEZE

Freeze the shrimp (make sure they have not been previously frozen) in the sweet chile syrup, but uncooked. Defrost thoroughly before broiling.

Asian-style soy and sesame fish bites

A great way to get children to eat fish, these sweet and sticky fish bites both look and taste utterly delicious.

10 mins, plus cooling and marinating   10 mins

SERVES 4 (as a light meal)

¼ cup soy sauce

¼ cup rice wine or dry sherry

2 tbsp rice vinegar or white wine vinegar

1 tbsp light brown sugar

1 tbsp honey

2 tsp sesame oil

1lb 2oz (500g) firm white-fleshed fish fillets, cut into ¾in (2cm) cubes

2 tbsp sesame seeds

| CALORIES: 210kcals/881kJ |
| CARBOHYDRATE: 8.5g |
| sugar: 8.5g |
| FAT: 7g |
| saturated: 1g |
| SALT: 2.9g |
| FIBER: 1g |

1 Combine the soy sauce, rice wine, vinegar, sugar, honey, and oil in a small, heavy-bottomed saucepan and bring it to a boil.

2 Reduce the heat to a simmer and cook, uncovered, for 5 minutes, until the sauce has reduced. Allow it to cool.

3 Turn the fish in the cooled sauce to coat, cover, and marinate in the fridge for 1 hour.

4 Preheat the broiler to its highest setting. Line a baking sheet or broiler pan with foil and spread out the marinated fish in a single layer. Sprinkle half the sesame seeds evenly over the fish.

5 Broil the fish for 3–4 minutes, until it is beginning to turn crispy at the edges, then turn it over carefully, sprinkle with the remaining sesame seeds, and broil for another 3–4 minutes.

VARIATION

Try this marinade with salmon, or even chicken pieces. Or reheat the leftover marinade until boiling, then use as a sauce for the fish bites.

Smoked mackerel pâté

This easy, quick pâté is a tasty and inexpensive way to get healthy, oily fish into the family diet.

10 mins

SPECIAL EQUIPMENT

food processor (optional)

SERVES 4

7oz (200g) hot-smoked mackerel fillets, skinned

¾ cup (7oz) low-fat crème fraîche

2 tsp horseradish sauce (optional)

2 tbsp roughly chopped dill

finely grated zest of 1 lime, plus juice of ½ lime

freshly ground black pepper

whole grain toast, to serve

CALORIES: 254kcals/1054kJ

CARBOHYDRATE: 0.5g
    sugar: 0.5g

FAT: 22g
    saturated: 7g

SALT: 1g

FIBER: 0g

1 Break the mackerel into pieces and place in a food processor (if using). Add the crème fraîche, horseradish sauce (if using), dill, and lime zest and juice. Process to a smooth paste. Or, for a chunkier pâté, combine all the ingredients in a large bowl, mashing with a fork.

2 Season to taste with pepper and transfer to a serving dish. Cover and chill until ready to serve.

3 Serve with hot, buttered whole grain toast.

VARIATION

Use peppered smoked mackerel fillets, or even smoked mackerel fillets with added chile, or honey, for a stronger flavored pâté.

CLEVER WITH LEFTOVERS

Once opened, smoked mackerel does not have a very long shelf life. If you have the odd fillet nearing use-by date, skin it, pop it in a freezer bag, and freeze until you have enough to make this recipe.

Smoked salmon pâté

Smoked salmon can be expensive, but cheaper packages of salmon trimmings work well for this recipe.

10 mins

SERVES 4

7oz (200g) low-fat cream cheese, at room temperature

7oz (200g) smoked salmon trimmings, very finely chopped

finely grated zest and juice of ½ lemon

2 tbsp chopped chives

freshly ground black pepper

crackers and cucumber sticks, to serve

CALORIES: 149kcals/623kJ

CARBOHYDRATE: 2g
    sugar: 2g

FAT: 8g
    saturated: 4g

SALT: 2.3g

FIBER: 0g

1 Place the cream cheese in a mixing bowl and break it up with a fork until smooth. Stir in the salmon, lemon zest and juice, chives, and plenty of pepper.

2 Transfer to a serving dish, cover with plastic wrap, and chill until ready to serve.

3 Spread the pâté on crackers and serve with cucumber sticks.

VARIATION

Use the zest and juice of ½ lime and 2 tbsp chopped dill instead of the lemon and chives.

COOK'S TIP

Smoked salmon freezes wonderfully, so pop a few packages of cheap trimmings in the freezer as a standby. They defrost in minutes and can be whipped into this delicious pâté or mixed with crème fraîche and tossed through hot pasta for an instant sauce.

Quick tuna pâté

This simple pâté can be ready in minutes, and makes an almost instant appetizer or light lunch.

10 mins   1 min

SPECIAL EQUIPMENT
food processor
4 x 5fl oz (150ml) ramekins

SERVES 4

4 tbsp butter

2 x 7oz (200g) cans tuna in spring water, drained

1 tbsp olive oil

finely grated zest and juice of ½ lemon

2 tbsp chopped flat-leaf parsley leaves

½ cup fresh white bread crumbs

salt and freshly ground black pepper

crudités and toast, to serve

1 Place the butter in a small microwave-proof bowl and heat it in a microwave on medium heat for 30 seconds to 1 minute, or until melted. (Or melt it in a small saucepan over very low heat.)

2 Put the tuna, melted butter, and oil in a food processor and blend until smooth. Add the lemon zest and juice, parsley, and bread crumbs. Season and pulse-blend to combine.

3 Spoon into four 5fl oz (150ml) ramekins, cover, and chill until ready to serve. Serve with crudités and toast.

Most children who don't like fish can be won over by the mild flavor and firm texture of canned tuna. Try making little servings of this pâté for lunch boxes, adding some cucumber or carrot sticks.

Fussy eaters!

CALORIES: 246kcals/1024kJ
CARBOHYDRATE: 5g
 sugar: 0.2g
FAT: 14g
 saturated: 7g
SALT: 0.6g
FIBER: 0.5g

Moules marinière

Discard any mussels that do not close firmly when sharply tapped on the sink.

25 mins   10 mins

SERVES 4 (as an appetizer)

1 tbsp olive oil

2 tbsp butter

1 onion, roughly chopped

2 celery stalks, finely chopped

1 carrot, finely chopped

2 garlic cloves, finely chopped

½ cup dry white wine

3lb 3oz (1.5kg) live mussels, scrubbed and beards removed

freshly ground black pepper

½ cup heavy cream

leaves from 1 bunch of flat-leaf parsley, finely chopped

baguette, to serve

1 Heat the oil and butter in a large pan, big enough easily to hold all the mussels, over medium heat, and gently cook the onion, celery, carrot, and garlic for 5 minutes, stirring occasionally.

2 Add the wine and mussels and season with pepper. Increase the heat and bring to a boil. Cover and cook for 5 minutes, shaking the pan occasionally. Discard any mussels that do not open, and warn your guests to do the same.

3 Stir in the cream and parsley. Serve immediately with chunks of baguette.

CLEVER WITH LEFTOVERS
Any leftover mussels that have opened on cooking can be taken from their shells and open-frozen on a baking sheet. Once frozen, transfer to a freezer bag and add up to 10 at a time to enrich dishes such as fish pies and fish crumbles.

CALORIES: 373kcals/1551kJ
CARBOHYDRATE: 8g
 sugar: 4g
FAT: 28g
 saturated: 15g
SALT: 1g
FIBER: 1.5g

Smoked fish chowder

This soup is like a stew, full of nourishing fish, potatoes, and corn. Omit the bacon if you do not eat meat.

25 mins **30 mins**

SERVES 4-6

½ tbsp olive oil

1 onion, finely chopped

1 leek, finely sliced

2 garlic cloves, finely chopped

4 strips bacon, chopped

2 celery stalks, finely sliced

1¼lb (550g) floury potatoes, such as Russets, cut into 1in (3cm) cubes

2½ cups fish stock

freshly ground black pepper

1 x 7oz (195g) can corn (no added salt or sugar), drained

1lb (450g) undyed smoked haddock fillet, skinned and chopped into bite-sized pieces

2 tbsp chopped flat-leaf parsley leaves

whole wheat bread, to serve

1 Heat the oil in a large pan over medium heat. Cook the onion and leek for 5 minutes, until soft, but not browned. Add the garlic, bacon, and celery. Cook for 2 minutes.

2 Add the potatoes and stock, season well with pepper, and bring to a boil. Reduce the heat, cover, and simmer for 15 minutes, or until the potatoes are tender when pierced with a sharp knife.

3 Stir in the corn and haddock, cover, and cook for 3–5 minutes, or until the fish just starts to flake. Be careful not to overcook the fish. Gently stir in the parsley.

4 Ladle into warmed bowls and serve with thickly sliced whole grain bread.

VARIATION

Make this extra special by adding cooked shrimp, shelled and deveined, with the haddock, heating them through thoroughly.

CALORIES: 348kcals/1472kJ

CARBOHYDRATE: 36g
  sugar: 8g

FAT: 5g
  saturated: 1g

SALT: 2.6g

FIBER: 7g

Seared tuna Niçoise

Although traditionally served without potatoes, the addition of small, warm new potatoes makes this a complete meal.

10 mins   **30 mins**

SERVES 4

10oz (300g) small new potatoes, halved

salt and freshly ground black pepper

3½oz (100g) thin green beans, halved

4 skinless tuna steaks, approx. 3½oz (100g) each

16 cherry tomatoes, halved

bag of mixed leaf salad, approx. 4oz (120g)

4 hard-boiled eggs, peeled and quartered

1¾oz (50g) pitted black olives

FOR THE DRESSING

3 tbsp olive oil, plus extra for brushing

1½ tbsp red wine vinegar

1 tsp granulated sugar

1 heaping tsp Dijon mustard

1 Cook the potatoes in a large pan of boiling salted water until tender (about 20 minutes). Drain.

2 Meanwhile, make the dressing in a large bowl. Whisk together the oil, vinegar, sugar, and mustard, and season well. Cook the green beans in a pan of boiling salted water for 2–3 minutes until just tender, then drain them, refresh under cold water, and drain again.

3 When the potatoes are ready, heat a grill pan or large frying pan. Brush the tuna with a little oil and season well. Cook over high heat for 2–3 minutes each side for medium-rare, or longer for well done. Rest the fish while you finish the salad.

4 Put the still-warm potatoes into the dressing and turn them through to coat. Add the green beans, tomatoes, and salad leaves and toss them all together.

5 Serve the salad on a platter, or individual plates. Place the egg around, scatter with the olives, and top with tuna, sliced into pieces.

FEEDING A CROWD

If you are having a summer lunch party or buffet, make double or triple quantities of this salad. Fresh tuna can be expensive, so don't double up on that, just cut it into strips and sear it for a minute on each side before scattering on top of the salad.

CALORIES: 432kcals/1805kJ

CARBOHYDRATE: 15g
  sugar: 4g

FAT: 27g
  saturated: 5g

SALT: 0.7g

FIBER: 3g

Warm herring, new potato, and beet salad

A modern version of a Swedish main course salad, this is even more delicious served while the potatoes are warm.

10 mins   20 mins

SERVES 4

14oz (400g) small new potatoes, peeled and halved

salt and freshly ground black pepper

12oz (300g) tub of marinated herrings

2 tbsp light olive oil

2 tbsp finely chopped dill

2 heaping tsp Dijon mustard

2 Little Gem lettuces, leaves separated (larger ones halved lengthwise)

7oz (200g) cooked baby beets (not in vinegar)

3 hard-boiled eggs, peeled and quartered

1 Cook the potatoes in a large pan of boiling salted water until they are tender (about 20 minutes, depending on the potato type). Drain and set aside.

2 Meanwhile, make the dressing in a large salad bowl. Whisk together ¼ cup of the herring marinade, the oil, dill, and mustard, and season well. Reserve 1 tbsp of the dressing.

3 While the potatoes are warm, toss them in the dressing. Gently toss through the fish and lettuce leaves. In a separate bowl, toss the beets with the reserved dressing, then decorate the salad with the eggs and beets.

COOK'S TIP

Marinated herrings and beets store, chilled, for weeks. Keep some in your fridge to have the basis of this dish.

CALORIES: 372kcals/1558kJ

CARBOHYDRATE: 27g
  sugar: 13g

FAT: 19g
  saturated: 2.5g

SALT: 2.1g

FIBER: 3g

Smoked mackerel salad

A package of smoked mackerel is a great fridge standby, and this healthy salad is a simple way of using it.

15 mins   10–15 mins

SERVES 4

salt and freshly ground black pepper

1¼lb (550g) new potatoes, well scrubbed and chopped into bite-sized chunks

7oz (200g) hot-smoked mackerel fillets, skinned

2oz (60g) baby salad leaves

2 tbsp chopped dill

2 tbsp chopped chives

7oz (200g) cooked beets (not in vinegar), roughly chopped

baguette, to serve

FOR THE DRESSING

¼ cup extra virgin olive oil

juice of 1 lemon

1 tsp whole grain mustard

1 tsp honey

1 garlic clove, finely chopped

1 Bring a large pan of salted water to a boil, add the potato chunks, and cook for 10–15 minutes, or until tender. Drain and set aside.

2 Meanwhile, break the mackerel into bite-sized pieces, removing any bones you find as you go, and place in a large serving bowl. Add the salad leaves and herbs, and gently toss together.

3 Place the dressing ingredients in a small bowl, season, and whisk together with a fork.

4 Add the warm potatoes to the serving bowl, pour in the dressing, and stir gently. Add the beets and serve immediately with the baguette.

CALORIES: 405kcals/1687kJ
CARBOHYDRATE: 27g
  sugar: 7.5g
FAT: 27g
  saturated: 5g
SALT: 1.2g
FIBER: 3.5g

Grilled salmon and salsa verde

A simple, tasty meal that takes just minutes to prepare but tastes piquant and sophisticated.

5 mins   5 mins

SPECIAL EQUIPMENT

small food processor

SERVES 4

4 salmon fillets, approx. 5½oz (150g) each

⅔ cup extra virgin olive oil, plus extra for rubbing

salt and freshly ground black pepper

2 tbsp chopped basil leaves

2 tbsp chopped flat-leaf parsley leaves

2 tbsp chopped mint leaves

3 tbsp lemon juice

6 anchovy fillets

1 tbsp capers, rinsed

2 tsp Dijon mustard

1 garlic clove, crushed

CALORIES: 541kcals/2242kJ
CARBOHYDRATE: 0.5g
  sugar: 0.5g
FAT: 46g
  saturated: 7g
SALT: 1g
FIBER: 0g

1 Preheat the broiler to its highest setting. Rub the salmon with a little oil and season it well on both sides. Broil for 3–5 minutes on each side (depending on thickness), until crispy outside and moist within.

2 Meanwhile, to make the salsa verde, put all the remaining ingredients except the oil into the bowl of a small food processor. Purée to a rough paste, then pour in the oil in a thin stream, still processing, until you have a thick, vibrant, green sauce (you may not need all the oil). Season to taste.

3 Serve the fish over mashed potatoes with the salsa verde on the side.

BATCHING AND FREEZING

Buying herbs can be expensive and you may not need to use the whole bunch. Try doubling or tripling this salsa verde recipe, to use as many of the herbs as possible. The sauce will store in a jar in the fridge for up to 1 week, and can be used on grilled meats, in sandwiches, or even mixed into mayonnaise for an instant dip for crudités or dressing for a warm potato salad.

Salmon in foil

Baking in foil keeps the flavors in the fish and the smells out of the kitchen, and saves on the cleaning up too!

10 mins   20-25 mins

SERVES 4

1 tbsp olive oil

4 salmon fillets, approx. 3½oz (100g) each

salt and freshly ground black pepper

2 lemons

4 tbsp butter, cut into cubes

bunch of chives

new potatoes and steamed green vegetables, to serve

1 Preheat the oven to 350°F (180°C). Line a shallow ovenproof dish, large enough to hold all the salmon fillets, with a piece of foil big enough to completely wrap over the top of the dish. Brush the foil with the oil.

2 Place the salmon on the foil, skin-side down, and season well. Squeeze the juice from one lemon and drizzle it over the fish. Slice the second lemon into four and place a slice centrally on each fillet, to release juice and baste the fish as it bakes.

3 Arrange the butter over and around the salmon and place the whole chives over the fish. Bring the edges of the foil together to make a sealed parcel.

4 Bake in the oven for 20–25 minutes, depending on the size of the fillets. Remove the lemon slices and chives from the foil and discard.

5 Transfer the fish to warmed serving plates. Drizzle the lemon butter from the foil over the salmon and serve with new potatoes and steamed green vegetables.

Cooking in individual foil parcels allows you to vary the seasonings within each. This way you can spice up your own portion, and keep others completely plain for those who prefer it that way.

Fussy eaters!

CALORIES: 300kcals/1234kJ	
CARBOHYDRATE: 0g	
sugar: 0g	
FAT: 24g	
saturated: 9g	
SALT: 0.3g	
FIBER: 0g	

Spice-rubbed salmon

This simple Cajun-inspired rub instantly livens up any fish, and is ideal for those who can find fish dull.

5 mins, plus resting   5-10 mins

SPECIAL EQUIPMENT
spice grinder (optional)

SERVES 4

1 tsp smoked paprika

1 tsp cayenne pepper

½ tsp dried thyme

1 tsp light brown sugar

½ tsp salt

4 skinless salmon fillets, approx. 5½oz (150g) each

2 tbsp olive oil

1 Combine the spices, thyme, sugar, and salt in a mortar and pestle or a spice grinder and grind to a fine powder.

2 Rub the mixture over both sides of the fish, cover with plastic wrap, and let rest in the fridge for 1 hour, so the flavors can sink into the fish.

3 Preheat the broiler to its highest setting and line a broiler pan with foil. Brush the fish with a little oil on both sides, being careful not to dislodge the spice rub, and broil for 3–4 minutes on each side, depending on thickness.

HOW TO FREEZE

The salmon can be marinated in the rub and frozen, uncooked. Defrost thoroughly before cooking from the start of step 3.

CALORIES: 324kcals/1384kJ
CARBOHYDRATE: 1g
  sugar: 1g
FAT: 22g
  saturated: 3.5g
SALT: 0.6g
FIBER: 0g

Salmon and potato gratin

This rich, creamy dish would convert anyone to the joys of eating oily fish. It's immensely comforting, too.

15 mins   1 hr

SPECIAL EQUIPMENT
10in (25cm) ovenproof dish

SERVES 4

1¾lb (800g) potatoes, peeled weight

salt and freshly ground black pepper

butter, softened, for greasing

2 heaping tbsp finely chopped dill

12oz (350g) skinless salmon fillets, cut into ¾in (2cm) chunks

¾ cup half-and-half

⅔ cup fish or vegetable stock (see p156)

1 Preheat the oven to 375°F (190°C). Cut the potatoes into ¼in- (5mm-) thick slices. Bring them to a boil in a large pan of boiling salted water and simmer for five minutes, until part-cooked. Drain well. Rub a 10in (25cm) ovenproof dish with the butter.

2 Layer half the potato slices in the dish. Sprinkle the dill on the potatoes, lay the salmon over in a single layer, and season well. Top with the rest of the potatoes, making sure that the final layer looks neat.

3 Whisk the half-and-half and stock together, pour it over the potatoes, and cook for 50 minutes to 1 hour, until the top is crispy and the potatoes cooked through.

COOK'S TIP

Salmon can be expensive, but should be part of a family's diet as it is rich in healthy omega-3 fatty acids. Try buying the more inexpensive tail fillets, which are perfect for this dish.

CALORIES: 423kcals/1769kJ
CARBOHYDRATE: 33g
  sugar: 2g
FAT: 22g
  saturated: 9g
SALT: 0.6g
FIBER: 3.5g

Baked fish with cherry tomatoes

Use really ripe tomatoes for this dish and they will partially break down to make an instant sauce.

10 mins   25–30 mins

SERVES 4

4 tuna steaks, approx. 5½oz (150g) each

salt and freshly ground black pepper

finely grated zest of 1 lime, plus juice of ½ lime

2 garlic cloves, finely chopped

7oz (200g) cherry tomatoes, halved

⅔ cup dry white wine

¾ cup (7oz) plain yogurt

3 tbsp chopped cilantro leaves

roast new potatoes and green beans, to serve

1 Preheat the oven to 350°F (180°C). Place the tuna steaks in a single layer in a shallow ovenproof dish. Season well and sprinkle with the lime zest.

2 Arrange the chopped garlic and tomatoes over and around the fish. Pour the wine into the dish and cover tightly with foil. Bake for 20–25 minutes.

3 Meanwhile, put the yogurt, lime juice, and cilantro in a small serving dish, season generously with pepper, and stir well.

4 Remove the tuna steaks from the dish and place on warmed serving plates. Arrange a few tomatoes on each plate and spoon over some of the cooking juices. Serve with the cilantro and lime sauce, and with roast new potatoes and green beans.

CALORIES: 277kcals/1167kJ

CARBOHYDRATE: 5g
  sugar: 5g

FAT: 9g
  saturated: 3g

SALT: 0.3g

FIBER: 0.7g

VARIATION

Instead of tuna, this also works well with haddock or cod fillet, or any sustainable fish with a firm texture.

Baked fish with a herby crust

This easy fish recipe looks amazing with its vivid green crust, and is an aromatic crowd-pleaser.

5 mins   10 mins

SPECIAL EQUIPMENT
small food processor

SERVES 4

1 cup fresh white bread crumbs

2 tbsp roughly chopped basil leaves

2 tbsp roughly chopped flat-leaf parsley leaves

2 tbsp roughly chopped chives

finely grated zest of ½ lemon

salt and freshly ground black pepper

¼ cup olive oil, plus extra for brushing

4 fillets firm-fleshed, white, sustainable fish, such as cod or haddock, approx. 5½ oz (150g) each

1 Preheat the oven to 425°F (220°C). In a small food processor, pulse the bread crumbs, herbs, lemon zest, and seasoning, until the bread crumbs are bright green.

2 Add the oil in a slow stream, with the food processor running, until it forms a thick, bright green paste.

3 Brush the fish fillets with a little oil on both sides and season them well. Press the herby crust onto the top (or skinless side) of the fillets, packing it down well. Place on a non-stick baking sheet and bake in the top of the oven for 10 minutes, or until cooked through and turning crispy on top.

CALORIES: 290kcals/1214kJ

CARBOHYDRATE: 9g
  sugar: 0g

FAT: 15g
  saturated: 2g

SALT: 0.5g

FIBER: 0.5g

HOW TO FREEZE

Use up extra herbs by making larger quantities of this bread crumb mix, and simply freeze in a sturdy freezer bag until needed. The bread crumbs can be used straight from the freezer.

Hake in green sauce

Add extra vegetables, such as lightly cooked peas or asparagus tips, to the sauce in keeping with its green theme.

10 mins · **14–16 mins**

SERVES 4

2 tbsp olive oil

2 garlic cloves, finely chopped

2 tbsp plain flour

⅔ cup dry white wine

¾ cup fish stock

¼ cup chopped flat-leaf parsley leaves

salt and freshly ground black pepper

4 skin-on hake fillets, approx. 5½oz (150g) each

sautéed potatoes and green beans, to serve

1 Heat the oil in a large, non-stick frying pan over medium heat. Gently cook the garlic for 1 minute.

2 Sprinkle the flour into the pan and stir thoroughly with a wooden spoon. Cook for 2 minutes, stirring until smooth. Gradually add the wine, followed by the stock, stirring constantly.

3 Stir in the parsley and simmer very gently over low heat for about 5 minutes.

4 Season the fish and add to the pan, skin-side down. Spoon some sauce over the top and cook for 2–3 minutes. Turn and cook for another 2–3 minutes, or until cooked through.

5 Transfer to warmed plates and serve immediately with sautéed potatoes and green beans.

CALORIES: 238kcals/998kJ

CARBOHYDRATE: 6g
  sugar: 0.3g

FAT: 9g
  saturated: 1.5g

SALT: 0.8g

FIBER: 0.3g

Keralan fish curry

The flavor and aroma of this exotic curry is beautifully subtle and fragrant, so try it with any firm white fish.

10 mins   15 mins

SERVES 4

1¾lb (800g) skinless haddock fillets, cut into bite-sized pieces

2 tsp ground turmeric

salt and freshly ground black pepper

1 tbsp vegetable oil

1 large onion, finely sliced

1 tsp black mustard seeds

5 curry leaves

1½in (4cm) fresh ginger, finely chopped

2 tbsp tamarind paste

¾ cup coconut milk

⅔ cup fish stock

2 scallions, finely sliced

1 red chile, seeded and finely chopped (optional)

basmati rice and chopped cilantro leaves, to serve

1 Place the haddock in a bowl, sprinkle with the turmeric, season, and stir to coat. Set aside.

2 Heat the oil in a large, non-stick frying pan over medium heat, and add the onion, black mustard seeds, and curry leaves. Cook gently for 10 minutes, stirring occasionally, until the onion is lightly brown.

3 Add the ginger and cook for 1 or 2 minutes, then add the tamarind paste, coconut milk, and stock, and stir well. Heat the sauce to a low simmer.

4 Add the fish and simmer gently for 3–4 minutes or until it is just cooked. Stir in the scallions and chile (if using).

5 Serve the curry with basmati rice, sprinkled with chopped cilantro leaves.

PREPARE AHEAD

Make the sauce (following steps 2 and 3) up to 2 days in advance. You can then reheat the sauce gently (do not boil or it may split, because of the coconut milk), and season and cook the fish just before you are ready to serve.

CALORIES: 213kcals/905kJ

CARBOHYDRATE: 5.5g
   sugar: 5g

FAT: 4.5g
   saturated: 0.5g

SALT: 0.8g

FIBER: 0.8g

Spinach and coconut shrimp curry

This mild, creamy curry flavored with coconut makes a light and fragrant supper dish that is easy to prepare.

15 mins   20 mins

SERVES 4

2 tbsp sunflower or vegetable oil

2 red onions, finely chopped

4 garlic cloves, finely chopped

2in (5cm) piece of fresh ginger, finely grated

¼–½ tsp chile powder

½ tsp turmeric

2 tsp ground cumin

1 tsp ground coriander

4 large tomatoes, peeled and finely chopped (see p191)

1 x 14fl oz (400ml) can coconut milk

10 fresh or dried curry leaves (optional)

5½oz (150g) spinach, shredded

14oz (400g) raw large shrimp, shelled and deveined

½ tsp granulated sugar

salt

basmati rice, warmed naan bread, and lime wedges, to serve

1 Heat the oil in a large, deep-sided frying pan or wok. Add the onions, garlic, and ginger and cook for 2–3 minutes over low heat until softened, but not browned. Add the spices and cook for another 1 or 2 minutes to release the flavors.

2 Add the tomatoes and continue to cook over low heat for another 2 minutes, until the tomato flesh starts to break down. Add the coconut milk and curry leaves (if using), and bring to a boil. Mix in the spinach and reduce the heat, continuing to cook until the spinach has wilted. Baby spinach will take 1 or 2 minutes, bigger leaves up to 4 minutes.

3 Add the shrimp, sugar, and a pinch of salt, and cook for another 2 minutes over high heat, or until the shrimp turns a bright pink color. Serve with basmati rice, warmed naan bread, and lime wedges on the side.

COOK'S TIP

A bag of shrimp in the freezer can be a life saver. To defrost them quickly, put them in a bowl of cold water for a few minutes, rubbing occasionally, until the ice starts to melt. Drain, put in one layer on a plate, and cover; they will be ready to cook in 30 minutes.

CALORIES: 204kcals/859kJ

CARBOHYDRATE: 14g
  sugar: 13g

FAT: 7g
  saturated: 1g

SALT: 0.9g

FIBER: 4g

Mackerel teriyaki

This Japanese-style mackerel is an affordable, tasty way to enjoy a fish high in healthy omega-3 fatty acids.

5 mins   15 mins

SERVES 4

2 garlic cloves, finely chopped

¾in (2cm) piece of fresh ginger, finely chopped

2 tbsp granulated sugar

¼ cup rice vinegar

¼ cup mirin

¼ cup sake

¼ cup soy sauce

salt and freshly ground black pepper

4 mackerel fillets, approx. 3½oz (100g) each

1 tbsp vegetable oil

chopped scallions, to garnish

noodles and stir-fried vegetables, to serve

1 Place the garlic, ginger, sugar, vinegar, mirin, sake, and soy sauce in a small pan and bring to a boil. Reduce the heat and simmer for about 10 minutes, until the mixture has thickened to a coating consistency.

2 Season the fish on both sides. Heat the oil in a large, non-stick frying pan over medium heat, add the mackerel skin-side down, and cook for 2 minutes until crisp.

3 Turn the fish over and cook for 1 minute. Add the sauce to the pan and cook for 2 minutes more.

4 Place the mackerel on serving plates, drizzle with a little of the sauce, and garnish with the scallions. Serve with noodles and stir-fried vegetables.

CALORIES: 317kcals/1320kJ

CARBOHYDRATE: 9g
  sugar: 9g

FAT: 19g
  saturated: 3.5g

SALT: 2.8g

FIBER: 0g

The strong taste of spinach means that children often don't like it. Try this creamy treatment of the iron-rich vegetable alongside chicken or fish.

Fussy eaters!

Salmon fishcakes

These are ideal as a main course, or you can form the mixture into small fishcakes to make bite-sized canapés.

20 mins, plus chilling   30 mins

SERVES 6

1lb (450g) potatoes, peeled and chopped into cubes

2lb (900g) skinless salmon fillets

1 onion, halved

2–3 bay leaves

1 tsp black peppercorns

4 scallions, finely chopped

2 tbsp horseradish cream

salt and freshly ground black pepper

juice and finely grated zest of 1 lemon

large handful of dill, chopped

pinch of cayenne pepper

FOR THE COATING

2 cups fresh bread crumbs

2 tbsp chopped chives (optional)

2 tbsp chopped parsley leaves (optional)

all-purpose flour, for coating

2 large eggs, lightly beaten

sunflower or vegetable oil, for frying

1 Place the potatoes in water and boil for 20 minutes, or until very tender. Drain and mash. Set aside.

2 Place the salmon in cold water with the onion, bay leaves, and peppercorns. Bring to a boil, simmer for 2 minutes, then turn off the heat and let cool for 20 minutes. Drain well, discarding the cooking liquid, and cool.

3 Flake the salmon into a large bowl. Fold in the cooled mashed potatoes and all the other fishcake ingredients. Mix well and shape into 12 round cakes. Cover with plastic wrap and chill for 1 hour before coating.

4 Mix the bread crumbs well with the herbs (if using). Season the flour, then put the flour, eggs, and bread crumbs in separate shallow bowls. Roll the salmon cakes in flour, dusting off excess, then in egg, then in bread crumbs.

5 Heat enough oil to cover the bottom of a frying pan and cook the fishcakes for 3–4 minutes on each side, or until crisp and hot. Drain on paper towels and serve.

CALORIES: 546kcals/2289kJ

CARBOHYDRATE: 43g
 sugar: 3.5g

FAT: 24g
 saturated: 4g

SALT: 1.1g

FIBER: 3g

Crispy trout with sweet tomato relish

This is a simple dish of fried fish made special with a homemade sweet-sour "ketchup."

10 mins, plus chilling   40 mins

SERVES 4

¼ cup all-purpose flour

1 tsp paprika

salt and freshly ground black pepper

2 large eggs, lightly beaten

1 cup panko bread crumbs or day-old bread crumbs

4 skinless trout fillets

sunflower or vegetable oil, for frying

Warm new potato salad (see p159), to serve

FOR THE TOMATO RELISH

¼ cup olive oil

½ red onion, finely chopped

2 large ripe tomatoes, peeled and roughly chopped (see p191)

2 tsp granulated sugar

2 tbsp balsamic vinegar

1 Sift the flour with the paprika and season well. Lay the flour, eggs, and bread crumbs out in 3 wide, shallow bowls.

2 Dust the fish fillets first with the flour, then coat them in egg, then in bread crumbs. Put them on a large plate, cover in plastic wrap, and rest in the fridge for 30 minutes. This helps the coating to stick.

3 Meanwhile, make the relish. Heat the olive oil in a heavy-bottomed saucepan. Cook the onion, covered, over low heat for up to 15 minutes, until soft and sweet but not brown. Add the tomatoes and cook for 10 minutes, until they break down. Add the sugar, vinegar, and 2 tbsp of water and cook over low heat for 5 minutes, until reduced to a thick relish. Season.

4 After the fish has rested, heat a ½in (1cm) depth of sunflower oil in a large frying pan. When it is hot, fry the fish for 2–3 minutes on each side, turning carefully, until golden brown and crispy. You will need to do this in two batches, so keep the first warm while you cook the rest. Serve with the relish and Warm new potato salad (see p159).

CALORIES: 536kcals/2244kJ

CARBOHYDRATE: 36g
 sugar: 8g

FAT: 26g
 saturated: 3g

SALT: 0.8g

FIBER: 2.5g

Fish pie

Try to use small, Gulf shrimp in this dish, which are tastier and also less likely to have been farmed.

20 mins 30–35 mins, plus resting

SPECIAL EQUIPMENT

7in (18cm) baking dish

SERVES 4

10oz (300g) skinless salmon fillet

7oz (200g) skinless smoked haddock fillet

4 tbsp unsalted butter

5 tbsp all-purpose flour, plus extra for dusting

1½ cups whole milk

salt and freshly ground black pepper

pinch of grated nutmeg

7oz (200g) cooked shrimp, shelled and deveined

3½oz (100g) baby spinach

9oz (250g) store-bought puff pastry, preferably all-butter

1 large egg, lightly beaten, for glazing

1 Preheat the oven to 400°F (200°C). Poach the salmon and haddock in simmering water for 5 minutes. Drain and cool.

2 Melt the butter in a pan. Remove from the heat and whisk in the flour until a paste is formed. Gradually add the milk, whisking to avoid any lumps. Season well and add the nutmeg. Bring the sauce to a boil, reduce the heat, and cook for 5 minutes, stirring.

3 Flake the fish into a bowl and add the shrimp. Spread the uncooked spinach over the top and pour the hot sauce over it. Season to taste. When the spinach has wilted, mix the filling together and transfer to a 7in (18cm) baking dish.

4 On a floured surface, roll out the pastry to a shape bigger than the baking dish, ⅛–¼in (3–5mm) thick. Cut a shape to fit the pie. Roll some of the trimmings out into long strips. Brush the rim of the dish with some egg and press the pastry strips around the rim.

5 Brush the edging with egg and top with the pastry lid. Press down to seal the lid and trim off any overhang. Brush the top with

egg and cut two slits in it. Bake in the top of the oven for 20–25 minutes until golden, and let rest for 5 minutes before serving.

PREPARE AHEAD

Leave the pie until cold, then cover, chill overnight, and reheat the next day. Make sure it is piping hot in the center, and cover the top with foil if the pastry is becoming too dark.

CALORIES: 694kcals/2908kJ

CARBOHYDRATE: 40g
  sugar: 5g

FAT: 39g
  saturated: 17g

SALT: 2.5g

FIBER: 2.8g

Cod in parsley and mustard sauce

This soothing white sauce is enlivened with the use of ample amounts of parsley and some piquant mustard.

 10 mins   30 mins

SERVES 4

3 tbsp butter

¼ cup all-purpose flour

1½ cups whole milk

6 tbsp chopped flat-leaf parsley leaves

2–3 tsp Dijon mustard

finely grated zest of 1 lemon

salt and freshly ground black pepper

4 skinless cod fillets, approx. 5½oz (150g) each

mashed potatoes and broccoli, to serve

1 Preheat the oven to 350°F (180°C). Melt the butter in a small, non-stick pan over low heat and whisk in the flour.

2 Cook, whisking constantly, for 2 minutes, until the mixture bubbles and separates.

3 Remove the pan from the heat and whisk in the milk, a little at a time, whisking well between each addition, until it has all been added and the sauce is smooth.

4 Return the pan to the heat and cook, stirring constantly, until the sauce thickens. Reduce the heat to low and cook, stirring occasionally, for 5 minutes. Whisk right into the edges of the sauce, as this is where it can burn.

5 Remove from the heat and add the parsley, mustard, lemon zest, and seasoning.

6 Place the cod fillets in a single layer in a shallow ovenproof dish. Pour the sauce over the top and cook in the oven for 20–25 minutes. Serve the cod with mashed potatoes and broccoli.

CALORIES: 290kcals/1211kJ

CARBOHYDRATE: 11g
  sugar: 4g

FAT: 13g
  saturated: 7.5g

SALT: 0.7g

FIBER: 0.4g

Sole with butter sauce

This sauce is perfect with flat fish or salmon steaks. Change it up by using tarragon or dill instead of parsley.

 15 mins   10 mins

SERVES 4

4 small whole sole, fins and tails trimmed

2 tbsp butter, melted

salt and freshly ground black pepper

1 small onion, finely chopped

2 tbsp cider vinegar

8 tbsp butter, cut into cubes

2 tbsp chopped parsley leaves

baby carrots and steamed new potatoes, to serve

1 Preheat the broiler. Line the broiler pan with foil. Lay the fish on the broiler pan and brush all over with butter. Season lightly on both sides. Broil for about 5 minutes on each side, turning carefully, until lightly golden and cooked through.

2 Meanwhile, put the onion in a small pan with 2 tbsp of water and the cider vinegar. Bring to a boil, reduce the heat, and simmer until the onion is soft and the liquid is reduced by one-half.

3 Whisk in the butter, a piece at a time, until the sauce is thickened. Stir in the parsley and season to taste.

4 Transfer the cooked fish to warmed plates, spoon over the sauce, and serve with baby carrots and steamed new potatoes.

CLEVER WITH LEFTOVERS

Fresh herbs can be expensive and sometimes they do not get used up before going bad. Finely chop leftover herbs and freeze them in ice cube trays with a little water, then transfer into freezer bags until needed. The flavor is not as aromatic as fresh herbs, but they are well suited to adding to sauces.

CALORIES: 500kcals/2079kJ

CARBOHYDRATE: 1.5g
  sugar: 1.5g

FAT: 34g
  saturated: 19g

SALT: 1.2g

FIBER: 0.3g

Smart shopping

You can save yourself and your family a lot of time, money, and effort with some smart shopping. This could mean shopping online to save time and fuel costs, or combing the shelves for in-store offers, last-minute discounts, and culinary inspiration. Buying in bulk can be effective, but only if you know you are going to use the items you are buying. Don't be attracted by supposed "offers" to buy things you don't need. For all smart shoppers, eating seasonally, planning ahead, and making a list can prevent waste and save money.

Cupboard love

A well-stocked pantry is a wonderful thing. It doesn't really matter whether you have a walk-in pantry or a few shelves in the kitchen, as long as you know where to find your culinary basics whenever you need them. Rotate the items in the cupboard regularly so that you move older items to the front and use them first. Throw out anything that's past its use-by-date, especially anything that's been opened. Simple, cheap plastic fasteners are great for keeping open packages airtight and spill free.

shopping on a budget

Grocery bills can be expensive for a growing family, so look carefully at items that are on sale. Break out of your usual routine and think about shopping in different places or buying store-brand alternatives.

Bulk buying This can be economical, as long as you have adequate storage. If you don't, consider buying commonly used items in larger, more cost-effective quantities and splitting the costs with friends or family.

shopping list

Keep your shopping list somewhere accessible—hanging up in the kitchen perhaps—so that all the family can add to it when they notice that something has run out.

Decant

Decanting bulk purchases into airtight storage containers makes them easier to store and to serve. For picky kids, try decanting store-brand cereal into clear containers and see if anyone detects the difference!

Eat seasonally and locally
Seasonal shopping isn't just good for the planet, it's also good for your health and your wallet. Food that has traveled shorter distances will be fresher, and seasonal gluts of fruit and vegetables bring prices down.

Check the sell-by dates before you buy. Make sure you choose items with the latest date—not only will they be fresher, but they will keep longer, too.

Special offers A good rule of thumb for a tempting offer is only to buy something if it is genuinely cheaper than usual, you use it regularly, or you've always wanted to try it but it was too expensive.

Keep in stock...

Stock up on these great pantry favorites—some are excellent bulk buys.

⭐ Dried pasta – various shapes and sizes

⭐ Dried beans – suitable for quick soups and stews

⭐ Rice – Arborio, basmati, white, and brown rice

⭐ Baking essentials – flours, rising agents, fast-acting dried yeast packages, dried fruits

⭐ Sugars – granulated, light brown, dark brown, and confectioners' sugar

⭐ Tomato products – canned tomatoes, tomato sauce, tomato paste

⭐ Oils – olive oil, extra virgin olive oil, sunflower oil, and vegetable oil

⭐ Vinegars – balsamic, cider, red, and white wine vinegars

⭐ Asian products – soy sauce, oyster sauce, sesame oil, chili oil, rice wine

⭐ Stocks – good quality chicken, beef, and vegetable stocks and stock powders

⭐ Canned fish – tuna, salmon, sardines, anchovies

Store-brand products Some brands are iconic for a reason—we love them because they taste good. Others are simply the result of good advertising. Experiment with store-brand products to find the ones that suit your family.

shop online

Shopping online can be a life saver for busy parents. Using a basic weekly list that you add extras to can prevent unnecessary purchases. Choose late-night delivery slots, which are sometimes cheaper or even free.

Shop around If you live close to an ethnic shop or supermarket, why not use it? Many Asian supermarkets sell dried herbs and spices at a fraction of the cost of big superstores, as well as bags of rice, dried beans, and an array of authentic ingredients at rock-bottom prices.

Chicken noodle soup

Make this with chicken stock (see right) to get a second delicious meal from a simple roast chicken.

  20 mins   20 mins

SERVES 4

2 tbsp olive oil

1 onion, finely chopped

1 leek, white part only, finely chopped

1 celery stalk, finely chopped

2 carrots, finely chopped

4 cups chicken stock (see right)

7oz (200g) cooked chicken, shredded, or the meat from making chicken stock (see right)

5½oz (150g) soup noodles, such as vermicelli

salt and freshly ground black pepper

2 tbsp finely chopped flat-leaf parsley leaves, to serve (optional)

CALORIES: 359kcal/1503kJ

CARBOHYDRATE: 35g
  sugar: 5.5g

FAT: 8g
  saturated: 1.5g

SALT: 0.9g

FIBER: 3g

1 Heat the oil in a large stock pot. Add the vegetables and cook over medium heat for 5–7 minutes until softened, but not browned.

2 Add the stock and bring to a boil. Reduce the heat to a gentle simmer and cook for about 10 minutes, until the vegetables are soft.

3 Add the chicken and noodles and continue to cook until the noodles are ready (follow the package instructions). Check the seasoning, add the parsley (if using), and serve.

CLEVER WITH LEFTOVERS

Save the green part of the leeks, wash them well, and store in the freezer. They have a more bitter taste than the white part, so are not good in this soup, but are excellent added to chicken stock (see right).

BATCHING AND FREEZING

If you have a lot of stock, double the recipe and cook it up to step 3. Add the chicken but leave out the noodles. Freeze it in portions. Defrost, bring to a boil, add the noodles, and cook until tender.

Chicken stock

Never throw away a chicken carcass. The bones make fantastic stock, which is the basis of many meals.

5 mins   1 hr 10 mins

MAKES 5½ CUPS

1 leftover cooked chicken carcass

1 celery stalk, roughly chopped

1 onion, quartered

1 large carrot, roughly chopped

1 leek, green part only

sprig of thyme, or some parsley sprigs, or both

1 bay leaf

½ tsp salt

1 heaping tbsp black peppercorns

CALORIES: 7kcals/27kJ

CARBOHYDRATE: 0g
  sugar: 0g

FAT: 0.7g
  saturated: 0.1g

SALT: 0.2g

FIBER: 0g

1 Put the chicken, vegetables, herbs, and seasoning into a large stock pot. Cover with 7 cups of water.

2 Bring to a boil, then reduce the heat to a simmer and cook, uncovered, for 1 hour, until reduced to a bit more than half the original volume. Skim off any impurities from the surface as necessary.

3 Strain the stock, cool completely, and chill or freeze. The stock can either be used as it is, or the meat can be picked from the carcass and used to make chicken noodle soup (see left).

COOK'S TIP

Use a raw chicken carcass to make a lighter, more refined stock suitable for sauces and Asian recipes. The darker stock recipe above, made from a cooked carcass, is more suitable for using in stews and soups.

Ribollita

Meaning "reboiled" in Italian, ribollita is a tasty and economical dish that is based on a traditional Tuscan soup.

10 mins, plus soaking   2 hrs

SERVES 4

3½oz (100g) dried navy beans, soaked overnight

2 tbsp extra virgin olive oil

1¾oz (50g) chopped pancetta

1 celery stalk, finely chopped

1 carrot, finely chopped

1 small onion, finely chopped

2 garlic cloves, crushed

2 sprigs of thyme

1 quantity chicken stock (see left)

2 handfuls or 3½oz (100g) kale, shredded

sea salt and freshly ground black pepper

scant 1oz (25g) finely grated Parmesan cheese

1 Rinse the soaked beans and place in a pan with plenty of cold water. Bring to a boil, skim off any foam, and reduce the heat to a simmer. Cook the beans for about 1 hour, until softened. Drain and set aside.

2 Heat the olive oil in a separate large saucepan and add the pancetta. Cook for 2–3 minutes over medium heat until crispy. Add the celery, carrot, and onion, then add the garlic and thyme. Continue to cook for another 2–3 minutes, until the vegetables are softened. Pour in the stock and add the drained beans. Simmer the stew for 30–40 minutes, uncovered, until the beans are very soft.

3 Add the kale, cover, and cook for 5 minutes until the leaves have wilted. Season to taste,

sprinkle with the Parmesan cheese, and serve with lots of chunks of crusty bread for dipping.

CALORIES: 206kcals/860kJ

CARBOHYDRATE: 15g
sugar: 4g

FAT: 11g
saturated: 3g

SALT: 1.3g

FIBER: 8g

Smoked chicken, bacon, and apple salad

This main course has a great smoky flavor, and plenty of crunch from the apple and walnuts.

20 mins   5 mins

SERVES 4

4 strips thick-cut bacon

1 crisp apple, such as Granny Smith

juice of ½ lemon

½ cup walnut pieces

7oz (200g) arugula or watercress

2 skinless smoked chicken breasts, approx. 10oz (300g) in total, sliced

FOR THE DRESSING

2 tbsp cider vinegar

¼ cup extra virgin olive oil

1 tsp Dijon mustard

2 tsp maple syrup

salt and freshly ground black pepper

CALORIES: 370kcals/1534kJ

CARBOHYDRATE: 7g
  sugar: 7g

FAT: 27g
  saturated: 5g

SALT: 1.1g

FIBER: 2g

1 Preheat the broiler to its highest setting. Broil the bacon until crisp, then drain on paper towels. When cold, break into large pieces.

2 Peel, core, quarter, and thinly slice the apple and drop into a bowl of water mixed with the lemon juice. Place a heavy-bottomed frying pan over medium heat, add the nuts, and stir to toast. Let cool.

3 Whisk together the dressing ingredients in a salad bowl until emulsified.

4 Put the arugula or watercress in the bowl and toss with the dressing. Drain and dry the apple and add to the salad with the chicken and three-quarters each of the walnuts and bacon. Gently toss the salad, then sprinkle with the remaining walnuts and bacon.

CLEVER WITH LEFTOVERS

Any leftover salad can be chopped up and mixed with good-quality mayonnaise to make an instant sandwich or wrap filling for a lunch box the following day.

Spicy Asian chicken salad

This vibrant salad is tasty as well as healthy, and a great dish to serve at a summer buffet.

25-30 mins   15 mins

SERVES 4-6

14oz (400g) boneless, skinless chicken breasts

salt

¼ cup lime juice (approx. 2 limes)

4 tsp Thai fish sauce

1 tbsp granulated sugar

pinch of chile flakes (optional)

1 Little Gem lettuce, shredded

3½oz (100g) beansprouts

1 large carrot, shaved using a vegetable peeler

6in (15cm) piece of cucumber, seeded and finely sliced

½ red bell pepper, finely sliced

½ yellow bell pepper, finely sliced

approx. 15 cherry tomatoes, halved

small handful of mint leaves, chopped

small handful of cilantro leaves, chopped

1¾oz (50g) salted peanuts, chopped (optional)

1 Poach the chicken in a large saucepan in plenty of simmering salted water or chicken stock (see p94) for 7–10 minutes, depending on thickness, until cooked through. Let cool, then thinly slice.

2 Whisk the lime juice, fish sauce, sugar, a pinch of salt, and the chile flakes (if using) together, until the sugar dissolves.

3 Mix together the salad vegetables, most of the herbs, and the chicken. Mix in the dressing and scatter with the remaining herbs and the peanuts (if using), to serve.

CALORIES: 245kcals/1031kJ

CARBOHYDRATE: 13g
  sugar: 12g

FAT: 8g
  saturated: 1.5g

SALT: 1.3g

FIBER: 4.5g

Grilled chicken Caesar salad

This has an easy version of the classic Caesar dressing, replacing the traditional recipe made with raw egg.

20 mins   20 mins

SPECIAL EQUIPMENT
mini food processor or
hand-held blender

SERVES 4

3½oz (100g) day-old baguette,
or other rustic white bread

4 tbsp olive oil

salt and freshly ground black
pepper

14oz (400g) boneless, skinless
chicken breasts

1 large Romaine lettuce, leaves
broken into bite-sized pieces

1oz (30g) Parmesan cheese shavings

FOR THE DRESSING

½ cup extra virgin olive oil

1 tbsp Dijon mustard

3 tbsp good-quality mayonnaise

4 anchovy fillets, chopped

½ tsp Worcestershire sauce

1 garlic clove, crushed

2 tbsp finely grated Parmesan
cheese

pinch of granulated sugar

1 Preheat the oven to 400°F
(200°C). Trim the bread
of any crusts and cut into ¾in
(2cm) cubes. Toss them with 3
tbsp of the olive oil, season well,
and spread them out on a large
baking sheet, in a single layer if
possible. Cook them at the top
of the oven for 6–8 minutes,
turning occasionally, until they
are golden brown on all sides.
Watch carefully so that they do
not burn. Set aside to cool. If you
do not have a grill pan, preheat
the broiler to its highest setting.

2 Meanwhile, rub the chicken
breasts with the remaining
olive oil, season well, and either
grill in a grill pan or broil them for
5 minutes on each side, or until
cooked through and nicely charred.
Set aside to cool, then slice.

3 To make the dressing, put all
the ingredients into the bowl
of a mini food processor, or into a
suitable container for a hand-held
blender, and process or blend
until they have emulsified into
a thick, creamy dressing. Season
with pepper. To serve, put the
lettuce in a large bowl and toss it
in the dressing. Scatter with the
croutons and Parmesan shavings
and arrange the warm chicken
slices on top.

CALORIES: 593kcals/2467kJ

CARBOHYDRATE: 15g
sugar: 2.5g

FAT: 45g
saturated: 9g

SALT: 1.5g

FIBER: 1.5g

Mild creamy chicken curry

Introducing children to more adventurous tastes can be hard, so start them off with this gently spiced curry.

15 mins   35-40 mins

SERVES 4

2 tbsp sunflower or vegetable oil

1 onion, finely chopped

2 garlic cloves, finely chopped

2-3 tbsp medium curry powder

1 tsp ground cumin

4 boneless, skinless chicken breasts, sliced lengthwise into 4-5 strips

2 cups chicken stock (see p94)

5½oz (150g) red lentils

⅔ cup (5oz) plain yogurt

salt and freshly ground black pepper

½ cup toasted sliced almonds

2 tbsp chopped cilantro leaves

basmati rice or naan breads, to serve

1 Heat half the oil in a large, non-stick frying pan that has a lid, and cook the onion for 5 minutes, or until softened, but not browned. Add the garlic and spices and cook for 2 minutes.

2 Add the remaining oil and the chicken and cook for 5-7 minutes, turning to coat the chicken in the spices and to seal it on all sides. Add the stock and lentils and bring to a boil. Cover, reduce the heat, and simmer for 20 minutes or until the chicken and lentils are cooked.

3 Stir in the yogurt, season to taste, and heat through for 2 minutes until piping hot once more. Do not return to a boil after adding the yogurt, or there is a risk that the curry sauce might separate.

4 Sprinkle the curry with the almonds and cilantro and serve with basmati rice or warmed naan bread.

CALORIES: 475kcals/1996kJ

CARBOHYDRATE: 26g
  sugar: 5.5g

FAT: 16g
  saturated: 2.5g

SALT: 0.7g

FIBER: 4g

Spicy chicken and tomato curry

Try making double or triple amounts of this fresh, zingy curry paste and freezing leftovers for another time.

20 mins   30-35 mins

SPECIAL EQUIPMENT
food processor

SERVES 4

FOR THE CURRY PASTE

1 onion, chopped

1in (2.5cm) fresh ginger, chopped

2 garlic cloves

juice of ½ lemon

2 tsp ground coriander

2 tsp ground cumin

½-1 tsp medium chili powder

1 tsp ground allspice

2 tsp garam masala

FOR THE CURRY

1 tbsp vegetable oil

1 onion, sliced

8 boneless, skinless chicken thighs

salt and freshly ground black pepper

2 tbsp tomato paste

2 potatoes, cut into ¾in (2cm) cubes

1 green bell pepper, sliced

1 red bell pepper, sliced

4 tomatoes, peeled, seeded, and chopped

1¼-1½ cups chicken stock (see p94)

rice and mini naan bread, to serve

1 Put the curry paste ingredients in a food processor. Blend to a paste. Set aside until needed.

2 For the curry, heat the oil in a large pan over medium heat and cook the onion for 5 minutes. Add the curry paste and chicken, season, and cook for 5 minutes.

3 Stir in the tomato paste, vegetables, and stock to cover. Cover. Simmer for 20-25 minutes. Serve with rice and warmed naan.

CALORIES: 344kcals/1450kJ

CARBOHYDRATE: 28g
  sugar: 11.5g

FAT: 8g
  saturated: 2g

SALT: 0.6g

FIBER: 6g

Chicken and coconut curry

This Thai-inspired curry is delicious. You can omit the eggplant and add cooked broccoli at the end instead.

20 mins, **25–30 mins**
plus marinating

SPECIAL EQUIPMENT
mini food processor

SERVES 4

FOR THE MARINADE
2 lemongrass stalks

3 garlic cloves, finely chopped

1 red chile, seeded and chopped

2 tbsp Madras curry paste

1 tbsp dark brown sugar

3 tbsp soy sauce

FOR THE CURRY
1lb (450g) boneless, skinless chicken
  thighs, cut into strips

½ tbsp vegetable oil

1 red onion, finely chopped

⅔ cup chicken stock (see p94)

1 x 14fl oz (400ml) can coconut
  milk

1 eggplant, cut into ¾in (2cm) cubes

2 zucchini, cut into ¾in (2cm) cubes

salt and freshly ground black
  pepper

Thai or regular basil leaves,
  to garnish

jasmine rice, to serve

1 Peel the lemongrass stalks to reveal the soft white centers; discard the tough outer layers and trim the ends of the stalks. Roughly chop the tender white inner layers of the lemongrass and place in a mini food processor with the garlic, chile, curry paste, sugar, and soy sauce. Blend well to a smooth paste, trying to remove all lumps as much as possible.

2 Place the chicken strips in a shallow dish and spoon over the marinade, stirring to coat thoroughly. Cover and set aside to marinate for 1 hour at room temperature. (You may marinate the chicken for up to 1 day if it is more convenient, but refrigerate if you plan to do so.)

3 Heat a large, non-stick frying pan that has a lid over high heat, add the oil, and reduce the temperature to medium. Add the onion and cook for 5 minutes, stirring occasionally, until softened, but not browned. Add the chicken and its marinade and cook for another 5 minutes, stirring occasionally to color the chicken on all sides.

4 Pour in the stock and coconut milk, then add the eggplant and zucchini. Season well, bring to a boil, cover, then reduce the heat and simmer gently for 15–20 minutes. Scatter with the Thai basil and serve with jasmine rice.

PREPARE AHEAD
Blend the marinade up to 2 days in advance, cover, and refrigerate. The flavors will deepen—especially the strengths of the chile and garlic tastes—the longer you leave it.

CALORIES: 387kcals/1623kJ

CARBOHYDRATE: 12g
  sugar: 8g

FAT: 24g
  saturated: 16g

SALT: 2.7g

FIBER: 2.5g

Easy chicken tikka skewers with cucumber and mint raita

This easy-to-make Indian dipping sauce can be a staple accompaniment to so many grilled or broiled dishes.

20 mins plus marinating — 10 mins

SPECIAL EQUIPMENT
8 bamboo skewers

SERVES 4

FOR THE MARINADE

6 tbsp plain low-fat yogurt

1 tbsp lemon juice

1 tsp ground cumin

1 tsp ground coriander

½ tsp turmeric

2 tsp cayenne pepper or chili powder

½ tsp salt

1 garlic clove, crushed

1in (3cm) fresh ginger, grated

1lb 5oz (600g) boneless, skinless chicken breast or thigh, cut into 1in (3cm) cubes

FOR THE RAITA

4in (10cm) piece of cucumber, seeded and grated

¾ cup (7oz) Greek-style yogurt

handful of mint leaves, finely chopped

1 small garlic clove, crushed

salt and freshly ground black pepper

1 Mix the marinade ingredients, except the chicken, in a bowl. Add the chicken, turning to coat. Cover and refrigerate for 1 hour.

2 Meanwhile, place 8 bamboo skewers in a large, shallow bowl of water, to keep them from burning.

3 Put the cucumber in a clean kitchen towel and squeeze well. Mix with the remaining raita ingredients and season to taste. Cover and chill.

4 Thread the chicken onto the soaked, drained skewers, distributing it evenly. Preheat the broiler and broil the chicken for 3–5 minutes on each side, or until starting to char. Serve with the raita.

VARIATION

For an even easier recipe, mix 2 tbsp of store-bought tikka paste with the yogurt and use that as the marinade.

CALORIES 242kcals/1019kJ
CARBOHYDRATE: 4.5g
  sugar: 4g
FAT: 7g
  saturated: 4g
SALT: 0.8g
FIBER: 0.5g

Easy General Tso's chicken

A healthier version of a take-out classic, try making this recipe as part of a weekend family feast.

15 mins plus marinating — 10 mins

SERVES 4

FOR THE MARINADE

1 tbsp soy sauce

1 tbsp rice wine or dry sherry

1 tsp granulated sugar

FOR THE CHICKEN

1lb 2oz (500g) boneless, skinless chicken thighs, cut into ¾in (2cm) cubes

2 heaping tbsp cornstarch

½ cup sunflower or vegetable oil, plus 1 tbsp

2 garlic cloves, finely chopped

1in (3cm) fresh ginger, finely chopped

shredded scallions, to serve

jasmine rice, to serve

FOR THE SAUCE

⅔ cup chicken stock (see p94)

1 tbsp tomato paste

2 tbsp soy sauce

1 tbsp hoisin sauce

1 tsp crushed chile flakes

1 tsp granulated sugar

1 Mix the marinade ingredients in a bowl, add the chicken, and turn to coat. Cover and refrigerate for 30 minutes. Whisk together the sauce ingredients. Set aside.

2 Put the cornstarch in a freezer bag. Add the chicken and shake to coat. Pour into a sieve to remove excess cornstarch.

3 Heat the ½ cup of oil in a wok. It's ready when an oil thermometer reads 350°F (180°C), or a cube of bread sizzles immediately. Fry the chicken in batches for 2–3 minutes each side, until crispy. Remove with a slotted spoon and drain on paper towels. Repeat to cook all the chicken.

4 Pour the oil from the wok and wipe it with paper towels. Heat another 1 tbsp of oil in the wok and cook the garlic and ginger for a minute. Mix the sauce ingredients, then pour into the wok and bring to a simmer. Return the chicken and cook for 2 minutes. Scatter with scallions and serve with rice.

CALORIES: 386kcals/1609kJ
CARBOHYDRATE: 10g
  sugar: 4.5g
FAT: 24.5g
  saturated: 3.5g
SALT: 2.5g
FIBER: 0.1g

Spicy stir-fried chicken with vegetables

This dish is quite spicy so, to reduce the heat for young or sensitive palates, cut down the amount of chile used.

15 mins
plus marinating

10 mins

SERVES 4

3 tbsp soy sauce

2 tbsp rice wine or dry sherry

1 tsp sugar

2½ tbsp sunflower or vegetable oil

14oz (400g) boneless, skinless chicken thighs, cut into ½in (1cm) strips

1¾oz (50g) thin green beans, halved

salt

1¾oz (50g) broccoli florets

2 garlic cloves, crushed

1in (3cm) fresh ginger, finely chopped

1 red chile, seeded and finely chopped

bunch of scallions, cut into ¾in (2cm) pieces

3½oz (100g) sugarsnap peas, halved on the diagonal

1 tbsp oyster sauce

1 Mix 1 tbsp of the soy sauce, 1 tbsp of the rice wine, the sugar, and ½ tbsp of the oil in a bowl. Stir in the chicken, cover, and refrigerate for 30 minutes.

2 Cook the green beans in a pan of boiling salted water for 1 minute. Add the broccoli and cook for another minute. Drain and refresh under cold water. Set aside.

3 Heat the remaining oil in a wok, add the garlic, ginger, and chile, and cook for 1 minute. Now add the chicken and stir for 2–3 minutes. Add the scallions and peas and stir-fry for another 2–3 minutes. Pour in the remaining soy sauce, rice wine, and the oyster sauce, and bubble up. Add in the blanched vegetables and heat through to serve.

CALORIES: 216kcals/904kJ

CARBOHYDRATE: 6g
sugar: 5g

FAT: 10g
saturated: 1.5g

SALT: 2.6g

FIBER: 2g

Stir-fried chicken and asparagus

The mild spicing in this dish complements the delicate flavor of the asparagus.

15 mins
plus marinating

10 mins

SERVES 4

2 tsp cornstarch

3 tbsp soy sauce

2 tbsp rice wine or dry sherry

2 tsp granulated sugar

1lb 2oz (500g) boneless, skinless chicken thighs, finely sliced

bunch of asparagus, woody ends removed, cut into 1in (3cm) pieces, stalks and tips separated

salt

2 tbsp sunflower or vegetable oil

2 garlic cloves, finely chopped

1½in (4cm) fresh ginger, finely chopped

bunch of scallions, cut into 1in (3cm) pieces

rice, to serve

1 Mix together 1 tsp of the cornstarch, 1 tbsp of the soy sauce, 1 tbsp of the rice wine, and 1 tsp of the sugar in a large bowl. Toss through the chicken, cover, and refrigerate for 30 minutes.

2 Meanwhile, cook the asparagus stalks in a pan of boiling salted water for 1 minute, then add the tips and blanch for another minute. Drain and refresh under cold water. Mix the remaining cornstarch with 1 tbsp of cold water. Set aside.

3 Heat the oil in a wok and, when it is hot, add the garlic and ginger and cook for 1 minute. Add the chicken and stir-fry for 3–4 minutes. Add the scallions and cook for another 2 minutes.

4 Add the remaining soy sauce, rice wine, sugar, and 2 tbsp of water, and bring to a boil.

5 Stir and add the cornstarch mixture, then the asparagus. Cook for another 2 minutes until the mixture thickens and the asparagus is hot. Serve over rice.

CALORIES: 241kcals/1008kJ

CARBOHYDRATE: 8g
sugar: 6g

FAT: 9.5g
saturated: 1.5g

SALT: 2.3g

FIBER: 2g

Sweet and sour chicken

Removing the pineapple chunks of the take-out version makes this a more sophisticated alternative.

15 mins, plus marinating   10 mins

SERVES 4

FOR THE MARINADE

1 tsp cornstarch

1 tbsp soy sauce

1 tbsp rice wine or dry sherry

1 tsp granulated sugar

FOR THE CHICKEN

1lb 2oz (500g) boneless, skinless chicken breast, cut into ½in (1cm) slices

2 tbsp sunflower or vegetable oil

2 garlic cloves, finely chopped

1in (3cm) fresh ginger, finely chopped

3½oz (100g) raw, unsalted cashews, roughly chopped

FOR THE SAUCE

2 tbsp rice wine vinegar or white wine vinegar

2 tbsp rice wine or dry sherry

3 tbsp ketchup

2 tbsp soy sauce

½ cup chicken stock (see p94)

1 tbsp granulated sugar

1 Mix the marinade ingredients in a bowl and turn the chicken to coat. Cover and refrigerate for at least 30 minutes.

2 Whisk together all the sauce ingredients and set aside.

3 Heat the oil in a wok, add the garlic and ginger, and stir-fry for 1 minute. Add the chicken and stir-fry until it turns pale.

4 Add the sauce and bring to a boil. Add the cashews and cook for 2–3 minutes until the mixture has thickened and the chicken is coated in a glossy sauce. Serve.

PREPARE AHEAD

If you want to get ahead, make this recipe without the cashews and freeze it. Defrost the chicken thoroughly, then reheat quickly until piping hot, stirring in the nuts just before serving.

CALORIES: 386kcals/1616kJ
CARBOHYDRATE: 14g
   sugar: 10g
FAT: 19g
   saturated: 3.5g
SALT: 2.7g
FIBER: 1g

Chicken and broccoli simmered in soy sauce and star anise

Deeply aromatic, this is a great recipe to cook for minimum fuss and easy clean-up.

10 mins   20-25 mins

SERVES 4

½ cup rice wine or dry sherry

¼ cup soy sauce

1¾ cups chicken stock (see p94)

1½in (4cm) fresh ginger, cut into matchsticks

2 garlic cloves, sliced

4 star anise

3 tbsp light brown sugar

4 boneless, skinless chicken breasts

1 tbsp cornstarch

5½oz (150g) broccoli rabe or broccoli florets

1 In a large, deep-sided frying pan or wok, mix the rice wine, soy sauce, stock, ginger, garlic, star anise, and sugar and bring to a boil over medium heat. Reduce the heat and simmer for 5 minutes.

2 Add the chicken in a single layer, making sure it is submerged as much as possible, and poach for 7–10 minutes, turning occasionally, until firm. Remove with a slotted spoon, cover, and keep warm.

3 Strain the liquid through a sieve and return it to the pan. Return it to a boil over medium heat, then reduce the heat to a simmer. Mix the cornstarch with 1 tbsp of water and add, whisking until it thickens. Add the broccoli and cook for 3–5 minutes until tender.

4 Pour the sauce over the chicken and arrange the broccoli around to serve.

VARIATION

Use quartered bok choy, Napa cabbage cut into wedges, or lengths of scallions instead of broccoli.

CALORIES: 282kcals/1192kJ
CARBOHYDRATE: 16g
   sugar: 12.5g
FAT: 2g
   saturated: 0.5g
SALT: 2.8g
FIBER: 1.5g

Pot-roast chicken

A simple one-pot, succulent, and tender variation of the traditional roast chicken loved by all.

10 mins   1 hr 45 mins

SPECIAL EQUIPMENT
large Dutch oven

SERVES 4

2 tbsp olive oil

1 large onion, cut into 8 wedges

1 leek, cut into 1in (3cm) pieces

1 celery stalk, cut into 1in (3cm) pieces

4 carrots, cut into 1in (3cm) pieces

2 garlic cloves, roughly chopped

8 new potatoes, skin on, halved

1½ cups chicken stock (see p94)

sprig of thyme

1 bay leaf

salt and freshly ground black pepper

1 chicken, approx. 3lb 3oz (1.5kg)

pat of butter

1. Preheat the oven to 350°F (180°C). Heat the oil in a large Dutch oven. Cook the onion, leek, celery, and carrots for 5 minutes until softened and browning. Stir in the garlic and potatoes and cook for 2 minutes.

2. Add the stock, herbs, black pepper, and a little salt. Rub the chicken with the butter and season the breast with salt and pepper.

3. Place the chicken on the vegetables. If it is close to the lid of the pan, cover it loosely with parchment paper to prevent it from sticking. Cover and cook in the oven for 1 hour.

4. Remove the lid, increase the oven temperature to 400°F (200°C), and cook for another 30 minutes, until the breast is golden brown and the sauce reduced. Remove the herbs before serving.

COOK'S TIP

Remove the chicken and vegetables and reduce the cooking liquid over high heat for 5 minutes to thicken.

HOW TO FREEZE

Remove the chicken from the bone in the largest pieces possible before freezing. (Smaller pieces can dry out in the freezer.)

CALORIES: 495kcals/2082kJ

CARBOHYDRATE: 27g
  sugar: 11.5g

FAT: 13.5g
  saturated: 3.5g

SALT: 0.7g

FIBER: 6g

Chicken with pancetta, peas, and mint

This delicious dish can be prepared in minutes and left in the oven to cook, with no extra attention needed.

15 mins   1 hr 45 mins

SPECIAL EQUIPMENT
large Dutch oven

SERVES 4

2 tbsp olive oil

4 large or 8 small skin-on bone-in chicken pieces

2 onions, finely chopped

7oz (200g) chopped pancetta or bacon

2 garlic cloves, grated or finely chopped

1 cup dry white wine

2 cups hot chicken stock (see p94)

salt and freshly ground black pepper

handful of flat-leaf parsley leaves, finely chopped

handful of mint leaves, finely chopped

8oz (225g) frozen peas

crusty bread and sautéed potatoes, to serve

1. Preheat the oven to 300°F (150°C). Heat 1 tbsp of the oil in a large Dutch oven over medium heat. Add the chicken and cook for about 8 minutes, turning, until golden all over. Remove from the Dutch oven and set aside.

2. Reduce the heat to low and add the remaining oil and onions to the Dutch oven. Cook gently for 5 minutes until soft and translucent, then add the pancetta. Increase the heat and cook for 5 minutes until the pancetta is golden. Stir in the garlic, then pour in the wine. Increase the heat to high and simmer for a few minutes until the alcohol has evaporated.

3. Add the stock and return to a boil. Season with salt and pepper and stir through. Return the chicken. Stir in half the parsley and mint, cover, and cook in the oven for 1½ hours. Check the level of liquid occasionally—it needs to be fairly dry, but if it needs more, add a little hot water. Stir in the peas and remaining chopped herbs 5 minutes before the end of cooking time. Serve hot with crusty bread or sautéed potatoes.

CALORIES: 510kcals/2125kJ

CARBOHYDRATE: 10g
  sugar: 4g

FAT: 26g
  saturated: 7g

SALT: 2.1g

FIBER: 4.5g

Chicken and barley stew

A nutritious, warming, and comforting one-pot dish that needs nothing more than mashed potatoes on the side.

10 mins   1 hr 15 mins

SPECIAL EQUIPMENT
large Dutch oven (optional)

SERVES 4

5½oz (150g) pearl barley

4 tbsp sunflower or vegetable oil

1 large onion, chopped

1 leek, sliced into ½in (1cm) rings

1 celery stalk, cut into
¾in (2cm) pieces

2 large carrots, cut into
¾in (2cm) pieces

1 parsnip, cut into ¾in (2cm) pieces

salt and freshly ground black pepper

1 tbsp all-purpose flour

8 skinless bone-in chicken thighs

2 cups chicken stock (see p94)

1 bouquet garni

1 Put the barley in a saucepan and cover it with cold water. Place over high heat and bring to a boil. Cook for 10 minutes, skimming off foam. Drain and rinse.

2 In a large Dutch oven or heavy-bottomed saucepan with a lid, heat 2 tbsp of the sunflower oil.

Cook the onion, leek, celery, carrots, and parsnip for 10 minutes over medium heat until they color at the edges. Remove from the pan and wipe it out with paper towels.

3 Heat the remaining 2 tbsp of oil in the pan. Season the flour. Dust the chicken with the flour, shaking off excess. Cook the pieces, spaced well apart, for 3–5 minutes each side until golden. You may need to cook in batches. Set aside.

4 Pour in the stock, scraping up the residue from the pan. Return the vegetables, barley, and chicken. Add the bouquet garni.

5 Bring to a boil, then reduce the heat to a gentle simmer and cook, covered, for about 45 minutes, until the chicken is cooked through. Remove the bouquet garni before serving.

CALORIES: 513kcals/2156kJ

CARBOHYDRATE: 45g
  sugar: 10g

FAT: 17g
  saturated: 3g

SALT: 0.8g

FIBER: 6g

Spanish chicken, chorizo, and pepper stew

A quick and satisfying crowd pleaser of a recipe that adds a dash of warming spice to family meal times.

10 mins   1 hr 15 mins

SPECIAL EQUIPMENT
large Dutch oven (optional)

SERVES 4

3 tbsp olive oil

1 tbsp all-purpose flour

salt and freshly ground black pepper

8 skinless bone-in chicken pieces, thighs, drumsticks, or a mixture

1 red onion, finely sliced

1 red bell pepper, finely sliced

1 yellow bell pepper, finely sliced

2 garlic cloves, chopped

5½oz (150g) dry Spanish-style chorizo, casing removed, cut into 1in (3cm) pieces

1 heaping tsp smoked paprika

1 x 14oz (400g) can chopped tomatoes

1¾ cups chicken stock (see p94)

2 heaping tbsp chopped flat-leaf parsley leaves

a few sprigs of thyme

1 In a large Dutch oven or pot with a lid, heat 2 tbsp of the olive oil. Season the flour with salt and pepper. Dust the chicken pieces with the flour, shaking off excess. Cook them in the pan, spaced well apart, for a few minutes each side, until golden brown. Remove from the pan.

2 Heat the remaining 1 tbsp of oil and cook the onion and peppers for 5 minutes until softened, but not browned. Add the garlic and cook for another minute. Add the chorizo and cook for a few minutes until it becomes crisp at the edges and the reddish oil starts to run. Sprinkle in the smoked paprika and stir well.

3 Add the tomatoes, stock, and herbs and season to taste. Finally, return the chicken to the pan, cover, and simmer over low heat for 40–45 minutes, until the chicken is cooked (pierce a thick piece to the bone to check; there should be no trace of pink). Remove the thyme and serve.

BATCHING AND FREEZING
To get ahead, make this meal when there are only two of you for dinner. Divide the remaining 2 portions into separate freezer- and microwave-safe containers and freeze. Defrosted, and reheated in a microwave, these frozen portions make ideal lunches on busy days, with no effort. Accompany with crusty bread.

CALORIES: 485kcals/2029kJ
CARBOHYDRATE: 13g
    sugar: 9g
FAT: 23g
    saturated: 6.5g
SALT: 1.4g
FIBER: 3g

Mediterranean chicken

This colorful one-pot meal is stuffed full of vitamin-rich vegetables, pleasing the eye as well as the palate.

20 mins   1 hr

SERVES 4

9oz (250g) butternut squash, peeled and cut into 1in (3cm) cubes

1 red bell pepper, cut into 1in (3cm) cubes

1 yellow bell pepper, cut into 1in (3cm) cubes

2 small red onions, quartered

14oz (400g) small new potatoes, halved

2 tbsp olive oil, plus extra for greasing

1 tbsp chopped flat-leaf parsley

salt and freshly ground black pepper

8 skin-on bone-in chicken thighs

10oz (300g) cherry tomatoes

2 tbsp chopped basil leaves

4 small sprigs of rosemary

1 Preheat the oven to 350°F (180°C). In a large metal roasting pan, mix the squash, peppers, onions, and potatoes with the olive oil and parsley. Season them well and spread out in a single layer.

2 Rub the chicken thighs with a little oil, season them, and poke into the layer of vegetables.

3 Roast in the oven for 40 minutes. Remove from the oven and increase the oven temperature to 200°C (400°F).

4 Mix in the tomatoes and basil, with another splash of olive oil if necessary, and tuck in the rosemary. Spread it all out and cook for another 15–20 minutes at the top of the oven, until the chicken is crisp and the tomatoes are just starting to burst. Remove the rosemary and serve.

CALORIES: 428kcals/1795kJ

CARBOHYDRATE: 29g
sugar: 12.5g

FAT: 18g
saturated: 4g

SALT: 0.4g

FIBER: 6g

FEEDING A CROWD

Casseroles are ideal for large numbers, as they can be prepared ahead and need little tending. Use 2 pieces of chicken per person, and add more vegetables. Do not crowd the pan: use 2, so the ingredients can be spread out in a single layer.

Coq au vin

A classic French dish that makes a comforting winter meal. The alcohol cooks off, leaving only a rich taste.

10 mins   1 hr 10 mins

SERVES 4

4 tbsp olive oil

3½oz (100g) chopped pancetta

5½oz (150g) small button mushrooms, wiped, and halved if necessary

12 small pearl onions or shallots, peeled

4 tbsp all-purpose flour

salt and freshly ground black pepper

8 skinless bone-in chicken pieces, thighs, drumsticks, or a mixture

¼ cup brandy (optional)

1¼ cups red wine

1¼ cups chicken stock (see p94)

1 tbsp redcurrant or sour cherry jelly

1 bouquet garni

CALORIES: 564kcals/2361kJ

CARBOHYDRATE: 17g
sugar: 5.5g

FAT: 20g
saturated: 4g

SALT: 1.3g

FIBER: 2g

1 In a large pot with a lid, heat 2 tbsp of the oil over medium heat. Cook the pancetta, mushrooms, and small onions for 5 minutes, until golden brown. Remove from the pan.

2 Heat the remaining 2 tbsp of oil in the pan. Season 1 tbsp of the flour with salt and pepper and put on a plate. Dust the chicken with the flour, shaking off excess. Cook the chicken, well spaced (you may have to do this in batches), for 3–5 minutes each side, until golden brown. Add the brandy (if using), take it off the heat, and ignite with a match to cook off the alcohol.

3 Remove the chicken from the pan and add it to the vegetables and pancetta. Add the remaining 3 tbsp of flour to the pan and stir for a minute. Add the wine, stock, redcurrant jelly, and bouquet garni.

4 Return the chicken, pancetta, and vegetables and bring to a boil. Reduce to a simmer, cover, and cook for 40–45 minutes, until cooked through. Remove the bouquet garni to serve.

Moroccan-spiced chicken

A gently spiced stew, sweet with squash and dried apricots, this is particularly appealing to younger children.

15 mins   1 hr 10 mins

SERVES 4

1 heaping tbsp all-purpose flour

salt and freshly ground black pepper

8 skinless bone-in chicken pieces,
   thighs, drumsticks, or a mixture

4 tbsp olive oil

1 large onion, finely chopped

1 red bell pepper, sliced

1 yellow bell pepper, sliced

2 garlic cloves, roughly chopped

1 tsp ground cumin

½ tsp ground coriander

½ tsp ground cinnamon

1 tsp smoked paprika

1 tsp dried thyme

1 x 14oz (400g) can chopped tomatoes

2 cups chicken stock (see p94)

1 tbsp honey

9oz (250g) butternut squash, peeled
   and cut into ¾in (2cm) cubes

1¾oz (50g) dried apricots,
   roughly chopped

handful of cilantro leaves,
   roughly chopped

1 Place the flour in a freezer bag and season it well. Toss the chicken in the bag until well coated. Pour out into a sieve and shake to remove excess flour.

2 Heat 2 tbsp of the oil over medium heat in a large, heavy-bottomed pot with a lid. Cook the chicken (you may need to do this in batches), spaced well apart, for 3–5 minutes each side, until golden brown all over. Set aside while you cook the remaining pieces.

3 Heat the remaining 2 tbsp of oil in the pan and cook the onion, peppers, and garlic for 3–5 minutes until softened, but not brown. Add all the spices and the thyme and cook for a minute or two until they release all their fragrances. Add the tomatoes, stock, and honey, and season to taste.

4 Return the chicken and bring to a boil. Reduce the heat to a low simmer and cook, covered, for 20 minutes. Add the squash and apricots and cook, covered, for another 20 minutes, stirring occasionally, until the chicken is cooked through. Stir in the cilantro leaves to serve.

PREPARE AHEAD

Stews or slow-cooked dishes often taste better the day after they are made, as time allows the flavors to develop. Cook this dish a day or two in advance and, when it is cold, remove the chicken from the bones and store it in an airtight container in the fridge. Removing the bones saves space and allows it to reheat more easily.

CALORIES: 414kcals/1739kJ

CARBOHYDRATE: 26g
   sugar: 20g

FAT: 16g
   saturated: 3g

SALT: 0.8g

FIBER: 6g

Chicken cacciatore

Chicken breasts can be dry. Cooking them in this rich, Italian sauce will give them a succulent texture.

10 mins   50-55 mins

SPECIAL EQUIPMENT
Dutch oven

SERVES 4

1 tbsp olive oil

4 skin-on bone-in chicken breasts

1 red onion, finely chopped

2 garlic cloves, finely chopped

1 red bell pepper, sliced

2 x (14oz) 400g cans chopped tomatoes

¾ cup chicken stock (see p94)

½ tsp dried rosemary

2½oz (75g) pitted black olives

salt and freshly ground black pepper

basil leaves, to garnish

pasta or cooked rice, to serve

1 Preheat the oven to 375°F (190°C). Place half the oil in a large, heavy-bottomed Dutch oven over medium heat and brown the chicken on all sides. Remove with a slotted spoon and set aside on a plate lined with paper towels.

2 Add the remaining oil and cook the onion for 5 minutes, stirring occasionally. Add the garlic and pepper and cook for another 2 minutes. Add the tomatoes, stock, rosemary, and olives, season well, and stir.

3 Return the chicken and coat in the sauce. Bring to a boil, cover, and bake in the oven for 30–35 minutes, or until the chicken is cooked. Sprinkle with basil and serve with pasta or cooked rice.

CALORIES: 301kcals/1267kJ
CARBOHYDRATE: 10g
  sugar: 9g
FAT: 10g
  saturated: 2g
SALT: 0.8g
FIBER: 4g

For a different texture, use two 15oz (425g) cans of tomato sauce instead of the canned chopped tomatoes. This gives a smoother sauce for children who are not keen on "lumps."

Fussy eaters!

Chicken and white bean stew

Soaking dried beans is preferable to using canned. They are far cheaper and tastier.

20 mins, plus soaking   2 hrs

SERVES 4

5½oz (150g) dried white beans, such as navy or cannellini

3 tbsp olive oil

1 tbsp all-purpose flour

salt and freshly ground black pepper

8 skinless bone-in chicken pieces, thighs, drumsticks, or a mixture

1 onion, finely chopped

2 garlic cloves, finely chopped

¾ cup white wine (optional)

2 cups chicken stock (see p94), or 2½ cups if not using wine

2 heaping tbsp chopped flat-leaf parsley leaves

1 tbsp finely chopped oregano leaves

sprig of rosemary

9oz (250g) cherry tomatoes

1 Soak the beans overnight in lots of cold water. Make sure they have plenty of room to swell. Drain, rinse, and place in a large pan of water. Bring to a boil over high heat, skim off any froth, then reduce the heat and simmer for 10 minutes. Drain and rinse.

2 In a large saucepan with a lid, heat 2 tbsp of the olive oil. Season the flour with salt and pepper. Dust the chicken in the flour and cook in the pan, spaced well apart, for a few minutes on each side, until golden brown all over. Set aside.

3 Heat the remaining 1 tbsp of oil and cook the onion for 5 minutes until softened, but not browned. Add the garlic and cook for another minute. Add the wine (if using) and stock, and stir to loosen the residue from the pan.

4 Return the beans to the pan with the herbs, cover, and simmer over low heat for up to 1 hour, or until the beans are tender. Return the chicken and simmer for another 30 minutes. Remove the lid and add the tomatoes. Cook for another 15 minutes, uncovered, until the sauce reduces. Remove the rosemary before serving.

CALORIES: 489kcals/2060kJ
CARBOHYDRATE: 24g
  sugar: 4.5g
FAT: 13g
  saturated: 2.5g
SALT: 0.8g
FIBER: 10g

One-pot Spanish chicken with rice

This simple supper dish is packed full of warmly spicy flavor and is a no-fuss recipe: it practically cooks itself.

20 mins 1 hr

SERVES 4–6

4 tbsp olive oil

1 heaping tbsp all-purpose flour

salt and freshly ground black pepper

2 tsp smoked paprika, plus extra for dusting

8 boneless, skinless chicken thighs, cut into large pieces

1 onion, finely chopped

1 red and 1 orange bell pepper, cut into ¾in (2cm) cubes

1 dry, Spanish-style chorizo, approx. 7oz (200g), casing removed, cut into 1in (3cm) slices

2 garlic cloves, chopped

½ tsp cayenne pepper (optional)

2¾ cups chicken stock (see p94)

3 heaping tbsp chopped flat-leaf parsley leaves

10oz (300g) long-grain or basmati white rice

2½oz (75g) frozen peas

1 tbsp butter

1 Heat 2 tbsp of the oil in a large, heavy-bottomed saucepan with a lid. Season the flour with salt, pepper, and a little smoked paprika to taste. Dust the chicken evenly with the flour, shaking off excess. Cook the chicken, well spaced apart, for 2–3 minutes on each side over medium heat, until golden brown all over (you may need to do this in batches). Set aside and keep warm.

2 Heat the remaining oil in the pan and cook the onion and peppers for 3–5 minutes until softened and turning brown. Add the chorizo (don't worry if it breaks up) and cook for a few minutes, until beginning to turn crispy at the edges. Add the garlic, smoked paprika, and cayenne pepper (if using) and cook for 1 minute, until fragrant.

3 Add the stock, scraping up the meaty residue from the pan. Return the chicken to the pan, add 2 tbsp of the parsley, and bring to a boil. Reduce to a low simmer, cover, and cook for 10 minutes.

4 Add the rice and stir well. Cover and cook over very low heat for about 15 minutes, until the rice has cooked and absorbed most of the liquid. Stir in the peas, butter, and remaining parsley and rest, off the heat but with the lid on, for 5 minutes before serving.

CALORIES: 815kcals/3400kJ
CARBOHYDRATE: 69g
  sugar: 8g
FAT: 31g
  saturated: 10g
SALT: 1.6g
FIBER: 3.6g

Ricotta-stuffed chicken breasts

A modest effort for an impressive midweek meal, or weekend treat chic enough to serve to friends.

20 mins · 20–25 mins

SERVES 4

¼ cup ricotta cheese

2 tbsp finely grated Parmesan cheese

2 tbsp finely chopped basil leaves

1 tbsp finely chopped flat-leaf parsley leaves

finely grated zest of 1 lemon

salt and freshly ground black pepper

4 boneless, skinless chicken breasts

1 tbsp olive oil

8 prosciutto slices

1 Preheat the oven to 400°F (200°C). In a bowl, mash the ricotta cheese with the Parmesan cheese, herbs, and lemon zest. Season well.

2 Take the chicken breasts and cut a pocket into the thickest side. Stuff each with one-quarter of the ricotta mixture, then rub with a little oil. Lay 2 prosciutto slices on a cutting board, overlapping slightly, and place the chicken on top. Carefully wrap the prosciutto around, making sure it meets on top. (If necessary, use a toothpick to secure.)

3 Flip the breasts over and place seam-side down on a baking sheet. Cook at the top of the oven for 20–25 minutes, until golden brown. When pressed with a finger, the meat should bounce back. Remove the toothpicks, if you used them, before serving.

CALORIES: 281kcals/1181kJ

CARBOHYDRATE: 0.3g
  sugar: 0.3g

FAT: 11g
  saturated: 4g

SALT: 1.4g

FIBER: 0g

Duck in orange sauce

Duck à l'orange is a classic, sadly fallen out of favor. This simpler recipe uses breasts for a modern twist.

20 mins · 20–30 mins

SERVES 4

4 skin-on boneless duck breasts

salt and freshly ground black pepper

⅓ cup brown sugar

finely grated zest and juice of 2 large oranges

2 tbsp cider vinegar

¾ cup chicken stock (see p94)

1 tbsp cornstarch

orange slices, to garnish

1 With a sharp knife, score the skin of the duck in a criss-cross pattern and season well. Heat a large, non-stick frying pan over medium heat and add the duck, skin-side down. Reduce the heat to low and cook for 8–10 minutes to release the fat.

2 Increase the temperature and cook for 3–5 minutes, or until the skin is golden brown.

3 Turn the duck over and cook over medium heat for another 5 minutes. Place on a warmed plate lined with paper towels, loosely cover with foil, and set aside. Pour the fat from the frying pan and wipe it clean with paper towels.

4 Put the sugar, orange zest and juice, vinegar, and stock in the frying pan. Stir well and boil for 8–10 minutes or until reduced. Season to taste. While there is still 5 minutes cooking time left, stir the cornstarch with 3 tbsp water and add to the sauce to thicken, stirring frequently from then on.

5 Arrange the duck on serving plates, drizzle with the sauce, and garnish with the orange slices.

CALORIES: 520kcals/2178kJ

CARBOHYDRATE: 27g
  sugar: 24.4g

FAT: 28.5g
  saturated: 8.5g

SALT: 0.7g

FIBER: 0.2g

Crispy duck char siu

Chinese roast duck is tasty, but it is tricky to cook a whole bird. Try this easy version with duck breasts instead.

5 mins, plus marinating　**25 mins**

SERVES 4

4 skin-on boneless duck breasts

3 garlic cloves, crushed

3 tbsp soy sauce

3 tbsp rice wine

1 tbsp hoisin sauce

2 tbsp honey

2 tsp five-spice powder

salt and freshly ground black pepper

noodles or a green salad, to serve

1 Score the skin of the duck breasts with a knife in a criss-cross pattern, being careful not to cut down into the meat.

2 Whisk all the remaining ingredients together in a wide, shallow dish. Turn the duck breasts through the marinade to coat them on all sides, cover with plastic wrap, and leave to marinate for 2–4 hours in the fridge.

3 Preheat the oven to 400°F (200°C). Line a baking sheet with foil, to make cleaning up easier later.

4 Put the duck, skin-side down, in a frying pan and place over medium heat. Cook for 8 minutes.

5 Place the duck, skin-side up, on the baking sheet and cook at the top of the oven for 10 minutes. Rest for 5 minutes.

6 Cut the duck into slices on the diagonal and serve with stir-fried noodles or a green salad.

HOW TO FREEZE

Freeze the raw duck in the marinade. Defrost thoroughly before continuing with the recipe from step 3.

BATCHING AND FREEZING

Duck breasts can be expensive, so if you find them at a good price it is worth buying more than you need. Cook double this recipe and bag it up in portions for the freezer for a near-instant addition to a quick stir-fry anytime.

CALORIES: 576kcals/2394kJ

CARBOHYDRATE: 8g
　sugar: 8g

FAT: 44g
　saturated: 13g

SALT: 2.5g

FIBER: 0g

Zesty roasted chicken pieces

A great last-minute recipe for when all you have is some chicken and a few pantry essentials.

10 mins, plus marinating | 40-45 mins

SERVES 4

finely grated zest of 1 lemon

finely grated zest of 1 orange

2 tbsp orange juice

2 tbsp olive oil

1 tbsp honey

1 tbsp soy sauce

2 heaping tbsp chopped flat-leaf parsley leaves (optional)

8 skin-on bone-in chicken thighs, drumsticks, or a mixture

CALORIES: 321kcals/13.7kJ

CARBOHYDRATE: 4.5g
sugar: 4.5g

FAT: 15g
saturated: 3.5g

SALT: 1.1g

FIBER: 0g

1 Preheat the oven to 400°F (200°C). Mix all the ingredients except the chicken in a large, shallow container.

2 Add the chicken, turning to coat. Cover and leave it in the fridge for at least 2 hours, but preferably 4 if possible.

3 Put the chicken in a large baking dish, spaced well apart and in a single layer. Roast at the top of the oven for 40–45 minutes, turning occasionally, until golden brown and crispy.

VARIATION

The parsley can be omitted, or replaced with other chopped herb leaves, such as cilantro, dill, or oregano.

HOW TO FREEZE

Freeze the raw chicken in the marinade. Defrost thoroughly before cooking, and follow the recipe from the start of step 3.

Parmesan-crusted chicken

This crispy, crunchy coating is a perfect foil to the succulent and juicy chicken beneath.

15 mins | 40-45 mins

SPECIAL EQUIPMENT
food processor

SERVES 4

1 cup day-old white bread crumbs

1¾oz (50g) finely grated Parmesan cheese

2 garlic cloves, crushed

handful of basil leaves

finely grated zest of 1 lemon

salt and freshly ground black pepper

1 large egg, beaten

1 heaping tbsp all-purpose flour

8 skin-on bone-in chicken thighs

2 tbsp olive oil

1 Preheat the oven to 400°F (200°C). In a food processor, place the bread crumbs, Parmesan, garlic, basil, zest, and salt and pepper, and process until the basil turns the mixture green. Transfer into a wide, shallow bowl.

2 Place the egg in a shallow bowl and the flour in a freezer bag. Season the flour well. Put the chicken in the freezer bag and toss to coat. Pour out into a sieve and shake to remove excess flour.

3 Dip each piece of chicken in the egg, then coat well in the bread crumbs.

4 Heat the olive oil on a large baking sheet for 5 minutes, then arrange the chicken on the sheet, spaced well apart and in a single layer. Cook for 40–45 minutes, turning occasionally, until golden brown and crispy.

To make bite-sized nuggets, use diced chicken breast and reduce the cooking time to 20-25 minutes.

Fussy eaters!

CALORIES: 423kcals/1777kJ

CARBOHYDRATE: 21g
sugar: 0.8g

FAT: 19g
saturated: 6g

SALT: 1.1g

FIBER: 1g

Cajun-spiced chicken

This sweet, spicy marinade can be used in the oven, on the barbecue, and even under the broiler.

10 mins, plus marinating   40-45 mins

SERVES 4

2 tbsp olive oil

2 tsp light brown sugar

2 tsp paprika

½–1 tsp cayenne pepper or chili powder, to taste

1 tsp ground cumin

1 tsp dried thyme

1 tsp ground coriander

salt and freshly ground black pepper

8 skin-on bone-in chicken pieces, thighs, drumsticks, or a mixture

CALORIES: 321kcals/1345kJ

CARBOHYDRATE: 2.5g
  sugar: 2.5g

FAT: 14g
  saturated: 3g

SALT: 0.4g

FIBER: 0g

1 To make the marinade, mix all the ingredients together, apart from the chicken.

2 Rub the chicken in the marinade. Place in a dish, cover, and refrigerate for at least 1 hour, or preferably up to 4 hours. When ready to cook, preheat the oven to 400°F (200°C).

3 Arrange the chicken on a roasting pan, spaced well apart and in a single layer. Cook at the top of the oven for 40–45 minutes, turning occasionally, until the chicken is dark golden brown and cooked through.

HOW TO FREEZE

Freeze the raw chicken in the marinade. Defrost thoroughly before cooking, and follow the recipe from the start of step 3.

Crispy southern-baked chicken

A healthier alternative to the great tasting but fatty fried chicken that everybody loves.

10 mins, plus chilling   45 mins-1 hr

SERVES 4

⅓ cup all-purpose flour

2 tsp paprika

salt and freshly ground black pepper

1 large egg, beaten

1 cup panko bread crumbs or day-old bread crumbs

1 tsp cayenne pepper

½ tsp celery salt

8 skin-on chicken drumsticks

2 tbsp sunflower or vegetable oil

1 Put the flour, 1 tsp of the paprika, and salt and pepper in a large freezer bag. Place the egg in a shallow bowl. Put the bread crumbs, remaining 1 tsp of paprika, the cayenne, celery salt, and a good grinding of black pepper into a separate bowl and mix well.

2 Put the chicken in the freezer bag and toss to coat. Pour out into a sieve and shake to remove excess flour.

3 Dip each chicken drumstick in the egg, then coat with bread crumbs. Cover and refrigerate for at least 30 minutes (this helps the coating to stick). Preheat the oven to 350°F (180°C).

4 Heat the oil in a large, heavy pan in the oven for 10 minutes.

5 Add the chicken to the pan, spacing it well apart. It should sizzle as it hits the oil. Cook in the center of the oven for 45 minutes to 1 hour, turning once the underside is golden brown and crusty. Drain on paper towels.

VARIATION

For more crunch, try using finely crushed cornflakes instead of bread crumbs in the chicken coating.

CALORIES: 338kcals/1422kJ

CARBOHYDRATE: 27g
  sugar: 1g

FAT: 13g
  saturated: 3g

SALT: 1.3g

FIBER: 1g

Spicy chicken fajitas

A quick recipe and a classic crowd pleaser, with the winning "hands-on" element that is so popular with children.

15 mins,
plus marinating

15 mins

SERVES 3-4

FOR THE MARINADE

2 tbsp olive oil

1 tbsp lime juice

2 tsp ground cumin

1 tsp smoked paprika, plus extra
for the onions

1 tsp dried oregano

1 tsp cayenne pepper or chili powder

salt and freshly ground black pepper

FOR THE FAJITAS

2 large boneless, skinless chicken
breasts, sliced

2 tbsp sunflower or vegetable oil

1 red onion, cut into ½in (1cm) slices

1 red and 1 yellow bell pepper, cut into
½in (1cm) slices

8 tortillas

TO SERVE

sour cream or plain yogurt

chili sauce

guacamole (see p290)

tomato salsa (see p288)

1 Whisk together the marinade
ingredients and pour over the
chicken in a bowl. Cover and
refrigerate for at least 30 minutes,
or up to 4 hours.

2 Preheat the broiler to its
highest setting. Broil the
chicken for 3–5 minutes on
each side until golden and
cooked. (It can also be grilled
for a smoky flavor.)

3 Meanwhile, heat the sunflower
oil in a large frying pan or wok
over high heat and cook the onion
and peppers for 5–7 minutes, or until
cooked through and colored on the
edges. Season with a little salt and
pepper, and smoked paprika.

4 Warm the tortillas in a
microwave or a low oven,
following the package instructions.
Serve the chicken on a platter with
the vegetables, tortillas, and the
sour cream and sauces, letting
everyone make their own fajita.

VARIATION

Try using this marinade with beef
or shrimp. The beef will need to be
very thinly sliced to cook through,
while the shrimp will only need to
be broiled for 1–2 minutes on each
side, or until pink.

These fajitas are
ideal for fussy eaters
because they can include
only what they like in their
wrap. Cooking the peppers
and chicken separately
makes it easy to pick
these out.

Fussy eaters!

CALORIES: 565kcals/2382kJ

CARBOHYDRATE: 75g
sugar: 9g

FAT: 14g
saturated: 2g

SALT: 1g

FIBER: 7g

Spicy chicken meatballs

These are perfect alongside a vegetable and noodle stir-fry. Finely chopped chile can be added for more heat.

10 mins   10 mins

SERVES 4

14oz (400g) ground chicken

¼ cup fresh white bread crumbs

2 scallions, finely chopped

1 garlic clove, crushed

¾in (2cm) fresh ginger, finely grated

1 tbsp finely chopped cilantro leaves

1 tbsp sweet chili sauce

1 tsp lime juice

1 tsp fish sauce

2 tbsp sunflower or vegetable oil

1 Mix all the ingredients, except the oil, together in a large bowl until evenly incorporated. It's easiest to use your fingers for this; you may prefer to wear plastic food preparation gloves. Cover and refrigerate for at least 30 minutes.

2 With damp hands, shape walnut-sized balls with the chicken mixture, placing them on a plate. At this point, you may cover and chill the meatballs for up to 1 day, if that is more convenient.

3 Heat the sunflower oil in a large frying pan and cook the meatballs over medium-high heat for about 3–5 minutes, turning to color all sides, until golden and cooked through (cut one through to the center to check there is no trace of pink). You may need to do this in batches, depending on the size of the pan. Serve.

VARIATION

Try making these meatballs with ground turkey instead of chicken, for a slightly deeper and richer flavor.

BATCHING AND FREEZING

Meatballs are an ideal ingredient to prepare in bulk. Double or triple the quantities suggested and prepare the meatballs to the end of step 2. Open-freeze on a large baking sheet (make sure that it fits in your freezer first); the meatballs should not touch. Once they are frozen solid (after 2–3 hours), transfer to large freezer bags and freeze. To defrost, remove the amount needed and place them in a single layer on a plate, cover, and put in the fridge on the morning you need them. They will be ready for supper that night.

CALORIES: 211kcals/888kJ

CARBOHYDRATE: 11.5g
  sugar: 3g

FAT: 7g
  saturated: 1g

SALT: 0.8g

FIBER: 0.5g

Chicken scallops with lemon sauce

This light, bright recipe is perfect with steamed spring vegetables and potatoes.

10-15 mins   15 mins

SERVES 4

4 boneless, skinless chicken breasts

1 tbsp olive oil

salt and freshly ground black pepper

3 tbsp all-purpose flour

1 tbsp butter

1 cup chicken stock (see p94)

juice of ½ lemon

¼ cup (2oz) crème fraîche

1 tbsp finely chopped thyme leaves

½ tsp granulated sugar

1 Preheat the oven to 400°F (200°C). Flatten each chicken breast gently with a rolling pin until ¾in (2cm) thick all over.

2 Heat the oil in a large, heavy-bottomed frying pan. Season 2 tbsp of the flour. Dust the chicken with the flour, shaking off excess. Cook the chicken for 2–3 minutes on each side over medium heat, until golden. Transfer to a baking dish and cook in the hot oven for 10 minutes until cooked.

3 Meanwhile, wipe the pan clean with paper towels. Melt the butter in the pan and scatter with the remaining 1 tbsp of flour, whisking over medium heat for 1 minute. Gradually add the stock and lemon juice, whisking constantly, and bring to a boil.

4 Add the crème fraîche, thyme, and sugar, and season to taste. Cook the sauce for 5 minutes, until thick and glossy, whisking. Remove the chicken from the oven and add its juices to the sauce. Slice the chicken on the diagonal and pour the sauce over to serve.

CALORIES: 323kcals/1356kJ
CARBOHYDRATE: 9g
  sugar: 1g
FAT: 13.5g
  saturated: 7g
SALT: 0.5g
FIBER: 0.5g

Chicken in leek and mustard sauce

A super-speedy midweek supper that looks as good as it tastes, with the gentle sweetness of leeks.

10-15 mins   25 mins

SERVES 4

2 tbsp olive oil

3 tbsp all-purpose flour

salt and freshly ground black pepper

4 boneless, skinless chicken breasts

2 tbsp butter

7oz (200g) leeks, white part only, finely sliced

1¼ cups chicken stock (see p94)

¼ cup half-and-half

1 tbsp Dijon mustard

1 Preheat the oven to 400°F (200°C). Heat the oil in a large, heavy-bottomed frying pan. Season 2 tbsp of the flour with salt and pepper. Dust the chicken with the flour, shaking off excess. Cook the chicken for 2–3 minutes on each side over medium heat, until golden brown. Transfer to a baking dish and cook in the hot oven for 10 minutes until cooked, then remove from the oven, cover with foil, and rest while you make the sauce.

2 Wipe the pan with paper towels and add the butter. Cook the leeks for 10 minutes over low heat, until they soften. Stir in the remaining 1 tbsp of flour and cook for another minute.

3 Add the stock and bring to a boil. Reduce to a simmer and cook the sauce until it thickens. Add the half-and-half and mustard and cook for 2–3 minutes until thick, adding juices from the chicken. Pour the sauce over the chicken to serve.

CALORIES: 364kcals/1526kJ
CARBOHYDRATE: 10g
  sugar: 2g
FAT: 17g
  saturated: 7g
SALT: 0.8g
FIBER: 2g

Chicken with a creamy mushroom sauce

A deliciously quick dinner, perfect served with fluffy mashed potatoes to soak up the delicious juices.

20–25 mins   15 mins

SERVES 4

3 tbsp olive oil

1 tbsp butter

7oz (200g) button mushrooms, sliced

1 onion, finely chopped

2 garlic cloves, finely chopped

1 heaping tbsp all-purpose flour

salt and freshly ground black pepper

1lb 5oz (600g) boneless, skinless chicken thighs, cut into 1in (3cm) pieces

½ cup white wine (optional)

¾ cup chicken stock (see p94)

1 tbsp finely chopped sage leaves

3 tbsp heavy cream

1 Heat 1 tbsp of the olive oil and the butter in a large, deep-sided frying pan. Cook the mushrooms for 5 minutes until they start to brown. Add the onion and cook for 2–3 minutes until it softens. Add the garlic, cook for 1 minute, then remove the vegetables from the pan. Wipe the pan clean with paper towels.

2 Heat the remaining 2 tbsp of oil in the pan. Season the flour with salt and pepper. Toss the chicken in the flour, shaking off excess. Cook the chicken for 8–10 minutes, turning, until golden all over. Add the wine (if using), stock, and sage and bring to a boil.

3 Add the mushroom mixture and simmer for 5 minutes, stirring occasionally, until the sauce starts to reduce. Add the cream and cook for 2–3 minutes until the chicken is cooked and the sauce is thick and creamy.

VARIATION

If cooking for young children, you can replace the wine with extra chicken stock.

CALORIES: 377kcals/1572kJ	
CARBOHYDRATE: 5g	
sugar: 1.8g	
FAT: 22g	
saturated: 8g	
SALT: 0.6g	
FIBER: 1.5g	

Tarragon chicken

This simple oven-roasted dish is given a classic French makeover with the use of tarragon and cream.

15 mins   40–45 mins

SERVES 4

FOR THE HERB BUTTER

1 tbsp olive oil

2 tbsp butter, softened

1 heaping tbsp Dijon mustard

2 garlic cloves, crushed

2 tbsp finely chopped tarragon leaves, plus extra to serve (optional)

finely grated zest and juice of 1 lemon

salt and freshly ground black pepper

FOR THE CHICKEN

8 skin-on bone-in chicken pieces, thighs, drumsticks, or a mixture

1 tbsp all-purpose flour

2 cups chicken stock (see p94)

⅓ cup half-and-half

1 Preheat the oven to 400°F (200°C). To make the herb butter, mash the oil, butter, mustard, garlic, tarragon, lemon zest, and salt and pepper until well combined.

2 Smear the butter over the chicken and put it in a large flameproof baking dish. Squeeze the lemon over the chicken. Roast the chicken in the hot oven for 40–45 minutes until golden brown with crispy skin. Remove from the pan and keep it warm.

3 Put the baking dish over low heat and whisk in the flour, stirring for 1 minute. Gradually pour in the stock, stirring all the time to loosen the sticky residue from the pan.

4 Bring to a boil and simmer for a few minutes until the stock has thickened. Add the cream and bubble for another minute or 2 before serving.

The sauce can be poured directly over the chicken, or passed through a strainer first for children who don't like "bits".

Fussy eaters!

CALORIES: 406kcals/1698kJ	
CARBOHYDRATE: 3.5g	
sugar: 1g	
FAT: 21g	
saturated: 8.5g	
SALT: 1.2g	
FIBER: 0.5g	

Chicken pot pies

Children often love individual portions, so these gently flavored pies, filled with vegetables, are ideal.

20 mins,
plus chilling

40 mins

SPECIAL EQUIPMENT
6 x 3in (7.5cm) round pie dishes

3in (7.5cm) round cutter

MAKES 6

FOR THE DOUGH
2 cups all-purpose flour,
  plus extra for dusting

12 tbsp butter, cut into cubes

½ tsp salt

1 egg, beaten

FOR THE FILLING
3½ cups chicken stock
  (see p94)

3 carrots, sliced

1lb 10oz (750g) Yukon Gold potatoes,
  cut into cubes

3 celery stalks, thinly sliced

6oz (175g) peas

1lb 2oz (500g) cooked boneless,
  skinless chicken

4 tbsp butter

1 onion, chopped

¼ cup all-purpose flour

⅔ cup heavy cream

nutmeg, to taste

sea salt and freshly ground
  black pepper

small bunch of flat-leaf parsley
  leaves, chopped

1 Preheat the oven to 400°F (200°C). To make the dough, rub the flour and butter together with your fingertips until the mixture resembles bread crumbs. Add the salt and enough cold water to form a soft dough. Wrap in plastic wrap and chill in the fridge for 30 minutes.

2 For the filling, bring the stock to a boil in a large saucepan. Add the carrots, potatoes, and celery, and simmer for 3 minutes.

Add the peas and simmer for another 5 minutes until all the vegetables are tender. Strain, reserving the stock. Cut the chicken into slivers and put in a bowl. Add the vegetables.

3 Melt the butter in a small pan over medium heat. Add the onion and cook for 3–5 minutes until softened, but not browned. Sprinkle the flour over the onions and cook for 1–2 minutes, stirring. Gradually add 2 cups of the stock, whisking all the time, and heat until the sauce comes to a boil and thickens.

4 Reduce the heat and simmer the sauce for 2 minutes, add the cream and a grating of nutmeg, then season. Now pour the sauce over the chicken and vegetables, add the parsley, and mix gently. Divide the filling evenly among six 3in (7.5cm) round pie dishes.

5 Roll the dough out on a well-floured surface to ¼in (5mm) thick. Cut out 6 circles using a 3in (7.5cm) round cutter. Brush the edge of each pie dish with water and place the dough circles on top, pressing down firmly to secure in place. Place the pies on a baking sheet and brush with the beaten egg. Cut a slit in the top of each pie and bake for 15–20 minutes.

HOW TO FREEZE
The pastry and the filling can be frozen separately for up to 1 month. Wrap the pastry in plastic wrap and then in foil to store securely in the freezer.

CALORIES: 903kcals/3771kJ
CARBOHYDRATE: 76g
  sugar: 7.5g
FAT: 52g
  saturated: 31g
SALT: 1.3g
FIBER: 9g

Vegetable and chicken pie

A pleasant change to a pastry-topped pie. Gently flavoring with turmeric turns this into something special.

20 mins   50 mins

SERVES 2

FOR THE TOPPING

1lb (450g) large potatoes, peeled and cut into large chunks

salt and freshly ground black pepper

large pat of butter

4–5 tbsp whole milk

FOR THE FILLING

5½oz (150g) green beans, cut into ¾in (2cm) pieces

3 tbsp butter

1 red bell pepper, thinly sliced

1 leek, sliced

¼ tsp turmeric

3 tbsp all-purpose flour

1 cup milk

¾ cup (7oz) crème fraîche

8oz (225g) cooked boneless, skinless chicken, sliced

1 Preheat the oven to 400°F (200°C). Cook the potatoes in boiling salted water for 15 minutes, or until tender when pierced with a sharp knife, adding the green beans for the last 3 minutes. Drain, return the potatoes to the pan, and mash with the butter and enough milk to make a smooth mash. Season with salt and set aside. Set the green beans aside separately.

2 For the filling, melt the butter in a large pan. Add the red bell pepper and leek, and cook for 3–4 minutes until soft. Stir in the turmeric, cook for a minute, then add the flour and cook for another 2–3 minutes.

3 Pour in the milk slowly, while stirring constantly, and cook for 4–5 minutes until the sauce has thickened and looks smooth, glossy, and golden in color. Add the crème fraîche, blanched green beans, and chicken and mix well to distribute all the ingredients equally through the sauce. Do not bring to a boil at this point, or the sauce may split.

4 Season well with salt and pepper and pour the filling into an ovenproof dish. Cover with the mashed potatoes, then cook in the oven for 25 minutes until the filling is piping hot and bubbling around the edges and the potato is golden brown.

CALORIES: 1161kcals/4830kJ

CARBOHYDRATE: 67g
    sugar: 17g

FAT: 76g
    saturated: 48g

SALT: 0.9g

FIBER: 10g

Batching and freezing

Batching and freezing meals is a great standby if you have a busy schedule and little time to cook during the week. Simple sauces and stews can be made in double, or even triple, quantities and portioned up for freezing. Stale bread can be ground in a food processor to make instant bread crumbs, combined with parmesan and basil for extra flavor, then used straight from the freezer. If you have time to bake on the weekend, consider making a large batch of cookie dough (as used for Double chocolate chip cookies, p404) then open freeze the formed, unbaked cookies. Once they are frozen solid, pack the dough shapes into a freezer bag, then defrost and bake as needed for almost instant home-baked cookies even during the busiest of weeks.

"Eat the freezer" week

Eat the freezer week is a great way to save money, organize the freezer, and challenge your culinary skills all at the same time. Once every month or so, make your weekly shopping list after first going through the freezer to see what you can find. Use those overlooked items at the bottom of the freezer as the basis of your weekly menu, and add only essential items to the weekly store trip. You may be amazed at what you discover lurking in the depths of your freezer!

Labeling

A roll of freezer-proof labels will help you recognize items you may have frozen weeks ago. There are also freezer-proof pens available, and freezer bags that you can write directly onto.

Ways of freezing

By using the correct method and preparing food carefully you can freeze almost anything—from herbs to fruit cordials—saving yourself time and money in the process.

Open freezing This is one of the best ways to preserve smaller items and ensure that they do not freeze into a solid mass. Spread them out, not touching each other, on a baking sheet and freeze; once frozen solid, pack into freezer bags.

Using freezer bags Have at least two sizes of sturdy freezer bags on hand to ensure you can freeze things quickly and efficiently. Dividing up food into portion sizes helps you to make the most of the economies of scale.

Using ice-cube trays Freezing foods such as herbs, pesto, or stock in ice-cube trays gives a ready supply of portion-sized amounts. Herbs work especially well in this way, as freezing will preserve their flavors.

Safe freezing

Plastics Not all plastics are suitable for freezing. Some become brittle with the low temperatures, and lids can shatter if removed while too cold. Try using freezer- and microwave-proof containers for items that can be defrosted in an emergency.

Defrosting The denser the item, the longer it will take to defrost. Ideally, long, slow overnight defrosting in the fridge is best for items such as larger pieces of meat, although smaller items can be defrosted at room temperature.

Freezer burn This occurs when food has not been adequately wrapped or stored in an airtight container. Throw away any food that has patches of discoloration on it, as the taste and quality will have been affected.

Freezing gluts Take advantage of gluts of seasonal fruit and vegetables by freezing any excess you have in pre-portioned freezer bags. Vegetables with a lower water content freeze better, but often need to be blanched first.

Freezing bread Frozen bread cuts quite easily with a sharp knife. If you use it to make sandwiches, it will defrost in time for lunch, keeping everything fresh and cool in the summer months.

Freezing liquids Liquids such as soups, stocks, and even cordials can be frozen in sturdy freezer bags or well washed, plastic milk containers. Be sure to leave a small amount of space at the top, as most liquids expand on freezing.

Handy things to have in the freezer

★ Frozen berry mixes, such as summer fruits

★ Ice cream

★ Frozen yogurt portions for quick lunch box fillers

★ Frozen sliced bread—see top tip, above

★ Slow-cooked tomato sauce for pasta (p34)

★ Packages of ground beef, lamb, chicken, or pork

★ Homemade burgers (p278), divided by waxed paper and stacked

★ Assorted vegetables, such as peas, broccoli, and corn

Thai beef salad

The bright, vibrant flavors of this salad really sing out, making it perfect for a summer lunch.

10 mins | 10 mins

SERVES 4

FOR THE SALAD

14oz (400g) thin-cut skirt or sirloin steak

1 tbsp sesame oil or sunflower oil

salt and freshly ground black pepper

2 Little Gem lettuces, leaves separated

large handful of watercress

8in (20cm) piece of cucumber, seeded and finely sliced on the diagonal

1 small red onion, finely sliced

handful of cilantro leaves, roughly chopped

handful of mint leaves, roughly chopped

1 red chile, seeded and finely chopped (optional)

FOR THE DRESSING

¼ cup lime juice

2 tbsp fish sauce

2 tsp light brown sugar

pinch of chile flakes (optional)

1 Heat a frying pan or grill pan. Rub the steak in the oil and season it well all over. Briefly sear over high heat on both sides so it is browned outside but still tender and juicy within. Set aside.

2 Whisk the dressing ingredients together until the sugar dissolves completely.

3 In a large bowl, mix the lettuce, watercress, cucumber, onion, herbs, and chile (if using). Slice the still-warm steak and add to the bowl with the dressing. Toss gently, then serve.

VARIATION

Large shrimp, deveined and sliced horizontally or butterflied, make a nice alternative to steak.

CALORIES: 190kcals/796kJ
CARBOHYDRATE: 5.5g
sugar: 5g
FAT: 7.5g
saturated: 2.5g
SALT: 1.6g
FIBER: 1g

Harissa-spiced lamb chops with chickpea mash

With spices and pantry ingredients, midweek lamb chops can be turned into something really special.

15 mins | 25 mins

SERVES 4

FOR THE LAMB

½ cup fresh white bread crumbs

finely grated zest of 1 lemon

1 tbsp harissa paste

2 tbsp finely chopped cilantro leaves

2 tsp olive oil

salt and freshly ground black pepper

8 x 3½oz (100g) lamb loin chops

FOR THE CHICKPEA MASH

1 tbsp olive oil

1 red onion, finely chopped

2 garlic cloves, finely chopped

2 x 14oz (400g) cans chickpeas, drained and rinsed

1½ tbsp lemon juice

2 tbsp extra virgin olive oil

2 tbsp finely chopped cilantro leaves

tomato salad, to serve

CALORIES: 594kcals/2489kJ
CARBOHYDRATE: 30g
sugar: 2.5g
FAT: 30g
saturated: 9g
SALT: 1.3g
FIBER: 8g

1 Place the bread crumbs, zest, harissa, cilantro, and olive oil in a bowl, season, and stir well to combine evenly.

2 Preheat the broiler. Place the chops on a foil-lined baking sheet and broil on one side for 8 minutes. Turn and press the bread crumb and harissa mixture onto the uncooked side of each chop. Broil for another 8 minutes.

3 Meanwhile, make the chickpea mash. Heat the oil in a saucepan over medium heat, add the onion, and cook for 5 minutes. Add the garlic and cook for 2 minutes. Stir in the chickpeas, lemon juice, and extra virgin olive oil, and gently heat.

4 Remove from the heat and mash roughly with a potato masher; it should not be smooth. Stir in the cilantro and season generously.

5 Serve the chops with the chickpea mash and a dressed tomato salad.

PREPARE AHEAD

Make the bread crumb topping up to 3 days ahead, cover, and store in an airtight container in the fridge.

Veal with creamy mushroom sauce

When buying veal, always try and find meat that has come from a source with a good animal welfare guarantee.

10 mins   20 mins

SERVES 4

4 veal scallops, approx.
3½oz (100g) each

salt and freshly ground black pepper

¼ cup all-purpose flour

2 tbsp olive oil

1 tbsp butter

9oz (250g) crimini mushrooms,
sliced

¾ cup chicken stock (see p94)

½ cup dry white wine

2 sprigs of thyme

¼ cup (2oz) heavy cream

rice, to serve

1 Place the veal between sheets of parchment paper and pound each with a meat mallet or wooden rolling pin until about ⅛in (3mm) thick. Season the scallops with salt and pepper. Place the flour on a plate, season it, and coat each scallop on both sides.

2 Heat the oil and butter in a large, non-stick frying pan that has a lid over medium heat and brown 2 of the scallops for 1 minute on each side. Set aside on a plate. Repeat to brown the remaining veal.

3 Add the mushrooms to the pan, stir well, and cook over medium heat for 5 minutes, stirring, until they have released their juices and the juices have evaporated. Add the stock, wine, and thyme, season, and bring to a boil.

4 Return the veal to the pan and gently shake to cover the scallops in the mushroom sauce.

5 Reduce the heat, cover the pan, and simmer for 5 minutes over low heat, carefully turning once halfway through cooking. Remove the veal from the pan and place on a warmed serving plate.

6 Bring the sauce to a boil and cook for 5 minutes to reduce. Stir in the cream and heat through. Pour the sauce and mushrooms over the veal and serve with rice.

CLEVER WITH LEFTOVERS

If you have any of this delicious dish left over, you can make a quick and tasty pasta sauce. Just slice the cold meat into thin slices and reheat it. Add chicken stock (see p94) to loosen the sauce and toss it through freshly cooked tagliatelle.

CALORIES: 345kcals/1440kJ

CARBOHYDRATE: 11.5g
sugar: 1g

FAT: 19g
saturated: 8.5g

SALT: 0.4g

FIBER: 1.5g

Slow-cooked Moroccan lamb

For an exotic take on a family meal, try serving this aromatic lamb with couscous salad.

10 mins, plus marinating 3 hrs 30 mins

SERVES 4–6

2 tbsp olive oil

juice of 1 lemon

2 tbsp harissa paste

2 tsp smoked paprika

1 tsp ground cinnamon

salt and freshly ground black pepper

1 bone-in shoulder of lamb, approx. 3lb 3oz–4½lb (1.5–2kg)

1 Mix the oil, lemon juice, harissa, and spices in a bowl and season well. Cut slashes all over the lamb, rub in the marinade, cover, and refrigerate for at least 4 hours, preferably overnight.

2 Preheat the oven to 350°F (180°C). Place the lamb in a roasting pan where it fits snugly and pour in water to a depth of ¾in (2cm). Place a piece of parchment paper on top, then cover tightly with foil, making sure there are no gaps.

3 Cook for 3 hours. Uncover the pan and cook for 20–30 minutes. If the pan is dry, add a little water.

4 When the lamb is crisp on the outside and falling off the bone, it is ready. Strain off the liquid and separate and discard the fat. Pour the juices over the sliced lamb before serving on a platter.

CLEVER WITH LEFTOVERS

Turn leftover lamb into a wrap: serve it warmed, with Greek yogurt mixed with chopped mint leaves, and warmed Middle Eastern flatbread.

HOW TO FREEZE

Freeze the lamb, in its marinade, uncooked. Defrost thoroughly before cooking from the start of step 2.

CALORIES: 516–344kcals/2152–1435kJ
CARBOHYDRATE: 0.7–0.5g
  sugar: 0.6–0.4g
FAT: 30–20g
  saturated: 11–7.5g
SALT: 0.6–0.4g
FIBER: 0.2–0.1g

Easy Chinese roast pork

Recreate this favorite restaurant choice at home, using some clever shortcuts.

10 mins, plus marinating 40 mins

SERVES 4

2 tbsp soy sauce

1 tbsp hoisin sauce

1 tbsp honey, plus 1 tbsp for glazing

1 tbsp rice wine or dry sherry

1 tsp sunflower or vegetable oil

1 tsp light brown sugar

2 garlic cloves, crushed

1lb (450g) piece of pork tenderloin

rice, to serve

1 Mix all the ingredients—except the honey for glazing and the pork—in a bowl. Rub the marinade all over the pork, cover, and refrigerate for at least 4 hours, but preferably overnight.

2 Preheat the oven to 400°F (200°C). Put the pork on a rack over a roasting pan half filled with hot water, making sure the water does not touch the rack. Brush the meat with the remaining honey on all sides.

3 Roast at the top of the oven for 40 minutes, turning occasionally, until glossy on all sides. Serve with rice.

HOW TO FREEZE

Freeze the meat, in its marinade, uncooked. Defrost thoroughly before cooking from the start of step 2.

CALORIES: 190kcals/804kJ
CARBOHYDRATE: 9g
  sugar: 9g
FAT: 5g
  saturated: 2g
SALT: 1.6g
FIBER: 0g

Chinese-spiced pork belly

A wonderful treatment turns an inexpensive cut of meat into an Asian feast, with the best crackling ever.

10 mins, plus marinating   1 hr 30 mins

SERVES 4

piece of boneless skin-on pork belly, approx. 1lb 10oz (750g)

2 tbsp soy sauce

1 tbsp light brown sugar

1 tbsp five-spice powder

2 tsp salt

1 tsp sunflower or vegetable oil

1 With a sharp knife, make criss-cross slits all over the skin of the pork, being careful not to cut through to the meat. (Or ask your butcher to do this.) Pat the skin dry.

2 Mix the soy sauce, sugar, five-spice powder, and 1 tsp of salt into a thick paste and rub it over the meat side of the pork, keeping all the skin dry. Refrigerate, skin-side up and uncovered, for at least 8 hours, or overnight.

3 Preheat the oven to 425°F (220°C). Place the meat, skin-side up, on a rack in a roasting pan lined with foil (making cleaning easier later). Rub the skin with the oil and remaining 1 tsp of salt. Fill the pan half full with hot water.

4 Roast the pork at the top of the oven for 30 minutes, then reduce the oven temperature to 400°F (200°C) and roast for another 45 minutes to 1 hour, until crispy. Keep an eye on the water level, and add more if it starts to get too low.

CALORIES: 507kcals/2109kJ
CARBOHYDRATE: 4g
  sugar: 4g
FAT: 39g
  saturated: 14g
SALT: 4g
FIBER: 0g

Chinese braised beef with ginger and soy sauce

For a simple supper, put some broccoli rabe in the sauce to braise for the last 5 minutes of cooking.

25 mins   2 hrs 30 mins

SERVES 4

4 tbsp sunflower or vegetable oil

2 onions, quartered

2in (5cm) fresh ginger, finely sliced

3 garlic cloves, finely sliced

2 heaping tbsp all-purpose flour

1 tsp five-spice powder

1lb 2oz (500g) beef stew meat, cut into 1in (3cm) cubes

1¼ cups beef stock

¼ cup rice wine or dry sherry

2 tbsp soy sauce

4 dried red chiles, left whole

1 tbsp light brown sugar

salt and freshly ground black pepper

steamed rice, to serve

cilantro leaves, to serve (optional)

1 Heat 2 tbsp of the oil in a large, heavy-bottomed saucepan with a lid. Cook the onions, turning with tongs until browned all over. Add the ginger and garlic and cook for another minute. Set aside.

2 Mix the flour and ½ tsp of five-spice powder in a freezer bag and add the beef. Toss until coated on all sides, then pour out into a sieve, shaking to remove excess flour.

3 Heat the remaining 2 tbsp of oil. Cook the beef, a few pieces at a time, until browned on all sides. Return the onion mixture.

4 Add the stock, rice wine, and soy sauce and bring to a boil, stirring to dislodge any residue from the pan. Add the chiles and sugar.

5 Cover and cook over very low heat for 2 hours, then uncover and cook for 30 minutes until the meat is meltingly tender and the sauce reduced and thickened slightly. Season to taste, remove the chiles, and serve with steamed rice and a sprinkling of cilantro leaves (if using).

CALORIES: 366kcals/1528kJ
CARBOHYDRATE: 13.5g
  sugar: 7g
FAT: 18g
  saturated: 4g
SALT: 1.7g
FIBER: 1g

Pot-roast beef

Try to find a piece of well-marbled beef that will be good and juicy. Round or chuck are both good.

20 mins   2 hrs 30 mins

SERVES 4

3 tbsp olive oil

2 onions, quartered

4 large carrots, cut into
   1in (3cm) pieces

2 garlic cloves, roughly chopped

salt and freshly ground black pepper

2¼lb (1kg) round roast

2 cups red wine, or beef stock,
   or a mixture

1 tbsp redcurrant or sour cherry jelly

2 sprigs of rosemary

handful of thyme

mashed potatoes, to serve

CALORIES: 511kcals/2146kJ
CARBOHYDRATE: 13.5g
   sugar: 12g
FAT: 15g
   saturated: 4g
SALT: 0.6g
FIBER: 4g

1 Preheat the oven to 350°F (180°C). Heat 2 tbsp of the oil in a large, heavy-bottomed saucepan with a lid. Cook the onions, carrots, and garlic over medium heat until they start to color. Set aside.

2 Heat the remaining 1 tbsp of oil in the pan. Season the beef well on all sides and sear it in the oil for 2–3 minutes, turning, until browned. Set aside.

3 Add the wine and/or stock to the pan. Stir in the redcurrant or sour cherry jelly and season well. Return the meat and vegetables. Tuck in the herbs.

4 Cover and cook in the oven for 2 hours until meltingly tender. Remove the herbs before serving with mashed potatoes.

COOK'S TIP

Feeding a family can sometimes be expensive. The cheaper cuts of meat are perfectly suited to pot roasting, as the long, slow cooking time allows the meat to cook to a melting softness.

Slow pot-roast lamb shoulder

Lamb shoulder is an affordable choice for a family. Pot roasting renders it succulent and provides gravy, too.

20 mins,   3 hrs 40 mins
plus marinating

SERVES 4

4½lb (2kg) bone-in shoulder of lamb

2 tbsp olive oil

salt and freshly ground black pepper

4 sprigs of rosemary, torn into
   small pieces

4 garlic cloves, halved lengthwise

1¾ cups lamb stock

1¾ cups red wine

4 carrots, roughly chopped

1 onion, roughly chopped

4 celery stalks, roughly chopped

CALORIES: 836–557kcals/3487–2324kJ
CARBOHYDRATE: 10–6.5g
   sugar: 9–6g
FAT: 40–27g
   saturated: 16–10g
SALT: 1.1–0.7g
FIBER: 4–3g

1 Using a sharp knife, make 8 incisions in the lamb, rub the oil all over, season well, and sprinkle with rosemary. Cover and set aside for 1 hour.

2 Preheat the oven to 325°F (160°C). Heat a roasting pan on the stove top over medium heat and sear the lamb on all sides. Place the garlic in the incisions.

3 Add the stock, wine, and vegetables. Seal tightly with foil and cook in the oven for 3–3½ hours, basting the meat and stirring the vegetables from time to time.

4 Transfer the meat and vegetables to a warmed serving plate and loosely cover with foil to keep warm and rest. Skim and discard the fat from the juices and pour into a serving bowl, along with any juices from the lamb.

5 Shred the meltingly tender lamb with 2 forks and serve with the vegetables and juices.

Braised lamb with spring vegetables

Lamb neck is an inexpensive cut, and the long, slow cooking here breaks it down to a melt-in-the-mouth texture.

30 mins   2 hrs

SPECIAL EQUIPMENT
4-quart (4-liter) heavy-bottomed Dutch oven

SERVES 4

2 tbsp all-purpose flour

salt and freshly ground black pepper

1lb 5oz (600g) lamb neck filet, excess fat trimmed, cut into 1in (3cm) pieces

2 tbsp olive oil

6 baby leeks, sliced

4 shallots, halved

2 garlic cloves, finely sliced

2½ cups lamb or chicken stock (see p94)

1 bay leaf

2 sprigs of rosemary

finely grated zest of 1 lemon

5½oz (150g) Chantenay carrots, ends trimmed and halved lengthwise if large

3½oz (100g) thin green beans, topped, tailed, and halved

5½oz (150g) fresh or frozen peas

5½oz (150g) fresh or frozen baby fava beans

new potatoes, to serve

1 Place the flour in a large freezer bag, season well, and add the meat. Shake to coat the meat. Pour into a sieve to remove excess flour.

2 Heat 1 tbsp of the oil in a 4-quart (4-liter) heavy-bottomed Dutch oven over medium heat. Brown the meat in 2 batches, turning to color all sides. Remove with a slotted spoon and set aside on a plate lined with paper towels.

3 Add the remaining 1 tbsp of oil to the dish and add the leeks, shallots, and garlic. Cook over medium heat for 3 minutes, stirring occasionally.

4 Return the meat and add the stock, bay leaf, rosemary, and lemon zest. Season well and bring to a simmer, skim off any foam, then cover and simmer gently for 1½ hours.

5 Add the carrots, return to a boil, then reduce the heat and simmer gently, uncovered, for 10 minutes to reduce the sauce. Add the green beans, peas, and baby fava beans. Return to a boil, reduce the heat, and simmer for another 10 minutes, or until all the vegetables are just tender and the sauce has thickened slightly. Do not overcook the vegetables.

6 Remove the rosemary and bay leaf and serve the braised lamb with new potatoes.

BATCHING AND FREEZING

This kind of stew is ideally suited to freezing ahead. Make double or triple quantities and freeze it in family-sized portions at the end of stage 4. Defrost it thoroughly, reheat it, and add the vegetables to serve.

CALORIES: 441kcals/1839kJ

CARBOHYDRATE: 18g
  sugar: 7g

FAT: 19g
  saturated: 6.5g

SALT: 0.8g

FIBER: 11g

Greek lamb stew

This unusual stew is a meal in itself, and only needs some crusty bread to soak up the delicious juices.

20 mins   2 hrs 5 mins

SPECIAL EQUIPMENT
large Dutch oven

SERVES 4

2 tbsp olive oil

1lb 9oz (700g) boneless shoulder or neck filet of lamb, excess fat trimmed, cut into bite-sized pieces

1 red onion, finely chopped

2 garlic cloves, finely chopped

¾ cup dry white wine

2 x 14oz (400g) cans chopped tomatoes

3½oz (100g) pitted Kalamata olives

3 sprigs of thyme

3½oz (100g) orzo pasta

3½oz (100g) feta cheese, finely chopped

small bunch of mint leaves, finely chopped

salt and freshly ground black pepper

1 Preheat the oven to 300°F (150°C). Heat 1 tbsp of the oil in a large, heavy-bottomed Dutch oven over medium heat. Brown the meat in 2 batches, remove with a slotted spoon, and set aside on a plate lined with paper towels.

2 Add the remaining 1 tbsp of oil to the casserole, stir in the onion, and cook for 5 minutes, stirring occasionally. Add the garlic and cook for 2 minutes.

3 Add the wine and tomatoes and stir. Return the lamb with the olives and thyme. Bring to a boil, season, and cover.

4 Cook in the oven for 1½ hours. Discard the thyme, add the pasta, and stir. Return to the oven for 15 minutes. Mix the feta and mint in a small dish. Season the stew to taste and serve sprinkled with the cheese mixture.

CALORIES: 576kcals/2412kJ
CARBOHYDRATE: 28g
  sugar: 8g
FAT: 29g
  saturated: 11g
SALT: 2g
FIBER: 4g

Irish stew

An economical dish that uses inexpensive cuts; with a long cooking time to ensure a rich flavor.

25 mins   3 hrs

SPECIAL EQUIPMENT
large Dutch oven

SERVES 4

2lb (900g) stewing lamb from the neck or shoulder, excess fat trimmed, cut into 1in (3cm) pieces

4¾oz (130g) pearl barley

1 large onion, roughly chopped

3 carrots, roughly sliced

7oz (200g) rutabaga, roughly chopped

4 potatoes, roughly chopped

4 sprigs of thyme

salt and freshly ground black pepper

3½ cups hot lamb stock

crusty bread, to serve

CALORIES: 714kcals/3003kJ
CARBOHYDRATE: 68g
  sugar: 9.5g
FAT: 20g
  saturated: 8g
SALT: 1.2g
FIBER: 8g

1 Place half the meat in a large, heavy-bottomed Dutch oven. Top with half the barley, half the vegetables, and 2 of the thyme sprigs and season well. Repeat the layers to use up the remaining meat, barley, vegetables, and thyme. Season well.

2 Pour in hot stock, place over high heat, and bring to a boil. Skim off any foam that rises.

3 Cover and reduce the heat to a gentle simmer. Cook for 3 hours, stirring occasionally. Taste and adjust the seasoning. Serve in bowls with crusty bread.

PREPARE AHEAD
It can take a surprisingly long time to prepare vegetables. To get ahead, peel and chop the carrots, rutabaga, and potatoes in advance and submerge under water in a large saucepan or bowl. Left like this, they will be fine for up to 1 day in all but the very hottest kitchens.

Lamb, apricot, and chickpea tagine

If you forget to soak the dried chickpeas overnight, just replace them with a can, drained and added at the end.

25 mins, plus marinating · 2 hrs 30 mins

SPECIAL EQUIPMENT
4-quart (4-liter) Dutch oven

SERVES 4

3½oz (100g) dried apricots, roughly chopped

1¾oz (50g) raisins

½ cup dry sherry (or lamb stock or orange juice)

1lb 5oz (600g) boneless shoulder of lamb, excess fat trimmed, cut into 1in (3cm) pieces

finely grated zest and juice of 1 orange

2 garlic cloves, finely chopped

salt and freshly ground black pepper

3½oz (100g) dried chickpeas, soaked overnight in water

2 tbsp olive oil

1 red onion, finely chopped

pinch of saffron strands

2 tsp ground coriander

2 tsp ground cumin

½ tsp paprika

1¾oz (50g) pine nuts

2 tbsp all-purpose flour

⅔ cup red wine

⅔ cup lamb or chicken stock (see p94)

1 x 14oz (400g) can chopped tomatoes

20 pitted black olives

juice of ½ lemon

couscous, to serve

1 Place the apricots and raisins in a small bowl and pour in the sherry (or lamb stock or orange juice). Set aside for 2 hours to plump up.

2 Place the lamb in a dish with the orange zest and juice, garlic, and seasoning. Stir well, cover, and set aside for 2 hours to marinate.

3 Drain and rinse the soaked chickpeas under running water. Place in a medium pan, cover with cold water, and bring to a boil. Reduce the heat, cover, and simmer for 1 hour. Drain. Preheat the oven to 350°F (180°C).

4 Remove the lamb from the marinade, using a slotted spoon, reserving the marinade. Heat 1 tbsp of the oil in a 4-quart (4-liter) Dutch oven and brown the meat in 2 batches, for 3 minutes each. Transfer each batch with a slotted spoon to a plate lined with paper towels.

5 Add the remaining 1 tbsp of oil to the casserole and cook the onion over medium heat. Add the spices and pine nuts and cook for 2 minutes. Stir in the flour and add the soaked fruit and sherry, reserved marinade, wine, stock, tomatoes, and chickpeas. Season.

6 Return the meat to the casserole and bring to a boil. Cover and cook in the oven for 1 hour. Remove from the oven and add the olives and lemon juice. Return to the oven for 15 minutes. Serve in warmed bowls, over couscous.

CLEVER WITH LEFTOVERS

A little leftover tagine can easily be stretched with some extra chicken stock (see p94) to make a great spicy soup.

CALORIES: 667kcals/2794kJ

CARBOHYDRATE: 42g
sugar: 25g

FAT: 30g
saturated: 7g

SALT: 0.8g

FIBER: 9g

Braised lamb shanks

This takes only minutes to make; hours of unattended slow cooking leave it succulent and falling off the bone.

15 mins   3 hrs 15 mins

SPECIAL EQUIPMENT
4-quart (4-liter) Dutch oven

SERVES 4

2 tbsp olive oil

4 lamb shanks

salt and freshly ground black pepper

3 celery stalks, roughly chopped

3 carrots, roughly chopped

4 shallots, roughly chopped

2 garlic cloves, finely sliced

2 sprigs of rosemary

1 bay leaf

1¼ cups red wine

2 cups lamb stock

mashed potatoes, to serve

1 Preheat the oven to 300°F (150°C). Heat the oil in a very large (4-quart/4-liter) heavy-bottomed Dutch oven over medium heat.

2 Add 2 of the shanks, season well, and brown for 5 minutes, turning occasionally. Transfer to a plate and set aside. Repeat for the remaining shanks.

3 Add the vegetables and garlic to the casserole and cook over medium heat for 5 minutes. Return the lamb and its juices and add the herbs, wine, and stock. Bring to a boil and cover. Cook in the oven for 2½–3 hours or until the meat is starting to fall off the bone.

4 Using a slotted spoon, carefully transfer the shanks and vegetables to a warmed serving dish. Remove the bay leaf and rosemary. Discard the fat from the sauce and pour it into a bowl. Serve the lamb and vegetables with mashed potatoes and the sauce.

HOW TO FREEZE

Freezing dishes that are cooked on the bone is far easier if the meat is cooled and taken off the bone first. The bones can be frozen separately to make a stock at another time, and the deboned meat will take up far less space in your freezer.

CALORIES: 468kcals/1951kJ
CARBOHYDRATE: 8g
  sugar: 7g
FAT: 22g
  saturated: 8g
SALT: 0.7g
FIBER: 3g

Blanquette de veau

This classic French dish has a rich, creamy sauce that is thickened with the careful addition of egg yolks.

15 mins   1 hr 40 mins

SPECIAL EQUIPMENT
2-quart (2-liter) Dutch oven

SERVES 4

1lb 5oz (600g) veal, cut into 1½in (4cm) pieces

1 bouquet garni

1 celery stalk, roughly chopped

1 carrot, roughly chopped

salt and freshly ground black pepper

½ cup white wine

12 pearl onions

10oz (300g) button mushrooms

2 large egg yolks

¼ cup heavy cream

chopped flat-leaf parsley leaves, to garnish

mixed basmati and wild rice, and steamed green vegetables, to serve

1 Place the veal, bouquet garni, celery, and carrot in a 2-quart (2-liter) heavy-bottomed Dutch oven. Season well and add the wine. Pour in 2 cups of water. Bring to a boil, then skim off any foam. Reduce the heat, cover, and simmer for 1 hour, stirring occasionally.

2 Add the onions and mushrooms, return to a boil, cover, and simmer for 30 minutes. Remove the bouquet garni.

3 Whisk together the egg yolks and cream in a bowl and whisk in a little of the hot cooking juices. Slowly pour the egg yolk and cream mixture into the casserole, stirring constantly. Cook gently until the sauce thickens.

4 Scatter the parsley over the veal and serve with mixed basmati and wild rice and steamed green vegetables.

Veal is a gentle-tasting meat, and often appeals to children. If children want just the creamy sauce, leave the mushrooms and onions whole so that they can be picked out easily.

Fussy eaters!

CALORIES: 311kcals/1303kJ
CARBOHYDRATE: 5g
  sugar: 4g
FAT: 14g
  saturated: 7g
SALT: 0.3g
FIBER: 2.5g

Venison and red wine stew

Venison is an excellent source of low-fat protein, and its treatment in this recipe gives it a rich, satisfying flavor.

15 mins | 2¼–2¾ hrs

SPECIAL EQUIPMENT
medium Dutch oven

SERVES 4

3 tbsp olive oil

4 shallots, halved

2 celery stalks, finely chopped

1 carrot, finely chopped

2 garlic cloves, finely chopped

2 tbsp all-purpose flour

½ tsp grated nutmeg

½ tsp ground allspice

salt and freshly ground black pepper

1½lb (675g) boneless shoulder or other stewing venison, cut into bite-sized chunks

¼ cup redcurrant or sour cherry jelly

finely grated zest and juice of 1 orange

1¼ cups red wine

⅔ cup beef stock

1 bay leaf

potato and celeriac mash, to serve

1 Preheat the oven to 300°F (150°C). Heat 1 tbsp of the oil in a medium Dutch oven and gently cook the shallots, celery, and carrot for 3 minutes. Add the garlic and cook for a couple more minutes. Remove from the pot using a slotted spoon and set aside.

2 Place the flour, nutmeg, and allspice in a large freezer bag, season well, and add the meat. Shake to coat the meat in the seasoned flour. Pour out into a sieve and shake to remove excess flour.

3 Add the remaining 2 tbsp of oil to the pot and brown the meat in batches over medium heat, removing each batch to the plate with the vegetables.

4 Add the jelly, orange zest and juice, wine, stock, and bay leaf to the pot, season, and stir until the jelly has melted.

5 Return the vegetables and venison, stir, and bring to a simmer. Cover and cook in the oven for 2–2½ hours or until the venison is tender. Remove the bay leaf and serve the stew with potato and celeriac mash, made with two-thirds potato to one-third celeriac.

CALORIES: 400kcals/1670kJ

CARBOHYDRATE: 21g
sugar: 16g

FAT: 11g
saturated: 2.5g

SALT: 0.4g

FIBER: 2g

Polish hunter's stew

This is considered the Polish national dish. Called *bigos* it has a bit of everything—fresh, dried, smoked, and pickled!

30 mins   3 hrs 30 mins

SPECIAL EQUIPMENT
large Dutch oven

SERVES 6–8

scant 1oz (25g) dried wild mushrooms

3 tbsp olive oil

7oz (200g) chopped pancetta

1lb 2oz (500g) pork shoulder, cut into 1in (3cm) cubes

9oz (250g) cured, smoked sausage, ideally Polish sausage such as Kiełbasa Czosnkowa, cut into chunks

1 onion, finely sliced

1 celery stalk, sliced

1 large carrot, sliced

1 leek, white part only, finely sliced

7oz (200g) green cabbage, sliced

5½oz (150g) crimini mushrooms

½ tsp caraway seeds

½ tsp juniper berries, roughly ground in a mortar and pestle

1 tsp paprika

1 bay leaf

large sprig of thyme

1 heaping tbsp all-purpose flour

salt and freshly ground black pepper

1¼ cups red wine

1¾ cups beef or chicken stock (see p94)

9oz (250g) sauerkraut, drained and rinsed

2 tbsp redcurrant jelly

1 bouquet garni

bread or boiled potatoes, to serve

1 Soak the dried mushrooms in 2 cups of boiling water. In a large Dutch oven, heat 1 tbsp of the oil over high heat. Add all the meat and sausage and brown on all sides. Remove from the casserole and set aside.

2 Heat another 1 tbsp of the oil over medium heat. Cook the onion, celery, carrot, leek, and cabbage for 10 minutes, until softened. Remove and set aside.

3 Heat the remaining 1 tbsp of oil over low heat, and cook the crimini mushrooms for 2 minutes. Return the meat and vegetables, add the caraway, juniper, paprika, bay leaf, thyme, and flour, and season well. Stir over medium heat for 2 minutes.

4 Stir in the dried mushrooms, their soaking water (leave behind any grit), wine, and stock. Add the sauerkraut, redcurrant jelly, and bouquet garni and bring to a boil. Reduce the heat to low, cover, and cook for 2 hours.

5 Remove the lid and cook for another hour, until the meat is almost falling apart. Remove the bay leaf, thyme, and bouquet garni. Serve with bread or boiled potatoes.

CALORIES: 472kcals/1967kJ
CARBOHYDRATE: 11g
  sugar: 8.5g
FAT: 27g
  saturated: 9g
SALT: 2.6g
FIBER: 5g

Brazilian pork and beans

Otherwise known as *feijoada* this, the national dish of Brazil, is made with a variety of cured and fresh pork.

15 mins,
plus soaking

1 hr 45 mins

SERVES 6

1lb 2oz (500g) dried black-eyed peas

2 pig's trotters, split, or 1 ham hock

9oz (250g) pork ribs

7oz (200g) can chopped tomatoes

1 tbsp tomato paste

1 bay leaf

salt and freshly ground black pepper

2 tbsp olive oil

7oz (200g) chopped pancetta

1lb 2oz (500g) lean pork tenderloin

1 small onion, finely chopped

2 garlic cloves, finely chopped

6oz (175g) chorizo, in small chunks

1 green chile, seeded (optional)

1 Soak the beans overnight. Drain and place in a large saucepan. Cover with water, bring to a boil, and boil for 10 minutes, skimming off any foam, then lower the heat, cover, and simmer for one hour.

2 Meanwhile, place the pig's trotters or ham hock and pork ribs in a saucepan with the tomatoes, tomato paste, bay leaf, and salt and pepper. Cover with water, bring to a boil, and skim off any foam. Cover, reduce the heat, and simmer for 50 minutes.

3 Drain the beans and reserve the liquid, then return the beans to the pan. Add the meats with their cooking liquid. Add enough liquid from the beans to cover. Cook, covered, over low heat, for another 20 minutes.

4 Heat 1 tbsp of the oil in a frying pan and add the pancetta. Cook for 5 minutes, until it starts to brown. Remove it and use the same fat to brown the pork tenderloin. Add the pork and pancetta to the meat and bean mixture and cook for 10 minutes, or until everything is tender. Wipe out the frying pan, add 1 tbsp of oil, and cook the onion and garlic over medium heat for 4 minutes, stirring, until translucent. Add the chorizo and chile (if using), increase the heat, and cook for 2 minutes, stirring.

5 Add 2–3 tbsp of the cooked beans to the frying pan and mash well with the back of a spoon. Add the contents of the frying pan to the meat and beans, stir, and cook for another 10 minutes.

6 Pick the meat from the trotters or hock (discard the bones and skin). Cut the pork tenderloin into pieces. Transfer them and the rest of the meat and beans to a warmed platter, season to taste, and serve.

VARIATION

Instead of using dried beans, use two 14oz (400g) cans of beans, drained and added in step 5. Instead of black-eyed peas, try black beans, adzuki beans, red kidney beans, or pinto beans.

CALORIES: 757kcals/3178kJ

CARBOHYDRATE: 46g
  sugar: 6g

FAT: 33g
  saturated: 11g

SALT: 2.8g

FIBER: 10g

Boeuf bourguignon

A simplified version of a French classic, the beef here is meltingly rich and tender.

30 mins   2 hrs 45 mins

SERVES 4–6

4 tbsp olive oil

3½oz (100g) chopped pancetta

2 onions, finely chopped

4 thin carrots, cut into ¾in (2cm) slices

1 celery stalk, finely chopped

5½oz (150g) button mushrooms, halved if large

2¼lb (1kg) beef stew meat, cut into 1in (3cm) cubes

2 tbsp all-purpose flour

salt and freshly ground black pepper

1½ cups red wine

1 cup beef stock

1 bouquet garni

buttered noodles, to serve

1 Preheat the oven to 300°F (150°C). Heat 2 tbsp of the oil in a large casserole or Dutch oven. Cook the pancetta for a few minutes until lightly browned. Add the onions, carrots, celery, and mushrooms, and cook for 5 minutes. Set aside.

2 Pat the beef dry with paper towels. Season the flour with salt and pepper and toss the beef in it to coat. Shake off the excess.

3 Heat the remaining oil in the pan and cook the beef, in batches, until well browned. Set aside.

4 Pour the wine and stock into the pan, scraping any browned bits stuck to the bottom.. Season well, add the bouquet garni, and return the meat and vegetables.

5 Cover and cook in the oven for 2½ hours, until very tender. Remove the bouquet garni and serve with buttered noodles.

CLEVER WITH LEFTOVERS

Freeze leftover wine in ice cube trays for use in cooking. Once frozen, transfer to a freezer bag. Add a cube or two to a casserole or stew for added flavor.

CALORIES: 663kcals/2766kJ

CARBOHYDRATE: 15g
  sugar: 8.5g

FAT: 32g
  saturated: 10g

SALT: 1.5g

FIBER: 4.5g

Beef stroganoff

This classic Russian dish with a rich creamy sauce is a quick alternative to a stew.

10 mins   15 mins

SERVES 4

4 tbsp olive oil

14oz (400g) steak, such as sirloin, very thinly sliced

1 onion, finely chopped

5½oz (150g) button mushrooms, sliced

1 tbsp butter

2 tbsp all-purpose flour

1¼ cups beef stock

¼ cup (2oz) crème fraîche or sour cream

1 heaping tsp paprika

salt and freshly ground black pepper

½ tbsp lemon juice

1 tbsp chopped dill (optional)

buttered tagliatelle, to serve

1 Heat 2 tbsp of the oil in a large, deep-sided frying pan. Sear the steak in batches over high heat, cooking until it just colors. Set aside.

2 Heat the remaining 2 tbsp of oil in the pan and cook the onion and mushrooms over medium heat for 5 minutes until the mushrooms are golden brown, making sure not to burn the onions.

3 Add the butter and sprinkle in the flour, stirring it in. Gradually stir in the stock and cook for a few minutes until the sauce thickens. Stir in the crème fraîche and paprika and season to taste.

4 Return the beef to the pan and heat it through. Add the lemon with the dill (if using). Serve over buttered tagliatelle or pappardelle.

VARIATION

This treatment works just as well with thinly sliced chicken or pork. Add tarragon for chicken and sage for pork in the place of dill, use chicken stock (see p94) instead of beef stock, and add a spoonful of Dijon mustard to the sauce.

CALORIES: 364kcals/1513kJ

CARBOHYDRATE: 8g
  sugar: 2g

FAT: 25g
  saturated: 9g

SALT: 0.4g

FIBER: 1.5g

Beef in beer

The type of beer used here will affect the flavor, but both light and dark beers work well.

25 mins   2 hrs 45 mins

SERVES 4–6

¼ cup olive oil

1 onion, finely chopped

1 celery stalk, finely chopped

1 large carrot, finely chopped

2 garlic cloves, finely chopped

2¼lb (1kg) beef stew meat, cut into 1in (3cm) cubes

salt and freshly ground black pepper

2 tbsp all-purpose flour

12oz (330ml) bottle dark beer

1 cup beef stock

1 tsp granulated sugar

a few sprigs of thyme

3 tbsp chopped flat-leaf parsley leaves

CALORIES: 536kcals/2240kJ
CARBOHYDRATE: 13g
  sugar: 7g
FAT: 25.5g
  saturated: 7.5g
SALT: 0.6g
FIBER: 2g

1 Preheat the oven to 300°F (150°C). Heat half the oil in a large Dutch oven. Cook the onion, celery, and carrot for 10 minutes over medium heat, until they start to color. Add the garlic and cook for another minute. Set aside.

2 Pat the meat dry with paper towels. Season the flour and toss the beef in it, to coat. Shake off excess flour.

3 Heat the remaining oil in the pan and cook the beef, in batches, until well browned. Do not crowd the pan. Set aside.

4 Pour the beer and stock into the pan, scraping any browned bits stuck to the bottom. Season well, add the sugar, thyme, and 2 tbsp of parsley, and return the meat and vegetables.

5 Cover and cook in the oven for 2½ hours. The beef should be almost falling apart. Remove the thyme and sprinkle with the remaining parsley to serve.

Chili con carne

A family favorite, and a good way to introduce your children to beans such as kidney beans.

25 mins   1 hr 45 mins

SPECIAL EQUIPMENT
large Dutch oven

SERVES 4

2 tbsp olive oil

1 onion, finely chopped

1 celery stalk, finely chopped

1 green bell pepper, finely chopped

2 garlic cloves, crushed

1lb 2oz (500g) ground beef

1 tsp dried oregano

2 tsp smoked paprika

½ tsp cayenne pepper

1 tsp ground cumin

1 tsp brown sugar

salt and freshly ground black pepper

1 x 14oz (400g) can chopped tomatoes

1 cup beef stock

1 tbsp tomato paste

1 x 14oz (400g) can kidney beans, drained and rinsed

sour cream and grated Cheddar cheese, to serve (optional)

1 Heat the oil over medium heat in a large Dutch oven. Cook the onion, celery, and green bell pepper for 10 minutes, until they start to color at the edges. Add the garlic and cook for 1 minute.

2 Add the beef and cook over high heat, breaking up any clumps with a wooden spoon, until well browned. Add the oregano, spices, sugar, and seasoning and cook until the spices are fragrant.

3 Add the tomatoes, stock, and tomato paste and bring to a boil. Cover and cook over low heat for 1 hour. Uncover, add the kidney beans, and cook for another 30 minutes over very low heat, until the sauce has thickened slightly. Serve with sour cream and grated Cheddar cheese (if you like).

CALORIES: 451kcals/1881kJ
CARBOHYDRATE: 19g
  sugar: 10g
FAT: 26g
  saturated: 10g
SALT: 1.2g
FIBER: 7.5g

Cider-braised pork with fennel

Pork shoulder is an inexpensive cut, and in this recipe a long, slow braise brings out all its flavor.

25 mins | 2 hrs

SERVES 4

4 tbsp olive oil

2 onions, quartered

1 fennel bulb, cut into similar-sized pieces as the onion

1lb 2oz (500g) pork shoulder, cut into 1in (3cm) cubes

salt and freshly ground black pepper

1 heaping tbsp all-purpose flour

12oz (330ml) bottle of hard cider

⅔ cup chicken stock (see p94)

1 tbsp Dijon mustard

2 tbsp finely chopped sage leaves

2 tbsp crème fraîche

1 Heat 2 tbsp of the oil in a large, heavy-bottomed saucepan with a lid. Cook the onions and fennel for 5–7 minutes, until they soften slightly. Set aside.

2 Pat the meat dry with paper towels. Season the flour and toss the pork in it, to coat. Shake off excess flour.

3 Heat the remaining 2 tbsp of oil in the pan and cook the pork, in batches, until browned. Set aside.

4 Pour the cider and stock into the pan, stirring well to dislodge any meaty residue. Season well, add the mustard and sage, and return the meat and vegetables.

5 Cover and cook over very low heat for 1½ hours until meltingly tender. Stir in the crème fraîche and heat through before serving.

COOK'S TIP

The cider in this dish can easily be replaced by apple juice, if preferred, or use half cider and half apple juice.

CALORIES: 358kcals/1496kJ
CARBOHYDRATE: 9g
  sugar: 6g
FAT: 19g
  saturated: 5g
SALT: 0.6g
FIBER: 2g

Creamy pork goulash

A delicious version of an old classic, the use of caraway adds extra depth to this rich, warming stew.

20 mins | 2 hrs

SERVES 4

1 tbsp all-purpose flour

2 tsp paprika

salt and freshly ground black pepper

1lb 2oz (500g) pork shoulder, cut into 1in (3cm) cubes

4 tbsp olive oil

5½oz (150g) button mushrooms, halved if large

1 onion, finely chopped

3½oz (100g) chopped pancetta

2 garlic cloves, crushed

1 tsp caraway seeds

2 cups chicken stock (see p94)

2 tbsp cider vinegar

2 heaping tbsp sour cream

mashed potatoes and cabbage, to serve

CALORIES: 393kcals/1638kJ
CARBOHYDRATE: 5g
  sugar: 2g
FAT: 24g
  saturated: 6g
SALT: 1.4g
FIBER: 1.5g

1 Put the flour in a freezer bag with ½ tsp of the paprika and some salt and pepper. Toss the pork in it. Pour out into a sieve, shaking to remove excess flour. Heat 2 tbsp of the olive oil in a large, heavy-bottomed saucepan with a lid. Cook the pork, in batches, for a couple of minutes on each side, until well browned. Set aside.

2 Heat the remaining 2 tbsp of oil in the pan and cook the mushrooms for a few minutes until they color. Add the onion and pancetta and cook for 5 minutes until the pancetta crisps up. Add the garlic, the remaining 2 tsp of paprika, and the caraway, and cook for 1 minute.

3 Stir in the stock and vinegar, scraping up any residue, and season. Return the pork and reduce the heat to a gentle simmer.

4 Cover and cook for 45 minutes to 1 hour, then uncover and cook for another hour, stirring occasionally, until the sauce has thickened and reduced and the meat is meltingly tender. Stir in the sour cream and serve with fluffy mashed potatoes and lightly steamed cabbage.

Easy cassoulet

Try this super family-friendly version of a far more complex French classic dish for a warming winter meal.

20 mins   1 hr 50mins

SPECIAL EQUIPMENT
2-quart (2-liter) Dutch oven

SERVES 4

1 tbsp olive oil

1lb (450g) pork belly slices

4 pork and herb sausages

3½oz (100g) chopped pancetta

1 onion, roughly chopped

2 carrots, roughly chopped

2 garlic cloves, roughly chopped

1 x 14oz (400g) can cannellini beans, drained and rinsed

1 tsp dried thyme

salt and freshly ground black pepper

2 tbsp sun-dried tomato pesto

1 cup hot chicken stock (see p94)

½ cup red wine

2 tbsp chopped flat-leaf parsley leaves

1 cup fresh white bread crumbs

crusty bread, to serve

1 Preheat the oven to 350°F (180°C). Heat the oil in a 2-quart (2-liter) Dutch oven over medium heat and brown the pork belly. Transfer to a plate lined with paper towels. Add the sausages to the pot and cook, turning to brown on all sides. Transfer to the plate.

2 Add the pancetta, onion, and carrots to the pot and cook gently, stirring occasionally, for 5 minutes. Add the garlic, beans, and thyme to the pot. Season and stir well.

3 Combine the tomato pesto, stock, and wine in a bowl and stir well. Pour into the pot and stir. Arrange the pork belly and sausages in the vegetable mixture. Cover and bake in the oven for 1 hour.

4 Mix the parsley into the bread crumbs with plenty of pepper. Remove the pot from the oven and sprinkle with the bread crumbs. Return to the oven, uncovered, for 30 minutes.

5 Spoon onto warmed plates, making sure each portion gets some crispy crumb topping, and serve with crusty bread.

VARIATION

Use 5½oz (150g) of dried beans instead of canned if you have time, soaking them overnight, then simmering according to the packet instructions. Add them to the cassoulet in step 3.

CALORIES: 716kcals/2988kJ

CARBOHYDRATE: 38g
  sugar: 7g

FAT: 41g
  saturated: 14g

SALT: 2.7g

FIBER: 7.5g

Toad in the hole with onion gravy

This gravy is perfect with toad in the hole, but also with grilled chops, mashed potatoes, or your favorite sausages.

25 mins   40-45 mins

SPECIAL EQUIPMENT
10 x 12 x 2¾in (25 x 30 x 7cm)
roasting pan

SERVES 4

FOR THE TOAD IN THE HOLE
¾ cup all-purpose flour

salt and freshly ground black pepper

4 large eggs

1¼ cups whole milk

½ tsp dried sage

½ tsp spicy brown mustard

2 tbsp beef dripping or butter

8 pork and herb sausages

FOR THE ONION GRAVY
2 tbsp olive oil

3 red onions, finely sliced

2 tbsp all-purpose flour

1¼ cups vegetable stock (see p156)

splash of red wine (optional)

1 Preheat the oven to 400°F (200°C). Place the flour in a mixing bowl and season well. Break the eggs, 1 at a time, into the flour, and stir with a fork to incorporate. Gradually add the milk, whisking vigorously with a fork after each addition. Stir in the sage and mustard. Set aside.

2 Start the gravy. Heat the oil in a small, non-stick pan over medium heat. Add the onions and cook for 5 minutes. Reduce the heat, cover, and cook very gently for 30 minutes, stirring occasionally.

3 Meanwhile, put the dripping in a non-stick, heavy-bottomed roasting pan and heat for 5 minutes. Add the sausages and cook in the oven for 15 minutes. Space the sausages out evenly in the pan, then carefully pour the batter over the top. Return to the oven for 25–30 minutes, or until well-risen and golden brown.

4 Meanwhile, stir the flour into the onions and cook over medium heat for 2 minutes, stirring with a wooden spoon. Gradually pour in the stock, stirring constantly. Season to taste and add the wine (if using). Serve with slices of toad in the hole.

VARIATION

Make a vegetarian version, using vegetarian sausages, and oil instead of dripping. These sausages will not need pre-cooking, so add the sausages and batter to the hot fat at the same time.

PREPARE AHEAD

Make the batter up to 1 day in advance, cover, and refrigerate. Return to room temperature; follow the recipe from step 2.

CALORIES: 705kcals/2941kJ

CARBOHYDRATE: 44g
    sugar: 9.5g

FAT: 45g
    saturated: 15g

SALT: 2.4g

FIBER: 3g

Sausage and butterbean goulash

This works best with German-style cooked or scalded sausages. Try cannellini beans instead of butterbeans.

10 mins   35 mins

SERVES 4

2 tbsp olive oil

1 onion, finely chopped

1 red bell pepper, cut into ¾in (2cm) cubes

1 yellow bell pepper, cut into ¾in (2cm) cubes

2 garlic cloves, crushed

1 tbsp all-purpose flour

½ tsp cayenne pepper

½ tsp smoked paprika

1½ cups tomato sauce

1¼ cups chicken stock (see p94)

salt and freshly ground black pepper

14oz (400g) mixed German wurst, cut into ¾in (2cm) chunks

1 x 14oz (400g) can butterbeans, drained, and rinsed

2 tbsp chopped flat-leaf parsley leaves

2 tbsp sour cream

white rice or crusty bread, to serve

1 In a large, heavy-bottomed saucepan, heat the oil over low heat and gently cook the onion and peppers for 5 minutes until softened but not browned. Add the garlic and cook for another 2 minutes.

2 Add the flour, cayenne pepper, and smoked paprika and stir well. Add the tomato sauce and chicken stock to the pan and mix thoroughly. Season with salt and pepper if needed (the stock may be salty). Bring to a boil, reduce the heat, and simmer for 10 minutes.

3 Add the wurst and continue to simmer for 10 minutes. Add the butterbeans and gently simmer for a final 5 minutes. Stir in the parsley and serve with the sour cream swirled on top, or on the side, with white rice or crusty bread.

CALORIES: 464kcals/1935kJ

CARBOHYDRATE: 25g
    sugar: 7g

FAT: 29g
    saturated: 10g

SALT: 2.1g

FIBER: 7g

All-American meatloaf

A sterling family meal. Any leftovers can be pan-fried with a little oil for a quick dinner the following day.

20 mins   1 hr

SPECIAL EQUIPMENT

food processor (optional)

9in x 5in (900g) loaf pan (optional)

SERVES 4

1 onion

1 celery stalk

1 carrot

2 tbsp olive oil, plus extra for greasing

1 garlic clove, crushed

½ cup fresh white bread crumbs

10oz (300g) ground beef

10oz (300g) ground pork

2 tbsp finely chopped parsley

½ tsp dried thyme, or 1 tbsp chopped thyme leaves

1 tsp Worcestershire sauce

2 tbsp ketchup

salt and freshly ground black pepper

1 Preheat the oven to 350°F (180°C). If you have a food processor, roughly chop the onion, celery, and carrot, then process until very finely chopped. If not, chop as finely as you can.

2 Heat the oil in a saucepan and cook the chopped vegetables over low heat for 5 minutes, until they darken slightly. Add the garlic and cook for 1 minute.

3 Next, mix the vegetables, bread crumbs, and remaining ingredients until well mixed, but not compacted.

4 Either line a shallow-sided baking sheet with waxed paper and shape the meat into an oval loaf with your hands, or lightly pack it into an oiled 9in x 5in (900g) loaf pan. Rub oil on top and bake in the middle of the oven for 45 minutes (1 hour if in a pan). Rest for 10 minutes, then slice with a sharp, serrated knife and serve with tomato sauce or creamy gravy.

HOW TO FREEZE

Freeze either whole, securely wrapped first in plastic wrap and then in foil, or in individually wrapped slices.

CALORIES: 429kcals/1788kJ

CARBOHYDRATE: 13g
    sugar: 4g

FAT: 28g
    saturated: 9g

SALT: 0.8g

FIBER: 1g

Moussaka

Good moussaka may take a while to prepare but the time taken to get the sauces right is well worth it.

1 hr   2 hrs 25mins

SPECIAL EQUIPMENT
8 x 8in (20 x 20cm) deep-sided
ovenproof dish

SERVES 4

FOR THE MEAT SAUCE

2 tbsp olive oil

1 onion, finely chopped

2 garlic cloves, finely chopped

1lb (450g) ground lamb

1 x 14oz (400g) can chopped tomatoes

1 cup beef, lamb, or chicken stock
(see p94)

¼ cup red wine (optional)

2 tbsp finely chopped parsley leaves

½ tsp dried thyme

½ tsp dried oregano

½ tsp ground cinnamon

salt and freshly ground black pepper

12oz (350g) waxy potatoes,
peeled weight

1 large eggplant, cut lengthwise
into ½in (1cm) thick slices

4 tbsp olive oil

FOR THE BÉCHAMEL SAUCE

4 tbsp butter

¼ cup all-purpose flour

1¾ cups whole milk

pinch of grated nutmeg

scant 1oz (25g) grated Parmesan
cheese

2 large eggs, beaten

1 To make the meat sauce,
heat the oil in a large, heavy-
bottomed saucepan. Cook the
onion over medium heat until it
softens, but does not color, then
add the garlic and cook for 1 minute.
Increase the heat and add the lamb.
Cook, using a wooden spoon to
break up the meat, until it browns.
Add the tomatoes, stock, wine

(if using), herbs, and cinnamon, and
season. Bring to a boil, reduce to a
simmer, and cook over low heat for
1–1¼ hours until all the liquid has
evaporated.

2 Meanwhile, boil the potatoes,
whole, in salted water, until
just cooked through. Drain, slice
lengthwise, and set aside. Preheat
the broiler to its highest setting.
Spread the eggplant on a baking
sheet, brush with 2 tbsp of the oil,
and broil until brown. Turn, brush
with the remaining 2 tbsp of oil,
and broil the other side. Set aside.

3 Preheat the oven to 350°F
(180°C). To make the béchamel
sauce, melt the butter in a small
pan over medium heat. Whisk in
the flour and cook for 2 minutes,
then take off the heat and gradually
whisk in the milk. Return to the
heat and cook, stirring, until it
thickens. Add the nutmeg, salt
and pepper, and the Parmesan

cheese, and cook over low heat for
10 minutes. Whisk in the beaten
eggs off the heat.

4 Spread half the meat into an
8 x 8in (20 x 20cm) ovenproof
dish. Cover it with half the eggplant,
then half the béchamel. Arrange
the potatoes in an overlapping
layer, then add the rest of the meat,
eggplant, and finally béchamel.
Bake for 1 hour until golden brown.
Rest for 10 minutes before serving.

CALORIES: 772kcals/3216kJ
CARBOHYDRATE: 35g
  sugar: 10g
FAT: 51.5g
  saturated: 20g
SALT: 1g
FIBER: 5g

Thursday —
Pasta with
peas and
pancetta
(p205)

Thursday

Friday —
Chili con
carne (p143)

Saturday —
Sausage and
sweet potato
(p302)

Saturday

A healthy variety

When planning, bear in mind not just the need for meals, but different tastes as well. Try different ingredients, but remember to keep the nutrition of the meals balanced for the whole family. Ensure that you aim for everyone to achieve their five a day; sufficient protein for growth; calcium for bones; and the essential vitamins and minerals we all need.

Fish is a good source of protein, along with meat, eggs, and pulses. Aim for at least two portions of fish a week, including one portion of oily fish such as salmon or mackerel, and not too much processed meat (for example, sausages, ham, and salami).

Check out the nutritional details on the recipes in this book and see pages 10–11 for more information on a balanced diet.

Keep it simple

Don't worry if you find planning the meals for the entire week tricky at first. Aiming for the whole family to sit down together at the weekend is a good first step to creating a weekly routine.

Vegetable stock

This simple stock is the basis for hundreds of delicious soups, stews, and sauces.

5 mins · 55 mins

MAKES 2 CUPS

1 tbsp olive oil

1 onion, roughly chopped

2 carrots, roughly chopped

1 celery stalk, roughly chopped (include any leaves)

1 leek, roughly chopped

¼ tsp black peppercorns

1 bay leaf

small handful of parsley

1 Heat the oil in a large, heavy-bottomed saucepan. Add the vegetables and cook them over low heat, stirring occasionally, for 10 minutes, until they soften and start to color at the edges.

2 Add 3½ cups of cold water, the peppercorns, and herbs, and bring to a boil. Reduce to a low simmer and cook for 45 minutes, or until the stock has reduced by half and tastes rich and flavorful.

Strain the stock through a sieve before using or cooling and freezing.

VARIATION

You can try adding some mushroom trimmings to give more depth to the stock.

COOK'S TIP

This stock is salt free, so is suitable for babies and young children. Salt can be added after it has reduced, if necessary. Never salt stock before cooking, as it will concentrate during the cooking process.

HOW TO FREEZE

Freezing the stock in icecube trays, then transferring them to a freezer bag, means that a few cubes at a time can be added to dishes for extra flavor.

CALORIES:	99kcals/407kJ
CARBOHYDRATE:	trace
sugar: trace	
FAT:	11g
saturated: 1.5g	
SALT:	trace
FIBER:	0g

Butternut squash soup

Make this rich, velvety soup more sophisticated with a garnish of sage leaves, quickly fried in light oil.

5 mins · 20 mins

SPECIAL EQUIPMENT
blender or hand-held blender

SERVES 4-6

3 tbsp olive oil

1 onion, chopped

1 leek, white part only, chopped

1 celery stalk, chopped

1lb 2oz (500g) butternut squash, peeled and cut into 1in (3cm) cubes

2½ cups vegetable or chicken stock (see left or p94)

½ tbsp chopped sage leaves

salt and freshly ground black pepper

1 Heat the oil in a large, heavy-bottomed saucepan with a lid. Add the onion, leek, and celery and cook for 5 minutes until they soften, but do not brown.

2 Add the squash, stock, and sage, and season well.

3 Bring to a boil, then reduce to a gentle simmer, cover, and cook for 15 minutes until the squash is tender.

4 Blend the soup, either in a blender or using a hand-held blender, until completely smooth. Check the seasoning and serve.

VARIATION

This soup can also be made with sweet potato or pumpkin, although the cooking times for those vegetables will be slightly less; try cooking for just 10 minutes in step 3.

CALORIES:	175–117kcals/734–490kJ
CARBOHYDRATE:	12–8g
sugar: 7–5g	
FAT:	8.5–6g
saturated: 1–0.8g	
SALT:	0.6–0.4g
FIBER:	4–3g

Harvest vegetable soup

Also known as "bottom of the fridge soup," this is a great way to use up odds and ends of vegetables.

10 mins   30 mins

SPECIAL EQUIPMENT
blender or hand-held blender

SERVES 4–6

3 tbsp olive oil

1 onion, chopped

1 leek, white part only, chopped

1 celery stalk, chopped

1lb 2oz (500g) mixed root vegetables, peeled weight, such as carrots, potatoes, parsnips, and turnips, cut into even-sized cubes

2½–3½ cups vegetable or chicken stock (see left or p94)

salt and freshly ground black pepper

1 Heat the oil in a large, heavy-bottomed saucepan with a lid. Add the onion, leek, and celery and cook for 5 minutes until they soften, but do not brown.

2 Add the mixed root vegetables and 2½ cups of the stock and season well.

3 Bring to a boil, then reduce the heat to a gentle simmer. Cover and cook for 20 minutes, until the vegetables are soft.

4 Blend the soup, either in a blender or using a hand-held blender, until it is completely smooth. Add more stock if you want a thinner soup. Check the seasoning and add a swirl of cream to serve.

CALORIES: 186–124kcals/778–519kJ

CARBOHYDRATE: 14–10g
sugar: 7–4.5g

FAT: 9–6g
saturated: 1–0.8g

SALT: 0.6–0.4g

FIBER: 4.5–3g

Minted split pea and tomato soup

This soup is full of goodness, warm, and nutritious, as well as being very delicious.

10 mins   1 hr

SPECIAL EQUIPMENT
blender or hand-held blender

SERVES 6

2 tbsp olive oil

1 large onion, finely chopped

2 garlic cloves, crushed

1 x 14oz (400g) can chopped tomatoes

3½ cups vegetable stock (see left)

9oz (250g) dried split peas

2 tsp dried mint

salt and freshly ground black pepper

1 Heat the oil in a large, heavy-bottomed saucepan with a lid. Cook the onion for 5 minutes over medium heat, until it has softened, but not browned. Add the garlic and cook for another minute.

2 Add the rest of the ingredients, season well, and bring to a boil. Reduce the heat to a low simmer and cook for up to 1 hour, stirring occasionally, or until the peas have softened. Keep an eye on it: start checking after 30 minutes, as different batches of split peas cook at varying rates.

3 Blend the soup, either in a blender or using a hand-held blender. You can process until completely smooth, or leave it a little chunky if you prefer.

VARIATION

If you eat meat, try using a good-quality beef stock instead of vegetable stock for a really rich taste.

CALORIES: 229kcals/954kJ

CARBOHYDRATE: 26g
sugar: 4g

FAT: 5g
saturated: 0.7g

SALT: 0.6g

FIBER: 4.5g

French onion soup

Deep-flavored and savory, this recipe creates a soup elegant enough to serve to friends.

20 mins   50 mins

SERVES 6

4 tbsp butter

1 tbsp olive oil

2lb 4oz (1kg) white onions, finely sliced

2 garlic cloves, crushed

salt and freshly ground black pepper

2 heaping tbsp all-purpose flour

⅔ cup white wine

7 cups beef stock

a few sprigs of thyme

12 slices of baguette, each ¾in (2cm) thick

5½oz (150g) grated Gruyère cheese

1 Heat the butter and oil in a large, heavy-bottomed pan. Add the onions and cook over medium-low heat for about 30 minutes, until dark golden brown and well softened. Add the garlic, season well, and stir in the flour for a minute or two.

2 Gradually stir in the wine and stock, add the thyme, and cook over very low heat, uncovered, for 40 minutes, until the onions are meltingly tender and the soup reduced. Remove the thyme.

3 Preheat the broiler. Broil the baguette slices on both sides. Divide the Gruyère cheese between the slices, then melt it under the broiler. Float 2 slices of cheesy toast on each warmed bowl of soup to serve.

CALORIES: 502kcals/2103kJ

CARBOHYDRATE: 47.5g
  sugar: 11g

FAT: 18g
  saturated: 10g

SALT: 2.3g

FIBER: 5g

Potato salad with celery and capers

A straightforward potato salad can easily be livened up with these tangy, fresh flavors.

10 mins   20-25 mins

SERVES 4-6

2lb 4oz (1kg) waxy potatoes, peeled

salt and freshly ground black pepper

¼ cup good-quality mayonnaise

2 tsp Dijon mustard

1 celery stalk, finely chopped

bunch of scallions, white part only, finely chopped

1 tbsp capers, drained or rinsed, and finely chopped

1 tbsp lemon juice

1 Cook the potatoes whole in a large pan of boiling salted water for 20–25 minutes until tender. Drain and set aside to cool. When cold, cut the potatoes carefully into 1in (3cm) cubes.

2 Mix the mayonnaise, mustard, celery, scallions, capers, and lemon juice, and season well.

3 Gently toss through the diced potatoes, being careful not to break them up.

VARIATION

Chopped hard-boiled egg, or canned tuna, can also be added to this versatile salad for added protein.

CALORIES: 303–202kcals/1272–848kJ

CARBOHYDRATE: 42–28g
  sugar: 3.5–2.5g

FAT: 12–8g
  saturated: 2–1g

SALT: 0.7–0.5g

FIBER: 5–3.5g

Mixed leaf salad with balsamic dressing

This slightly sweet version of a standard salad dressing is popular with adults and children alike.

5 mins

SERVES 4

5½oz (150g) mixed salad leaves

FOR THE DRESSING

2 tbsp extra virgin olive oil

1 tbsp balsamic vinegar

½ tsp honey

1 tsp Dijon mustard

salt and freshly ground black pepper

1 Make the dressing by whisking all the ingredients together in a salad bowl until the mixture emulsifies.

2 Gently toss through the salad leaves to serve.

PREPARE AHEAD

Try doubling or tripling the quantities of salad dressing and seal the leftovers in a jam jar. It will store in the fridge for up to a week, and is great on steamed green vegetables and new potatoes as well as on salad.

CALORIES: 64kcals/263kJ
CARBOHYDRATE: 2.5g
  sugar: 2.5g
FAT: 6g
  saturated: 0.8g
SALT: trace
FIBER: 0.5g

Warm new potato salad with caramelized red onions

With its sweet onions and sharp dressing, this salad is perfect with barbecued beef brisket (see p282).

10 mins   15 mins

SERVES 4–6

2lb 4oz (1kg) small new potatoes, halved lengthwise

salt and freshly ground black pepper

2 tbsp olive oil

2 red onions, finely sliced

2 tbsp balsamic vinegar

1 tsp light brown sugar

FOR THE DRESSING

¼ cup extra virgin olive oil, plus extra if needed

2 tbsp red wine vinegar

2 tsp Dijon mustard

1 tsp granulated sugar

1 Cook the potatoes in plenty of boiling salted water until just tender, 10–15 minutes depending on their size. Drain well.

2 Meanwhile, heat the oil in a large, deep-sided frying pan. Cook the onions over low heat for about 10 minutes until they soften, then add the vinegar and sugar and cook for another 10 minutes until dark and glossy. Season well.

3 Whisk together the dressing ingredients in a salad bowl and season well. While the potatoes are still warm, but not too hot, toss them through the dressing. Add the red onions and serve. (If you are not serving immediately you may need a little extra oil, as the potatoes often absorb all the dressing once cool.)

CALORIES: 364–243kcals/1524–1016kJ
CARBOHYDRATE: 45–30g
  sugar: 10–7g
FAT: 17.5–12g
  saturated: 2.5–2g
SALT: 0.3–0.2g
FIBER: 4–3g

New potato, sweet potato, and tarragon salad

Delicious served with herby barbecued chicken and a green salad for a summer lunch.

10 mins   10–15 mins

SERVES 4–6

1lb 2oz (500g) small new potatoes, halved lengthwise

salt and freshly ground black pepper

1lb 2oz (500g) sweet potatoes, peeled and cut into similar-sized pieces as the new potatoes

FOR THE DRESSING

¼ cup extra virgin olive oil

3 tbsp balsamic vinegar

2 tsp Dijon mustard

2 tbsp finely chopped tarragon leaves

1 Cook the new potatoes in plenty of boiling salted water for about 12 minutes, until tender. Cook the sweet potatoes in another pan of simmering water for about 8 minutes, until tender. Do not cook them in the same pan, as the sweet potatoes are delicate and need less cooking time. Drain both well, separately.

2 In a salad bowl, whisk together all the dressing ingredients and season well. Mix through the warm new potatoes to coat. Gently mix in the sweet potatoes with your hands, making sure they do not break up. Serve warm or cold.

CALORIES: 312kcals/1314kJ

CARBOHYDRATE: 46g
  sugar: 11g

FAT: 12g
  saturated: 2g

SALT: 0.4g

FIBER: 6g

Classic coleslaw

Infinitely superior to store-bought coleslaw, this makes a great topping for baked potatoes, with grated cheese.

5 mins

SERVES 6

¼ cup good-quality mayonnaise

½ tbsp white wine vinegar

1 tsp granulated sugar

salt and freshly ground black pepper

¼ white cabbage, approx. 9oz (250g), shredded

2 large carrots, shredded

½ sweet white onion, very finely sliced

1 Mix together the mayonnaise, vinegar, and sugar until well combined. Season well.

2 Mix the shredded and sliced vegetables into the mayonnaise well, until every strand is coated in the seasoned mayonnaise.

CALORIES: 105kcals/435kJ

CARBOHYDRATE: 7g
  sugar: 7g

FAT: 8g
  saturated: 1g

SALT: 0.15g

FIBER: 3g

Spicy Asian slaw

This is fantastic served as a barbecue accompaniment, or as part of a summer buffet.

20 mins

SERVES 4

FOR THE COLESLAW

¼ red cabbage, approx. 9oz (250g), shredded

2 large carrots, shredded

½ red onion, finely sliced

1 tbsp finely chopped cilantro leaves

1 tbsp finely chopped mint leaves

FOR THE DRESSING

3 tbsp white wine vinegar or rice wine vinegar

3 tbsp light olive oil

1 tsp light brown sugar

½ tsp salt

pinch of chile flakes

1 In a large bowl, whisk together all the ingredients for the dressing until the sugar dissolves.

2 Toss through the shredded and sliced vegetables and herbs, keeping a few herbs back to scatter over the top before serving.

PREPARE AHEAD

Prepare the vegetables and store them in freezer bags in the fridge for up to 2 days. Spicy Asian slaw dressing will keep in a jar in the fridge for up to 1 week. At the last minute, simply toss the vegetables and dressing together with the just-chopped herbs.

CALORIES: 116kcals/482kJ

CARBOHYDRATE: 8g
  sugar: 7g

FAT: 8.5g
  saturated: 1g

SALT: 0.6g

FIBER: 4g

Carrot and beet salad

This richly colored salad is packed with beneficial antioxidants. Young, fresh vegetables are ideal for this.

30 mins   3–4 mins

SERVES 4–6

1lb 5oz (600g) carrots, scrubbed

bunch of beets, approx. 1lb 5oz (600g), peeled and halved

small bunch of flat-leaf parsley, leaves picked and chopped, or 1 bunch of cress, snipped

FOR THE VINAIGRETTE

6 tbsp extra virgin olive oil, plus 1 tsp for toasting the seeds

¼ cup balsamic vinegar

1 garlic clove, crushed (optional)

1¾oz (50g) sunflower or pumpkin seeds

1 tsp soy sauce (optional)

salt and freshly ground black pepper

1 Coarsely grate the raw vegetables and combine in a large bowl.

2 For the vinaigrette, whisk the oil, vinegar, and garlic (if using), together until emulsified.

3 Gently heat the remaining 1 tsp of oil in a small frying pan and toast the seeds for 3–4 minutes over medium heat, stirring frequently. Add the soy sauce at the end of cooking (if using). Most of the soy sauce will evaporate, leaving a salty taste and extra browning for the seeds.

4 Add the parsley or cress to the carrot and beets. Shake the vinaigrette again, pour over the vegetables, then season to taste. Toss the salad gently, scatter the toasted seeds over, and serve.

PREPARE AHEAD

The vegetables, vinaigrette, and seeds can be prepared and stored separately in the fridge for up to 24 hours. Return to room temperature and combine before serving.

CALORIES: 350kcals/1453kJ

CARBOHYDRATE: 27g
  sugar: 24g

FAT: 24g
  saturated: 3.5g

SALT: 0.6g

FIBER: 10g

Roasted beet, goat cheese, and walnut salad

Roasted beets have a fabulously rich, earthy flavor, and are great served warm with tangy goat cheese.

10 mins   40 mins

SERVES 4

6 small raw beets, peeled and quartered

2 tbsp olive oil

2½oz (75g) walnut halves

5½oz (150g) mixed salad leaves

3½oz (100g) crumbly goat cheese

FOR THE DRESSING

¼ cup extra virgin olive oil

2 tbsp cider vinegar

1 tsp Dijon mustard

1 tsp honey

salt and freshly ground black pepper

1 Preheat the oven to 400°F (200°C). Coat the beets in the oil and spread out on a large baking sheet. Bake at the top of the oven for 30–40 minutes, turning occasionally, until tender and browning slightly at the edges. Let cool.

2 Meanwhile, toast the walnuts in a dry frying pan over medium heat until they start to brown slightly at the edges, but do not burn. Take them off the heat, cool, then roughly chop.

3 In a large salad bowl, whisk together all the ingredients for the dressing until it has emulsified. Season to taste.

4 When the beets have cooled, toss the salad leaves through the dressing. Gently mix in the beets and walnuts and crumble the goat cheese over the top to serve.

CALORIES: 399kcals/1650kJ

CARBOHYDRATE: 8g
  sugar: 8g

FAT: 36g
  saturated: 8g

SALT: 0.6g

FIBER: 3g

Oven-roasted tomato bruschetta

This is a great dish to serve when tomatoes are at their peak. Use several different varieties, if possible.

10 mins   20 mins

SERVES 4

2lb 4oz (1kg) mixed ripe tomatoes, such as cherry, plum, yellow, or heirloom

6 tbsp olive oil

salt and freshly ground black pepper

8 slices ciabatta bread, each ¾in (2cm) thick

1 garlic clove, halved horizontally

handful of basil leaves, roughly torn

1 tbsp good-quality balsamic vinegar

1 Preheat the oven to 425°F (220°C). Cut the tomatoes in half, or quarter if large, and spread them out over 1 or 2 baking sheets in a single layer. Drizzle them with 4 tbsp of the oil, and season well. Turn carefully with your hands, to coat in the oil and seasoning, making sure that they are all lying cut-side up. Cook in the middle of the oven for 20–25 minutes until they start to soften, but still hold their shape.

2 Meanwhile, brush the ciabatta slices on both sides with the remaining 2 tbsp of oil and spread them out in a single layer on a baking sheet. Cook them at the top of the oven for 5–7 minutes on each side, until they start to brown and are crispy on both sides. Watch them carefully—they should be golden, not dark brown or scorched. Remove them from the oven and rub them on 1 side with the cut sides of the garlic.

3 Put the warm tomatoes in a bowl and gently toss in the basil and vinegar. Distribute the tomatoes evenly on the garlic-rubbed sides of the ciabatta and serve while still warm.

VARIATION

Add feta or goat cheese, crumbled on top, for a light lunch, and serve with a crisp green salad.

CALORIES: 365kcals/1530kJ

CARBOHYDRATE: 38g
  sugar: 10g

FAT: 20g
  saturated: 3g

SALT: 0.9g

FIBER: 5.5g

Zucchini fritters

To offset wateriness, salt larger zucchini as in the recipe. Smaller zucchini won't need salting.

20 mins, plus draining | 10 mins

MAKES 12

7oz (200g) zucchini, coarsely grated

salt and freshly ground black pepper

3½oz (100g) ricotta cheese

1 large egg

2 tbsp all-purpose flour

3 garlic cloves, crushed

small handful of basil leaves, chopped

small handful of flat-leaf parsley leaves, chopped

light olive oil, to fry

FOR THE TZATZIKI

2 tbsp finely chopped dill fronds

7oz (200g) Greek-style yogurt

juice of ½ lemon

1 Sprinkle the zucchini with 1 tsp salt and leave to drain in a sieve over the sink for 1 hour. Water will leach out of the zucchini, leaving them firmer. Rinse and squeeze dry in a clean kitchen towel.

2 In a bowl, whisk together the ricotta cheese, egg, and flour. Add 2 of the crushed garlic cloves, the basil, and parsley, and season well. Mix in the zucchini.

3 Fill a frying pan with oil to a depth of ½in (1cm) and fry tablespoons of the zucchini batter over medium heat for 2–3 minutes on each side, until golden brown. Drain on paper towels.

4 To make the tzatziki, mix ½ of the last clove of garlic with the dill, salt and pepper, and yogurt. Add a squeeze of lemon juice, season to taste. Serve with the hot fritters.

Children may be much more willing to try some "unusual" vegetables, such as zucchini, when they are disguised in tasty fried morsels like these.

Fussy eaters!

CALORIES: 71kcals/293kJ

CARBOHYDRATE: 3g
  sugar: 1g

FAT: 5g
  saturated: 2g

SALT: trace

FIBER: 0.3g

Pea pancakes

A simple dish to prepare, the bright peas and asparagus contrast beautifully with the golden yolk of the egg.

10 mins | 30 mins

SPECIAL EQUIPMENT
food processor

SERVES 4 (MAKES 8)

14oz (400g) fresh peas, shelled weight, or frozen peas, defrosted

large handful of mint leaves, finely chopped

4 tbsp melted butter, plus extra for frying

¼ cup all-purpose flour

¼ cup heavy cream

2 tbsp finely grated Parmesan cheese

6 large eggs

salt and freshly ground black pepper

large bunch of asparagus spears, woody ends removed

1 tsp extra virgin olive oil

CALORIES: 539kcals/2238kJ

CARBOHYDRATE: 23g
  sugar: 4.5g

FAT: 38g
  saturated: 19g

SALT: 0.8g

FIBER: 9g

1 Put the fresh peas in a pan and blanch in boiling water for 1–2 minutes, then drain and let cool. Frozen peas will not need this step.

2 Put the peas and mint into a food processor and pulse to a rough texture. Add the butter, flour, cream, Parmesan, and 2 of the eggs, and season. Process once more to form a stiff paste.

3 Heat a little butter in a large frying pan and add a couple of tablespoonfuls of the mixture for each pancake. Cook over medium heat and use the back of a spoon to smooth the top. After 3–4 minutes, the edges will change color and show a brownish tinge. Carefully turn them over and cook for another couple of minutes.

4 Meanwhile, bring a large pan of water to a boil and lightly poach the remaining 4 eggs until just set. Remove them with a slotted spoon.

5 As the eggs are cooking, grill the asparagus in a hot grill pan with the extra virgin olive oil, seasoning while cooking, until golden. Serve on warmed plates with the pancakes, carefully placing a poached egg on each serving.

Glazed carrots with nutmeg

A favorite accompaniment to roast chicken, the nutmeg and sugar make these carrots extra special.

5 mins   10 mins

SERVES 4

10oz (300g) thin, young carrots, peeled weight, cut into ½in (1cm) rounds

salt and freshly ground black pepper

1 tbsp butter

½ tsp granulated sugar

pinch of nutmeg

CALORIES: 56kcals/233kJ
CARBOHYDRATE: 6g
 sugar: 6g
FAT: 3.5g
 saturated: 2g
SALT: 0.1g
FIBER: 2.5g

1 Cook the carrots in plenty of boiling salted water for about 7 minutes until they are really soft. Drain well.

2 Put the butter in the pan in which you cooked the carrots and allow it to melt over a low heat. Stir in the sugar and nutmeg and cook gently until the sugar dissolves. Return the carrots, season well, and turn them in the butter until well glazed.

PREPARE AHEAD

If you have a large meal to prepare, cook the carrots to the end of step 1 ahead of time, cover, and refrigerate for up to 3 days. Reheat them in the melted butter glaze, following step 2, for 2–3 minutes until hot throughout.

Creamed spinach

This is the perfect recipe to introduce children to this healthy and nutritious green leaf.

5 mins   10 mins

SERVES 4

1 tbsp butter

1 tbsp olive oil

1 small garlic clove, crushed

14oz (400g) baby spinach leaves

½ cup heavy cream

salt and freshly ground black pepper

We all know how healthy spinach is, yet its strong taste will often put children off. Try this creamy treatment of the iron-rich vegetable alongside chicken or fish for more hard-to-please palates.

Fussy eaters!

1 Melt the butter and oil in a large, deep-sided frying pan. Cook the garlic for 1 minute, then add the baby spinach. Turn it through the oil and sauté it for 2–3 minutes, until cooked through.

2 Add the cream, season well, bring to a boil, and reduce before serving.

CALORIES: 202kcals/830kJ
CARBOHYDRATE: 2g
 sugar: 2g
FAT: 20g
 saturated: 11g
SALT: 0.4g
FIBER: 3g

Zucchini with garlic and mint

Zucchini, when eaten small, are sweet and juicy. The secret to cooking them well is in this recipe.

5 mins   5 mins

SPECIAL EQUIPMENT
large Dutch oven (optional)

SERVES 4

2 tbsp olive oil

1 tbsp butter

10oz (300g) small zucchini, sliced into ½in (1cm) rounds

1 garlic clove, crushed

1 tbsp finely chopped mint

salt and freshly ground black pepper

1 Melt the oil and butter in a large Dutch oven or heavy-bottomed saucepan with a lid, ideally one that will fit the zucchini in a single layer.

2 Add the zucchini and stir them around so that as many as possible are touching the bottom of the pan. Cover and cook over medium-high heat for 3 minutes.

3 Remove the lid, stir in the garlic and mint, and season well. Cover again and cook for another 2 minutes, shaking occasionally, until the zucchini are just cooked and golden brown in places.

CALORIES: 91kcals/373kJ

CARBOHYDRATE: 1.5g
    sugar: 1g

FAT: 9g
    saturated: 3g

SALT: trace

FIBER: 1g

Slow-cooked red cabbage

A really warming winter dish, this goes equally well with game or sausages.

10 mins   2 hrs

SPECIAL EQUIPMENT
large Dutch oven

SERVES 4–6

4 tbsp butter

2 tbsp granulated sugar

1 tsp salt

6 tbsp white wine vinegar

1 red cabbage, approx. 2lb 4oz (1kg), shredded

2 tbsp redcurrant or sour cherry jelly

2 apples, peeled and grated

salt and freshly ground black pepper

1 Preheat the oven to 325°F (160°C). Heat the butter, sugar, salt, vinegar, and 6 tbsp of water in a large Dutch oven. Bring to a boil, then reduce to a simmer and cook for just 2 minutes.

2 Add the red cabbage and stir it through. Seal the pan with a thick piece of foil, then put on the lid.

3 Cook in the center of the oven for 1½ hours. Remove the lid and stir in the jelly and apples, adding a little more water if the cabbage looks dry. Season generously, cover, and return to the oven for a final 30 minutes before serving.

CALORIES: 228–152kcals/958–639kJ

CARBOHYDRATE: 28–18g
    sugar: 28–18g

FAT: 11–7.5g
    saturated: 6.5–4.5g

SALT: 1.5–1g

FIBER: 10.5–7g

BATCHING AND FREEZING

This is one of the few vegetable dishes that freeze well. If you have a large red cabbage, just weigh it and increase the other ingredients accordingly. Cook it all and freeze leftovers for another meal.

Savoy cabbage with onions and garlic

This delicious cabbage is the perfect accompaniment to mashed potato and a warming winter stew.

5 mins   20 mins

SPECIAL EQUIPMENT
large Dutch oven (optional)

SERVES 4

2 tbsp olive oil

1 tbsp butter

1 onion, finely sliced

1 garlic clove, crushed

14oz (400g) Savoy cabbage, shredded

salt and freshly ground black pepper

CALORIES: 237kcals/998kJ

CARBOHYDRATE: 40g
  sugar: 1.5g

FAT: 6g
  saturated: 0.8g

SALT: trace

FIBER: 4.5g

1 Heat the oil and butter in a large Dutch oven or heavy-bottomed saucepan with a lid. Add the onion, cover, and cook over medium heat, stirring frequently, for 10 minutes, until it is well softened, but not brown. Add the garlic and cook for another minute.

2 Add the cabbage, seasoning, and ¼ cup of water. The water will practically sizzle away. Mix it all together and cover. Cook over low heat for 10 minutes, stirring occasionally, until the cabbage is cooked through.

VARIATION

For an Eastern European version, try adding ½ tsp of aromatic caraway seeds to the pan with the garlic. This version is delicious with pork, ham, or sausages.

Stir-fried green vegetables

Serve alongside many Chinese dishes, such as Chinese braised beef with ginger and soy sauce (see p133).

5 mins   5 mins

SERVES 4

salt

3½oz (100g) thin green beans

3½oz (100g) broccoli spears, or small florets

1 tbsp sesame oil or sunflower oil

3½oz (100g) sugarsnap peas, halved diagonally

bunch of scallions, cut into 1in (3cm) lengths

2 tbsp oyster sauce

1 tbsp soy sauce

1 tbsp rice wine or dry sherry

CALORIES: 66kcals/278kJ

CARBOHYDRATE: 5.5g
  sugar: 4g

FAT: 3g
  saturated: 0.5g

SALT: 1.5g

FIBER: 2.5g

1 In a large pan of boiling salted water, blanch the beans for 1 minute. Add the broccoli and blanch for another minute. Drain and refresh in cold water, then drain once more and set aside.

2 Heat the oil in a wok and stir-fry the sugarsnaps for 1 minute. Add the scallions and cook for another minute. With the wok off the heat, add the oyster sauce, soy sauce, and rice wine. Be careful, it will sizzle.

3 Return the wok to the heat and heat the sauce until it bubbles. Toss in the blanched vegetables and heat for another minute until they are warmed through and the sauce is reduced.

Perfect mashed potatoes

Mashed potatoes may seem easy to make but try this for a really creamy mash.

10 mins   20–30 mins

SERVES 4-6

2lb 4oz (1kg) floury potatoes, such as Russets, peeled and cut into large chunks

salt and freshly ground black pepper

¼ cup whole milk or half-and-half

2 tbsp butter

pinch of granulated sugar

1 Bring the potatoes to a boil in a large pan of cold salted water. Reduce the heat to a brisk simmer and cook, uncovered, for 20–25 minutes until soft, but not breaking up. Drain well in a colander.

2 Heat the milk and butter over low heat until the butter melts and the milk is hot, but not boiling. Add the sugar and season well. Return the potatoes to the pan and mash them well with a masher, or for a perfectly smooth result press them through a potato ricer.

3 Finally, use a wooden spoon to beat the potatoes really well. This helps make them super-smooth and fluffy.

CLEVER WITH LEFTOVERS

If you have leftover mashed potato, add any of the following in any combination for some different flavors: a handful of chopped spring onions, a handful of chopped flat-leaf parsley, 1 tbsp rinsed and chopped capers, finely grated zest of ½ lemon, and a pinch of chile flakes.

CALORIES: 255–170kcals/1074–716kJ

CARBOHYDRATE: 41–28g
  sugar: 2.5–1.7g

FAT: 7–5g
  saturated: 4–3g

SALT: 0.17–0.1g

FIBER: 4–3g

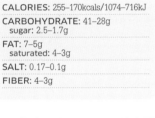

Mashed carrots and rutabaga

An accompaniment that works well with meat dishes, this is a good way to encourage kids to try rutabaga.

10 mins   20 mins

SERVES 4

10oz (300g) carrots, cut into small pieces

7oz (200g) rutabaga, cut into small pieces

salt and freshly ground black pepper

2 tbsp butter

1 tsp light brown sugar (optional)

pinch of grated nutmeg

1 Boil the vegetables together in a large pan of boiling salted water for about 20 minutes, or until soft. Drain well and return them to the pan.

2 Add the remaining ingredients and mash the vegetables well before serving.

CALORIES: 89kcals/371kJ

CARBOHYDRATE: 9g
  sugar: 9g

FAT: 5.5g
  saturated: 3.5g

SALT: 0.16g

FIBER: 4g

Rutabaga on its own has a strong taste. Yet mashed with a little butter, sugar, and some sweet carrots, it becomes a delicious, child-friendly dish.

Fussy eaters!

Green beans with toasted almonds

Liven up humble green beans with this simple twist that uses flaked almonds.

5 mins 5 mins

SERVES 4

10oz (300g) thin green beans

salt and freshly ground black pepper

2 tbsp sliced almonds

1 tbsp butter

1 Cook the green beans in plenty of boiling salted water for 3–5 minutes, or until they are tender. Drain well.

2 Meanwhile, dry-fry the almonds for a couple of minutes in a large frying pan over medium heat, turning constantly, until they begin to color, but not burn.

3 When the beans are ready, melt the butter in the pan with the almonds and toss the beans through. Season well with salt and pepper to serve.

COOK'S TIP

The same trick in this recipe can be used to liven up all types of green vegetable dishes. Simply adding a few toasted sliced almonds—or even hazelnuts—will add taste and texture.

CALORIES: 92kcals/380kJ

CARBOHYDRATE: 3g
   sugar: 2g

FAT: 7.5g
   saturated: 2.5g

SALT: trace

FIBER: 2g

Best roast potatoes

Completely indispensable with a Sunday roast; the best roast potatoes are cooked in goose fat.

10 mins 1 hr 10 mins

SERVES 4

2lb 4oz (1kg) white potatoes, such as Russet, peeled and halved

sea salt

3 heaping tbsp goose or duck fat

1 Preheat the oven to 400°F (200°C). Bring the potatoes to a boil in a large pan of salted water. Reduce the heat to a brisk simmer and cook, uncovered, for 10 minutes, until softening at the edges. Drain, return to the pan, and place over low heat for a minute to remove excess water, then remove from the heat, cover, and shake to rough up the edges.

2 Meanwhile, put the fat in a roasting pan big enough to take the potatoes in a single layer. Heat in the oven for 5 minutes.

3 Carefully remove the pan from the oven and add the potatoes. Turn to coat in fat, spread out, and sprinkle generously with salt. Roast for 45 minutes to 1 hour, turning them after they form a crust underneath.

CALORIES: 300kcals/1254kJ

CARBOHYDRATE: 40g
   sugar: 1.5g

FAT: 13g
   saturated: 8g

SALT: 0.3g

FIBER: 4.5g

Roast potatoes with rosemary and garlic

The Italians have a wonderful way of cooking potatoes in a large pan, but it is tricky. This is an easy version.

10 mins   40–45 mins

SERVES 4

2lb 4oz (1kg) waxy potatoes, peeled weight, cut into 2in (5cm) cubes

2 tbsp olive oil

2 garlic cloves, crushed

2 tbsp finely chopped rosemary

salt and freshly ground black pepper

1 Preheat the oven to 400°F (200°C). Toss all the ingredients together and spread them out in a single layer in a large roasting pan.

2 Cook for 40–50 minutes, turning occasionally, until golden brown and crispy at the edges.

FEEDING A CROWD

These simple Italian-style roast potatoes are an ideal dish for larger numbers. Just dice up as many potatoes as you need, and cook them on several baking sheets in the oven, switching the pans around during cooking so they all get to spend time at the top of the oven.

CALORIES: 237kcals/998kJ

CARBOHYDRATE: 40g
  sugar: 1.5g

FAT: 6g
  saturated: 0.8g

SALT: trace

FIBER: 4.5g

Boulangère potatoes

Try these for a healthy alternative to the more indulgent Gratin dauphinoise (see p170).

20 mins   1 hr 10 mins

SPECIAL EQUIPMENT

food processor (optional)

8 x 8in (20 x 20cm) deep-sided ovenproof dish

SERVES 4–6

2 tbsp butter, plus extra for greasing

1 tbsp olive oil

1 onion, finely sliced

1 garlic clove, crushed

2lb (900g) waxy, or yellow, potatoes, such as large Yukon Golds

salt and freshly ground black pepper

1¼ cups vegetable stock (see p156)

1 Preheat the oven to 350°F (180°C). Melt half the butter and the oil in a frying pan and cook the onion over medium heat for 5–7 minutes until softened, but not brown. Add the garlic and cook for another minute.

2 Finely slice the potatoes, using a food processor with a slicing attachment or a mandolin.

3 Rub an 8 x 8in (20 x 20cm) deep-sided ovenproof dish with the remaining butter. Spread in half the potatoes. Arrange the onions and garlic over the top, season well, and cover with the remaining potatoes. When you get to the top layer, arrange the potatoes nicely. Pour in the stock and dot with the remaining butter.

4 Put the ovenproof dish on a large baking sheet and cook in the center of the oven for 1 hour, or until the potatoes are soft and the top golden brown. Rest for 10 minutes before serving.

CALORIES: 284–190kcals/1191–794kJ

CARBOHYDRATE: 38–25.4g
  sugar: 3–1.8g

FAT: 10.5–7g
  saturated: 5–3.5g

SALT: 0.4–0.3g

FIBER: 4.5–3g

Cajun-spiced potato wedges

The spicy coating to these potato wedges works well with steak or just with a soured cream dip.

10 mins   40-50 mins

SERVES 6

4 potatoes, unpeeled and scrubbed

salt and freshly ground black pepper

1 lemon, cut into 6 wedges

12 garlic cloves

3 red onions, each cut into 8 wedges

4 bay leaves

3 tbsp lemon juice

1 tbsp tomato paste

1 tsp paprika

½ tsp cayenne pepper

1 tsp dried oregano

1 tsp dried thyme

½ tsp ground cumin

6 tbsp olive oil

1 Preheat the oven to 400°F (200°C). Cut the potatoes into thick wedges. Cook in a large pan of boiling salted water for 3 minutes, drain well, and place in a large roasting pan with the lemon, garlic, onions, and bay leaves.

2 Whisk together the remaining ingredients with 6 tbsp of water and pour evenly over the potatoes. Toss well to coat.

3 Roast for 30–40 minutes, or until the potatoes are tender and the liquid has been absorbed. Gently and frequently turn the potatoes during cooking, using a spatula. Serve hot.

CALORIES: 329kcals/1374kJ

CARBOHYDRATE: 38g
  sugar: 6g

FAT: 17g
  saturated: 2.5g

SALT: trace

FIBER: 5g

Gratin dauphinoise

Rich, creamy, and heady with garlic, this is a wonderful treat and the perfect side dish to any lamb recipe.

20 mins   1 hr

SPECIAL EQUIPMENT

food processor (optional)

8 x 8in (20 x 20cm) deep-sided ovenproof dish

SERVES 4-6

2lb 4oz (1kg) waxy, or yellow, potatoes, such as large Yukon Golds

1 tbsp butter, softened

2 garlic cloves, chopped

salt and freshly ground black pepper

1¾ cups half-and-half

1 Preheat the oven to 350°F (180°C). Finely slice the potatoes in a food processor with a slicing attachment, or a mandolin.

2 Rub an 8 x 8in (20 x 20cm) deep-sided ovenproof dish with some butter. Spread in half the potatoes. Sprinkle with the garlic, season, and arrange the remaining potatoes nicely on top.

3 Pour in the cream. You should just be able to see the cream coming up around the edges. Dot the top with the remaining butter.

4 Put the dish on a large baking sheet and cook in the center of the oven for 1 hour until the potatoes are soft, the cream has evaporated, and the top is golden. Rest for 10 minutes before serving.

PREPARE AHEAD

For an impressive side dish, make the potatoes the day before. When cold, use a ring to cut out individual servings and reheat to serve.

CALORIES: 408–272kcals/1708–1138kJ

CARBOHYDRATE: 42–28g
  sugar: 3.5–2.5g

FAT: 33–15g
  saturated: 14–9.5g

SALT: 0.2–0.1g

FIBER: 4–3g

Herby roasted roots

Most root vegetables become sweeter when roasted and can be a delicious alternative to simple roast potatoes.

10 mins   45-55 mins

SERVES 4

2lb 4oz (1kg) mixed root vegetables, such as waxy potatoes, carrots, parsnips, or butternut squash, cut into large wedges

1 large red onion, cut into wedges

3 tbsp olive oil

handful of mixed herb leaves, such as parsley, sage, and thyme, finely chopped

salt and freshly ground black pepper

1 Preheat the oven to 400°F (200°C). Mix all the vegetables, the oil, and herbs, and season well.

2 Arrange in a single layer in a large roasting pan and roast at the top of the oven for 45–55 minutes, turning occasionally, until browned at the edges and cooked through.

Roasting vegetables brings out their natural sweetness. Children who are not fond of vegetables may enjoy them roasted.

Fussy eaters!

CALORIES: 223kcals/936kJ

CARBOHYDRATE: 31g
   sugar: 13.5g

FAT: 9.5g
   saturated: 1.5g

SALT: trace

FIBER: 9g

Potato rosti

These fabulous potato pancakes always feel like a treat. Make 4 individual-sized rosti if you prefer.

10 mins   30 mins

SPECIAL EQUIPMENT
8-8½in (20-22cm) frying pan

SERVES 4

14oz (400g) waxy potatoes, such as Yukon Golds, peeled

salt and freshly ground black pepper

1 tbsp butter

1 tbsp olive oil

1 Bring the whole, peeled potatoes to a boil in a large pan of salted water. Reduce to a simmer and cook for 7–10 minutes, depending on size, until part-cooked but still firm. Leave to cool, then grate coarsely and toss with salt and pepper.

2 Melt the butter and oil in an 8–8½in (20–22cm) frying pan. Put the potato in the pan and squash it down with a spatula to make a large, flat pancake. Cook over medium heat for 5–7 minutes, until crispy underneath.

3 To turn, slide the potato pancake onto a large plate. Put another plate on top and flip the whole thing over, so the cooked side is on top. Slide back into the pan and cook for another 5–7 minutes until crispy underneath. Cut into wedges to serve.

VARIATION

These can be made with raw, grated potato, but the potato must be squeezed dry in a clean kitchen towel first, and the rosti will need to be cooked slowly for 35–40 minutes.

CALORIES: 128kcals/534kJ

CARBOHYDRATE: 16g
   sugar: 0.6g

FAT: 6g
   saturated: 2.5g

SALT: trace

FIBER: 2g

Baked shallots with cream and Parmesan

These are delicious served alongside a simple roast chicken, or with roast beef, ham, or pork.

10 mins   30–35 mins

SERVES 4

butter, for greasing

16 large shallots, peeled and left whole

1¼ cups heavy cream

1¾oz (50g) finely grated Parmesan cheese

freshly ground black pepper

¼ cup fresh bread crumbs

CALORIES: 390kcals/1611kJ

CARBOHYDRATE: 10g
  sugar: 5g

FAT: 35g
  saturated: 22g

SALT: 0.5g

FIBER: 2g

---

1 Preheat the oven to 350°C (180°C). Butter a small ovenproof dish, big enough to hold the shallots in a single, tight layer.

2 Put the shallots in a small pan of simmering water and cook them gently for 10 minutes. Drain well. Lay the shallots in the ovenproof dish.

3 In a bowl, stir together the cream and three-quarters of the Parmesan. Season with pepper and pour the cream over the shallots.

4 In a small bowl, toss together the bread crumbs, the remaining Parmesan, and plenty of pepper. Scatter it over the shallots.

5 Bake for 20–25 minutes, or until the shallots are soft and the top is golden brown and crispy.

Creamy cauliflower cheese

A classic cold weather dish, this needs nothing more than a baked potato to turn it into a main meal.

20 mins   15-20 mins

SPECIAL EQUIPMENT

10in (25cm) ovenproof dish

SERVES 4

1 cauliflower, cut into florets

4 tbsp butter

¼ cup all-purpose flour

2 cups whole milk

3½oz (100g) grated aged Cheddar cheese

salt and freshly ground black pepper

1 tbsp Dijon mustard (optional)

CALORIES: 408–272kcals/1694–1129kJ

CARBOHYDRATE: 21–14g
  sugar: 11.5–7.5g

FAT: 27–18g
  saturated: 16–11g

SALT: 1.1–0.7g

FIBER: 5–3.5g

---

1 Steam the cauliflower for about 7 minutes until it is tender, but still firm, then drain and arrange it in a 10in (25cm) ovenproof dish, with the stems underneath and the florets fitting together. Preheat the oven to 350°F (180°C).

2 Meanwhile, melt the butter in a small, heavy-bottomed saucepan. Whisk in the flour over low heat and cook for 2 minutes, whisking. Take off the heat and slowly whisk in the milk until smooth.

3 Return to the heat and cook, stirring constantly right into the edges of the saucepan, for 5 minutes. Add 2½oz (75g) of the cheese, the seasoning, and mustard (if using), and cook for 2 minutes until the cheese has melted and the sauce is creamy.

4 Pour the sauce over the cauliflower, scatter with the remaining cheese, and bake at the top of the oven for 15–20 minutes, or until golden brown all over.

VARIATION

Mix ¼ cup of bread crumbs with the cheese for the topping, if desired, for more crunch.

Spring vegetable stew

Serve this with simple grilled chicken or fish. The stew brings a lovely garlic flavor of its own.

10 mins   5 mins

SERVES 4

salt and freshly ground black pepper

8–10 asparagus stalks, woody ends broken off, chopped into ¾in (2cm) lengths, tips and stalks kept separate

3½oz (100g) frozen petits pois

1 tbsp butter

1 tbsp olive oil

2 small zucchini, quartered lengthwise, cut into ½in (1cm) cubes

4 large scallions, white part only, cut into ½in (1cm) pieces

1 garlic clove, finely chopped

3–4 tbsp white wine

½ cup half-and-half

1 tbsp finely chopped mint leaves

1 In a large pan of boiling salted water, blanch the asparagus stalks together with the petits pois for 1 minute. Add the asparagus tips and cook for another 1 minute. Drain the vegetables and refresh immediately in a large bowl of cold water, then drain again.

2 In the same pan, melt the butter with the oil. Add the zucchini and scallions and cook for 2–3 minutes until they start to brown at the edges. Add the garlic and cook for another minute. Add the wine (it will bubble up and almost evaporate), then the cream, and season well.

3 Add the blanched vegetables to the pan and cook for another minute or two over high heat until the sauce has reduced and thickened. Stir in the mint to serve.

CALORIES: 163kcals/672kJ
CARBOHYDRATE: 6g
    sugar: 4g
FAT: 11.5g
    saturated: 5.5g
SALT: trace
FIBER: 4g

Braised lentils

A healthy dish that works particularly well with sausages or pork, or as an alternative to many potato side dishes.

10 mins   50 mins

SERVES 4

10oz (300g) brown lentils, washed and drained

salt and freshly ground black pepper

2 tbsp olive oil

1 onion, finely chopped

1 large carrot, finely chopped

1 celery stalk, finely chopped

1 garlic clove, finely chopped

1 heaping tbsp all-purpose flour

2 cups vegetable stock (see p156)

1 Cook the lentils in a large pan of boiling salted water for 20–30 minutes (depending on the type of lentils), until cooked, but still firm. Drain and set aside.

2 Heat the oil in a large, heavy-bottomed saucepan. Cook the onion, carrot, and celery for 7–10 minutes until softened, but not browned. Add the garlic and cook for another minute.

3 Sprinkle in the flour, stir, and cook for another minute or two, before stirring in the stock.

4 Add the lentils and season well. Bring them to a boil, then reduce the heat to a gentle simmer and cook for 7–10 minutes until the lentils are soft and the braise has thickened slightly.

BATCHING AND FREEZING

This is not only tasty, it is also good for you. Prepare double or triple quantities and freeze it in family-sized portions.

CALORIES: 171kcals/718kJ
CARBOHYDRATE: 19g
    sugar: 4.5g
FAT: 6.5g
    saturated: 1g
SALT: trace
FIBER: 6g

Sweet potato, red onion, and thyme galettes with chile

A store-bought butter-based puff pastry is a great time saver, all but indistinguishable from homemade pastry.

20 mins   50 mins

MAKES 6

FOR THE FILLING

2 sweet potatoes, approx. 10oz (300g) peeled weight, cut into ½in (1cm) cubes.

2 red onions, cut into ½in (1cm) cubes

1 tbsp olive oil

salt and freshly ground black pepper

½ red chile, seeded and finely chopped

1 tsp finely chopped thyme leaves

FOR THE PASTRY

12oz (375g) store-bought puff pastry

all-purpose flour, for dusting

1 egg yolk, beaten

1 Preheat the oven to 400°F (200°C). Toss the sweet potatoes and red onions in the oil in a large bowl and season well with salt and pepper. Turn the vegetables out onto a baking sheet and bake for 30 minutes until softened and golden at the edges.

2 Roll out the puff pastry on a lightly floured surface into a square about 12 x 16in (30 x 40cm)

and cut it into quarters. Lay the pastry rectangles on baking sheets. Brush them with the egg yolk.

3 Toss the cooked vegetables with the chile and thyme and divide equally between the pastries. Spread the vegetables out, leaving a ½in (1cm) clear border to each pastry.

4 Bake for 20 minutes, or until the pastry is puffed up and golden brown at the edges, and the bases are firm to the touch. The pastries are best eaten hot, but set aside to cool the most ferocious heat of the oven for 5 minutes before serving with a leafy green salad.

PREPARE AHEAD

The cooked galettes can be covered and stored in the fridge for up to 2 days. Warm through again just before serving.

CALORIES: 317kcals/1329kJ

CARBOHYDRATE: 34g
    sugar: 5g

FAT: 18g
    saturated: 8g

SALT: 0.6g

FIBER: 3.5g

Whole wheat spinach and potato pasties

Chill these pasties in the fridge before baking; this helps firm up the pastry and hold them together during cooking.

45 mins   **30–35 mins**

MAKES 4

FOR THE PASTRY

1 cup whole wheat flour

1 cup all-purpose flour, plus extra for dusting

11 tbsp butter, chilled and diced

½ tsp salt

1 egg, beaten, to glaze

FOR THE FILLING

10oz (300g) unpeeled waxy potatoes, such as Yukon Golds, cut into small chunks

8oz (225g) spinach

1 garlic clove, finely chopped

9oz (250g) ricotta cheese

2½oz (75g) finely grated Grana Padano cheese

grated nutmeg

salt and freshly ground black pepper

1 To make the pastry, rub the flours and butter together with your fingertips until the mixture resembles bread crumbs. Add the salt and about ¼ cup of cold water to form a soft dough. Wrap in plastic wrap and chill for 30 minutes.

2 For the filling, cook the potato in a small saucepan of boiling water for 10 minutes. Drain and set aside to cool. Place the spinach in a colander and pour boiling water over it from a teapot to wilt. Squeeze out the liquid and chop finely. Place in a large bowl with the garlic, cheeses, nutmeg, salt and pepper, and stir well. Set aside.

3 Preheat the oven to 375°F (190°C). Line 2 baking sheets with parchment paper. Mix the potato and spinach mixture.

4 On a well-floured surface, cut the dough into 4 equal pieces. Roll each piece into a circle 8in

(20cm) across and ¼in (5mm) thick. Using a plate about 8in (20cm) in diameter, cut out a circle from each rolled circle of dough.

5 Arrange one-quarter of the filling on half of each circle, leaving a ½in (1cm) border around the edge. Brush the edges with the beaten egg, then bring them together to seal, and crimp. Chill for 10 minutes.

6 Place the pasties on the prepared baking sheets and brush with the remaining beaten egg. Cut a slit in the top of each pasty and bake for 20–25 minutes. Serve the pasties either hot or cold.

For children, try using butternut squash or sweet potatoes in place of the potatoes for a sweeter taste to this healthy filling.

Fussy eaters!

CALORIES: 795kcals/3321kJ

CARBOHYDRATE: 69g
  sugar: 4g

FAT: 47g
  saturated: 28g

SALT: 1.8g

FIBER: 6.5g

Vegetarian kids

With some careful planning, it's possible to ensure that a vegetarian child receives all the nutrients necessary to grow and thrive. You will need to ensure that their diet contains adequate amounts of protein and iron—this can be achieved by providing two to three portions of vegetable proteins (see opposite) or nuts each day (don't give whole nuts to children under five). For family meals, it's easier to cook just once. If other members of the family are meat eaters, try serving a roast chicken or cooking a pork chop alongside a vegetarian meal, or adapt to eating less meat overall as a family, a healthy option for all.

Types of vegetarianism

Some vegetarians avoid meat but eat fish; some avoid meat and fish; and vegans choose to avoid all animal products, including dairy. If you are a vegan household, or your child becomes a vegan, you will need to provide high-calorie foods to meet the energy needs of a growing child, such as bananas and peanut butter. Use vegetable oils in cooking, such as canola and avocado oils, which are a good source of healthy monounsaturated fats. Parents of vegetarian or vegan children are well advised also to seek specialist advice from their doctor or nutritionist.

Meat-free days

It is increasingly acknowledged that a little less meat is a good thing. So if a child becomes a vegetarian, take your cue from them and have at least two meat-free family meals a week.

Get kids cooking

The teenage years are often when people choose to cut meat from their diet. Use this interest in food as an opportunity to teach them how to cook in preparation for adulthood.

The importance of a balanced diet

If your child wishes to follow a vegetarian diet, it's vital that they are aware of the importance of eating a balanced diet that includes all the essential nutrients.

Vitamins and minerals Iron is found in dark green vegetables, beans, fortified cereals, and dried fruit. Vitamin C, which aids iron absorption, is found in citrus and kiwis, broccoli, tomatoes and bell peppers. Dairy products contain vitamin A, and vitamin D can be found in fortified cereals, eggs, and oily fish such as salmon.

Vitamins and Minerals

Protein

Protein Beans and legumes, such as lentils, chickpeas, and kidney beans, are good sources of proteins for vegetarians. Nut and seed butters also provide protein.

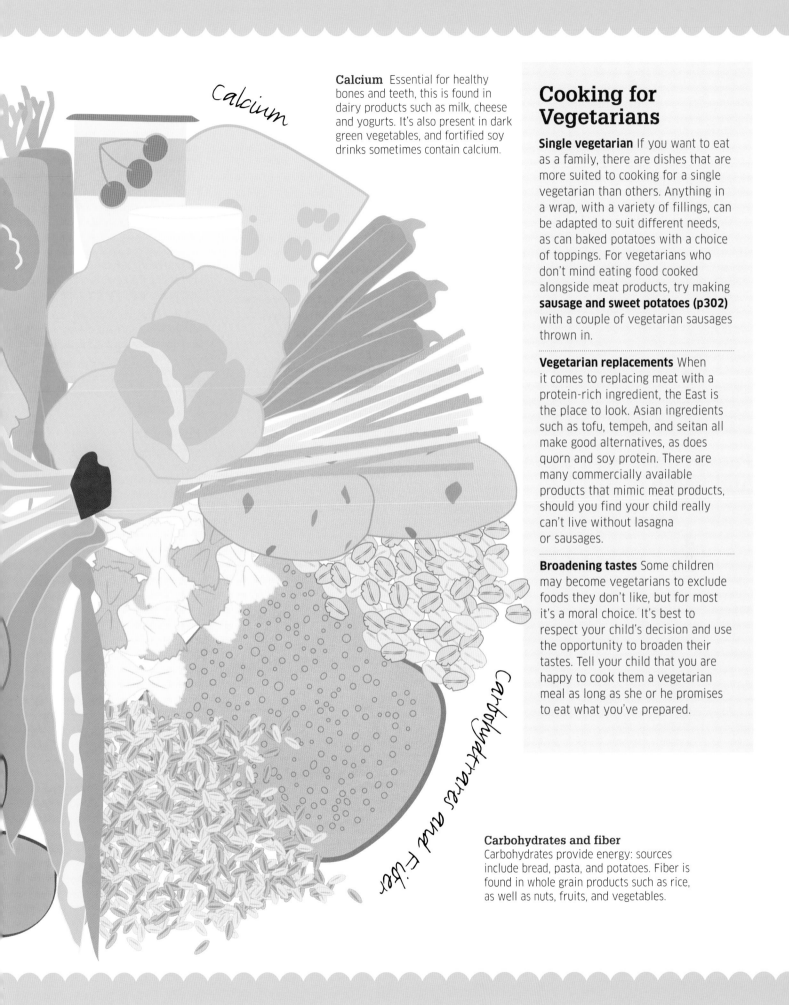

Calcium Essential for healthy bones and teeth, this is found in dairy products such as milk, cheese and yogurts. It's also present in dark green vegetables, and fortified soy drinks sometimes contain calcium.

Calcium

Carbohydrates and Fiber

Cooking for Vegetarians

Single vegetarian If you want to eat as a family, there are dishes that are more suited to cooking for a single vegetarian than others. Anything in a wrap, with a variety of fillings, can be adapted to suit different needs, as can baked potatoes with a choice of toppings. For vegetarians who don't mind eating food cooked alongside meat products, try making **sausage and sweet potatoes (p302)** with a couple of vegetarian sausages thrown in.

Vegetarian replacements When it comes to replacing meat with a protein-rich ingredient, the East is the place to look. Asian ingredients such as tofu, tempeh, and seitan all make good alternatives, as does quorn and soy protein. There are many commercially available products that mimic meat products, should you find your child really can't live without lasagna or sausages.

Broadening tastes Some children may become vegetarians to exclude foods they don't like, but for most it's a moral choice. It's best to respect your child's decision and use the opportunity to broaden their tastes. Tell your child that you are happy to cook them a vegetarian meal as long as she or he promises to eat what you've prepared.

Carbohydrates and fiber
Carbohydrates provide energy: sources include bread, pasta, and potatoes. Fiber is found in whole grain products such as rice, as well as nuts, fruits, and vegetables.

Pasta salad with shrimp and pesto

Homemade pesto takes just minutes to prepare and the flavor is far superior to store-bought varieties.

20 mins   10-12 mins

SPECIAL EQUIPMENT
food processor

SERVES 4

salt and freshly ground black pepper

7oz (200g) dried pasta, such as fusilli

2oz (60g) basil leaves

scant 1oz (25g) toasted pine nuts

scant 1oz (25g) grated Parmesan

2 garlic cloves, roughly chopped

⅓ cup extra virgin olive oil

finely grated zest of 1 lemon, plus 1 tbsp lemon juice

9oz (250g) cooked, peeled large shrimp

1 Bring a large pan of salted water to a boil and cook the pasta according to the package instructions. Drain and rinse under cold running water until the pasta is cold. Drain well and set aside.

2 Place the basil, pine nuts, Parmesan cheese, garlic, oil, and lemon zest and juice in a food processor and pulse until well blended.

3 Place the pasta in a large serving bowl and stir in the pesto. Season well with pepper and stir to combine. Carefully stir in the shrimp. Serve with hunks of whole grain bread.

BATCHING AND FREEZING
Try making double quantities of this pesto and freezing it in small portions. It can be used over pasta, to liven up a pizza crust, or can even be kneaded into some simple homemade ciabatta bread.

CALORIES: 420kcals/1759kJ
CARBOHYDRATE: 36g
    sugar: 1.5g
FAT: 22g
    saturated: 4g
SALT: 1g
FIBER: 2.5g

Summer pasta salad

Kids love pasta, so try to expand their horizons with this tasty Italian-style pasta salad.

20 mins   10-12 mins

SERVES 4

salt and freshly ground black pepper

9oz (250g) dried pasta, such as farfalle

5½oz (150g) cherry tomatoes

5½oz (150g) bocconcini (mini mozzarella cheese balls), drained

2 avocados, cut into large chunks

2oz (60g) pitted black olives

large handful of basil leaves

juice of 1 lemon

¼ cup extra virgin olive oil

1 tsp Dijon mustard

2 tbsp chopped chives

1 garlic clove, finely chopped

1 Bring a large pan of salted water to a boil and cook the pasta according to the package instructions. Drain and rinse under cold running water until the pasta is cold. Drain well and set aside.

2 Place the tomatoes, bocconcini, avocados, and olives in a large serving bowl. Tear the basil leaves and add to the bowl. Season well and toss carefully to combine.

3 In a bowl, combine the lemon juice, oil, mustard, chives, and garlic. Season and stir well.

4 Add the cold pasta to the bowl and pour in the dressing. Stir gently but well and serve with warm ciabatta.

COOK'S TIP

If you find it hard to get hold of bocconcini, buy a ball of fresh mozzarella and dice it into pieces the same size as the cherry tomatoes.

CALORIES: 611kcals/2554kJ
CARBOHYDRATE: 47g
    sugar: 3g
FAT: 40g
    saturated: 10g
SALT: 0.6g
FIBER: 7g

Bean thread noodle salad

This light yet vibrant summer salad is refreshing and perfect as part of an Asian-inspired meal or buffet lunch.

20 mins

SERVES 4

7oz (200g) dried Chinese bean thread noodles or thin rice noodles

1 large carrot, shaved using a vegetable peeler

4in (10cm) cucumber, halved lengthwise, seeded, and finely sliced on the diagonal

4 scallions, white parts only, finely sliced on the diagonal

1 mango, not too ripe, finely julienned

handful of mint leaves, roughly chopped

handful of cilantro leaves, roughly chopped

FOR THE DRESSING

juice of 2 limes

2 tbsp white wine vinegar or rice wine vinegar

1 tsp granulated sugar

pinch of salt

1 Put the noodles in a large bowl and cover with boiling water. Leave for 4 minutes, or according to the package instructions, until they are soft but still have a bite to them. Stir and separate the strands with chopsticks when you first pour the water over them, and once or twice afterwards. Drain and refresh under cold water, then drain thoroughly.

2 Meanwhile, assemble the rest of the salad ingredients in a bowl, keeping back a few herbs to serve. Preparing the salad vegetables over the bowl means you will capture all the juices. Pat the noodles completely dry with paper towels and add the cold, drained noodles to the bowl.

3 Whisk together the dressing ingredients and toss it through the salad. Serve, scattered with the reserved herbs.

VARIATION

Adding cooked large shrimp, shelled, deveined, and halved horizontally, makes this a lovely light summer lunch.

COOK'S TIP

If you can locate only the fatter ⅛in- (3mm-) wide variety of dried rice noodles, soak them for about 10 minutes, or according to the package instructions, being sure to separate them well with chopsticks, as in step 1.

CALORIES: 228kcals/957kJ

CARBOHYDRATE: 48g
  sugar: 10g

FAT: 0.5g
  saturated: 0.1g

SALT: 0.5g

FIBER: 3g

Tomato, bean, and pasta soup

If you make this ahead of time, you may need to add more water when reheating, as it thickens on standing.

15 mins   **45–50 mins**

SERVES 4–6

1 tbsp olive oil

1 onion, finely chopped

1 carrot, finely chopped

2 garlic cloves, finely chopped

2 x 14oz (400g) cans chopped tomatoes

1 x 14oz (400g) can butterbeans, drained and rinsed

1 x 14oz (400g) can cannellini beans, drained and rinsed

2 cups vegetable stock (see p156)

salt and freshly ground black pepper

2½oz (75g) mini dried pasta shapes

1 tsp finely chopped basil leaves

grated Cheddar cheese, to serve

1 Heat the oil in a large saucepan over medium-low heat. Add the onion and carrot and cook for about 5 minutes, stirring occasionally, until softened, but not browned. Add the garlic and cook for another minute, or until it is fragrant, but not browned.

2 Add the tomatoes, beans, and stock. Season, cover, and simmer gently for 25 minutes, stirring occasionally.

3 Add the pasta and cook the soup for another 15 minutes, stirring occasionally so it does not stick to the pan. Add a little more water if the soup seems to be becoming too thick.

4 Add the basil and stir it through, then ladle the soup into warmed bowls and sprinkle with grated cheese to serve.

COOK'S TIP

Cooking your own beans is cheaper and tastier. For every 14oz (400g) can, soak ½ cup of dried beans overnight. Cook according to the package instructions (without salt) before adding them to the soup.

CALORIES: 242kcals/1024kJ

CARBOHYDRATE: 38g
    sugar: 10g

FAT: 4.5g
    saturated: 0.5g

SALT: 1.6g

FIBER: 11.5g

Raw tomato and basil sauce

This super-quick sauce is perfect for using up flavorful, ripe tomatoes, if you are lucky enough to have a glut.

10 mins

SPECIAL EQUIPMENT
food processor

SERVES 4

1lb 2oz (500g) very ripe tomatoes

¼ cup olive oil

1 tbsp tomato paste

1 garlic clove, crushed

handful of basil leaves

salt and freshly ground black pepper

finely grated Parmesan cheese,
  to serve

CALORIES: 123kcals/510kJ

CARBOHYDRATE: 4g
  sugar: 4g

FAT: 11.5g
  saturated: 2g

SALT: trace

FIBER: 2g

1 Cut a small slit in the bottom of each tomato and place in a large bowl. Cover with boiling water. Set aside for 1 minute, until the skins start to peel back.

2 Transfer with a slotted spoon to a bowl of cold water. Peel the tomatoes. (At this point you can quarter each and remove the seeds with a teaspoon, if you want a dryer sauce.) Cut the flesh into cubes.

3 Put the tomatoes and other ingredients in a food processor, season generously, and process to a rough sauce.

4 Toss the sauce through cooked pasta and serve with finely grated Parmesan cheese.

VARIATION

For a special dish, sauté small bay scallops in butter for a couple of minutes, and toss them through cooked pasta with this sauce (this version is better without Parmesan).

Slow-cooked tomato sauce

A classic tomato sauce is the basis of so many good family meals. The secret is in the long cooking time.

10 mins   45 mins–1hr

SERVES 4

3 tbsp olive oil

1 onion, finely chopped

2 garlic cloves, crushed

1 x 14oz (400g) can chopped tomatoes

1 tbsp tomato paste

1 tsp granulated sugar

2 tbsp roughly chopped
  flat-leaf parsley leaves

salt and freshly ground black pepper

2 tbsp roughly chopped basil leaves

1 Heat the oil in a heavy-bottomed saucepan and cook the onion over medium heat for about 5 minutes until softened, but not browned. Add the garlic and cook for 1 minute.

2 Add the tomatoes, then fill the empty can with water and pour it in. Stir in the tomato paste, sugar, and parsley, and season well.

3 Bring the sauce to a boil, reduce the heat to a low simmer, and cook, uncovered, for 45 minutes to 1 hour, until thickened. If the tomatoes are taking a while to break down, mash with a potato masher to help them along. Stir in the basil to serve.

For young children who don't like "chunks," it can be a good idea to blend the sauce until smooth with a hand-held blender.

Fussy eaters!

CALORIES: 106kcals/440kJ

CARBOHYDRATE: 6g
  sugar: 5.5g

FAT: 8.5g
  saturated: 1g

SALT: 0.1g

FIBER: 1.5g

Arrabbiata sauce

This is traditionally served with penne. Alter the amount of chile flakes depending on how spicy you like it.

10 mins   1 hr

SERVES 4–6

3 tbsp olive oil

1 onion, finely chopped

2 garlic cloves, crushed

1 tsp dried chile flakes

1 x 14oz (400g) can chopped tomatoes

½ cup red wine (optional)

1 tbsp tomato paste

1 tsp granulated sugar

2 tbsp roughly chopped flat-leaf parsley leaves

salt and freshly ground black pepper

2 tbsp chopped basil leaves (optional)

1 Heat the oil in a heavy-bottomed saucepan and cook the onion over medium heat for about 5 minutes, until softened, but not browned. Add the garlic and chile flakes and cook for 1 minute.

2 Add the tomatoes, then fill the empty can three-quarters full with water and pour it in with the wine (if using). If not using wine, add a whole canful of water. Stir in the tomato paste, sugar, and parsley, and season well.

3 Bring to a boil, reduce the heat to a low simmer, and cook, uncovered, for 45 minutes to 1 hour, stirring occasionally, until thickened. If the tomatoes are taking a while to break down, mash with a potato masher to help them along. Stir through the basil (if using) and serve.

HOW TO FREEZE

It is best to freeze this sauce without the basil, adding it after defrosting, or the green herb will oxidize and turn black in the freezer.

CALORIES: 127kcals/529kJ

CARBOHYDRATE: 6g
  sugar: 5.5g

FAT: 8.5g
  saturated: 1g

SALT: 0.1g

FIBER: 1.5g

Tomato and mascarpone pasta

This is a perfect way to use up overripe tomatoes, and is made beautifully creamy by the mascarpone.

10 mins   10-15 mins

SERVES 4

salt and freshly ground black pepper

10oz (300g) dried pasta

4 large, overripe tomatoes, approx. 1lb 5oz (600g) in total

2 tbsp olive oil

2 garlic cloves, crushed

¼ cup mascarpone

¼ cup finely grated Parmesan cheese

2 tbsp roughly chopped basil leaves

1 Bring a large pan of salted water to a boil to cook the pasta. Before adding the pasta, use the boiling water to help peel the tomatoes (see p191). Cut them into fairly small cubes.

2 Use the boiling water to cook the pasta according to the package instructions.

3 Heat the oil in a large frying pan. Add the tomatoes and garlic and cook for 2 minutes until they start to break down.

4 Add ¾ cup of water and cook over high heat for about 5 minutes, or until the tomatoes have completely broken down and the sauce is very thick. (You can use a potato masher to help this process along.) Drain the pasta and return it to the pan.

5 Season the sauce well and stir in the mascarpone. Cook for another minute or two until the mascarpone has dispersed and the sauce is thick and creamy. Toss through the pasta and cook over low heat for 2 minutes until the pasta has absorbed some of the sauce. Take it off the heat, toss through the Parmesan cheese and basil, and serve.

CALORIES: 460kcals/1942kJ

CARBOHYDRATE: 58g
  sugar: 7g

FAT: 18g
  saturated: 8g

SALT: 0.4g

FIBER: 5g

Pasta primavera

This delicate, tasty sauce is an easy and delicious way to get plenty of green vegetables into your family's diet.

10 mins   20 mins

SERVES 4

salt and freshly ground black pepper

3½oz (100g) sugarsnap peas

4½oz (125g) thin asparagus spears, halved

3½oz (100g) baby zucchini, quartered lengthwise

14oz (400g) dried linguine or fettuccine

1 tbsp olive oil

2 garlic cloves, finely sliced

1 shallot, finely chopped

2 tbsp extra virgin olive oil

⅔ cup (5oz) low-fat crème fraîche

½ tsp grated nutmeg

finely grated zest of 1 lemon, plus juice of ½ lemon

2 tbsp torn basil leaves

2 tbsp chopped flat-leaf parsley leaves

3½oz (100g) baby spinach

Parmesan cheese shavings and ciabatta, to serve

1 Bring a large pot of salted water to a boil and add the sugarsnap peas, asparagus, and zucchini. Return to a boil and cook for 3 minutes, or until the vegetables are just tender, but still brightly colored and al dente. Drain well, then run under cold water to set the color. Drain once more, and set aside in a colander over the kitchen sink.

2 Refill the pot used for cooking the vegetables with more salted water and bring it to a boil. Cook the pasta according to the package instructions. Meanwhile, heat the olive oil in a small pan over medium heat and sauté the garlic and shallot for 2 minutes.

3 In a medium bowl, combine the extra virgin olive oil, crème fraîche, nutmeg, lemon zest and juice, basil, and parsley. Add the cooked garlic and shallot. Stir well and season generously with pepper.

4 Drain the pasta well in the same colander as the vegetables to reheat them slightly, then return the pasta and vegetables to the pot. Add the spinach and stir until it wilts. Add the herby sauce to the pasta and stir to coat.

5 Transfer to warmed serving bowls, top with Parmesan shavings, and serve with ciabatta.

PREPARE AHEAD

The herby sauce can be prepared up to 1 day in advance, covered, and kept in the fridge until needed. Whisk it once more to emulsify before use.

CALORIES: 505kcals/2135kJ	
CARBOHYDRATE: 73g sugar: 4.5g	
FAT: 15g saturated: 5g	
SALT: 0.1g	
FIBER: 6.5g	

Angel hair pasta with arugula pesto

Homemade pesto is great, but can be expensive to make using just basil. Try this arugula-basil version instead.

10 mins, plus resting

10 mins

SPECIAL EQUIPMENT
food processor

SERVES 4

3½oz (100g) pine nuts

1¾oz (50g) arugula leaves

large handful of basil leaves, approx. ½oz (15g)

1¾oz (50g) finely grated Parmesan cheese, plus extra for serving

1 garlic clove, crushed

¾ cup extra virgin olive oil

salt and freshly ground black pepper

10oz (300g) dried angel hair or other long, thin pasta

CALORIES: 820kcals/3416kJ
CARBOHYDRATE: 54g
  sugar: 3g
FAT: 59g
  saturated: 9g
SALT: 0.3g
FIBER: 4g

1 Dry-fry the pine nuts in a frying pan over medium heat for 2 minutes, stirring constantly, or until golden brown, but not burnt. Pour out of the pan and set aside to cool.

2 Once the nuts are cold, put them in a food processor with the arugula, basil, Parmesan, and garlic, and grind to a medium-coarse paste. With the motor running, pour in the oil in a slow, steady stream until you have a loose, vivid green paste. Check the seasoning and adjust if necessary. The pesto tastes better if you can rest it, covered, for 30 minutes to allow the flavors to develop.

3 Boil the pasta according to the package instructions, drain it (reserving a ladleful of the cooking water), and return it to the pan with the reserved water. Stir the pesto through the pasta and serve, sprinkled with extra Parmesan cheese.

VARIATION

After step 1, set aside ¾oz (20g) of the pine nuts, sprinkling them over just before serving, for more texture.

Pantry spaghetti

A great recipe to cook when you have nothing—you'll probably have at least these essentials.

10 mins

15 mins

SPECIAL EQUIPMENT
food processor

SERVES 4

10oz (300g) dried spaghetti

salt and freshly ground black pepper

7oz (200g) good-quality day-old white bread or baguette

3 tbsp olive oil, plus extra if needed

2 tbsp butter

2 garlic cloves, crushed

1¾oz (50g) finely grated Parmesan cheese

CALORIES: 572kcals/2413kJ
CARBOHYDRATE: 79g
  sugar: 3g
FAT: 20g
  saturated: 7g
SALT: 1.1g
FIBER: 5g

1 Cook the spaghetti in a large pan of boiling salted water according to the package instructions.

2 Cut the bread into large chunks and pulse it in a food processor to coarse bread crumbs. (Leaving the crusts on gives larger crumbs and so a better texture to the finished dish.)

3 Heat the oil and butter in a large frying pan. Cook the garlic for a minute over medium heat until fragrant. Add the bread crumbs and continue to cook until golden brown and crispy, adding a little extra oil if the bread crumbs appear dry.

4 Drain the pasta and return to the pan, with a little oil tossed through to keep it from sticking together. Toss through the bread crumbs and Parmesan cheese and season well to serve.

VARIATION

Try adding a pinch of chile flakes with the garlic, or 4 chopped anchovies, or a handful of black olives.

Pasta with butternut squash

This dish is perfect for those slightly cooler days, as it has the comfort of cream and the warmth of red chiles.

20 mins   30 mins

SPECIAL EQUIPMENT
blender or food processor

SERVES 4

7oz (200g) butternut squash, peeled and diced

1–2 tbsp olive oil

salt and freshly ground black pepper

1 garlic clove, crushed

½ red chile, seeded and finely chopped

8 sage leaves

⅔ cup half-and-half

scant 1oz (25g) Parmesan cheese, grated, plus extra to serve

12oz (350g) dried conchiglie pasta

CALORIES: 451kcals/1906kJ

CARBOHYDRATE: 66g
sugar: 5g

FAT: 14g
saturated: 7g

SALT: 0.2g

FIBER: 5g

1 Preheat the oven to 400°F (200°C). Toss the squash in a little oil, season it well with salt and pepper, and roast for about 30 minutes, or until soft. Remove it from the oven and leave to cool for a few minutes.

2 Meanwhile, gently cook the garlic, chile, and sage in a little oil for 2–3 minutes.

3 Once the butternut squash has cooled slightly, put it into a blender or food processor. Add the half-and-half, Parmesan, garlic, chile, sage leaves, plenty of pepper, and a little salt. Blend it all to a coarse purée, adding 1–2 tbsp water if it looks too thick.

4 Cook the pasta until al dente and drain it. Quickly reheat the sauce in the pasta pan, adding more water if it seems a little stiff. Put the pasta back into the pan and mix it well, allowing the sauce to coat the pasta. Serve with plenty of Parmesan.

Pasta with creamy zucchini

If your children are wary of eating zucchini, try grating it into the sauce instead.

15 mins   15 mins

SERVES 4

2 tbsp butter

1 tbsp olive oil

1 garlic clove, crushed

14oz (400g) baby zucchini, quartered lengthwise

10oz (300g) long dried pasta, such as spaghetti, linguine, fettuccine, or pappardelle

salt and freshly ground black pepper

1¼ cups half-and-half

finely grated zest and juice of 1 lemon

¾oz (20g) finely grated Grana Padano cheese, plus extra to serve

pinch of grated nutmeg

CALORIES: 530kcals/2224kJ

CARBOHYDRATE: 56g
sugar: 5g

FAT: 27g
saturated: 15g

SALT: 0.3g

FIBER: 4g

1 Heat the butter and oil in a large, non-stick frying pan over medium heat. Add the garlic and zucchini and cook gently for 10 minutes, stirring occasionally.

2 Meanwhile, cook the pasta in boiling salted water according to the package instructions.

3 Return to the zucchini mixture and add the half-and-half, lemon zest and juice, Grana Padano cheese, nutmeg, salt, and plenty of pepper. Heat through gently.

4 Drain the pasta and serve immediately, with the sauce tossed through and extra grated Grana Padano cheese.

VARIATION

For a crispy garnish, broil 8 slices of prosciutto under a hot broil until crisp. Break into small pieces and sprinkle over the pasta just before serving.

Blue cheese and broccoli pasta sauce

This is a delicious sauce to stir through pasta shapes. Cook 14oz (400g) of dried pasta to serve four people.

10 mins   15 mins

SPECIAL EQUIPMENT
food processor

SERVES 4

9oz (250g) broccoli, in bite-sized florets

¾ cup (7oz) low-fat crème fraîche

7oz (200g) Dolcelatte or gorgonzola cheese, rind removed and roughly chopped

finely grated zest of 1 lemon, plus 1 tbsp lemon juice

freshly ground black pepper

¼ tsp ground nutmeg

3 tbsp chopped walnuts, to serve

1 Place the broccoli in a steamer and cook until just tender (up to 5 minutes). Drain well. Transfer to a food processor and blend to a bright green purée.

2 Place the crème fraîche and cheese in a medium saucepan over low heat and stir until the cheese has melted to form a smooth sauce. Stir in the lemon zest and juice, plenty of pepper, and the nutmeg.

3 Scrape the broccoli purée into the pan and stir well. Pour the sauce over cooked pasta and sprinkle with the walnuts to serve.

Blue cheese has a strong flavor. For very young children, try replacing it with cream cheese and a handful of grated Parmesan, for a milder sauce.

Fussy eaters!

CALORIES: 707kcals/2971kJ
CARBOHYDRATE: 72g
  sugar: 3.5g
FAT: 33g
  saturated: 16g
SALT: 2.1g
FIBER: 7g

Classic carbonara

Even when you think you have nothing in the fridge, you may have the ingredients for this creamy sauce.

15 mins   25 mins

SERVES 4

7oz (200g) thick-cut bacon

salt and freshly ground black pepper

14oz (400g) dried long pasta, such as spaghetti, linguine, fettuccine, or pappardelle

¾ cup half-and-half

4 large eggs, lightly beaten

1¼oz (40g) finely grated Parmesan cheese, plus extra to serve

2 tbsp chopped flat-leaf parsley leaves, to garnish

tomato and basil salad, to serve

1 Heat a large, non-stick frying pan over medium heat. Add the bacon and cook, turning, until crisp. Transfer to a plate lined with paper towels.

2 Bring a large pan of salted water to a boil and cook the pasta according to package instructions.

3 Meanwhile, measure the half-and-half into a large liquid measuring cup and stir in the eggs, Parmesan cheese, and pepper. Snip the bacon into pieces with kitchen scissors, and stir into the egg.

4 Drain the pasta and return to the pan, pour in the egg mixture, and place over low heat. Stir for 2 minutes, or until the sauce has thickened and clings to the strands of pasta. Divide between warmed bowls, season with pepper, and sprinkle with parsley. Serve with extra Parmesan and a tomato and basil salad.

CALORIES: 716kcals/3011kJ
CARBOHYDRATE: 72g
  sugar: 3g
FAT: 33g
  saturated: 14g
SALT: 2g
FIBER: 4g

Three cheese pasta

This rich, cheesy sauce is a heartening recipe to make on a cold day. The pine nuts add crunch and texture.

10 mins   15 mins

SERVES 4

salt and freshly ground black pepper

14oz (400g) dried long pasta, such as spaghetti, linguine, fettuccine, or pappardelle

1lb 2oz (500g) fat-free ricotta

9oz (250g) cream cheese with garlic and herbs

1oz (30g) finely chopped flat-leaf parsley leaves

scant 1oz (25g) finely grated Pecorino Romano cheese

1¾oz (50g) toasted pine nuts, very finely chopped

pinch of grated nutmeg

1 Bring a large pan of salted water to a boil and cook the pasta according to the package instructions.

2 Meanwhile, place the ricotta and cream cheese in a saucepan over very low heat, stirring occasionally, until a smooth sauce is formed.

3 Stir in the parsley, Pecorino Romano, and pine nuts, and heat through, stirring constantly, until piping hot.

4 Drain the pasta (reserving a ladleful of the cooking water) and return it to the pan with the reserved water.

5 Season the cheese sauce well with pepper and nutmeg, pour over the cooked pasta, stir, and serve immediately.

VARIATION

This tasty sauce can be varied to suit whatever odds and ends of cheese you have available. Just grate small pieces and add to the heating ricotta.

CALORIES: 796kcals/3335kJ
CARBOHYDRATE: 76g
  sugar: 8g
FAT: 42g
  saturated: 21g
SALT: 0.7g
FIBER: 4.5g

Easy carbonara

This simple, delicious sauce can be tossed together in less time than the pasta takes to cook.

10 mins   10 mins

SERVES 4

3½oz (100g) prosciutto slices

salt and freshly ground black pepper

14oz (400g) quick-cook dried long pasta, such as spaghetti, linguine, fettuccine, or pappardelle

⅔ cup (5oz) low-fat crème fraîche

⅔ cup half-and-half

1¼oz (40g) finely grated Parmesan cheese, plus extra to serve

arugula salad, to serve

1 Preheat the broiler to its highest setting. Line a baking sheet with foil. Place the slices of prosciutto on the foil-lined pan and broil for 3–4 minutes on one side until crispy. Set aside.

2 Bring a large pan of salted water to a boil and cook the pasta according to package instructions.

3 Drain the pasta and return it to the pan. Crumble in the crispy broiled ham and stir in the crème fraîche, half-and-half, and cheese. Season well with pepper. Serve with extra Parmesan and an arugula salad.

PREPARE AHEAD

This simple yet luxurious dish is ideal for midweek entertaining. To get ahead, the prosciutto can be broiled, crumbled up, and stored in the fridge in an airtight container for up to 2 days.

CALORIES: 578kcals/2439kJ
CARBOHYDRATE: 71g
  sugar: 3g
FAT: 20g
  saturated: 11g
SALT: 1.5g
FIBER: 4g

Smoked salmon and crème fraîche pasta

A simple yet stylish way to pull together a fabulous supper with just a few ingredients from the fridge.

 5 mins   10 mins

SERVES 4

10oz (300g) dried pasta

salt and freshly ground black pepper

¾ cup (7oz) low-fat crème fraîche

4oz (120g) smoked salmon, finely chopped

1 tbsp finely chopped capers, rinsed, or more to taste

finely grated zest of ½ lemon

2 tbsp finely chopped dill

finely grated Parmesan cheese, to serve

1 Cook the pasta in a large pan of boiling salted water according to the package instructions.

2 Meanwhile, beat the crème fraîche in a bowl until smooth. Add the smoked salmon, capers, lemon zest, and dill, and season.

3 Drain the pasta (reserving a ladleful of the cooking water) and return it to the pan with the reserved water. Toss the sauce through the pasta and return it to the heat, stirring just long enough both for the pasta to soak up some of the sauce and for the sauce to heat through. Serve with the Parmesan cheese.

Sometimes children will surprise you with a liking for stronger, piquant flavors but for those who don't, you can exclude the dill and capers.

Fussy eaters!

CALORIES: 510kcals/2142kJ

CARBOHYDRATE: 54g
  sugar: 3g

FAT: 25g
  saturated: 15g

SALT: 1.2g

FIBER: 2.2g

Spaghetti alle vongole

The classic Italian dish is made with fresh clams, but this version uses a can for a pantry supper.

 15 mins   1 hr 5 mins

SERVES 4

3 tbsp olive oil

1 onion, finely chopped

2 garlic cloves, crushed

1 x 7oz (280g) can clams

1 x 14oz (400g) can chopped tomatoes

1 tbsp tomato paste

1 tsp granulated sugar

2 tbsp roughly chopped flat-leaf parsley leaves

salt and freshly ground black pepper

10oz (300g) dried spaghetti

1 Heat 2 tbsp of the oil in a heavy-bottomed saucepan and cook the onion over medium heat for about 5 minutes, until softened, but not browned. Add the garlic and cook for a minute. Drain the clams, reserving the liquid. Cover and refrigerate the clams.

2 Add the tomatoes and clam liquid to the onions. Stir in the tomato paste, sugar, and parsley, and season well. Bring to a boil, reduce the heat to a low simmer, and cook for about 1 hour until thickened and reduced. If the tomatoes are taking a while to break down, mash with a potato masher to help them along.

3 When the sauce is nearly ready, cook the spaghetti in a large pan of boiling salted water according to the package instructions. Drain the spaghetti (reserving a ladleful of the cooking water), and return it to the pan with the reserved water.

4 Add the clams and remaining oil to the sauce and allow to heat through, before tossing in the cooked spaghetti.

CALORIES: 387kcals/1634kJ

CARBOHYDRATE: 59g
  sugar: 8.5g

FAT: 10g
  saturated: 1.5g

SALT: 0.3g

FIBER: 5g

Tuna, tomato, and black olive pasta sauce

Another pantry recipe, the addition of tuna and black olives to a basic tomato sauce gives added flavor.

15 mins | 1 hr 10 mins

SERVES 4

2 tbsp olive oil

1 onion, finely chopped

2 garlic cloves, crushed

1 x 14oz (400g) can chopped tomatoes

1 tbsp tomato paste

1 tsp granulated sugar

2 tbsp roughly chopped flat-leaf parsley leaves

salt and freshly ground black pepper

1 x 7oz (185g) can tuna, drained, and flaked with a fork

1¾oz (50g) pitted black olives, roughly chopped

2 tbsp roughly chopped basil leaves

finely grated Parmesan cheese, to serve

1 Heat the oil in a heavy-bottomed saucepan and cook the onion over medium heat for about 5 minutes, until softened but not browned. Add the garlic and cook for 1 minute.

2 Add the tomatoes, then fill the empty can with water and pour it in. Stir in the tomato paste, sugar, and parsley, and season well. Bring the sauce to a boil, reduce it to a low simmer, and cook for about 1 hour, until thickened and reduced, stirring occasionally. If the tomatoes are taking a while to break down, mash with a potato masher to help them along.

3 When the sauce has reduced and is rich and thick, add the tuna and olives and heat through.

4 Remove from the heat and stir in the basil before serving over your favorite pasta, with the Parmesan cheese.

CALORIES: 178kcals/742kJ

CARBOHYDRATE: 6g
  sugar: 6g

FAT: 11g
  saturated: 1.5g

SALT: 0.4g

FIBER: 2g

Linguine with spicy shrimp and tomato sauce

Adding Parmesan cheese is not traditional with shellfish pasta recipes, but feel free to have some if you want!

20 mins   1 hr

SERVES 4

14oz (400g) shell-on, cooked shrimp

2 tbsp olive oil

1 onion, finely chopped

2 garlic cloves, crushed

1 tsp chile flakes

1 x 14oz (400g) can chopped tomatoes

1 tbsp tomato paste

1 tsp granulated sugar

2 tbsp roughly chopped flat-leaf parsley leaves

salt and freshly ground black pepper

10oz (300g) dried linguine

1 First, shell the shrimp and devein them. Cover and refrigerate. Put the shells in a saucepan and pour in a 2in (5cm) depth of water. Bring to a boil, reduce to a low simmer, and cook for 25–30 minutes until the liquid has reduced by about half. Strain.

2 Heat the oil in a heavy-bottomed saucepan and cook the onion over medium heat for about 5 minutes, until softened but not browned. Add the garlic and chile flakes and cook for 1 minute.

3 Add the tomatoes and shrimp stock. Stir in the tomato paste, sugar, and parsley, and season well. Bring the sauce to a boil, reduce the heat to a low simmer, and cook for about 45 minutes until thickened and reduced. If the tomatoes are taking a while to break down, mash gently with a potato masher to help them along.

4 When the sauce is nearly ready, cook the linguine in boiling salted water according to the package instructions. Drain (reserving a ladleful of the cooking water) and return it to the pan with the reserved water.

5 Add the shrimp to the sauce and cook for 2 minutes, or until heated through, being careful not to overcook. Toss the sauce through the linguine to serve.

CLEVER WITH LEFTOVERS

Whenever you are peeling shrimp, don't throw the shells away; they have an amazing flavor. Bag them up and freeze them until you have enough to prepare the stock for this dish, or for the basis of hundreds of shellfish soups and sauces.

CALORIES: 467kcals/1971kJ

CARBOHYDRATE: 59g
    sugar: 7g

FAT: 11g
    saturated: 1.5g

SALT: 0.2g

FIBER: 4.5g

Spaghetti Bolognese

A household standard, but the long, slow cooking time here turns the everyday into something special.

20 mins   1 hr

SERVES 4

2 tbsp olive oil

1 onion, finely chopped

1 celery stalk, finely chopped

1 carrot, finely chopped

2 garlic cloves, crushed

1lb 2oz (500g) ground beef

1 x 14oz (400g) can chopped tomatoes

1 cup beef stock

1 tbsp tomato paste

1 tsp granulated sugar

2 tbsp roughly chopped flat-leaf parsley leaves

1 tsp dried oregano

salt and freshly ground black pepper

10oz (300g) dried spaghetti

finely grated Parmesan cheese, to serve

1 Heat the oil in a large, heavy-bottomed saucepan and cook the onion, celery, and carrot over medium heat for 5 minutes, until softened, but not browned. Add the garlic and cook for 1 minute. Add the ground beef and cook it over high heat, breaking any clumps up with a wooden spoon and turning to brown all over.

2 Add the tomatoes and stock. Stir in the tomato paste, sugar, parsley, and oregano, and season generously. Slowly bring to a boil, then reduce the heat to a low simmer, and cook for about 1 hour, or more if needed, until the sauce has thickened and reduced, and smells rich.

3 When the sauce is nearly ready, cook the spaghetti until just al dente in boiling salted water according to the package instructions. Drain the pasta (reserving about a ladleful of the cooking water) and return it to the pan along with the reserved water.

4 Toss the sauce through the spaghetti and serve with plenty of Parmesan cheese.

VARIATION

Substitute some of the stock with a small glass of red wine for a richer flavor, if you are cooking for adults.

CALORIES: 641kcals/2692kJ

CARBOHYDRATE: 60g
  sugar: 10g

FAT: 27g
  saturated: 10g

SALT: 0.6g

FIBER: 6g

Conchigliette with sausage and tomato sauce

Sausages are an easy standby, but can get boring. Remove the casing and mix into this child-friendly pasta sauce.

10 mins   30–40 mins

SERVES 4

1 tbsp olive oil

1 red onion, finely chopped

2 garlic cloves, finely chopped

8 pork and herb sausages

1 tsp dried oregano

1 tsp dried marjoram

½ tsp fennel seeds

salt and freshly ground black pepper

2 x 15oz (500g) cans tomato sauce

5½oz (150g) dried conchigliette or other small pasta shapes

finely grated Parmesan cheese, garlic bread, and salad, to serve

1 Heat the oil in a large pan over medium heat and cook the onion for 5 minutes, until translucent and softened, but not browned.

2 Add the garlic, sausages, oregano, marjoram, and fennel seeds. Season and stir well, breaking the sausages up with a wooden spoon so the meat browns all over. Cook over medium heat for 5 minutes, stirring constantly so it does not stick. Add the tomato sauce, cover, and simmer for 10 minutes.

3 Add the conchigliette and cook over low heat for 10 minutes, or until cooked, stirring regularly. If the mixture threatens to become too dry, add a splash of water.

4 Spoon into bowls, sprinkle generously with Parmesan cheese, and serve with garlic bread and a green salad.

BATCHING AND FREEZING

A frozen portion of Slow-cooked tomato sauce (see p191) works well here. For a quick version, defrost the sauce in the morning. Add it to cooked pasta and sausages for an instant family supper.

CALORIES:	510kcals/2136kJ
CARBOHYDRATE:	48g
sugar:	4g
FAT:	25g
saturated:	8.5g
SALT:	2.1g
FIBER:	5g

Spaghetti and meatballs

It's best to make the meatballs fairly small for this dish, as it makes it easier to pick them up with the spaghetti.

30 mins, plus chilling   1 hr 10 mins

SERVES 4

FOR THE MEATBALLS

½ cup fresh bread crumbs

5½oz (150g) ground pork

5½oz (150g) ground beef

¾oz (20g) finely grated Parmesan cheese, plus extra for serving

1 tbsp finely chopped parsley leaves

1 large egg yolk

salt and freshly ground black pepper

FOR THE SAUCE AND PASTA

4 tbsp olive oil

1 onion, finely chopped

2 garlic cloves, crushed

1 x 14oz (400g) can chopped tomatoes

1 tbsp tomato paste

1 tsp granulated sugar

2 tbsp roughly chopped flat-leaf parsley leaves

10oz (300g) dried spaghetti

2 tbsp roughly chopped basil leaves (optional)

1 In a large bowl, mix all the meatball ingredients until well combined, seasoning generously. Cover and chill for at least 30 minutes.

2 For the sauce, heat 2 tbsp of the oil in a heavy-bottomed saucepan and cook the onion over medium heat for about 5 minutes, until softened, but not browned. Add the garlic and cook, stirring, for another minute.

3 Add the tomatoes, then fill the empty can with water and pour it in. Stir in the tomato paste, sugar, and parsley, and season well. Bring to a boil, reduce it to a low simmer, and cook for about 1 hour, until

thickened. If the tomatoes are taking a while to break down, mash with a potato masher.

4 When the sauce is nearly ready, cook the spaghetti in boiling salted water according to the package instructions. Drain the pasta (reserving a ladleful of the cooking water) and return it to the pan with the reserved water.

5 Meanwhile, heat the remaining 2 tbsp of oil in a large, heavy-bottomed frying pan. Roll the meat mixture into 1in (3cm) balls and cook for 5 minutes over medium heat, shaking frequently, until browned all over and cooked through. They should be springy to the touch. Drain on paper towels.

6 Mix the sauce through the spaghetti with the basil (if using) and turn it into a large, wide, warmed serving bowl. Scatter in the meatballs (this helps to portion

out the meatballs when serving), and serve with plenty of grated Parmesan cheese.

VARIATION

Use all ground pork, or all ground beef, or even substitute ground turkey for the ground pork, to suit your family's diet and budget.

HOW TO FREEZE

Open-freeze the raw meatballs on a baking sheet, then transfer to a freezer bag and keep for up to 3 months. You can then remove only as many as you want. The cooked sauce can be frozen separately and kept for up to 6 months.

CALORIES: 606kcals/2548kJ

CARBOHYDRATE: 64g
sugar: 7g

FAT: 26g
saturated: 7.5g

SALT: 0.6g

FIBER: 5g

Lasagna Bolognese

No one ever gets tired of lasagna. If you have time to assemble the different parts, it will always be appreciated.

30 mins | 2 hrs, plus resting

SPECIAL EQUIPMENT
10in (25cm) ovenproof dish

SERVES 4–6

3½oz (100g) dried lasagna sheets
green salad and crusty bread, to serve

FOR THE BOLOGNESE SAUCE
2 tbsp olive oil
1 onion, finely chopped
1 celery stalk, finely chopped
1 carrot, finely chopped
2 garlic cloves, crushed
1lb 5oz (600g) ground beef
1 x 14oz (400g) can chopped tomatoes
1 cup beef stock
1 tbsp tomato paste
1 tsp granulated sugar

2 tbsp chopped flat-leaf parsley leaves
1 tsp dried oregano
salt and freshly ground black pepper

FOR THE CHEESE SAUCE
5 tbsp butter
⅓ cup all-purpose flour
2 cups whole milk
2½oz (75g) grated aged Cheddar cheese

1 Cook the meat sauce as for Spaghetti Bolognese (see p201).When the sauce is nearly ready, preheat the oven to 350°F (180°C).

2 For the cheese sauce, melt the butter in a small, heavy-bottomed saucepan. Whisk in the flour over low heat and cook for 2 minutes, whisking constantly, until the mixture bubbles and separates. Take the pan off the heat and whisk in the milk, a little at a time, whisking well between each addition, until it has all been added and the sauce is smooth. Return to the heat and cook, stirring constantly, until it thickens.

3 Reduce the heat to low and cook, stirring occasionally, for 5 minutes. Be sure to whisk right into the edges of the saucepan, as this is where the sauce can burn if left undisturbed. Add 1¾oz (50g) of the cheese, season well, and cook for another 2 minutes until the cheese has melted and the sauce is smooth, thick, and creamy.

4 Spread one-third of the meat sauce over a 10in (25cm) ovenproof dish. Top with a layer of lasagna sheets and one-third of the cheese sauce. Repeat twice more, finishing with the cheese sauce. Sprinkle the scant 1oz (25g) of reserved cheese on top and cook in the middle of the oven for 45 minutes to 1 hour until golden brown and a knife goes easily through the center. Rest for 10 minutes, then serve with green salad and plenty of crusty bread.

BATCHING AND FREEZING

Getting ahead with supper can be easy if you have made a double or triple batch of Bolognese sauce (see p201) and frozen it in family-sized portions. Defrost a portion and you can make this lasagna in half the time.

CALORIES: 892kcals/3716kJ
CARBOHYDRATE: 44.5g
  sugar: 13.5g
FAT: 57g
  saturated: 28g
SALT: 1.4g
FIBER: 4g

Roasted vegetable lasagna

Meat-free days are a good thing, but sometimes difficult to manage for the whole family. This makes them easy.

25 mins   30 mins

SPECIAL EQUIPMENT
11 x 8 x 2in (28 x 20 x 5cm) ovenproof dish

SERVES 4

3 tbsp olive oil

2 red onions, roughly chopped

1 eggplant, cut into 1in (3cm) cubes

1 red and 1 yellow bell pepper, cut into 1in (3cm) pieces

1 zucchini, cut into 1in (3cm) cubes

1 bulb fennel, finely sliced

3 garlic cloves, roughly chopped

1 tsp dried rosemary

1 tsp dried basil

salt and freshly ground black pepper

2 cups tomato sauce

1¾ cups (14oz) low-fat crème fraîche

2 large eggs, beaten

2oz (60g) finely grated Parmesan cheese

8oz (225g) fresh lasagna sheets

3½oz (100g) grated mozzarella cheese

garlic bread, to serve

1 Preheat the oven to 400°F (200°C). Pour the oil into a large roasting pan and heat in the oven for 5 minutes.

2 Add all the vegetables to the pan with the garlic, herbs, and plenty of seasoning. Stir well and return the pan to the oven for 30 minutes, stirring occasionally. Remove, then stir the tomato sauce into the roasted vegetables.

3 Meanwhile, place the crème fraîche, eggs, and Parmesan in a bowl, season with pepper, and whisk together with a fork. Place half the vegetables in the bottom of a 11 x 8 x 2in (28 x 29 x 5cm) ovenproof dish and top with half the lasagna. Repeat the layers.

4 Pour the egg mixture over the lasagna and top with the mozzarella cheese. Place the dish on a baking sheet and bake for 30 minutes. Serve with garlic bread.

CALORIES: 635kcals/2660kJ

CARBOHYDRATE: 46g
  sugar: 9g

FAT: 36g
  saturated: 17g

SALT: 0.7g

FIBER: 6g

Spinach and ricotta cannelloni

This soothing vegetarian dish makes a welcome change to the more usual meat-filled lasagna. Great on cold days.

25 mins   50 mins

SERVES 4

4 tbsp butter, plus extra for greasing

10oz (300g) spinach

2 garlic cloves, finely chopped

salt and freshly ground black pepper

15oz (425g) ricotta cheese, drained

½ tsp grated nutmeg

16 dried cannelloni tubes

¼ cup all-purpose flour

2 cups whole milk

1¼oz (40g) finely grated Grana Padano cheese

1 Preheat the oven to 350°F (180°C). Butter a medium, shallow ovenproof dish.

2 Bring a large pan, containing a ½in (1cm) depth of water, to a boil, add the spinach, and stir until wilted. Drain and press out excess water. Chop the spinach.

3 Melt 1 tbsp of the butter in a medium pan and sauté the garlic for 2 minutes. Add the spinach, season, and stir well. Remove from the heat and stir in the ricotta cheese and nutmeg. Carefully fill the cannelloni with the spinach mixture and place the tubes in the buttered dish.

4 Meanwhile, melt the remaining 3 tbsp of the butter in a large pan. Whisk in the flour over low heat and cook for 2 minutes, whisking constantly. Take the pan off the heat and whisk in the milk, a little at a time, whisking well between each addition, until it has all been added. Return to the heat and cook, stirring constantly, until it thickens.

5 Reduce the heat to low and cook, stirring occasionally, for 5 minutes. Be sure to whisk right into the edges of the saucepan, as this is where the sauce can burn if left undisturbed. Season well and pour over the filled cannelloni. Sprinkle the cheese over the top in an even layer. Place on a baking sheet and bake for 30 minutes.

VARIATION

Reduce the amount of ricotta to 13oz (375g), and add 1¾oz (50g) finely chopped sun-dried tomatoes to the filling mixture.

CALORIES: 761kcals/3191kJ
CARBOHYDRATE: 78g
  sugar: 10g
FAT: 36g
  saturated: 22g
SALT: 1.1g
FIBER: 6g

Cheesy tuna and corn pasta bake

Tuna is a great pantry essential, being relatively inexpensive, yet packed full of low-fat protein.

10 mins   35 mins

SPECIAL EQUIPMENT

2-quart (2-liter) flameproof casserole

SERVES 4

salt and freshly ground black pepper

12oz (350g) dried fusilli

4 tbsp butter

¼ cup all-purpose flour

2 cups whole milk

5¾oz (160g) grated white Cheddar cheese

2 x 14oz (400g) cans tuna in spring water, drained and flaked

1 x 7oz (195g) can corn (no added salt or sugar), drained

1 tbsp tomato paste

1 tsp dried thyme

1¼oz (40g) cheese tortilla chips, roughly crushed

steamed green beans, to serve

CALORIES: 984kcals/4132kJ
CARBOHYDRATE: 92g
  sugar: 11g
FAT: 34g
  saturated: 18g
SALT: 1.9g
FIBER: 6g

1 Preheat the oven to 350°F (180°C). Bring a large pan of salted water to a boil, add the pasta, and cook according to the package instructions. Drain.

2 Meanwhile, melt the butter in a 2-quart (2-liter) flameproof casserole dish. Whisk in the flour over low heat. Cook for 2 minutes, whisking constantly until the mixture bubbles and separates.

3 Take the pan off the heat and whisk in the milk, a little at a time, whisking well between each addition, until it has all been added and the sauce is smooth. Return to the heat and cook, stirring, until it thickens. Reduce the heat to low and cook, stirring occasionally, for 5 minutes. Be sure to whisk right into the edges of the saucepan, as this is where the sauce can burn.

4 Add 3oz (90g) of the cheese and stir until melted. Add the tuna, corn, tomato paste, and thyme. Season and stir well.

5 Add the cooked pasta to the sauce and stir well to coat. Sprinkle the crushed tortilla chips over the pasta and top with the remaining cheese. Bake in the oven for 15 minutes. Serve with steamed green beans.

Chicken and broccoli pasta bake

A fantastic idea for leftovers, and perfect for making Sunday's roast chicken stretch to Monday night's supper.

20 mins

30 mins,
plus resting

SPECIAL EQUIPMENT
10in (25cm) ovenproof dish

SERVES 4

10oz (300g) small dried pasta
  shapes, such as mini conchigliette
  or macaroni

7oz (200g) small broccoli florets

5 tbsp butter

⅓ cup all-purpose flour

2 cups whole milk

1¾oz (50g) grated aged
  Cheddar cheese

salt and freshly ground black pepper

leftover roast chicken (ideally
  10oz/300g), chopped small

1 cup day-old bread crumbs

scant 1oz (25g) finely grated
  Parmesan cheese

1 Preheat the oven to 400°F (200°C). Boil the pasta according to the package instructions. A couple of minutes before it is ready, throw in the broccoli and cook until al dente. Drain the pasta and broccoli and return them to the pan.

2 Meanwhile, melt the butter in a small, heavy-bottomed saucepan. Whisk in the flour over low heat. Continue to cook for 2 minutes, whisking constantly, until the mixture bubbles and separates. Take the pan off the heat and whisk in the milk, a little at a time, whisking well between each addition, until it has all been added and the sauce is smooth.

3 Return to the heat and cook, stirring constantly, until it thickens. Reduce the heat to low and continue to cook, stirring occasionally for 5 minutes.

Be sure to whisk into the edges of the saucepan, as this is where the sauce can burn if left undisturbed.

4 Add the Cheddar cheese, season well, and cook for 2 minutes until the cheese has melted and the sauce is smooth, thick, and creamy.

5 Pour the sauce over the pasta and broccoli, add the chicken, and stir until well combined. Be gentle, so as not to break up the broccoli florets. Check the seasoning and pour the mixture into a 10in (25cm) ovenproof dish. Mix the bread crumbs and Parmesan and sprinkle an even layer on top.

6 Cook the pasta at the top of the oven for 20–25 minutes, until golden brown on top with crisp bread crumbs, and bubbling around the edges. Rest for at least 5 minutes before serving.

VARIATION

If you do not have leftover chicken, or your family does not eat meat, try adding a large can of drained, flaked salmon or tuna to the pasta in step 5 before baking.

CALORIES: 800kcals/3365kJ

CARBOHYDRATE: 82g
  sugar: 8g

FAT: 31.5g
  saturated: 18g

SALT: 1.2g

FIBER: 6g

"Mac and cheese"

A thick, creamy mac and cheese is everybody's idea of a tasty supper. This is the ultimate family favorite.

10 mins 15 mins

SERVES 4

10oz (300g) dried macaroni

salt and freshly ground black pepper

4 tbsp butter

¼ cup all-purpose flour

2 cups whole milk

5½oz (150g) grated aged
   Cheddar cheese

1¾oz (50g) finely grated
   Parmesan cheese

steamed broccoli, to serve

1 Cook the macaroni in boiling salted water according to the package instructions. Drain and transfer to a shallow ovenproof dish.

2 Meanwhile, melt the butter in a saucepan. Whisk in the flour over low heat and cook for 2 minutes, whisking constantly, until the mixture bubbles and separates.

3 Take the pan off the heat and whisk in the milk, a little at a time, whisking well between each addition, until it has all been added and the sauce is smooth. Return to the heat and cook, stirring until it thickens. Reduce the heat to low and cook, stirring occasionally, for 5 minutes. Be sure to whisk right into the edges of the saucepan, as this is where the sauce can burn if left undisturbed. Add 3½oz (100g) of the Cheddar cheese and stir until it has melted. Preheat the broiler to its highest setting.

4 Pour the sauce over the macaroni, season with pepper, and stir well to coat. Sprinkle in the remaining 1¾oz (50g) of Cheddar cheese and the Parmesan. Place on a baking sheet and broil for 5 minutes, or until bubbling. Serve with steamed broccoli.

CALORIES: 679kcals/2847kJ

CARBOHYDRATE: 67g
   sugar: 7g

FAT: 33g
   saturated: 20g

SALT: 1.2g

FIBER: 3.5g

Mac and cheese is an easy, ever-popular way to ensure children are getting enough calcium and protein.

Fussy eaters!

Singapore noodles

This vegetable-packed dish is mildly spiced with curry powder, which you can reduce or omit as preferred.

25-30 mins   25 mins

SERVES 4

2 tbsp vegetable oil

5½oz (150g) boneless, skinless chicken breast, cut into strips

16 raw tiger shrimp, shelled and deveined

1 onion, finely sliced

2 garlic cloves, finely chopped

1in (3cm) piece of fresh ginger, finely chopped

1 red chile, seeded and finely chopped

1 red bell pepper, finely sliced

3½oz (100g) baby corn

3½oz (100g) sugarsnap peas

3½oz (100g) beansprouts

1 tsp turmeric

2 tsp mild curry powder

2 tbsp soy sauce

10oz (300g) fresh vermicelli rice noodles

3 large eggs, lightly beaten

salt and freshly ground black pepper

sliced scallions, to garnish

1 Heat half the oil in a wok or very large, non-stick frying pan over medium heat. Add the chicken and cook for 5 minutes or until cooked through, stirring. Remove from the wok and place on a plate lined with paper towels.

2 Add the shrimp to the pan and cook for 2–3 minutes until the shrimp turn pink and are cooked through, stirring occasionally. Transfer to the plate with the chicken.

3 Pour in the remaining 1 tbsp of oil and, over medium heat, cook the onion for 2 minutes. Add the garlic, ginger, and chile, and cook for 1 minute.

4 Add the remaining vegetables, turmeric, and curry powder and stir-fry for 5 minutes.

5 Stir in the soy sauce and noodles and cook for 3 minutes. Push the mixture in the wok to one side and pour the egg into the other

side of the pan. Stir constantly and, once cooked, stir the egg into the noodles. Season.

6 Return the chicken and shrimp to the pan and stir until heated through. Serve the noodles garnished with scallions.

CALORIES: 549kcals/2299kJ

CARBOHYDRATE: 68g
  sugar: 6g

FAT: 12g
  saturated: 2g

SALT: 1.9g

FIBER: 3g

After school

Preschool children usually need to eat between 5 and 6pm, and school aged children often return home ravenous. In addition, long working days for many parents have the unfortunate consequence that, for many families, sitting down together to eat rarely happens midweek. It would be lovely if families could sit down and eat together every night, but if that's not a realistic idea, then a bit of planning and a few simple recipes can help you.

Children's dinners

Cooking for children and adults separately can be tiresome and time-consuming, so if you can't sit down to a family meal, try to cook things that you will all enjoy, even at different times. Mild curries or chilis can be spiced up after the children have eaten, and easily reheated. Leftovers from an adult meal can often be used to make the children's dinner the following day, with chicken folded into a pasta sauce or fish used as a basis for fishcakes. When time is short, quick cook pasta with butter and cheese, cheese on toast, or ham and cheese quesadillas all make a tasty and nutritious meal. Alternatively, for an almost instant snack, arrange a platter with pick-and-mix food, such as hummus, pita bread, hard-boiled eggs, and chopped raw vegetables.

Drinks

Children often drink a lot of fruit juices. Try sticking to water as the drink of choice between mealtimes, and water down fresh juices to help prevent tooth decay.

Meals for kids

To help you keep your sanity and avoid spending hours in the kitchen, plan ahead and keep weekday meals fairly simple.

Spicy chicken and tomato curry (p98) This colorful dish makes a tasty adult supper and can be served to children the next day with garlic bread, rice, and some yogurt to temper the spices, if necessary.

Mac and cheese (p210) Easy to prepare and universally loved by children, this comforting dish is a weekday winner. You can add variety with extra ingredients such as bacon, tomatoes, or broccoli.

Breakfast may be rushed and it's hard to be certain what children have eaten for their lunch at school, so snack time is the best way of making sure your children have a balanced meal and include some vegetables and fruit in their diet.

Variety

It's easy to get stuck in a rut when preparing children's meals, especially when time is short. Planning ahead helps to ensure that you give them a good spread of meat, fish, and vegetarian dishes throughout the week.

After-school snacks

Healthy snacks are an important part of a child's diet, but make sure that they don't overload on sugary, processed foods that keep them from eating well-balanced, home-cooked meals. Try the following quick bites:

Granola breakfast bars (p474)

Homemade hummus (p388) andvegetable sticks

Grissini (p444)

Mixed nuts, dried fruit, and seeds

A full fruit bowl

Banana, mango, and yogurt smoothie (p32)

Toasted muffins and crumpets

Rice cakes

Frittata

Fruity ice pops (p59)

Banana and date mini muffins (p58) A substantial and healthy after-school snack, such as these delicious muffins, should keep your children going until you've had a chance to prepare the evening meal at a time to suit you.

No-cook desserts

Chopped up fruit with added juice make a colorful fruit salad, or serve favorite fruits with thick yogurt and honey. Keep a bag of frozen banana chunks on hand to whip up banana ice cream (see p328) in a minute.

Assemble fruit such as grapes, pineapple, apple, and strawberries onto skewers.

Jeweled rice salad

This pretty salad is a fantastic centerpiece at a buffet, along with some grilled meats and leafy green salads.

20 mins, plus cooling   20 mins

SERVES 4

9oz (250g) mixed basmati and wild rice

2 cups vegetable stock (see p156)

seeds from 2 pomegranates

finely chopped flesh of 1 orange

2oz (60g) dried apricots, chopped

1¼oz (40g) sliced almonds

6 scallions, finely chopped

3 tbsp chopped cilantro leaves

2 tbsp chopped flat-leaf parsley leaves

FOR THE DRESSING

finely grated zest and juice of 1 orange

juice of 1 lemon

2 tbsp extra virgin olive oil

1 tsp Dijon mustard

1 garlic clove, finely chopped

salt and freshly ground black pepper

1 Cook the rice in the stock according to the package instructions (about 20 minutes). Set aside to cool.

2 For the dressing, in a small bowl combine the orange zest and juice, lemon juice, oil, mustard, garlic, and seasoning. Whisk together with a fork to combine.

3 Transfer the cooled rice to a serving dish and stir in the dressing. Add the remaining ingredients and stir well. Cover and keep in the fridge until ready to serve.

COOK'S TIP

To free the seeds from the pomegranates quickly and easily, first cut them in half. Then hold each pomegranate-half cut-side down over a bowl and, using a wooden spoon, bash the skin until the shell is empty. Pick out and discard any white pith.

CALORIES: 429kcals/1795kJ

CARBOHYDRATE: 66g
  sugar: 19g

FAT: 12g
  saturated: 1g

SALT: 0.1g

FIBER: 6g

Curried rice salad

Serve this with Easy chicken tikka skewers and raita (see p100) for an Indian-inspired summertime meal.

15 mins, plus cooling   25 mins

SERVES 4

9oz (250g) brown basmati rice

2 cups vegetable stock (see p156)

1 tbsp medium curry powder

1¾oz (50g) raisins

1 red onion, very finely sliced

2¾oz (80g) dried cranberries

1¾oz (50g) shelled pistachio nuts

1oz (30g) flaked coconut

1 green bell pepper, finely chopped

FOR THE DRESSING

3 tbsp mango chutney

1 tbsp olive oil

juice of ½ lemon

salt and freshly ground black pepper

1 Place the rice, stock, curry powder, and raisins in a saucepan and cook the rice according to the package instructions (about 25 minutes). Set aside.

2 In a small bowl, combine the dressing ingredients. Whisk together with a fork to combine. Transfer the cooled rice to a serving dish and pour in the dressing.

3 Add the onion, cranberries, nuts, coconut, and green bell pepper to the rice and stir well. Cover and keep in the fridge until ready to serve.

CLEVER WITH LEFTOVERS

A near-instant version of this salad can be made using leftover cooked and chilled rice (see the guidelines for cooked rice, p9). Simply mix the curry powder with the dressing ingredients and toss it through the cold rice with the nuts, fruits, and vegetables.

CALORIES: 524kcals/2208kJ

CARBOHYDRATE: 67g
  sugar: 19g

FAT: 16g
  saturated: 6g

SALT: 0.4g

FIBER: 7g

Simple Parmesan risotto

This basic but fabulous risotto relies as much on the cooking method as the ingredients.

15 mins　30–35 mins

SERVES 4

2 tbsp olive oil

1 onion, finely chopped

1 garlic clove, finely chopped

2½ cups hot vegetable or chicken stock (see p156; p94)

10oz (300g) risotto rice, such as Arborio or Carnaroli

¼ cup white wine (optional)

2oz (60g) finely grated Parmesan cheese, plus extra to serve

1 tbsp butter

salt and freshly ground black pepper

1 Heat the oil in a large, heavy-bottomed, deep-sided frying pan. Cook the onion over medium heat for five minutes. Add the garlic and cook for another minute.

2 Keep the stock gently simmering on the stove near the risotto pan.

3 Add the rice to the onion pan and stir it in the oil and onions to coat. When it begins to sizzle, pour in the wine (if using) and allow it to evaporate.

4 Now pour in the stock a ladleful at a time, stirring the rice constantly, for about 20 minutes, allowing all the liquid to evaporate from the pan between ladlefuls.

5 When the rice is cooked but still al dente, stop adding the liquid and continue to cook it, stirring, until it is quite dry (the cheese and butter will loosen it up again).

6 Take off the heat and stir in the Parmesan and butter, season, then serve with extra Parmesan.

VARIATION

Once you have mastered a basic risotto, try adding leftover chicken, handfuls of herbs, or different cheeses as you like.

CALORIES: 484kcals/2017kJ
CARBOHYDRATE: 58g
 sugar: 2g
FAT: 13g
 saturated: 6g
SALT: 0.9g
FIBER: 0.5g

Butternut squash risotto

It's well worth roasting the squash before adding it to the risotto; it gives a lovely deep, rich, sweet flavor.

10 mins　1 hr 25 mins

SPECIAL EQUIPMENT
food processor (optional)

SERVES 4–6

1 butternut squash, approx. 1¾lb (800g) prepared weight

2 tbsp olive oil, plus extra for drizzling

1 onion, finely chopped

1 garlic clove, finely chopped

2½ cups hot vegetable or chicken stock (see p156; p94)

10oz (300g) risotto rice, such as Arborio or Carnaroli

¼ cup white wine (optional)

2 tbsp chopped sage leaves

2oz (60g) finely grated Parmesan cheese, plus extra to serve

1 tbsp butter (optional)

salt and freshly ground black pepper

CALORIES: 553kcals/2316kJ
CARBOHYDRATE: 73g
 sugar: 10g
FAT: 14g
 saturated: 6g
SALT: 0.8g
FIBER: 5g

1 Preheat the oven to 400°F (200°C). Slice the squash in half lengthwise and scoop out the seeds. Place on a baking sheet, drizzle with oil, and cover with foil. Bake for 1 hour, until soft.

2 When the squash is nearly cooked, start the risotto. Heat the oil in a large, heavy-bottomed, deep-sided frying pan. Cook the onion over medium heat for 5 minutes. Add the garlic and cook for another minute.

3 Keep the stock simmering on the stove near the risotto pan. Add the rice to the onion pan, and stir. When it sizzles, pour in the wine (if using) and allow to evaporate. Continue to add stock a ladleful at a time, stirring, for 20 minutes, allowing the liquid to evaporate between ladlefuls.

4 Scoop out the squash flesh and mash it, or purée in a food processor with 2 tbsp of stock.

5 Add the squash and sage to the risotto and cook for five minutes, until most of the liquid has evaporated. The rice should be cooked, but still al dente. Add the Parmesan and butter (if using), and season. Serve with extra Parmesan.

Minted pea and shrimp risotto

Sweet peas and shrimp contrast well with the sharp Parmesan and creamy rice.

10 mins   25 mins

SPECIAL EQUIPMENT
food processor or hand-held blender

SERVES 4

14oz (400g) frozen peas

salt and freshly ground black pepper

2½ cups fish or vegetable stock (see p156)

1 tbsp olive oil

1 onion, finely chopped

1 garlic clove, finely chopped

10oz (300g) risotto rice, such as Arborio or Carnaroli

½ cup white wine (optional)

10oz (300g) cooked, shelled, and deveined large shrimp

1oz (30g) finely grated Parmesan cheese, plus extra to serve

2 tbsp chopped mint leaves

1 tbsp butter (optional)

CALORIES: 542kcals/2262kJ
CARBOHYDRATE: 68g
  sugar: 4g
FAT: 11g
  saturated: 4.5g
SALT: 1.9g
FIBER: 7g

1 Cook the peas in boiling salted water for 2 minutes, until just cooked. Drain, refresh under cold water, then purée with about ¾ cup of the stock in a food processor, or with a hand-held blender, until smooth. Put the remaining stock in a saucepan over low heat, and keep it simmering on the stove with a ladle nearby.

2 Heat the oil in a large, heavy-bottomed, deep-sided frying pan. Cook the onion over medium heat for 5 minutes until it softens, but does not brown. Add the garlic and cook for another minute.

3 Add in the rice and stir to coat. When it sizzles, stir in the wine (if using) and allow it to evaporate.

4 Add the stock a ladleful at a time, stirring constantly, for 20 minutes, allowing the liquid to evaporate between ladlefuls.

5 Add the puréed peas and cook for 2 minutes, or until most of the liquid evaporates. The rice should be al dente. Add the shrimp and another ladle of stock and heat through for 2 minutes.

6 Take the pan off the heat, add the Parmesan, mint, and butter (if using), and season well to taste. Sprinkle with extra Parmesan to serve.

Oven-baked risotto

If you don't have time to stir a risotto for 20 minutes, try this trouble-free baked version instead.

10 mins   25-30 mins

SPECIAL EQUIPMENT
large, heavy-bottomed Dutch oven

SERVES 4

2 tbsp butter

1 tbsp olive oil

1 onion, finely chopped

2 garlic cloves, finely chopped

10oz (300g) mixed mushrooms, such as crimini, shiitake, and oyster, roughly chopped

14oz (400g) risotto rice

2½ cups vegetable or chicken stock (see 156; p94)

⅔ cup dry white wine

salt and freshly ground black pepper

10oz (300g) cooked chicken, chopped into bite-sized pieces

1¼oz (40g) grated Grana Padano cheese, plus extra to serve

¼ cup chopped parsley leaves

CALORIES: 670kcals/2801kJ
CARBOHYDRATE: 78g
  sugar: 2g
FAT: 16g
  saturated: 7g
SALT: 1.4g
FIBER: 2g

1 Preheat the oven to 400°F (200°C). Heat the butter and oil in a large, heavy-bottomed Dutch oven over low heat. Once the butter has melted, add the onion and garlic and cook gently for 5 minutes.

2 Add the mushrooms and rice and stir well to coat in the butter and oil. Pour in the stock and wine, bring to a boil, season, and stir well.

3 Cover and cook in the oven for 20 minutes or until the rice is tender, stirring a couple of times.

4 Remove from the oven and stir in the chicken, Grana Padano cheese, and parsley. Return to the oven for 5 minutes, or until the chicken is heated through. Serve with pepper and extra Grana Padano, for sprinkling.

VARIATION

For a spinach and hot-smoked salmon risotto, omit the mushrooms and chicken, and stir in 10oz (300g) flaked, hot-smoked salmon fillets, and 3½oz (100g) spinach 5 minutes before the end of the cooking time.

Mozzarella-stuffed risotto balls

A fantastic way to use up leftover risotto, these Italian *arancini* make a great snack that children love.

20 mins, plus resting   10 mins

MAKES 12

14oz (400g) cooked, cold Simple Parmesan risotto (see p219)

2oz (60g) mozzarella cheese, cut into 12 x ½in (1cm) cubes

¼ cup all-purpose flour

1 large egg, beaten

1 cup day-old bread crumbs or panko bread crumbs

3½ cups sunflower or vegetable oil, for deep-frying

1 Keep your hands damp to mold the risotto balls. Take a walnut-sized spoonful of risotto and mold it in your palm so it creates a flattened circle. Place a piece of the mozzarella in the middle of the rice and mold the rice around it, rolling it to make a ball. Make sure the mozzarella is well covered, and be sure to pack the risotto down well. Continue until you have 12 balls.

2 Put the flour, egg, and bread crumbs in 3 wide, shallow bowls. Roll each risotto ball first in the flour, then in the egg, and finally coat it well in the bread crumbs. Place on a plate, cover with plastic wrap, and rest in the fridge for at least 30 minutes (this will help the coating to stick).

3 When you are ready to cook the risotto balls, preheat the oven to 300°F (150°C). Heat the oil in a large, heavy-bottomed saucepan to a depth of 4in (10cm). It will be ready to use when a small piece of bread dropped in sizzles and turns golden brown.

4 Cook the risotto balls a few at a time for two minutes until golden brown all over. Remove with a slotted spoon and drain on paper towels. Keep warm in the oven while you cook the rest.

VARIATION

Try this with other risottos, but make sure they are fairly smooth in texture, as these will adhere more easily to the bread crumb coating. Adding a spicy tomato sauce for dipping cuts through the richness of the risotto balls.

CALORIES: 188kcals/789kJ
CARBOHYDRATE: 18g
  sugar: 0.5g
FAT: 10g
  saturated: 3g
SALT: 0.9g
FIBER: 0.5g

Crispy risotto cakes

These are stylish leftovers. Serve with grilled fish and a poached egg on top for a simple, sophisticated meal.

5 mins   30 mins

SPECIAL EQUIPMENT

4in (10cm) cookie cutter or ring mold

SERVES 4

1¾lb (800g) cooked, cold risotto, such as Simple Parmesan risotto (see p219)

1¾oz (50g) finely grated Parmesan cheese

handful of flat-leaf parsley or basil leaves, finely chopped (optional)

salt and freshly ground black pepper

olive oil, for brushing

1 Preheat the oven to 450°F (230°C). In a bowl, mix together the risotto, Parmesan, and herbs (if using), and season well.

2 Use a 4in (10cm) round cutter or mold to make cakes of the mixture: place the cutter or mold on a work surface and spoon in one-quarter of the risotto mixture, squashing it in and flattening it off nicely. Remove the cutter or mold. Repeat to make four cakes.

3 Brush each risotto cake with a little oil on one side and place oil-side down on a non-stick baking sheet. Brush the upper side with oil and bake at the top of the oven for 25 minutes, turning carefully after 15 minutes, or until golden and crispy on the outside but soft and yielding within.

VARIATION

Make bite-sized Crispy risotto cakes for an instant canapé, serving them with arugula pesto (see p194).

CALORIES: 646kcals/2710kJ
CARBOHYDRATE: 66g
  sugar: 2g
FAT: 33g
  saturated: 12g
SALT: 4.9g
FIBER: 1g

Paella

As with any recipe involving fresh clams or mussels, discard any that do not close when firmly tapped on a sink.

35 mins   35 mins

SERVES 4

2 tbsp olive oil

4 boneless, skinless chicken thighs, halved

1¾oz (50g) chorizo, thinly sliced

1¾oz (50g) chopped pancetta

2 garlic cloves, finely chopped

1 Spanish onion, finely chopped

1 green bell pepper, sliced

1 red bell pepper, sliced

9oz (250g) Spanish short-grain rice, such as paella rice

generous pinch of saffron strands

1 tsp smoked paprika

2 tbsp dry sherry

¾ cup dry white wine

2 cups chicken stock (see p94)

4 tomatoes, peeled, seeded, and roughly chopped (see p191)

salt and freshly ground black pepper

3½oz (100g) fresh or frozen peas

12–16 fresh mussels or clams, scrubbed, rinsed, and beards removed

7oz (200g) raw, shelled, and deveined large shrimp

5½oz (150g) scallops

¼ cup chopped flat-leaf parsley leaves

juice of ½–1 lemon

1 Heat half the oil in a very large non-stick frying pan with a lid over medium heat. Cook the chicken for 5 minutes. Set aside.

2 Add the chorizo, pancetta, garlic, and onion and cook for 3 minutes, stirring occasionally. Add the peppers and cook for 1 minute.

3 Stir in the rice and spices for 1 minute. Add the sherry, wine, stock, tomatoes, and seasoning, and bring to a boil. Reduce the heat to a simmer, return the chicken, cover, and cook for 15 minutes. Add the peas and mussels, cover, and cook for 5 minutes. Discard any mussels that don't open.

4 Meanwhile, in a small pan, heat the remaining 1 tbsp of oil over medium heat and cook the shrimp and scallops for only 2 or 3 minutes, until just cooked through and opaque. Add to the paella and stir well. Stir the parsley and lemon juice into the paella and serve immediately.

CALORIES: 663kcals/2774kJ

CARBOHYDRATE: 61g
  sugar: 10g

FAT: 16g
  saturated: 4g

SALT: 1.7g

FIBER: 5g

Quick paella

Frozen foods can often help you out when time is short, and frozen seafood adds flavor and body to this dish.

10 mins 35-40 mins

SERVES 4

1 tbsp olive oil

7oz (200g) boneless, skinless chicken breast, cut into strips

14oz (400g) frozen seafood mix, defrosted and drained

1 Spanish onion, sliced

2 garlic cloves, finely chopped

1 tsp turmeric

1 tsp smoked paprika

salt and freshly ground black pepper

10oz (300g) long-grain white rice

3½ cups hot chicken stock (see p94)

3½oz (100g) frozen thin green beans

3½oz (100g) frozen peas

juice of ½ lemon

1 Heat half the oil in a very large, non-stick frying pan with a lid over medium heat. Add the chicken and cook for 5 minutes, stirring occasionally. Remove from the pan and set aside.

2 Add the seafood mix to the pan and cook for 2 minutes, stirring occasionally. Remove from the pan using a slotted spoon and set aside with the chicken.

3 Wipe the pan dry with paper towels and add the remaining ½ tbsp of oil. Add the onion and cook for 5 minutes. Add the garlic and cook for 1 minute.

4 Add the spices, seasoning, and rice to the pan and stir to coat for 1 minute. Add the stock, bring to a boil, cover, and simmer for 10–15 minutes.

5 Add the beans to the pan, stir well, and cook for another 3 minutes, then add the peas and cook for 2 minutes.

6 Return the cooked chicken and seafood to the pan and heat through over high heat for a final 2 minutes, stirring constantly. Squeeze in the lemon and serve immediately.

CALORIES: 522kcals/2188kJ
CARBOHYDRATE: 62g
    sugar: 2.5g
FAT: 6g
    saturated: 1g
SALT: 1.3g
FIBER: 3g

Cashew and zucchini rice

You can serve this nutty, gingery pilaf on its own or as an accompaniment to grilled lamb or fish.

15 mins 40 mins

SERVES 4

1-2 tbsp olive oil

1 onion, finely chopped

salt and freshly ground black pepper

4in (10cm) piece of fresh ginger, finely grated

4 zucchini, quartered lengthwise and chopped into bite-sized pieces

3 garlic cloves, finely chopped

1 tbsp cider vinegar

pinch of cayenne pepper

7oz (200g) long-grain white rice

approx. 3 cups hot vegetable stock (see p156)

2½oz (75g) cashew nuts, roughly chopped

bunch of scallions, green part only, thinly sliced

bunch of cilantro, leaves only, chopped

1 Heat 1 tbsp of oil in a large, heavy-bottomed pan with a lid over medium heat, add the onion, and cook for 3 minutes until soft. Season with salt and pepper, increase the heat, and stir in the ginger and zucchini.

2 Cook for 5 minutes until the zucchini are lightly golden (adding more oil, if necessary), then add the garlic and cook for another 3 minutes.

3 Increase the heat, add the vinegar, let it cook for 1 minute, then stir in the cayenne pepper and rice. Add a little stock and turn it so all the grains are coated.

4 Bring to a boil, add enough stock to cover, cover with a lid, and simmer gently for about 20 minutes, or until the rice is tender. Add more stock when needed.

5 Stir in the cashew nuts, scallions, and half the cilantro, taste, and season as needed. Sprinkle with the remaining cilantro to serve.

HOW TO FREEZE

Grated fresh ginger freezes well, so wrap small quantities in plastic wrap, freeze, and you'll always have some on hand.

CALORIES: 356kcals/1484kJ
CARBOHYDRATE: 44g
    sugar: 4.5g
FAT: 13g
    saturated: 2.5g
SALT: 0.2g
FIBER: 3g

Jamaican rice and peas

The kidney beans in this tasty dish are known as "gungo peas" in Jamaica and "pigeon peas" in Trinidad.

10 mins   45 mins

SERVES 4

1 x 14oz (400g) can kidney beans, drained and rinsed

1 x 14oz (400ml) can coconut milk

1 large onion, finely chopped

1 green bell pepper, finely chopped or sliced

salt and freshly ground black pepper

4½oz (125g) long-grain white rice

chile powder, to garnish

1 Put the beans, coconut milk, onion, and green bell pepper in a saucepan. Season to taste with salt and pepper and simmer over low heat for 5 minutes.

2 Stir in the rice, cover, and cook gently for 35 minutes, or until the rice is tender, stirring. Serve sprinkled with chile powder.

PREPARE AHEAD

The dish can be prepared in advance (but cool it quickly and store it carefully, following the guidelines on the Clever with Leftovers feature on pp322–323). To reheat, place in a shallow dish and tightly cover with foil. Reheat in a preheated oven at 350°F (180°C) for 15 minutes, or until piping hot.

CALORIES: 379kcals/1590kJ
CARBOHYDRATE: 42g
  sugar: 6g
FAT: 18g
  saturated: 15g
SALT: 0.6g
FIBER: 7g

Chinese fried rice with shrimp and chicken

If your family has favorite crunchy vegetables, vary the ingredients here according to what they like.

15 mins   40 mins

SERVES 8

2lb (900g) white basmati rice

salt and freshly ground black pepper

5 tbsp sunflower or vegetable oil

1lb (450g) raw, shelled, and deveined shrimp, chopped

4 large boneless, skinless chicken breasts, cut into 1in (2.5cm) strips

15oz (425g) chopped pancetta

8oz (225g) mushrooms, chopped

3in (7.5cm) piece of fresh ginger, finely sliced

8oz (225g) frozen peas, defrosted

4 large eggs, lightly beaten

2 tbsp dark soy sauce

2 tbsp mirin

bunch of scallions, finely sliced

small handful of flat-leaf parsley leaves, finely chopped

CALORIES: 733kcals/3057kJ
CARBOHYDRATE: 88g
  sugar: 2g
FAT: 24g
  saturated: 6g
SALT: 2.7g
FIBER: 2g

1 Rinse the rice, then place in a large pan, cover with boiling water, and add salt. Cover with a lid, bring to a boil, and cook for 15–20 minutes, or until done. Drain well and set aside to cool completely.

2 Meanwhile, heat 1 tbsp of the oil in a wok over high heat, add the shrimp, season, and cook until pink. Set aside. Heat another 1 tbsp of the oil, add the chicken, season, and stir-fry for 5 minutes, or until no longer pink. Set aside.

3 Heat another 1 tbsp of the oil, add the pancetta, and cook over medium-high heat until crispy and golden. Set aside. Wipe the wok with paper towels, then heat another 1 tbsp of the oil. Add the mushrooms and ginger and stir-fry for 5 minutes. Add the peas for the last minute. Set aside.

4 Heat the final 1 tbsp of oil in the wok, then pour in the eggs and cook gently, stirring, for 1 minute. Add the rice and stir well, then stir in the shrimp, chicken, pancetta, mushrooms, and peas. Add the soy sauce and mirin and stir for 5 minutes. Transfer to a serving dish, top with the scallions and parsley, and serve.

Moroccan spiced rice

This exotic rice dish is full of flavor, and would be delicious with Slow-cooked Moroccan lamb (see p132).

15 mins   20-25 mins

SERVES 4

1 tbsp olive oil

1 onion, very finely sliced

2 garlic cloves, finely chopped

2 tsp ras el hanout spice mix

9oz (250g) long-grain white rice

2 cups vegetable stock (see p156)

1 x 14oz (400g) can chickpeas, drained

2¼oz (70g) dried apricots, chopped

2¼oz (70g) dried figs, finely chopped

1 preserved lemon, finely chopped

salt and freshly ground black pepper

1oz (30g) toasted sliced almonds

2 tbsp chopped cilantro leaves

2 tbsp chopped mint leaves

1 Heat the oil in a large pan over medium heat. Add the onion and cook for 5 minutes, until it has softened. Add the garlic and cook for 1 minute.

2 Stir in the spice mix and cook for 1 minute. Add the rice and stir to coat in the spices.

3 Add the stock, chickpeas, apricots, figs, and preserved lemon. Season, bring to a boil, stir well, cover, and cook according to the package instructions (about 10–15 minutes).

4 Remove from the heat and stir in the almonds, cilantro, and mint. Serve hot, or cool and chill and serve cold. (If serving cold, add the herbs only once the rice has cooled, and follow the guidelines for cooked rice, see p9.)

CALORIES: 374kcals/1568kJ
CARBOHYDRATE: 63g
  sugar: 16g
FAT: 8g
  saturated: 0.7g
SALT: 0.6g
FIBER: 3.5g

Mexican red rice

Try this as a side dish for dishes that have a little heat, such as Spicy pork and beans (see p146).

5 mins   30 mins,
           plus resting

SERVES 4

2 tbsp olive oil

1 onion, finely chopped

1 garlic clove, finely chopped

1 red chile, seeded and finely chopped

7oz (200g) long-grain white rice

1 cup tomato paste

2 cups vegetable stock (see p156)

2 tsp smoked paprika

salt and freshly ground black pepper

1 tbsp butter

1 heaping tbsp chopped cilantro leaves (optional)

1 Heat the oil in a heavy-bottomed saucepan with a lid. Cook the onion over medium heat for 5 minutes, until it softens, but does not brown. Add the garlic and chile and cook for another minute.

2 Add the rice and cook it over low heat, stirring constantly, for 2–3 minutes, until it starts to turn translucent. Add the tomato paste, stock, and smoked paprika and season well.

3 Bring the rice to a boil, reduce the heat to low, cover, and simmer for 25 minutes until the rice is tender and all the liquid has been absorbed.

4 Take the rice off the heat, stir in the butter, cover, and rest for 5 minutes. Serve, scattered with cilantro (if using).

CALORIES: 286kcals/1190kJ
CARBOHYDRATE: 41g
  sugar: 3g
FAT: 9g
  saturated: 3g
SALT: 0.4g
FIBER: 1g

CLEVER WITH LEFTOVERS

If you have leftover cooked rice, use this recipe as the inspiration for a Mexican-style refried rice, using a combination of just enough paste and chicken stock (see p94) to color and flavor the dish, without making it too moist.

Dirty rice

A classic recipe from the Deep South, this dish gets its name from the color given by the meat.

15 mins   1 hr, plus resting

SPECIAL EQUIPMENT
large Dutch oven, ideally cast-iron

SERVES 6

4 tbsp olive oil

1 onion, finely chopped

½ celery stalk, finely chopped

1 green bell pepper, finely chopped

9oz (250g) ground pork

7oz (200g) chicken livers, trimmed and finely chopped

1 green chile, seeded and finely chopped

2 garlic cloves, finely chopped

1 tsp smoked paprika

1 tsp coriander seeds, crushed

10oz (300g) long-grain white rice

salt and freshly ground black pepper

2½ cups hot chicken stock (see p94)

large sprig of thyme

handful of flat-leaf parsley leaves, finely chopped

1 tbsp finely chopped oregano leaves

1 Preheat the oven to 325°F (160°C). Heat 3 tbsp of the oil in a large Dutch oven and add the onion, celery, and green bell pepper. Cook gently for 5 minutes, until soft. Set aside.

2 Add the remaining oil, then the pork and chicken livers. Increase the heat to high and cook, turning, until the meat is well browned, about 5 minutes.

3 Add the chile, garlic, smoked paprika, and coriander seeds and cook for 2 minutes. Return the vegetables, then stir in the rice. Season well and add the hot stock and thyme. Bring to a boil, stir, cover, and cook in the oven for 30–40 minutes, stirring once or twice, until the rice is cooked and the stock absorbed.

4 Remove and rest for 5 minutes. Remove the thyme, stir in the chopped herbs, taste for seasoning, and serve.

CALORIES: 326kcals/1360kJ
CARBOHYDRATE: 27g
   sugar: 2.5g
FAT: 12.5g
   saturated: 3g
SALT: 0.5g
FIBER: 1g

Thai coconut rice

Traditional flavorings of coconut and kaffir lime leaves are mixed with plain rice to make this popular Asian dish.

25 mins   40 mins

SERVES 4–6

¼oz (10g) bunch of cilantro

2 tbsp olive oil

2 tbsp butter

1 red chile, finely chopped (seed it if you want a milder dish)

2 shallots, finely chopped

2½oz (75g) Thai red curry paste

finely grated zest of 1 lime

14oz (400g) Thai jasmine rice

1 tsp salt

1 14oz (400ml) can coconut milk

large pinch of shredded kaffir lime leaves

2 scallions, thinly sliced

CALORIES: 684kcals/2855kJ
CARBOHYDRATE: 80g
   sugar: 1.5g
FAT: 32g
   saturated: 19g
SALT: 1.8g
FIBER: 0.3g

1 Pick the cilantro leaves from the stalks, finely chop the stalks, and reserve the leaves.

2 Heat the oil and butter in a large frying pan with a lid over low heat. Add the chile and shallots and cook, stirring, for 5 minutes, or until they start to turn golden. Stir in the curry paste and cook for 30 seconds.

3 Add the lime zest, cilantro stalks, rice, and salt and mix together until the grains of rice are coated in the curry paste. Pour in the coconut milk, then fill the empty can with water and add that too. Stir well. Bring to a simmer over medium heat, stirring occasionally so the rice doesn't stick. Scatter in the lime leaves and simmer, uncovered, for 5 minutes.

4 Stir the rice thoroughly, then cover the pan and leave over very low heat for 15 minutes, or until the rice is tender. If all the liquid has been absorbed but the rice is still not quite ready, add a little extra water until it is tender. When ready to serve, stir in the scallions and sprinkle with the reserved cilantro leaves.

Chinese chicken and rice

Simply serve with some steamed bok choy for an aromatic and deliciously different one-pot meal.

10 mins | 30 mins, plus resting

SERVES 4

1 tsp sesame oil

1 tbsp soy sauce

2 tbsp rice wine or dry sherry

14oz (400g) boneless, skinless chicken thighs, cut into 1in (3cm) chunks

2 tbsp sunflower or vegetable oil

1 bunch of scallions, finely sliced

2 garlic cloves, finely chopped

1in (3cm) piece of fresh ginger, finely chopped

1 red chile, seeded and finely chopped

1 tsp five-spice powder

2½ cups chicken stock (see p94)

10oz (300g) long-grain white rice, or jasmine rice

steamed bok choy, to serve

1 Mix together the sesame oil, soy sauce, and half the rice wine in a shallow dish. Add the chicken, stir to coat, cover, and refrigerate in the marinade for up to 1 hour.

2 Heat the sunflower oil in a heavy-bottomed saucepan with a lid. Drain the chicken from its marinade (reserve any of the remaining marinade) and cook it for 2–3 minutes, until colored all over. Add the scallions, garlic, ginger, and chile and cook for another 2 minutes. Now add the five-spice powder and cook for 1 minute.

3 Add the stock, remaining rice wine, and any marinade and stir in the rice. Bring the rice to a boil, then reduce the heat to a low simmer and then cook, covered, for 20–25 minutes, until the rice is cooked and all the liquid has evaporated.

4 Take it off the heat and rest it, covered, for 5 minutes before serving with steamed bok choy.

VARIATION

If you can find Chinese sausages, add a couple of these, casings peeled and sliced, with the chicken.

CALORIES: 464kcals/1945kJ

CARBOHYDRATE: 57g
  sugar: 1g

FAT: 5g
  saturated: 1g

SALT: 1.4g

FIBER: 0.5g

Chicken and chickpea pilaf

This one-pot rice dish is full of flavor and easy to make. It just needs a crisp green salad on the side.

20 mins | 35 mins

SERVES 4

pinch of saffron threads

2 tsp vegetable oil

6 boneless, skinless chicken thighs, cut into small pieces

2 tsp ground coriander

1 tsp ground cumin

1 onion, sliced

1 red bell pepper, chopped

2 garlic cloves, crushed

8oz (225g) long-grain white rice

2½ cups hot chicken stock (see p94)

2 bay leaves

1 x 14oz (400g) can chickpeas, drained and rinsed

2oz (60g) golden raisins

2oz (60g) sliced almonds or pine nuts, toasted

3 tbsp chopped flat-leaf parsley leaves

1 Crumble the saffron threads into a small bowl, add 2 tbsp of boiling water, and set aside for at least 10 minutes.

2 Meanwhile, heat half the oil in a large saucepan, then add the chicken, coriander, and cumin and cook over medium heat for 3 minutes, stirring frequently.

3 Remove from the pan and set aside. Lower the heat, add the rest of the oil, the onion, red bell pepper, and garlic, and cook for 5 minutes, or until softened.

4 Stir in the rice, return the chicken to the pan, and pour in about three-quarters of the stock. Add the bay leaves and saffron with its soaking water and bring to a boil. Simmer for 15 minutes, or until the rice is almost cooked, adding more stock as needed.

5 Stir in the chickpeas and golden raisins and continue cooking until the rice is tender. Transfer to a warmed serving platter and serve hot, sprinkled with the toasted nuts and chopped parsley.

CALORIES: 566kcals/2371kJ

CARBOHYDRATE: 66g
  sugar: 14g

FAT: 14g
  saturated: 2g

SALT: 1g

FIBER: 5g

Vegetable biryani

This tasty Indian dish is packed full of vegetables, and the cashew nuts add protein for vegetarians, too.

20–30 mins   40–45 mins

SERVES 4–6

14oz (400g) white basmati rice

salt and freshly ground black pepper

2 tbsp vegetable oil

1 large onion, finely chopped

1in (2.5cm) piece of fresh ginger, finely chopped

2 garlic cloves, finely chopped

1 tsp ground coriander

2 tsp ground cumin

1 tsp turmeric

½–1 tsp chile powder

3 cups vegetable stock (see p156)

2 sweet potatoes, finely chopped

7oz (200g) thin green beans, halved

7oz (200g) small cauliflower florets

1 tsp garam masala

juice of 1 lemon

handful of cilantro leaves, chopped

1¾oz (50g) unsalted cashew nuts

raita and poppadoms, to serve

1 Rinse the rice, then pour into a large pan of salted water, and cook according to the package instructions. Drain and set aside.

2 Meanwhile, heat the oil in a large pan over medium heat and cook the onion for 5 minutes. Add the ginger and garlic and cook for 2 minutes. Add the spices and cook for 1 minute, stirring.

3 Stir in the stock, season, and bring to a boil. Add the sweet potatoes, cover, and simmer for 10 minutes. Stir in the beans and cauliflower and cook for another 10 minutes.

4 Return the rice to heat through. Stir in the garam masala and lemon juice. Season to taste and stir in the cilantro and nuts. Serve with raita and poppadoms.

VARIATION

Instead of the sweet potatoes use 3 sliced carrots or ½ chopped butternut squash.

CALORIES: 621kcals/2598kJ

CARBOHYDRATE: 102g
    sugar: 10g

FAT: 13g
    saturated: 2g

SALT: 0.2g

FIBER: 7g

Vietnamese stir-fried ground pork and rice

Fresh mint leaves, sour lime, salty fish sauce, and a touch of sweetness make this stir-fry extremely tasty.

10 mins   15 mins

SERVES 4

3½oz (100g) thin green beans, chopped into ¾in (2cm) pieces

salt

3½oz (100g) small broccoli florets

3½oz (100g) sugarsnap peas, chopped into ¾in (2cm) pieces

4 tbsp sunflower or vegetable oil

1 tsp sesame oil

4 scallions, finely sliced

2 garlic cloves, finely chopped

1in (3cm) piece of fresh ginger, finely chopped

14oz (400g) ground pork

1¾lb (800g) cooked, cold white rice, such as basmati or jasmine

1 tbsp Thai fish sauce

juice of 1 lime, plus 1 extra lime, to serve

2 tbsp soy sauce

2 tbsp oyster sauce

1 tsp granulated sugar

2 tbsp finely chopped mint leaves

2 tbsp finely chopped cilantro leaves

1 Blanch the beans in boiling salted water for 1 minute, then add the broccoli and sugarsnap peas and blanch for another minute. Drain, refresh under cold water, then drain again.

2 In a wok, heat 2 tbsp of the sunflower oil and the sesame oil and cook the scallions, garlic, and ginger over high heat for 2 minutes. Add the pork and cook for 5 minutes, until brown, then remove from the wok. Wipe the wok with paper towels.

3 Heat the remaining sunflower oil and cook the green vegetables for 2 minutes. Return the pork.

4 Add the rice, fish sauce, lime juice, soy sauce, oyster sauce, and sugar, and cook for another 2 minutes until heated through. Stir in the herbs and serve with extra lime wedges to squeeze over.

CALORIES: 565kcals/2373kJ

CARBOHYDRATE: 59g
    sugar: 1.5g

FAT: 24g
    saturated: 6g

SALT: 0.9g

FIBER: 2g

Jambalaya

This one-pot meal captures the authentic Creole and Cajun flavors of Louisiana in the Deep South.

30 mins 45 mins

SPECIAL EQUIPMENT
large Dutch oven

SERVES 4–6

4 tbsp sunflower or vegetable oil

4 boneless, skinless chicken thighs, cut into bite-sized pieces

8oz (225g) mix of garlic and spicy sausages, (and smoked, if liked), cut into thick slices

1 onion, finely chopped

2 garlic cloves, finely chopped

1 red bell pepper, finely chopped

1 green bell pepper, finely chopped

1 celery stalk, thinly sliced

1 Scotch bonnet chile, seeded and chopped, or to taste

12oz (350g) long-grain white rice

1 tsp chile powder

1 tsp Worcestershire sauce

2 tbsp tomato paste

2 bay leaves

2 tsp dried thyme

1 tsp salt

½ tsp smoked paprika

pinch of sugar

freshly ground black pepper

1 x 14oz (400g) can chopped tomatoes

2 cups vegetable stock (see p156)

12 large raw shrimp, shelled and deveined

hot pepper sauce, to serve

1 Heat half the oil in a large Dutch oven over high heat. Cook the chicken for 10 minutes, or until the juices run clear. Set aside on paper towels.

2 Add the remaining oil to the pan and heat. Add the sausages, except the smoked sausages (if using), and cook, stirring, for 5 minutes, or until browned. Remove with a slotted spoon and set aside with the chicken.

3 Add the onion, garlic, peppers, celery, and chile to the pan and cook for 5 minutes, or until softened, stirring frequently. Add the rice and chile powder and cook, stirring, for 2 minutes. Add the Worcestershire sauce and tomato paste and cook, stirring, for another minute.

4 Return the chicken to the Dutch oven with all the sausages, including smoked (if using), the bay leaves, thyme, salt, paprika, and sugar, and season to taste with pepper. Pour in the tomatoes and the stock and bring to a boil, stirring. Reduce the heat to its lowest setting, cover, and simmer for 12–15 minutes, or until the peppers are tender.

5 Add the shrimp, cover, and simmer for 3 to 5 minutes, or until the shrimp are pink. The rice should be tender and the mixture a little soupy. Transfer to a warmed serving bowl and serve with hot pepper sauce.

CALORIES: 734kcals/3068kJ

CARBOHYDRATE: 78g
 sugar: 11g

FAT: 25g
 saturated: 6g

SALT: 2.6g

FIBER: 3.5g

The hard-working fridge

A hard-working, well-organized fridge can save you time as well as being more energy efficient, allowing cool air to circulate to keep food at the right temperature. It can be helpful to go through the fridge just before a supermarket trip, and throw out anything that is past its use-by-date, or make a mental note to use up anything that has been hanging around a little too long (these items can form the basis of your next few meals).To prevent germs multiplying, your fridge should be kept clean, and all food should be wrapped or stored in covered containers. When refrigerating leftovers, allow hot food to cool first.

What goes where

Storing things in designated spaces in your fridge means that you can see at a glance when you are running low of a staple item. Most modern fridges have special storage areas for cheese, eggs, and vegetables—using these frees up space for bulkier items. Fridges often have movable shelves, too. Try positioning these at different heights to optimize the space that you have. A small top shelf is ideal for shorter things like jars, for example.

Best chilled

Many items say "refrigerate after opening". Storing items such as ketchup, mustard, and jelly will prolong their shelf life and keep them tasting fresher for longer.

How to store

Ensure that items are accessible, visble, and not too crammed. The back of the fridge will be colder than the door, so plan carefully to make your food last longer.

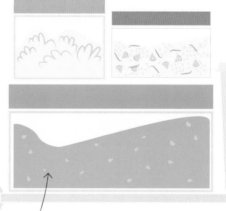
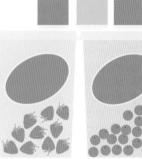
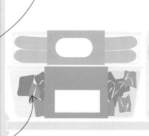

Leftovers Most leftovers will keep for 2-3 days in the fridge, providing they are well wrapped or stored in an airtight container. Delicate items such as shellfish and fish should be kept overnight only.

Meat Meat must always be carefully stored. For hygiene reasons you should try and store it separately from other foodstuffs, if not on its own shelf then at least in a designated area, well wrapped.

Vegetables Most vegetables are best stored in the large drawers at the bottom of the fridge. Keeping one side for the tougher root vegetables means that more delicate items such as lettuce can be protected from damage.

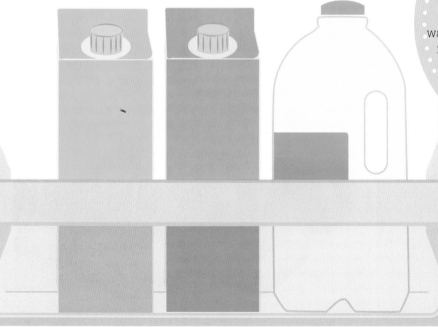

Essential fridge stock

⭐ Cheeses – a hard cheese (such as cheddar), a soft cheese (such as brie), feta, and parmesan

⭐ Butter – salted and unsalted for baking

⭐ Eggs – try using free range or organic, if possible

⭐ Yogurts – flavored, plain, and Greek yogurt

⭐ Creams – heavy cream and sour cream

⭐ Curry pastes

⭐ Good quality sauces – such as tartar, horseradish, and hollandaise

⭐ Mustards – English, Djon, and grain mustards

⭐ Good-quality mayonnaise

⭐ Prepared ginger, chile paste, and garlic in tubes or jars

Temperature check

The wrong temperature not only wastes energy, it can result in spoiled food. Use a fridge thermometer to make sure that the fridge stays between 37–41°F.

Inviting layout

Make the inside of the fridge look appealing to kids. Ensure that there's fresh, colorful fruit for snacking, so that when they're hungry, they head to the fridge rather than the cookie jar.

Zucchini and goat cheese omelet

The vibrant green of zucchini combines with the creamy white of goat cheese in this tasty omelet.

10 mins   5 mins

SERVES 1

3 large eggs, lightly beaten

1 small zucchini, grated

salt and freshly ground black pepper

pat of butter

1¾oz (50g) soft goat cheese, crumbled

small handful of thyme, leaves picked (optional)

1 Put the eggs and zucchini in a bowl. Season with salt and pepper. Melt the butter in a small, non-stick frying pan over medium-high heat until foaming, then pour in the egg mixture, swirling it around the pan to cover the bottom. Gently slide a rubber spatula under the edges.

2 When the omelet is beginning to cook around the edges, scatter in the goat cheese so that it is evenly covered. Continue cooking until the center is still just a little wet. Remove from the heat and leave for 2 minutes to set;

the heat of the pan will continue to cook the omelet. (Do not overcook it; you do not want it to be rubbery in texture.)

3 Evenly sprinkle in a little black pepper and scatter with the thyme leaves (if using). Carefully slide the omelet out of the pan (a rubber spatula will help with this) and serve immediately.

Try serving vegetables grated, well cooked, and disguised in a dish such as this. Omit the fresh thyme for fussy eaters, as it has a rather "grown-up" taste.

Fussy eaters!

CALORIES: 514kcals/2135kJ

CARBOHYDRATE: 2g
  sugar: 2g

FAT: 41g
  saturated: 20g

SALT: 1.6g

FIBER: 1g

Herby feta and spinach filo pie

Spinach works well with strong, sharp cheeses. In this Greek pie it is encased in crispy filo pastry with herbs.

30 mins   1 hr, plus cooling

SPECIAL EQUIPMENT
8in (20cm) round springform pan

SERVES 6

FOR THE FILLING

2lb (900g) spinach

7 tbsp butter, plus extra for greasing

2 onions, finely chopped

2 garlic cloves, finely chopped

4oz (120g) roasted peppers in oil, drained and chopped

handful of basil leaves, torn

3 tbsp chopped mint leaves

3 tbsp chopped parsley leaves

salt and freshly ground black pepper

10oz (300g) feta cheese, crumbled

FOR THE PASTRY

6 sheets store-bought filo pastry, 16 x 12in (40 x 30cm)

1 Pack the spinach into a large saucepan, cover, and cook, stirring occasionally, until just wilted. Drain well in a colander. Set aside, still draining, to cool.

2 Melt scant 1oz (25g) of the butter and cook the onions for 3 minutes. Add the garlic and cook for one minute. Stir in the peppers and herbs and set aside. Preheat the oven to 400°F (200°C). Grease and line an 8in (20cm) round springform pan.

3 Chop the spinach. Stir into the onion mixture and season. Melt the remaining butter. Brush the pan with butter. Cover with a sheet of pastry, leaving it overhanging, and brush with butter. Repeat to use all the pastry, arranging each sheet at an angle to the one beneath. Add half the onion mixture, the feta, then the remaining onion. Pull the overhanging pastry over the top, brushing with the last of the butter.

4 Place on a baking sheet. Bake for 35–40 minutes, until crisp. Leave for 10 minutes, then release from the pan. Serve hot or warm.

CALORIES: 438kcals/1814kJ

CARBOHYDRATE: 28g
  sugar: 8g

FAT: 28g
  saturated: 16g

SALT: 3.2g

FIBER: 5g

Broiled halloumi salad

Halloumi, a Cypriot sheep cheese, is delicious served warm. Work quickly, as it hardens on cooling.

10 mins, plus marinating   5-10 mins

SERVES 4 (as an appetizer)

9oz (250g) halloumi cheese with mint, cut into 8 slices

finely grated zest and juice of 1 lime

2 tbsp extra virgin olive oil

1 red chile, seeded and finely chopped (optional)

freshly ground black pepper

1¾oz (50g) pitted Kalamata olives

5½oz (150g) cherry tomatoes, halved

2 tbsp chopped cilantro leaves

2 tbsp chopped flat-leaf parsley leaves

¾oz (20g) toasted pine nuts

2¼oz (70g) arugula

4 pita breads, warmed, to serve

CALORIES: 305kcals/1270kJ
CARBOHYDRATE: 8g   sugar: 1.5g
FAT: 27g   saturated: 12g
SALT: 1.9g
FIBER: 1g

1 Place the sliced cheese in a single layer in a shallow dish. Evenly sprinkle over the lime zest and juice, oil, chile, and a good grinding of pepper and turn the cheese slices to coat them. Cover and set aside to marinate for 30 minutes at room temperature.

2 Meanwhile, place the remaining ingredients (except the pita bread) in a large bowl and toss to combine. Divide the salad between 4 plates. Preheat the broiler to its highest setting.

3 Line a baking sheet with foil. Using a slotted spoon, remove the cheese from the marinade (reserve the marinade) and place on the sheet. Broil for 3–5 minutes on each side, turning carefully, until golden brown. The cheese will not melt, but should soften slightly.

4 Place 2 slices of halloumi on top of each plate of salad. Drizzle the reserved marinade evenly over each portion, to act as a dressing, and serve with warmed pita bread.

Herby goat cheese spread

A simple spread to serve as an appetizer or dip, or even to make an interesting sandwich filling.

5 mins

SERVES 4–6

9oz (250g) soft goat cheese, at room temperature

9oz (250g) cream cheese, at room temperature

3 heaping tbsp finely chopped basil leaves

3 heaping tbsp finely chopped chives

finely grated zest of 1 lemon

salt and freshly ground black pepper

toasted baguette, to serve (optional)

1 Put the 2 cheeses in a large bowl and beat with a wooden spoon until any lumps have been removed and the mixture is completely smooth and evenly blended together.

2 Add the herbs and lemon zest and mix them in. Season well with pepper and a little salt (the goat cheese can be quite salty). Serve with toasted baguette (if using), or in a sandwich with roasted vegetables.

CLEVER WITH LEFTOVERS

Use this recipe as a guide to use up any soft cheese and herbs you may have, varying the taste with the addition of smoked paprika, pesto (see p194), or a handful of finely grated Parmesan cheese.

CALORIES: 474kcals/1960kJ
CARBOHYDRATE: 0.6g   sugar: 0.6g
FAT: 46g   saturated: 30g
SALT: 1.4g
FIBER: 0g

Herby baked feta with pita chips

A wonderfully simple appetizer or snack. Leave out the chile if you are feeding young children.

5 mins   20 mins

SERVES 4 (as an appetizer)

7oz (200g) package of feta cheese

1 tsp finely grated orange zest

1 tsp finely chopped red or green chile

1 tbsp finely chopped mint leaves

½ tbsp honey

3-4 tbsp olive oil

freshly ground black pepper

3 pita breads

1 Preheat the oven to 400°F (200°C). Put the cheese in a small ovenproof dish and sprinkle evenly with the zest, chile, and mint. Drizzle in the honey and 1 tbsp of the oil and season well with pepper (feta cheese is quite salty, so you shouldn't need any salt). Bake for 20 minutes until softened and golden brown.

2 Meanwhile, with a sharp knife, carefully pry and cut apart the 2 layers of each pita bread. Brush each side of the bread with a little of the oil, then pile them on top of each other. Use a large knife to cut them into irregular triangle-shaped pieces, each about 2in (5cm) large. Spread them out in 1 layer across 2 baking sheets and bake at the top of the oven for 5–7 minutes, turning once, until golden brown and crisp. Swap the positions of the baking sheets halfway, so each spends time at the top of the oven.

3 Use the pita chips to scoop up the baked feta while it is still hot (it will harden as it cools).

VARIATION

Serve the baked feta as a light lunch with a green salad and some fresh, crusty bread, instead of the pita chips.

CALORIES: 340kcals/1423kJ

CARBOHYDRATE: 29g
    sugar: 4g

FAT: 19g
    saturated: 8g

SALT: 2.5g

FIBER: 1g

Baked ricotta

Try this easy vegetarian dish as a light lunch, scooping it up with plenty of warm, crusty bread.

10 mins   30 mins

SPECIAL EQUIPMENT

4 x 5fl oz (150ml) ramekins

SERVES 4

vegetable oil, for greasing

1lb 2oz (500g) ricotta cheese, drained

1 large egg, beaten

1¾oz (50g) finely grated Parmesan cheese

3 tbsp thyme leaves

1 tbsp chopped rosemary leaves

salt and freshly ground black pepper

⅓ cup fresh white bread crumbs

breadsticks or crackers, to serve

1 Preheat the oven to 350°F (180°C). Brush four 5fl oz (150ml) ramekins with oil and place on a baking sheet.

2 Put the ricotta, egg, Parmesan, thyme, rosemary, and plenty of seasoning in a mixing bowl and beat well. Divide among the prepared ramekins.

3 Season the bread crumbs and sprinkle over the ricotta mixture. Bake in the oven for 30 minutes. Serve hot with breadsticks or crackers for dipping.

PREPARE AHEAD

These make a fantastic vegetarian lunch choice. They can be prepared ahead and stored in the fridge for up to 1 day. For best results, bring to room temperature before baking.

CALORIES: 271kcals/1131kJ

CARBOHYDRATE: 6g
    sugar: 2.5g

FAT: 19g
    saturated: 11g

SALT: 0.7g

FIBER: 0g

Mozzarella en carrozza

These Italian-style fried sandwiches are rich, crispy, and oozing with melted mozzarella.

15 mins   10–15 mins

SERVES 4

2 balls of mozzarella cheese, approx. 4½oz (125g) each, sliced

8 thick slices of white bread, crusts removed

¼ cup all-purpose flour

salt and freshly ground black pepper

2 large eggs

2 tbsp milk

2 tbsp olive oil

1 Carefully pat each of the mozzarella slices dry with paper towels; be gentle and try not to tear them. Arrange them evenly over 4 slices of the bread, leaving a ½in (1cm) gap all round the edges to act as a border.

2 Place the remaining slices of bread on top of the cheese and press the bread together all around the edges.

3 Put the flour on a plate and season well. Beat the eggs and milk in a shallow dish, large enough for a sandwich to fit in, and whisk together with a fork until well combined.

4 Heat half the oil in a large, non-stick frying pan over medium heat. Coat one of the sandwiches in the flour and then in the egg mixture. Add to the pan. Repeat with the second sandwich. Cook for 2–3 minutes on each side, turning once, until golden brown. Do not let them burn; reduce the heat slightly if they threaten to do so. Remove and keep warm.

5 Add the remaining oil to the pan and cook the last 2 sandwiches. Serve immediately.

CALORIES: 500kcals/2092kJ

CARBOHYDRATE: 48g
  sugar: 2.5g

FAT: 23g
  saturated: 11g

SALT: 1.8g

FIBER: 2.2g

VARIATION

Thinly spread each slice of bread with sundried tomato pesto and add a slice of prosciutto to 4 of the slices before topping with the mozzarella and remaining bread.

Brie and cranberry walnut toasts

This combination of nutty bread, tart cranberries, and oozing melted cheese is simply delicious.

5 mins   5 mins

SERVES 4 (as a snack)

8 slices of walnut bread

½ cup cranberry sauce

9oz (250g) soft, ripe Brie cheese, cut into thin slices

leafy green salad, to serve (optional)

1 Preheat the broiler to a medium-hot setting. Lay the slices of bread on a baking sheet or in the broiler pan and toast them under the broiler on each side until golden brown, making sure they don't burn. (Or toast the bread in a toaster.)

2 Spread each slice of toast evenly with 1 tbsp of cranberry sauce and cover evenly with the slices of Brie.

3 Put the toasts back under the broiler and cook for 2–3 minutes, or until the Brie is melted and bubbling. (You may have to do this in batches.) Serve as a snack or with a leafy green salad.

CLEVER WITH LEFTOVERS

This is a really great way to use up leftover cranberry sauce and cheeses after Christmas, when small, easy-to-prepare snacks come into their own.

CALORIES: 444kcals/1861kJ

CARBOHYDRATE: 39g
  sugar: 13g

FAT: 24g
  saturated: 12g

SALT: 1.7g

FIBER: 1.5g

Cheese croquettes

Inspired by a Spanish tapa, these croquettes are loved by children and adults alike. Try adding ham, if you like.

25 mins, plus chilling   20 mins

SERVES 4

3 tbsp butter

1½ cups all-purpose flour

1¼ cups whole milk

9oz (250g) coarsely grated manchego cheese

pinch of nutmeg

salt and freshly ground black pepper

2 large eggs, beaten

1 cup day-old white bread crumbs or panko crumbs

vegetable oil, for deep-frying

Tomato salsa (see p288), or ketchup, to serve

1 Line a baking sheet with parchment paper. Melt the butter in a small, non-stick pan over low heat. Whisk in ½ cup of the flour and cook for 2 minutes.

2 Take the pan off the heat and whisk in the milk a little at a time, whisking well between each addition, until the sauce is smooth.

3 Return to the heat and cook, stirring constantly, until it thickens. Reduce the heat to low and cook, stirring occasionally, for 5 minutes.

4 Add the cheese, nutmeg, and seasoning, remove from the heat, and stir until the cheese has melted. Cover and cool, then chill in the fridge for at least 1 hour.

5 Stir ½ cup more of the flour into the chilled mixture and divide it into 8 equal portions. Place the remaining ½ cup of flour, the eggs, and the bread crumbs in 3 shallow dishes, seasoning the flour well.

6 Using a spooon and your fingers, shape one portion of the mixture into a sausage shape. Coat in the flour, dip in the egg, then in the bread crumbs. Place on the baking sheet. Repeat to make 8. Cover and chill for 1 hour.

7 Heat the oil to 350°F (180°C) in a medium, heavy-bottomed pan. To check the temperature of the oil without a thermometer, add a cube of bread. It should turn golden after 1 minute. Cook the croquettes in 2 batches for 3 minutes or until golden. Transfer to a plate lined with paper towels. Serve with Tomato salsa (see p288) or ketchup.

VARIATION

To make the perfect classic cheese sauce, follow the method for making the croquettes base, but use ¼ cup of flour, 2 cups of milk, and 2½oz (75g) grated sharp Cheddar cheese. Omit the nutmeg, but season well.

CALORIES: 815kcals/3398kJ
CARBOHYDRATE: 49g
    sugar: 5g
FAT: 56g
    saturated: 25g
SALT: 1.7g
FIBER: 2.5g

Twice-baked cheese soufflés

A true soufflé can be nerve-wracking to serve at a dinner party, but twice-baked soufflés are a fail-safe alternative.

10 mins, plus chilling

40 mins

SPECIAL EQUIPMENT

4 x 5fl oz (150ml) ramekins or soufflé dishes

electric hand-held mixer

SERVES 4

2 tbsp butter, plus extra for greasing

2 tbsp all-purpose flour

¾ cup whole milk

½ tsp ground mustard

pinch of grated nutmeg

salt and freshly ground black pepper

2 large eggs, separated

1¾oz (50g) grated Gruyère cheese

2 tbsp finely grated Parmesan cheese

1 Preheat the oven to 350°F (180°C). Butter four 5fl oz (150ml) ramekins or soufflé dishes and place in a small baking dish.

2 Melt the butter in a small, non-stick pan over low heat. Whisk in the flour and cook for 2 minutes, whisking constantly, until the mixture bubbles.

3 Take the pan off the heat and whisk in the milk a little at a time, whisking well between each addition, until it has all been added and the sauce is smooth.

4 Return the pan to the heat and bring to a boil, then reduce the heat and simmer for 2 minutes to thicken, stirring constantly. Be sure to whisk right into the edges of the saucepan as this is where the sauce can burn.

5 Remove from the heat and add the ground mustard, nutmeg, seasoning, egg yolks, and Gruyère cheese. Stir well. Whisk the egg whites with an electric hand-held mixer until stiff, then carefully fold into the cheese mixture.

6 Divide between the ramekins. Pour a ¾in (2cm) depth of just-boiled water into the baking dish. Carefully transfer to the oven and bake for 20 minutes.

7 Remove from the oven and cool completely. Use a knife to loosen the soufflés from the ramekins, then invert onto a buttered heatproof dish. Chill.

8 Preheat the oven to 400°F (200°C). Sprinkle each soufflé with Parmesan and bake for 10 minutes. Serve immediately.

HOW TO FREEZE

After the first cooking at the end of step 6, cool, unmold, and open-freeze the soufflés, then transfer to a large freezer bag. When ready to serve, remove as many as you need, stand them separately on a plate or tray, cover, and defrost thoroughly in the fridge (not at room temperature). Cook the soufflés within 1 day.

CALORIES: 288kcals/1199kJ

CARBOHYDRATE: 10g
    sugar: 2.5g

FAT: 21g
    saturated: 12g

SALT: 0.8g

FIBER: 0.5g

Cheesy potato bake

The ultimate in comfort food and a great recipe for cold days. It is equally good on its own, or as a rich side dish.

20 mins   35 mins, plus resting

SPECIAL EQUIPMENT

8in (20cm) deep-sided, ovenproof dish

SERVES 4–6

1¾lb (800g) waxy or yellow potatoes, such as large Yukon Golds

salt and freshly ground black pepper

2 tbsp butter, plus extra for greasing

2 tbsp all-purpose flour

2 cups whole milk

4½oz (125g) grated sharp cheese, such as Cheddar

green salad, to serve

1 Preheat the oven to 375°F (190°C). Peel and slice the potatoes into ⅛–¼in (3–5mm) slices. Put them in a large pan of boiling salted water and return to a boil. Reduce to a gentle simmer and cook for 5 minutes until the slices are tender, but not breaking up. Drain well.

2 Meanwhile, make the cheese sauce. Melt the butter in a small, heavy-bottomed saucepan. Whisk in the flour over low heat. Continue to cook for 2 minutes, whisking constantly, until the mixture bubbles and separates.

3 Take the pan off the heat and slowly whisk in the milk, a little at a time, whisking well between each addition, until it has all been added and the sauce is smooth. Return to the heat and cook, stirring constantly, until it thickens. Continue to cook, stirring now and then, for 5 minutes. Be sure to whisk right into the edges of the saucepan as this is where the sauce can burn if left undisturbed.

4 Add 1¾oz (50g) of the cheese, season well, and cook for another 2 minutes until the cheese has melted and the sauce is smooth, thick, and creamy.

5 Rub the inside of an 8in (20cm) deep-sided, ovenproof dish with the butter. Layer one-third of the potato slices in the dish, then top with one-third of the sauce and one-third (scant 1oz/25g) of the remaining grated cheese. Repeat twice more, seasoning as you go. When you get to the last layer of potatoes, arrange the slices so that the dish will look attractive after it has been baked.

6 Put the dish on a large baking sheet and cook in the oven for 30 minutes, until the potatoes are soft when pierced with the tip of a knife and the top is golden brown and bubbling. Rest for 5 minutes before serving with a green salad.

CALORIES: 437kcals/1826kJ

CARBOHYDRATE: 38g
  sugar: 7g

FAT: 24g
  saturated: 15g

SALT: 0.9g

FIBER: 3.5g

Cheese and onion pie

Soft and sweet slow-cooked onions make the perfect foil for the buttery pastry and rich cheeses in this pie.

20 mins | 1 hr, plus resting

SERVES 4–6

1 tbsp olive oil

2 tbsp butter

2 garlic cloves, finely chopped

2 red onions, finely sliced

salt and freshly ground black pepper

2lb (900g) floury potatoes, such as Russets, peeled and cut into bite-sized chunks

5½oz (150g) grated mozzarella cheese

3½oz (100g) grated Emmental cheese

¼oz (40g) finely grated Parmesan cheese

2 x 7½oz (215g) sheets (8½ x 11in/ 22 x 28cm) store-bought puff pastry

1 large egg, beaten

mixed salad, to serve

1 Preheat the oven to 400°F (200°C). Line a baking sheet with parchment paper.

2 Heat the oil and butter in a large, non-stick frying pan over medium heat and gently cook the garlic and onions for 25 minutes, stirring occasionally, until softened and just beginning to be tinged with gold. They should be sweet and not too brown. If they seem to be browning too fast, reduce the heat to its lowest setting and cover the pan, so the onions sweat.

3 Meanwhile, bring a large pan of salted water to a boil, add the potatoes, and cook for 10 minutes, or until just tender to the point of a knife. Drain.

4 Add the cooked potatoes to the frying pan and cook over medium heat for 5 minutes, turning carefully halfway through. Remove the pan from the heat, season well, and stir in the cheeses.

5 Place one of the rectangles of pastry on the lined baking sheet. Spoon the filling into the center, leaving a ¾in (2cm) border around the edges. Brush the edges with water. Place the second pastry sheet over the filling and gently stretch it to cover the first sheet. Press the pastry sheets firmly together to seal. Brush with the egg and, using a sharp knife, make three 1½in (4cm) slashes in the top crust to allow the steam to escape.

6 Place on a baking sheet and bake for 20–25 minutes, or until browned. Remove from the oven and place the sheet on a wire rack to rest for 5 minutes. Serve hot, with a mixed salad.

VARIATION

For alternative fillings, you can try half Russets and half sweet potatoes, or half potato and half butternut squash.

HOW TO FREEZE

If you intend to freeze the pie, use chilled pastry, not pre-frozen, for the crust (you should not freeze pastry that has already been frozen). Assemble the pie and freeze at the end of step 5, omitting the egg glaze. Defrost, glaze, and follow step 6.

CLEVER WITH LEFTOVERS

If you have some odds and ends of different cheeses to use up, they can easily be part of this dish.

CALORIES: 622kcals/2596kJ

CARBOHYDRATE: 53g
  sugar: 4.5g

FAT: 36g
  saturated: 19g

SALT: 1.2g

FIBER: 3.5g

Cheesy soufflé omelet

This is an easy but impressive standby for a light supper or lunch dish. Serve with a green salad.

5 mins | 5-10 mins, plus resting

SPECIAL EQUIPMENT
10in (25cm) non-stick frying pan

SERVES 2

4 large eggs, separated

1 tbsp heavy cream

scant 1oz (25g) finely grated Parmesan cheese

salt and freshly ground black pepper

1 tbsp butter

1¾oz (50g) grated aged cheese, such as Cheddar (any sharp cheese will be good)

CALORIES: 449kcals/1864kJ	
CARBOHYDRATE: 0.3g	
sugar: 0.3g	
FAT: 38g	
saturated: 18g	
SALT: 1.3g	
FIBER: 0g	

1 Whisk the egg whites to soft peaks. In a separate bowl, whisk the cream and Parmesan into the egg yolks and season well. Fold in the egg whites gently until they are well combined.

2 Heat the butter in a 10in (25cm) non-stick frying pan. Add the egg mixture and cook over low heat for 5 minutes, until the sides have set, without moving it. Scatter the cheese over the omelet and carefully fold it in half.

3 Continue to cook for another couple of minutes, then turn it out onto a plate and rest it for a minute or two. The middle will continue to cook as it rests. Cut in half to serve.

COOK'S TIP

Any simple omelet can be made to look far more substantial simply by separating the eggs and whisking the whites. Fold them in gently, without knocking out the air, for a fluffy, voluminous omelet.

Spanish tortilla

Slices of these thick omelets are served in bars all over Spain. They are best eaten at room temperature.

10 mins | 40 mins, plus cooling

SPECIAL EQUIPMENT
8in (20cm) non-stick frying pan

SERVES 4

3 tbsp olive oil

1 large Spanish onion, finely chopped

4 large eggs

9oz (250g) cooked, cooled new potatoes, cut into ½in (1cm) cubes

salt and freshly ground black pepper

CALORIES: 222kcals/925kJ	
CARBOHYDRATE: 13g	
sugar: 3g	
FAT: 15g	
saturated: 3g	
SALT: 0.2g	
FIBER: 2g	

1 Heat 2 tbsp of the oil in an 8in (20cm) non-stick frying pan. Cook the onion over low heat for 10 minutes, until softened. Set aside. Wipe the pan with paper towels.

2 Beat the eggs in a large bowl. Add the onions and potatoes and season well, stirring gently.

3 Heat the remaining oil in the pan. Pour in the egg mixture and cook over low heat for 20 minutes, covered, until the edges start to pull away from the pan. The middle will not be cooked.

4 Loosen the tortilla with a spatula and put a plate on top. Turn the tortilla onto the plate. Slide it back into the pan, uncooked-side down, and cook for 10 minutes over low heat, or until cooked through. Serve at room temperature.

VARIATION

Although not strictly authentic, it is fun to add other ingredients to a tortilla. Try roasted peppers from a jar, drained, olives, or whole roasted garlic cloves.

Ham and cheese family omelet

When you need a quick meal and don't want to cook individual omelets, try this easy family recipe.

5 mins   5–10 mins

SPECIAL EQUIPMENT

10in (25cm) heavy-bottomed, ovenproof frying pan

SERVES 4

6 large eggs

1 tbsp heavy cream

salt and freshly ground black pepper

1 tbsp butter

1¾oz (50g) ham, chopped

2½oz (75g) grated cheese, such as Cheddar or Monterey Jack

CALORIES: 272kcals/1129kJ
CARBOHYDRATE: 0.2g
  sugar: 0.2g
FAT: 22g
  saturated: 10g
SALT: 1g
FIBER: 0g

---

1 Preheat the broiler to its highest setting. Beat the eggs and cream in a bowl and season well.

2 Heat the butter in a 10in (25cm) heavy-bottomed, ovenproof frying pan over medium heat. When it is bubbling, pour in the egg mixture. Cook the omelet over medium heat for 2–3 minutes, moving it gently with a spatula.

3 When the edges of the omelet start to set, take it off the heat. Scatter in the ham and cheese.

4 Transfer the pan to the broiler and cook for 2–3 minutes until the top has set and is golden brown. Cut into wedges to serve.

CLEVER WITH LEFTOVERS

Some odds and ends of cheese and a few slices of ham can be turned into a quick family lunch using this easy recipe. Add leftover boiled potatoes, fried until crispy, to make it more substantial.

Pancetta and pea frittata

A frittata is basically a broiled omelet, and a mainstay of Italian family cooking. This one makes a great lunch.

10 mins   15 mins, plus resting

SPECIAL EQUIPMENT

10in (25cm) heavy-bottomed, ovenproof frying pan

SERVES 4–6

1 tbsp olive oil

3½oz (100g) chopped pancetta

6 large eggs

1 tbsp heavy cream

scant 1oz (25g) finely grated Parmesan cheese

salt and freshly ground black pepper

3½oz (100g) frozen peas

1 tbsp butter

CALORIES: 318kcals/1318kJ
CARBOHYDRATE: 3g
  sugar: 0.7g
FAT: 26g
  saturated: 10g
SALT: 1.3g
FIBER: 2g

---

1 Heat the oil in a 10in (25cm) heavy-bottomed, ovenproof frying pan. Cook the pancetta for 3–5 minutes until it starts to brown at the edges. Transfer to a plate. Wipe the pan with paper towels. Preheat the broiler to its highest setting.

2 Whisk together the eggs, cream, and Parmesan and season well (go easy on the salt, as the Parmesan and pancetta are salty). Add the peas (they will cook in the frittata) and pancetta, and mix well.

3 Melt the butter in the frying pan over medium heat and pour in the egg mixture. Cook for 5 minutes, without moving it, until the edges start to set.

4 Transfer the pan to the broiler and cook for 5 minutes until the frittata is set and golden brown. Rest for at least 5 minutes. Cut into wedges and serve warm or at room temperature.

Easy entertaining

Easy entertaining

Whether it's a Sunday lunch with extended family, dinner with friends, or a children's birthday party, there are times when you want to do something a little special. What you cook will depend on the occasion but also on the season, the number of guests, and the time you have available. If you're hosting a large gathering, for example, try to serve dishes that can be prepared ahead, so you have more time to spend with your guests.

Rally the troops

A large part of entertaining is the serving and clearing of the meal, as well as the preparation. If you are planning a big gathering, try to ensure that some of your nearest and dearest (family, friends, or children) are happy to help in some way so that everything doesn't fall to you. Give each person a specific job beforehand, and make sure the work is distributed evenly and appropriately, so no one feels over-burdened and everyone is able to fulfill their role. Even small children can pass around appetizers or snacks—if you don't mind a few of them disappearing along the way!

Something for everyone

Family gatherings will often include everyone from toddlers to grandparents, so you'll need to serve a selection of dishes that will cater to all tastes. A platter of child-friendly bites such as Chicken patties (p56), carrot and cucumber sticks, and some

Texas-style barbecue spare ribs (p280) are ideal for entertaining friends in the summer. Serve with Barbecued corn-on-the cob (p287) on the side, some tasty salsas, and plenty of green salad.

Pumpkin and cinnamon waffles (p265) make a mouthwatering weekend brunch. Served warm with maple syrup and apple slices they are an appealing and indulgent treat for guests.

cut-up grapes and strawberries, should keep the under-fives happy at a get-together. Find out, too, if any of your guests have food allergies or specific dietary requirements so that you can provide something they can eat. Avoid serving any dishes that contain raw eggs, for example, to pregnant women.

Planning the menu

Choose light but tasty starters to whet the appetite, perhaps some Home-cured gravlax (p309) or, if you're having a barbecue Lemongrass-marinated shrimp skewers (p274), followed by a main course that makes a good centerpiece. For special occasions Boeuf en croute (p318) or a Roast turkey with all the trimmings (p314 and pp316-7) will make a splash. For a Sunday supper there are favorites such as Crispy pork belly with applesauce (p299), or spice things up with Chinese roast duck pancakes (p321) that people can assemble themselves. If you want a vegetarian main course, try an impressive Mediterranean vegetable and goat cheese timbale (p305) or make a casserole without the meat.

Cooking for a crowd

If the weather is good and you choose to barbecue, you can prepare a variety of meat, vegetarian, and side dishes to suit all palates, and which your guests can mix and match for themselves. In winter, casseroles, one-pots, or a large roast might fit the bill. When you are feeding a crowd, select more economical cuts of meat, such as a whole pork shoulder, and cook it long and slow to bring out its full flavor. Try Slow-cooked shoulder of pork with cider gravy, p301. If you opt to provide a buffet for your guests, be sure to include vegetarian options such as Individual mushroom and leek pies (p304) and hold these back especially to serve to your vegetarian guests.

Knock-out desserts

Some easy-to-prepare desserts are real crowd pleasers. A pavlova (Strawberry pavlova, p345) can be made as large as you need it to be. Prepare the fruit and whip the cream then the whole thing can be assembled at the last minute. Homemade ice creams, such as Quick banana ice cream (p328), served in cones will please most guests on a hot summer's day. A fruity crumble such as Berry and banana crumble (p350) is perfect on a cold winter's day, or you could pile up Raspberry cream meringues (p484) for an impressive display on a buffet table.

Strawberry pavlova (p345) is a perennial favorite that can be topped with seasonal fruits at any time of the year. It makes a fine centerpiece and can be quickly put together on the day.

Entertaining with children

While meeting up with friends and family is great fun for adults, grown-up conversation over a lingering lunch isn't always the way children want to spend their day. To make sure that everyone enjoys the event, spend a little time thinking about what might keep the little ones out of trouble while you catch up with friends.

Get them involved

Getting children to design and draw table place cards and write people's names on them before the party is a good way to get them excited and help them feel involved.

Give them their own table

A children's table can be a good idea—but set it up like the adults' one so they don't feel left out. They can eat at their own pace, although you will need to keep checking on them. Make the table fun by covering it with white paper and distributing crayons to the younger guests, so they can draw and color their own tablecloth.

Timing

Be aware that younger children need to eat earlier than adults, they may like different things, and will often finish their meal much sooner too. Catering to their tastes and timing will give your adult guests a more enjoyable time.

Stay spill free

It may not be elegant, but serving juice boxes to small children instead of drinks in glasses makes sense, especially as they often end up walking around with them.

Keep them busy

Have a plan for what to do with the kids once they have finished eating. Provide a selection of games and toys for younger children, or ask an older child to lead some games or perhaps do a bit of babysitting so that the children are happily occupied for a little longer.

Get the kids to help make this colorful Rainbow popcorn (p367) to serve when the guests arrive.

Eggs Benedict with smoked salmon

Follow the advice on partially-cooked eggs (see p11) when feeding pregnant women.

10 mins   5 mins

SPECIAL EQUIPMENT
blender

SERVES 2

FOR THE HOLLANDAISE SAUCE
7 tbsp unsalted butter
1 large egg yolk
½ tbsp lemon juice
salt and freshly ground black pepper

FOR THE REST
4 large eggs
2–4 English muffins
5½oz (150g) smoked salmon

CALORIES: 913kcals/3826kJ
CARBOHYDRATE: 29g
  sugar: 2.5g
FAT: 70g
  saturated: 34g
SALT: 3.6g
FIBER: 2g

1 To make the sauce, melt the butter over low heat, making sure it does not split. Put the egg yolk, lemon juice, and seasoning into a blender and blend briefly. With the motor running, pour in the melted butter drop by drop, accelerating to a thin stream, until it has emulsified to a thick sauce. Serve it as soon as possible.

2 Meanwhile, boil a large pan of salted water, then reduce the heat to a low simmer. Crack an egg into a teacup and gently slide into the bubbling water. Repeat for all the eggs. Poach for 3 minutes, until the white is set but the yolk is still runny. Remove with a slotted spoon.

3 At the same time, toast the muffins. If you like thick muffins use 4, cutting a thin slice off each one to add the egg, otherwise split 2 muffins horizontally to make 4 halves. When they are toasted, divide the salmon between them and top each with a poached egg and a little hollandaise sauce.

Eggs Benedict with crispy bacon

Try this version of Eggs Benedict with salty, crisp bacon and crunchy walnut bread.

10 mins   5 mins

SPECIAL EQUIPMENT
blender

SERVES 2

FOR THE HOLLANDAISE SAUCE
7 tbsp unsalted butter
1 large egg yolk
½ tbsp lemon juice
salt and freshly ground black pepper

FOR THE REST
6 slices thick-cut bacon
4 large eggs
4 thick slices of walnut bread, or
  multigrain bread, crusts removed

CALORIES: 934kcals/3913kJ
CARBOHYDRATE: 37g
  sugar: 2g
FAT: 73g
  saturated: 36g
SALT: 3.1g
FIBER: 1.5g

1 Make the hollandaise sauce as for Eggs Benedict with smoked salmon (see left).

2 Meanwhile, preheat the broiler to its highest setting. Cut each bacon slice in half horizontally, to make 12 short slices, and broil until crisp. Keep warm.

3 Next, poach the eggs. Boil a large pan of salted water and reduce the heat to a low simmer. Crack an egg into a teacup and gently slide into the bubbling water. Repeat for all the eggs. Poach for 3 minutes, until the white is set but the yolk is still runny. Remove with a slotted spoon.

4 Meanwhile, toast the bread. Top each piece with 3 half slices of crispy bacon, a poached egg, and a little hollandaise sauce.

PREPARE AHEAD

You could broil the bacon 1 day in advance and reheat it in a microwave until it sizzles.

Huevos rancheros

A classic Mexican dish of "ranch-style eggs" makes a substantial breakfast with a fabulous chile kick.

20 mins   50 mins

SERVES 4

6 tbsp olive oil

1 onion, finely chopped

2 garlic cloves, crushed

2 dried chiles, finely chopped

1 scant tsp smoked paprika

1 x 14oz (400g) can chopped tomatoes

½ tsp granulated sugar

1 tbsp chopped flat-leaf parsley leaves

salt and freshly ground black pepper

10oz (300g) cooked new potatoes, cut into ¾in (2cm) cubes

7oz (200g) spicy chorizo, casing removed, cut into ¾in (2cm) cubes

4 large eggs

2 tbsp chopped cilantro leaves

CALORIES: 452kcals/1881kJ

CARBOHYDRATE: 21g
  sugar: 6g

FAT: 32g
  saturated: 8g

SALT: 1g

FIBER: 3g

1 Heat 4 tbsp of the oil in a small saucepan. Add the onion and cook over medium heat for 5 minutes until softened. Add the garlic, chiles, and paprika and cook for one minute. Add the tomatoes, sugar, and parsley and bring to a boil. Season, reduce the heat, and simmer for 30 minutes. Set aside.

2 In a large, heavy-bottomed frying pan, heat the remaining 2 tbsp of oil over medium heat. Cook the potatoes for 5 minutes, add the chorizo, and cook for 5 minutes.

3 Remove the pan from the heat and stir in the tomato salsa. Make 4 large holes in the mixture and crack the eggs into the holes. Return to the heat and cook for 5 minutes. Sprinkle with the cilantro and serve from the pan.

PREPARE AHEAD

This recipe can be made in advance up to the point you put the eggs into the mixture. Cover and chill the cooked chorizo and tomato base overnight in the fridge, then add the eggs in the morning and cook for a quick, tasty breakfast treat.

Eggs Florentine

A great vegetarian option; make sure you drain the spinach before serving to keep the toast dry.

15 mins   5 mins

SPECIAL EQUIPMENT
blender

SERVES 2

FOR THE HOLLANDAISE SAUCE

14 tbsp unsalted butter, plus 1 tbsp extra for the spinach

2 large egg yolks

¾–1 tbsp lemon juice, to taste

salt and freshly ground black pepper

FOR THE REST

9oz (250g) baby spinach leaves

4 large eggs

4 thick slices of whole wheat bread, crusts removed

CALORIES: 1169kcals/4894kJ

CARBOHYDRATE: 31g
  sugar: 4g

FAT: 104g
  saturated: 59g

SALT: 1.6g

FIBER: 5.3g

1 Make the sauce as for Eggs Benedict with smoked salmon (see far left), adding lemon to taste.

2 Next, cook the spinach. Heat the extra 1 tbsp of butter in a large saucepan and add the spinach. Season it well and cook for a minute or two, stirring frequently, until it wilts completely. Drain well, squeezing out excess water, then return to the pan, mix in 2 tbsp of the hollandaise sauce, and put the lid on to keep it warm.

3 Next, poach the eggs. Boil a large pan of salted water and reduce the heat to a low simmer. Crack an egg into a teacup and gently slide into the bubbling water. Repeat for all the eggs. Poach gently for 3 minutes, until the white is set but the yolk still runny. Remove with a slotted spoon.

4 Meanwhile, toast the slices of bread. When they are toasted, top each piece with a spoonful of creamy spinach, a poached egg, and a little hollandaise sauce.

Croque-madame

A once-in-a-while treat, this is the ultimate ham and cheese sandwich—try it and see.

10 mins · 10 mins

SERVES 4

2 tbsp butter, plus extra for the bread

8 slices of good-quality white bread

7oz (200g) grated Gruyère cheese

1 tbsp Dijon mustard (optional)

salt and freshly ground black pepper

4 thick slices of good-quality ham, or 5½oz (150g) thinly sliced ham

1 tbsp sunflower or vegetable oil

4 small eggs

1 Butter each slice of bread on both sides. Set aside 1¾oz (50g) of the cheese. Make sandwiches by spreading 4 slices of bread with a little mustard, (if using), then a layer of grated cheese, firmly pressed down. Season well, then add a piece of ham, another layer of cheese, and a second piece of bread.

2 Melt the 2 tbsp of butter in a large, non-stick frying pan and cook 2 sandwiches carefully over medium heat for 2–3 minutes each side, pressing them gently with a spatula, until golden brown. Keep warm while you cook the remaining 2 sandwiches. Wipe the pan with paper towels.

3 Preheat the broiler to its highest setting. Place the cooked sandwiches on a baking sheet and top each with one-quarter of the reserved grated cheese. Broil until the cheese has melted and is bubbling.

4 Meanwhile, heat the sunflower oil in the frying pan and cook the eggs how you like them. Top each sandwich with a fried egg and serve with a pile of shoestring fries.

VARIATION

A classic croque-madame uses béchamel sauce in place of the melted cheese on top of the sandwich. Make a little classic cheese sauce (see p244), and try grilling 1–2 tbsp on top of each sandwich instead of the grated cheese.

CALORIES: 555kcals/2319kJ
CARBOHYDRATE: 31g
  sugar: 2.9g
FAT: 34g
  saturated: 17g
SALT: 3.3g
FIBER: 1.8g

Cheesy scrambled eggs on English muffins

Turn simple scrambled eggs into an attractive brunch dish with melting cheese, herbs, and toasted muffins.

5 mins · 5 mins

SERVES 4

8 large eggs

¼ cup heavy cream

salt and freshly ground black pepper

4 English muffins

4 tbsp butter

3½oz (100g) finely grated Gruyère cheese

2 tbsp finely chopped chives, plus extra to serve (optional)

1 Whisk the eggs and cream together, then season well. Slice the muffins in half and toast. Melt the butter in a non-stick frying pan.

2 When the butter has melted, pour the egg mixture into the pan. Cook gently for a minute or two, moving it around slowly with a wooden spoon. Scatter the cheese and chives on top and continue to cook until the eggs are soft and just set and the cheese has melted.

3 Pile the cheesy scrambled eggs on the toasted muffins and serve with chives sprinkled over (if using).

VARIATION

If your family eats meat, cook chopped bacon in the pan before adding the egg mixture for a new twist on eggs and bacon.

CALORIES: 599kcals/2499kJ
CARBOHYDRATE: 29g
  sugar: 2.6g
FAT: 41g
  saturated: 21g
SALT: 1.8g
FIBER: 2g

Banana and oatbran muffins

These muffins are a tasty and healthy choice for a late leisurely brunch; delicious eaten when they're still warm.

20 mins | 20 mins

SPECIAL EQUIPMENT

12 paper muffin liners and/or
12-hole muffin pan

electric hand-held mixer

MAKES 12

8 tbsp butter, softened, plus extra
for greasing (if using a pan)

1¼ cups all-purpose flour

1 tsp baking soda

1 tsp baking powder

1 tsp ground cinnamon

¾ cup oatbran

1¾oz (50g) chopped walnuts (optional)

½ cup brown sugar

2 large eggs, lightly beaten

3 ripe bananas, mashed

½ cup whole milk

1 Preheat the oven to 375°F (190°C). Place 12 paper muffin liners in a 12-hole muffin pan, or simply place the liners on a baking sheet, or grease a 12-hole muffin pan with butter.

2 Sift the flour, baking soda, baking powder, cinnamon, and oatbran into a large bowl. Pour in any bran left in the sieve. Add the walnuts (if using). Stir well.

3 Place the butter and brown sugar in a separate mixing bowl and cream together, using an electric hand-held mixer, until very light and fluffy. (This could take as much as 5 minutes, so be patient!) Add the eggs and mix well. Stir in the bananas and milk.

4 Pour the wet mixture into the dry and stir to combine. Do not over-mix or the muffins will be heavy. Divide the mixture between the paper liners or muffin pan holes.

5 Bake for 20 minutes (start checking after 15), or until a toothpick inserted into a muffin comes out clean. Transfer to a wire rack to cool.

HOW TO FREEZE

As soon as the muffins have cooled, open-freeze them on a baking sheet. When they are frozen solid (after about 3 hours), transfer them to a large freezer bag and seal. This way you can remove and defrost only as many as you need, and they won't turn stale.

CALORIES: 192kcals/811kJ

CARBOHYDRATE: 29g
 sugar: 14g

FAT: 6g
 saturated: 1.5g

SALT: 0.4g

FIBER: 2g

Cinnamon rolls

Let these rolls proof overnight in the fridge so they are ready to bake in time for a brunch treat.

40 mins, plus proving 25-30 mins

SPECIAL EQUIPMENT
12in (30cm) springform cake pan

MAKES 10-12

½ cup whole milk

7 tbsp unsalted butter, plus extra for greasing

2 tsp dried yeast

¼ cup granulated sugar

3¾ cups all-purpose flour, sifted, plus extra for dusting

1 tsp salt

1 large egg, plus 2 large egg yolks

vegetable oil, for greasing

FOR THE FILLING AND GLAZE

2 tbsp ground cinnamon

½ cup light brown sugar

2 tbsp unsalted butter, melted

1 large egg, lightly beaten

¼ cup granulated sugar

1 In a pan, heat ½ cup of water, the milk, and butter until melted. Let it cool to just warm, then whisk in the yeast and 1 tbsp of the sugar. Cover for 10 minutes.

2 Place the flour, salt, and remaining sugar in a large bowl. Make a well in the center of the dry ingredients and pour in the warm milk mixture. Whisk the egg and egg yolks and add to the mixture. Combine to form a rough dough. Place on a floured surface and knead for 10 minutes. Add extra flour if it's too sticky.

3 Put in an oiled bowl, cover with plastic wrap, and keep in a warm place for 2 hours until well risen. Meanwhile, prepare the filling by mixing the cinnamon with the brown sugar.

4 When the dough has risen, turn it out onto a floured work surface and gently knock it back. Roll it out into a rectangle, measuring about 16 x 12in (40 x 30cm). Brush with

the melted butter. Scatter with the filling, leaving a ½in (1cm) border on one long side. Brush this with the egg.

5 Press the filling with the palm of your hand to ensure it sticks to the dough. Roll the dough up, working toward the egg-brushed border. Do not roll too tightly.

6 Cut into 10–12 equal pieces with a serrated knife, being careful not to squash the rolls. Grease and line a 12in (30cm) springform cake pan. Pack in the rolls, cut-sides up. Cover and proof for 1–2 hours until well risen.

7 Preheat the oven to 350°F (180°C). Brush with egg and bake for 25–30 minutes. Heat 3 tbsp of water with the sugar for the glaze until sugar has dissolved. Brush on the rolls and let cool for at least 15 minutes before serving.

HOW TO FREEZE
You can open-freeze the rolls when just baked, then transfer to a large freezer bag. This way you can defrost only as many as you need each time. You can also freeze the uncooked rolled dough at the end of step 5.

CALORIES: 400kcals/1685kJ

CARBOHYDRATE: 60g
 sugar: 22g

FAT: 14g
 saturated: 8g

SALT: 0.5g

FIBER: 2.5g

Buttermilk biscuits

These biscuits are a staple served at breakfast with bacon, sausage, or scrambled eggs.

10 mins   10–12 mins

SPECIAL EQUIPMENT
food processor (optional)

2¾in (7cm) round biscuit cutter

MAKES 6

1⅔ cups self-rising flour, sifted, plus extra for dusting

2 tsp baking powder

½ tsp fine salt

8 tbsp butter, chilled and cut into cubes

¾ cup buttermilk

1 large egg, lightly beaten

1 Preheat the oven to 450°F (230°C). In a large bowl, or the bowl of a food processor, mix together the flour, baking powder, and salt. Add the butter and rub it in, or pulse-blend, until the mixture resembles fine bread crumbs.

2 Make a well in the center of the flour mixture and stir in the buttermilk. You will need to use your hands to bring the dough together. Gently knead the mixture on a floured work surface to form a soft dough.

3 Gently roll the dough out to a thickness of 1in (3cm). Cut rounds out of the dough with a 2¾in (7cm) biscuit cutter. Gently bring the dough back together and re-roll it to cut out as many as possible.

4 Brush each biscuit with a little of the egg. Bake in the top of the oven for 10–12 minutes, until they have risen and are golden brown.

COOK'S TIP

The secret to light, fluffy biscuits is to handle the dough as little as possible, so cut them out close together to minimize the need to re-roll. Also, cut straight down with the biscuit cutter when you cut the biscuits out. If you twist the cutter as you work the dough, the edges of the biscuits will become compressed, stick together, and rise unevenly.

HOW TO FREEZE

Open-freeze the biscuits on a baking sheet the moment they are cool. When frozen solid, transfer to a freezer bag. This way you can defrost only as many as you need each time, and they won't turn stale.

CALORIES: 318kcals/1336kJ

CARBOHYDRATE: 37g
  sugar: 2g

FAT: 16g
  saturated: 9g

SALT: 1.5g

FIBER: 2g

Cooking for allergies

If your child has an allergy, follow to the letter the specific advice given by your doctor, who will have detailed guidance about what to avoid and how to cater for your child safely. Whether or not your own child has an allergy, sooner or later your child will have a playdate or throw a party with a friend who has some kind of food allergy. The most common childhood allergies are often to wheat, dairy, eggs, or nuts. Ideally, the parent of a child with an allergy should inform you in advance of what they cannot eat, along with some easy advice as to how to cook for them. Also, if the child has allergy medication, don't forget to get this from their parent, with instructions on how to use it.

What to cook

This will very much depend on the severity of the child's allergy. Sometimes excluding a certain food from your guest's plate will be enough. At other times it will be easier, and safer, if you avoid serving anyone any foods containing the allergen during the visit. However, some small children who have an allergy to uncooked or undercooked egg whites can easily consume items such as cakes, which contain eggs that have been well cooked. In this case, double check with their parent first.

Allergen-free kitchens

Depending on the severity of your guest's allergy, kitchen hygiene can play a part in ensuring a healthy and happy playdate. Be sure to use knives and boards fresh from the dishwasher, and avoid preparing any foods with the allergen in it using the same equipment. Try not to serve packaged or processed foods, if possible, and if you do serve them do so only after you have carefully read through the list of ingredients on the label.

Common allergens

Once you know what your guest is allergic to, take time to find out which food products contain that ingredient. Always read the label carefully because sometimes these allergens can be found in the most surprising things.

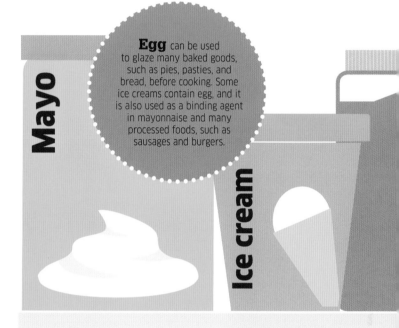

Egg can be used to glaze many baked goods, such as pies, pasties, and bread, before cooking. Some ice creams contain egg, and it is also used as a binding agent in mayonnaise and many processed foods, such as sausages and burgers.

Milk may well be in cheese, butter, margarine, cream, yogurt, and ice cream, but it can also appear in some more surprising products. Check foodstuffs made using milk or milk powder, such as chocolate, cakes, cookies, soups, and even sausages.

Peanuts are classified as a legume and do not come under the same grouping as tree nuts. Peanuts can produce some of the most severe reactions in an allergic child, so it is wise to be especially cautious when buying pre-packaged food. Always check the label carefully and if in doubt, leave it out.

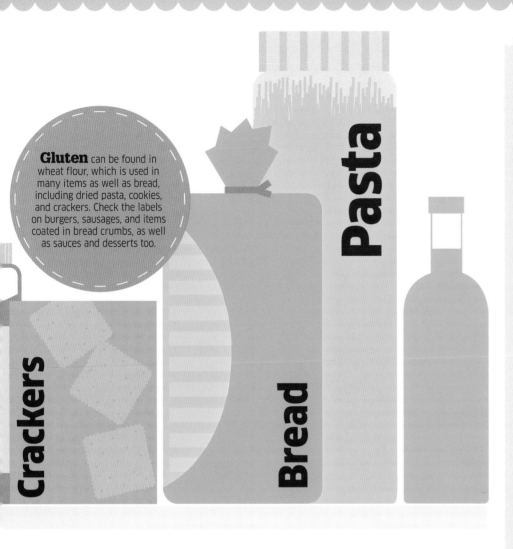

Gluten can be found in wheat flour, which is used in many items as well as bread, including dried pasta, cookies, and crackers. Check the labels on burgers, sausages, and items coated in bread crumbs, as well as sauces and desserts too.

Crackers

Pasta

Bread

Common substitutes

⭐ **Gluten** These days there are many specially produced wheat-free items to buy, from cookies and cakes to bread and pasta. However, don't forget to consider simple things such as oats and rice as a natural substitute if you can't get ahold of these products.

⭐ **Milk** Many children who are allergic to dairy products, or cows' milk, can happily consume goats' milk, soy milk, or even almond milk. Remember, too, that many delicious cheeses are made from sheeps' milk.

⭐ **Eggs** These can be easily avoided when served just as plain eggs, but they are present in cakes, cookies, and pastries. Eggs are used in baking to add air and moisture, so for best results look for egg-free recipes that use ingredients that produce equivalent effects, such as baking powder and milk or yogurt.

⭐ **Peanuts** These are also fairly easy to avoid in their simple state, and there are some good substitutes available. Health food stores sell many nut butters, such as almond, cashew, or macadamia. If the child is allergic to tree nuts, it's probably best to avoid peanuts, too.

Cereal

Tree nuts is a common food allergy in both children and adults and can cause severe allergic reactions. Many cakes and cookies may contain nuts, and some products produced in the same factory may have trace elements that can trigger a reaction.

Pesto includes pine nuts so avoid this if your guest is allergic to tree nuts.

Pesto

Read food labels

Read the labels on foodstuffs very carefully and check with a reputable website so that you know exactly which ingredients you are looking for, for each allergy. Some labels also specify allergens in the "contains" line.

Chicken satay with peanut sauce

This traditional Malaysian street food is incredibly addictive. Leave out the chile if making it for children.

15 mins, plus marinating   10 mins

SPECIAL EQUIPMENT
blender
8 bamboo skewers

SERVES 4

12oz (350g) boneless, skinless chicken breast, finely sliced

lime wedges, to serve

FOR THE MARINADE

1 stalk lemongrass, peeled of hard layers and finely chopped

2 scallions, white part only, roughly chopped

¾in (2cm) fresh ginger, roughly chopped

1 garlic clove, roughly chopped

½ tsp turmeric

1 tbsp light brown sugar

2 tbsp soy sauce

½ tbsp fish sauce

1 tbsp sunflower or vegetable oil

FOR THE PEANUT SAUCE

⅔ cup crunchy peanut butter

½ cup coconut milk

1 tbsp sweet chili sauce

1 tbsp soy sauce

1 tbsp fish sauce

1 tsp chile flakes (optional)

juice of ½ lime

1 Purée the marinade ingredients in a blender to a paste. Pour over the chicken and toss. Leave for 1 hour. Soak 8 bamboo skewers. Prepare the grill for cooking.

2 Meanwhile, put the ingredients for the sauce in a pan and stir over low heat until it loosens.

3 Thread the chicken onto the skewers, folding each piece of meat if necessary. Grill on a hot barbecue for 2–3 minutes on each side, until crispy. Serve with the sauce and lime wedges.

COOK IN THE OVEN
Preheat the broiler to its highest setting and line a broiler pan with foil. Broil the chicken for 2-3 minutes on each side.

HOW TO FREEZE
The uncooked, marinated chicken can be frozen for up to 3 months. Defrost thoroughly before cooking the recipe from the start of step 2.

CALORIES: 422kcals/1759kJ

CARBOHYDRATE: 12g
    sugar: 9g

FAT: 27g
    saturated: 9g

SALT: 3.7g

FIBER: 0g

Lemongrass-marinated shrimp skewers

Serve these alongside Chicken satay skewers (see left) for an Asian-inspired family feast.

15 mins, plus marinating   10 mins

SPECIAL EQUIPMENT
blender or food processor
8 bamboo skewers

SERVES 4

2 garlic cloves, roughly chopped

½ red chile, seeded and roughly chopped

2 lemongrass stalks, bottom (thickest) one-third only, peeled of hard layers and roughly chopped

1in (3cm) fresh ginger, finely chopped

1 tbsp chopped cilantro roots or stalks

2 tbsp fish sauce

2 tsp light brown sugar

1 tbsp lime juice, plus lime wedges, to serve

40 raw, shelled, and deveined large shrimp

1 Prepare the grill for cooking. To make the marinade, simply put all the ingredients, except the shrimp, in a blender or food processor and pulse to a fine paste.

2 Toss the shrimp in the marinade, cover, and leave in the fridge to marinate for 1 hour. Meanwhile, soak 8 bamboo skewers in water, as this will help to keep them from burning on the grill.

3 Thread 5 shrimp onto each skewer, threading through the top and bottom of the shrimp to make a curved "C"-shape. Grill the shrimp on the barbecue for 2–3 minutes on each side, until pink and charred in places. Serve with a squeeze of lime.

COOK IN THE OVEN
Preheat the broiler to its highest setting and line the broiler pan with foil. Lay the shrimp skewers on the pan and broil for 2-3 minutes on each side.

HOW TO FREEZE
Wrap well and freeze the marinated, uncooked shrimp. Defrost thoroughly, covered, in the fridge before use.

CALORIES: 128kcals/541kJ

CARBOHYDRATE: 3g
    sugar: 3g

FAT: 1g
    saturated: 0.1g

SALT: 2g

FIBER: 0g

Beef teriyaki

Try this delicious, all-purpose Japanese-style marinade with chicken, fish, and shrimp, as well as with beef.

15 mins, plus marinating   15 mins

SPECIAL EQUIPMENT
4 bamboo skewers

SERVES 4

1 garlic clove, finely chopped

¾in (2cm) fresh ginger, finely chopped

3 tbsp mirin

3 tbsp soy sauce

3 tbsp sake

1lb (450g) sirloin steak, trimmed of any fat and cut into 1in (2.5cm) cubes

1 red bell pepper, cut into 1in (2.5cm) pieces

1 yellow bell pepper, cut into 1in (2.5cm) pieces

vegetable oil, for brushing

1 tbsp olive oil

Jeweled rice salad (see p218), to serve

1 Soak 4 bamboo skewers in water, to keep them from burning on the grill. Prepare the grill for cooking.

2 Combine the garlic, ginger, mirin, soy sauce, and sake in a small bowl and whisk together. Place the beef in a shallow dish, pour in the marinade, and stir well.

Cover and set aside to marinate, at room temperature, for about 30 minutes.

3 Using a slotted spoon, remove the beef from the marinade and place on a plate. Pour the remaining marinade into a small pan. Place the pan over high heat, bring to a boil, and simmer for 10 minutes.

4 Meanwhile, thread the beef onto the skewers, alternating with pieces of pepper.

5 Brush a little vegetable oil on the grill rack. Brush the skewers with olive oil and cook for 2–3 minutes on each side until slightly charred.

6 Serve the skewers with Jeweled rice salad (see p218), with the sauce drizzled over the top.

COOK IN THE OVEN

Preheat the broiler to its highest setting and line a broiler pan with foil. Place the kebabs on the and broil them for 2–3 minutes on each side.

CALORIES: 217kcals/909kJ
CARBOHYDRATE: 6g sugar: 6g
FAT: 8g saturated: 2.5g
SALT: 2.2g
FIBER: 2g

Barbecued mackerel with fennel, tomato, and herb salad

The strong flavors of mackerel are complemented well by this robust marinade and the bright, zingy salad.

20 mins, plus marinating   6 mins

SERVES 4 (as a light meal)

1 hot red chile, seeded and finely chopped

1 tbsp small capers, rinsed, dried, and chopped

2 tbsp olive oil, plus extra for brushing

juice of 1 lemon, plus extra lemon wedges to serve

4 large skin-on mackerel fillets

salt and freshly ground black pepper

FOR THE SALAD

1 bulb fennel, thinly sliced

9oz (250g) cherry tomatoes, halved

2 red chiles, seeded and thinly sliced lengthwise

½ bunch chives, snipped into 1in (2.5cm) lengths

large handful of flat-leaf parsley, chopped

4 sprigs of dill, chopped

2 tbsp olive oil

juice of ½ lemon

1 garlic clove, crushed

1 Mix together the chile, capers, olive oil, and lemon juice in a wide, shallow bowl. Add the mackerel fillets and season well on both sides. Rub the mixture over the fish, cover, and marinate in the fridge for 1 hour.

2 Prepare the grill for cooking, and brush the rack lightly with oil. Cook the fish, skin-side down, for 2–3 minutes, or until the skin is golden brown and crispy. Turn it gently, brush the cooked sides with the excess marinade, and cook for another 2–3 minutes. Remove from the heat and divide between 4 warmed serving plates.

3 Put the salad ingredients in a serving bowl, toss gently, and serve with the fish, with lemon wedges for squeezing.

CALORIES: 504kcals/2089kJ

CARBOHYDRATE: 3g
  sugar: 2.5g

FAT: 40g
  saturated: 7g

SALT: 0.6g

FIBER: 2.1g

Blackened salmon

A spice rub, rather than a marinade, is useful to have in your grilling repertoire, and works for meat and fish.

5 mins, plus resting   10 mins

SERVES 4

1 tsp cayenne pepper

1 tsp celery salt

2 tsp dried oregano

1½ tbsp light brown sugar

freshly ground black pepper

4 skinless salmon fillets, approx. 5½oz (150g) each

1 tbsp olive oil

lemon or lime wedges, to serve

1 Prepare the grill for cooking. Grind all the dry ingredients together in a mortar and pestle to a fine consistency.

2 Rub all sides of the salmon fillets with the spice rub, cover, and rest in the fridge for 1 hour to let the flavors soak into the fish. Drizzle each piece of fish with a little oil and rub it gently all over.

3 Grill the salmon on the barbecue for 2–3 minutes on each side, until brown and crispy, but still moist. Serve with lemon or lime wedges to squeeze over.

COOK IN THE OVEN

Preheat the broiler to its highest setting. Broil the salmon fillets for 3–4 minutes on each side, or less if you like them rare in the middle (although for this the fish must be very fresh).

HOW TO FREEZE

The spice-rubbed, uncooked salmon fillets can be well wrapped and frozen for up to 3 months. Defrost thoroughly in the fridge before cooking.

CALORIES: 316kcals/1316kJ

CARBOHYDRATE: 5.5g
  sugar: 5.5g

FAT: 19g
  saturated: 3g

SALT: 1.2g

FIBER: 0g

Barbecued tuna steaks with cucumber and red onion relish

Tuna is a fabulous fish to cook on the grill; its robust, meaty texture means the steaks hold together well.

10 mins,
plus marinating

10 mins

SERVES 4

6in (15cm) piece of cucumber

2 tbsp rice wine or white wine vinegar

1 tsp granulated sugar

pinch of chile flakes

pinch of salt

¼ red onion, finely sliced

4 tuna steaks, approx.
3½oz (100g) each

1 tbsp olive oil

1 tsp smoked paprika

salt and freshly ground black pepper

lemon or lime wedges, to serve

1 Prepare the grill for cooking. Slice the cucumber in half lengthwise and scoop out the seeds with a spoon. Slice each half again lengthwise to make 4 long, thin pieces. Slice thinly on a diagonal.

2 In a bowl, whisk together the vinegar, sugar, chile flakes, and salt. Mix in the sliced cucumber and red onion, cover, and leave in the fridge to rest for 30 minutes (this helps soften the taste of the raw onion).

3 Rub each tuna steak on both sides with a little oil and smoked paprika and season them well. Cook the tuna on the hot grill for 2–3 minutes on each side for medium, or 3–4 minutes for well

done (and less for rare tuna, but only serve it this way if it is very fresh). It is easy to see if the tuna has cooked on one side, as the fish will turn opaque from the bottom upward when looked at from the side. Remember that the fish will continue to cook when removed from the grill.

4 Serve with the cucumber relish and a wedge of lemon or lime to squeeze over.

COOK IN THE OVEN

Preheat the broiler to its highest setting. Broil the tuna for 3-4 minutes on each side for medium-rare, or 2-3 minutes each side, if you prefer them rare.

PREPARE AHEAD

Preparing this cucumber relish a few hours ahead of time will not only save time when you are finishing the dish, but also help the flavors to develop.

CALORIES: 174kcals/729kJ	
CARBOHYDRATE: 2g	
sugar: 1.5g	
FAT: 7.5g	
saturated: 1.5g	
SALT: 4g	
FIBER: 0.8g	

Lamb koftes

These fragrantly spiced Middle Eastern kebabs are made of ground lamb, and take only minutes to cook.

15 mins   10–15 mins

SPECIAL EQUIPMENT
8 bamboo skewers

SERVES 4

vegetable oil, for greasing

1lb 2oz (500g) ground lamb

1 onion, finely chopped

1 garlic clove, finely chopped

½ tsp cayenne pepper

2 tsp ground cumin

2 tsp ground coriander

salt and freshly ground black pepper

warmed pita breads and coleslaw (see p160), to serve

1 Before you start, soak 8 bamboo skewers in water for 30 minutes. This will help keep them from burning on the grill. Prepare the grill for cooking. Brush a little oil on the grill rack.

2 Place the lamb, onion, garlic, cayenne, cumin, and coriander in a medium bowl, season well, and mix together with a fork.

3 Divide the mixture into 8 equal portions and shape them into chubby sausages, each 4–5in (10–12cm) long. Then thread the sausages onto the pre-soaked bamboo skewers.

4 Cook the lamb koftes on the grill for 10–15 minutes, turning frequently to ensure even cooking. Serve the koftes in warmed pita breads with coleslaw.

COOK IN THE OVEN

Preheat the broiler to its highest setting and line a baking sheet with foil. Place the koftes on the lined baking sheet and broil them for 10–15 minutes, turning frequently to ensure even cooking.

HOW TO FREEZE

Open-freeze the koftes raw at the end of step 3. Transfer to a freezer bag for up to 3 months. Defrost before cooking.

CALORIES: 254kcals/1059kJ

CARBOHYDRATE: 2g
  sugar: 1g

FAT: 17g
  saturated: 8g

SALT: 0.2g

FIBER: 0.5g

Beef burgers

Do not use very lean meat for a burger, or it will be dry. A little fat keeps the burger juicy, basting it from within.

15 mins, plus chilling   10 mins

SERVES 4

14oz (400g) good-quality ground beef

¼ cup fresh white bread crumbs

1 large egg yolk

½ red onion, very finely chopped

½ tsp ground mustard

½ tsp celery salt

1 tsp Worcestershire sauce

freshly ground black pepper

TO SERVE

4 burger buns

lettuce

tomato

finely sliced red onions

mayonnaise

mustard

relish

CALORIES: 290kcals/1208kJ

CARBOHYDRATE: 10g
  sugar: 1g

FAT: 18g
  saturated: 7g

SALT: 1g

FIBER: 0.6g

1 Prepare the grill for cooking. In a large bowl, mix together all the ingredients for the burgers until well combined.

2 With damp hands (to help keep the mixture from sticking to your fingers), divide the mixture into 4 balls and roll each between your palms until smooth. Flatten each ball out into a large, fat disk, 1in (3cm) high, and pat the edges in to tidy them up.

3 Place the burgers on a plate, cover with plastic wrap, and chill for 30 minutes (this helps them keep their shape while cooking).

4 Cook over a hot grill for 6–8 minutes, turning as needed, until the meat is springy to the touch and the edges charred.

5 Serve with a selection of buns and accompaniments and let everyone assemble their own burgers as they prefer.

COOK IN THE OVEN

These can be cooked under a hot, preheated broiler, or in a large, non-stick frying pan, for 3–4 minutes on each side, until they are springy to the touch and well browned.

Minted lamb burgers

A real favorite, these burgers are exceptionally tasty and always juicy, as ground lamb has extra fat.

10 mins, plus chilling   10 mins

SERVES 4

14oz (400g) ground lamb

¼ cup fresh white bread crumbs

1 large egg yolk

½ red onion, very finely chopped

1 tbsp dried mint, or 2 tbsp finely chopped mint leaves

½ tsp ground cinnamon

½ tsp ground cumin

salt and freshly ground black pepper

TO SERVE

4 burger buns, or 2 large pita breads, halved

lettuce

tomato

finely sliced red onions

Tzatziki (see p290)

mustard

relish

1 Prepare the grill for cooking. In a large bowl, mix together all the ingredients for the burgers until well combined.

2 With damp hands (to help keep the mixture from sticking to your fingers), divide the mixture into 4 balls and roll each one between your palms until smooth. Flatten each ball out to a large, fat disk, 1in (3cm) high, and pat the edges in to tidy them up.

3 Place the burgers on a plate, cover with plastic wrap, and chill for 30 minutes (this helps them keep their shape on cooking).

4 Cook over a hot grill for 6–8 minutes, turning as needed, until the meat is springy to the touch and the edges charred.

5 Serve with a selection of buns or pita breads and the suggested accompaniments, and let everyone assemble their own burgers as they prefer.

COOK IN THE OVEN

These can be cooked under a hot, preheated broiler, or in a large, non-stick frying pan, for 3–4 minutes on each side, until they are springy to the touch and well browned.

CALORIES: 260kcals/1087kJ

CARBOHYDRATE: 10g
sugar: 1g

FAT: 15g
saturated: 7g

SALT: 0.4g

FIBER: 1g

Spicy turkey burgers

Try making small versions of these Asian-inspired burgers, serving with sweet chili sauce, as a canapé.

15 mins, plus chilling   10 mins

SERVES 4

14oz (400g) ground turkey

⅓ cup fresh white bread crumbs

1 tbsp sweet chili sauce

4 scallions, white part only, finely sliced

¼ cup finely chopped cilantro leaves

¾in (2cm) fresh ginger, finely grated

1 red chile, seeded and finely chopped

salt and freshly ground black pepper

TO SERVE

4 burger buns

lettuce

tomato

finely sliced red onions

mayonnaise

Greek yogurt

sweet chili sauce

1 Prepare the grill for cooking. In a large bowl, mix together all the ingredients until well combined.

2 With damp hands (to help keep the mixture from sticking to your fingers), divide the mixture into 4 balls and roll each one between your palms until smooth. Flatten each ball out to a large, fat disk, 1in (3cm) high, and pat the edges in to tidy them up. Place the burgers on a plate, cover with plastic wrap, and chill for 30 minutes (this helps them keep their shape while cooking).

3 Cook over a hot grill for 6–7 minutes, turning as needed, until the meat is springy to the touch and the edges charred.

4 Serve with a selection of buns and accompaniments, and let everyone build their own burgers.

COOK IN THE OVEN

These can be cooked under a hot broiler, or in a large, non-stick frying pan, for 3 minutes on each side, until they are springy to the touch and well browned.

HOW TO FREEZE

The burgers can be open-frozen, uncooked, then transferred to a freezer bag for up to 3 months. You can defrost just as many as you need.

CALORIES: 244kcals/1027kJ

CARBOHYDRATE: 16g
sugar: 2.5g

FAT: 7g
saturated: 3g

SALT: 0.5g

FIBER: 0.8g

Butterflied leg of lamb

A whole, grilled leg of lamb is an easy yet impressive way to feed a crowd. Ask the butcher to butterfly the leg.

10 mins,
plus marinating   35-45 mins

SPECIAL EQUIPMENT

2 large metal skewers

SERVES 6

½ cup red wine

2 tbsp olive oil

4 garlic cloves, roughly chopped

zest of 1 orange, peeled off with a potato peeler, plus its juice

4 sprigs of rosemary, scrunched up (this will let the essential oils out)

freshly ground black pepper

boned leg of lamb, butterflied, approx. 2¾lb-3lb 3oz (1.2-1.5kg)

sea salt

1 Make the marinade by mixing together all the ingredients except the lamb and sea salt in a large, shallow dish big enough to hold the lamb in a single layer.

2 Rub the marinade over the meat. Leave it skin-side down and cover with plastic wrap. Leave in the fridge to marinate for at least 8 hours, or overnight.

3 Prepare the grill for cooking. Remove the meat from the marinade and wipe off any garlic, orange, or herb pieces. Use 2 large metal skewers to skewer it from corner to corner.

4 Sprinkle liberally with sea salt and grill it over a medium barbecue for 35–45 minutes, turning occasionally using the skewers. Place the lamb on a warmed platter, lightly cover with foil, and rest for 10 minutes before serving.

COOK IN THE OVEN

The lamb can be cooked in a roasting pan in a preheated oven at 400°F (200°C) for 35-45 minutes, depending on how you like your meat. You will not need to skewer it if cooked in an oven.

CALORIES: 591kcals/2450kJ

CARBOHYDRATE: 0.4g
sugar: 0.2g

FAT: 47g
saturated: 11g

SALT: 1.2g

FIBER: 0g

Texas-style barbecued spare ribs

This Southern-style sauce has a dark, sweet, smoky flavor that is universally popular.

30 mins,
plus marinating   40-50 mins

SERVES 4

2 tbsp sunflower or vegetable oil

1 red onion, finely chopped

2 garlic cloves, crushed

½ cup ketchup

2 tbsp red wine vinegar

2 tbsp molasses

1 tsp Worcestershire sauce

2 tsp smoked paprika

½ tsp cayenne pepper

¼ tsp celery salt

freshly ground black pepper

8-12 meaty pork spare ribs

1 Heat the oil in a small pan and cook the onion over medium heat for 5 minutes until softened. Add the garlic for one minute. Add the remaining ingredients, apart from the ribs, with ½ cup of water and whisk. Bring the mixture to a boil, reduce the heat to a low simmer, and cook, uncovered, for 20 minutes until it has reduced to a thick sauce. Let it cool.

2 Reserve half of the sauce for serving. Rub the rest into the ribs, cover, and leave to marinate in the fridge for at least 2 hours. Prepare the grill for cooking.

3 Grill the ribs over a medium barbecue for 20–30 minutes, turning frequently, and basting with any remaining sauce from the marinade bowl, until tender and charred in places. Warm up the remaining sauce to serve alongside.

COOK IN THE OVEN

Cook in a preheated oven at 400°F (200°C) for 20-25 minutes, turning once, until tender and charred in places.

BATCHING AND FREEZING

The cooked, cooled sauce can be frozen for up to 6 months, or make double the recipe and freeze half for another time.

CALORIES: 541kcals/2251kJ

CARBOHYDRATE: 15g
sugar: 14g

FAT: 36g
saturated: 11g

SALT: 1.8g

FIBER: 0.8g

Slow-cooked shoulder of pork

Also known as pulled pork, this is cooked until it falls apart juicily, shredded, then smothered in delicious sauce.

30 mins, plus marinating   3 hrs, plus resting

SPECIAL EQUIPMENT
hand-held blender or food processor

SERVES 6–8

2 tbsp sunflower or vegetable oil, plus extra for rubbing

1 onion, finely chopped

2 garlic cloves, crushed

½ cup ketchup

¼ cup cider vinegar

1 tsp Tabasco or other hot sauce

1 tsp Worcestershire sauce

1 tsp ground mustard

2 tbsp honey

4½lb (2kg) bone-in pork shoulder

salt, for rubbing

selection of flour tortillas, sour cream, Tomato salsa (see p288), Guacamole (see p290), lettuce, and finely sliced red onions, to serve

1 Heat the oil in a small, heavy-bottomed pan. Cook the onion over medium heat for 5 minutes until softened. Add the garlic gand cook for 1 minute. Add the remaining ingredients, apart from the pork and salt, with ½ cup of water, and whisk well.

2 Bring to a boil, reduce the heat to a simmer, and cook, uncovered, for 20 minutes until reduced to a thick sauce. Use a hand-held blender or food processor to blend it until smooth. Cool.

3 Rub the pork in the sauce, cover, and marinate in the fridge for at least 4 hours, but preferably overnight. Preheat the oven to 350°F (180°C). Put the pork and marinade in an oven pan just big enough to fit it. Put a piece of waxed paper over the top (to keep the skin from sticking to the foil) and seal with a double layer of foil. Cook the pork for 2½ hours.

4 Prepare the grill for cooking. Remove the meat from the oven. Pat the skin dry with paper towels and rub in a little oil, then some salt. Grill it over a hot barbecue for 10–15 minutes on each side, skin-side down first; carefully turn with tongs, but do not turn it until the crackling is crispy and charred in places.

5 Meanwhile, pour the juices from the oven pan into a saucepan and first pour, then skim off all the fat. Reduce the sauce over medium heat to a thick pouring consistency.

6 Cut the crackling off the meat and leave it uncovered (or it will go soft) while you rest the meat wrapped in foil for 10 minutes. When ready to serve, cut the crackling into shards. Shred the pork into a juicy pile, pour the sauce over the top, and serve, with the tortillas and accompaniments.

COOK IN THE OVEN
After step 3, remove the meat from the oven, strain off the juices into a saucepan, and skim off the fat. Rub the meat with a little oil and scatter it with sea salt. Increase the oven temperature to 450°F (230°C) and cook the pork, uncovered, for 30 minutes, until the crackling is crisp. Reduce the juices as in step 5 to serve with the shredded meat.

CALORIES: 335kcals/1411kJ

CARBOHYDRATE: 7g
  sugar: 7g

FAT: 12g
  saturated: 3.5g

SALT: 1.1g

FIBER: 0.4g

Barbecued beef brisket

This "two-heat" method of cooking brisket ensures that it is crispy on the outside but remains tender within.

30 mins, plus marinating   3 hrs 15 mins

SERVES 4–6

1 tbsp sunflower or vegetable oil

½ onion, finely chopped

1 garlic clove, crushed

3–4 tbsp ketchup

2 tbsp balsamic vinegar

2 tbsp dark brown sugar

1 tsp Worcestershire sauce

1 tsp ground cumin

½ tsp cayenne pepper

freshly ground black pepper

piece of beef brisket, approx. 2¼lb (1kg)

1 Heat the oil in a small pan. Cook the onion over low heat for 10 minutes, until softened. Add the garlic and cook for 1 minute.

2 Add the remaining ingredients, apart from the brisket, with 3–4 tbsp of water. Bring to a boil, reduce the heat, and simmer for 10 minutes to give a thick sauce.

3 Place the brisket in a bowl, rub it all over with the sauce, cover,

and marinate in the fridge for at least 4 hours, or overnight.

4 Preheat the oven to 325°F (160°C). Put the brisket in a roasting pan, cover it with the marinade, and seal with a double layer of foil. Cook for 3 hours.

5 Prepare the grill for cooking. Unwrap the meat, baste with the cooking juices, then grill it over a hot barbecue for 5–7 minutes each side until a crust develops. Serve sliced thinly with pickles, mustard, coleslaw (see p160), and Potato salad (see p158).

COOK IN THE OVEN

Cook the brisket as described in step 4, then unwrap it, increase the oven temperature to 450°F (230°C), and cook for another 30 minutes.

CALORIES: 284kcals/1195kJ

CARBOHYDRATE: 9g
  sugar: 8.5g

FAT: 12g
  saturated: 4.5g

SALT: 0.6g

FIBER: 0.2g

Dry-rubbed barbecued steak

Rubbing the steak with this spicy mix and allowing it to rest lets the flavors really permeate the meat.

5–10 mins, plus resting   5–10 mins, plus resting

SPECIAL EQUIPMENT

spice grinder (optional)

SERVES 4

2 tsp smoked paprika

2 tsp ground mustard

1 tsp garlic salt

1 tsp dried thyme

1 tbsp light brown sugar

freshly ground black pepper

4 steaks, such as flank or sirloin, approx. 5½oz (150g) each

1 tbsp olive oil

1 In a mortar and pestle or a spice grinder, mix the dry ingredients together to form a fine powder.

2 Rub each steak all over with the spice mix and wrap each one with plastic wrap. Let rest in the fridge for 4–6 hours. Prepare the grill for cooking.

3 Unwrap the steaks and allow them to come to room temperature. Drizzle with a little oil and grill on a hot barbecue for 2–3 minutes on each side if you want medium-rare (3–4 minutes for medium, or 4–5 for well done), turning only after the underside has crusted up.

4 Remove from the heat and allow to rest for 5 minutes, covered with foil, before serving.

COOK IN THE OVEN

These can be rubbed in a little olive oil and pan-fried for 4–8 minutes, turning occasionally, depending on thickness and how you like steak cooked.

HOW TO FREEZE

The rubbed, uncooked steaks can be well wrapped individually, as in step 2, then frozen for up to 3 months. Defrost thoroughly before cooking.

CALORIES: 226kcals/949kJ

CARBOHYDRATE: 4g
  sugar: 4g

FAT: 9g
  saturated: 3g

SALT: 1.2g

FIBER: 0g

Classic barbecued chicken

This barbecue sauce is really easy to adapt to your particular taste, by adding more chili sauce, honey, or mustard.

40 mins,
plus marinating   30-40 mins

SPECIAL EQUIPMENT
hand-held blender (optional)

SERVES 4

2 tbsp sunflower or vegetable oil

1 onion, finely chopped

2 garlic cloves, crushed

⅔ cup ketchup

3-4 tbsp cider vinegar

1 tsp Tabasco or other hot chili sauce

1 tsp Worcestershire sauce

2 tbsp honey

1 tbsp Dijon mustard

1 tsp smoked paprika

8 skin-on bone-in chicken drumsticks
or thighs

1 Heat the oil in a small, heavy-bottomed saucepan. Cook the onion gently over medium heat for 5 minutes, until it is softened, but not browned. Add the garlic and cook for another minute.

2 Add the remaining ingredients, apart from the chicken, with ⅔ cup of water, and whisk, being sure to get into all the corners of the pan where honey can stick and burn.

3 Bring the mixture to a boil, reduce the heat to a low simmer, and cook, uncovered, for 25–30 minutes until it has reduced to a thick sauce. You can at this stage use a hand-held blender to purée the sauce completely smooth, if you prefer (some children don't like "chunks"). Allow to cool.

4 Cut 2–3 slashes on each side of the chicken pieces, where the meat is thickest. Toss the chicken in the cooled barbecue sauce, cover, and marinate, if you have time, for at least a few hours, or overnight, in the fridge. Prepare the grill for cooking.

5 Grill the chicken over a medium barbecue for about 30 minutes for drumsticks and 40 minutes for thighs, turning frequently, and basting with leftover sauce as it cooks. The meat will separate slightly where it has been slashed, which enables it to cook right through and gives a bigger surface area for the sauce. Check to see if the meat is cooked by gently piercing it with a sharp knife up to the bone. The juices should run clear.

COOK IN THE OVEN
These can be cooked in a preheated oven at 375°F (190°C) for 40-45 minutes, turning halfway through.

BATCHING AND FREEZING
Make double or triple quantities of this simple sauce and freeze what you don't need for another day, using it up within 6 months. The sauce can also be used to make a quick dish of oven-roasted chicken wings.

CALORIES: 404kcals/1696kJ

CARBOHYDRATE: 19.5g
    sugar: 19g

FAT: 16g
    saturated: 3.5g

SALT: 2.3g

FIBER: 1g

Lemon, garlic, and herb grilled chicken

This flavorful Mediterranean-inspired marinade is also great for rubbing on rabbit before grilling.

10 mins, plus marinating   30–40 mins

SERVES 4

juice of 1 lemon

2 tbsp olive oil

2 garlic cloves, crushed

1 tbsp Dijon mustard

2 heaping tbsp thyme leaves

2 heaping tbsp finely chopped flat-leaf parsley leaves

1 heaping tbsp finely chopped rosemary leaves

salt and freshly ground black pepper

8 skin-on bone-in chicken drumsticks or thighs

1 Mix together all the ingredients except the chicken and season the marinade well.

2 Cut 2–3 slashes on each side of the chicken pieces, where the meat is thickest. Toss the chicken in the herby sauce, cover, and marinate for at least 2 hours in the fridge. Prepare the grill for cooking.

3 Grill the chicken over a medium barbecue for about 30 minutes for drumsticks and 40 minutes for thighs, turning frequently, and basting with leftover sauce as it cooks. The meat will separate slightly where it has been slashed, which enables it to cook right through and gives a bigger surface area for the sauce. Check if the meat is cooked by gently piercing it with a sharp knife up to the bone. The juices should run clear.

COOK IN THE OVEN

The chicken can be cooked in a preheated oven at 375°F (190°C) for 40–45 minutes, turning halfway through.

HOW TO FREEZE

The marinated, uncooked chicken can be frozen for up to 3 months. Defrost in the fridge before cooking as in step 3.

CALORIES: 338kcals/1411kJ

CARBOHYDRATE: 0.5g
  sugar: 0.2g

FAT: 18g
  saturated: 4g

SALT: 0.5g

FIBER: 0g

Chinese barbecued chicken wings

Chicken wings are inexpensive, and are an easy and ever-popular way to feed a hungry family.

10 mins, plus marinating   25 mins

SERVES 4

2 tbsp soy sauce

1 tbsp rice wine or dry sherry

1 tbsp brown sugar

1 tbsp sunflower or vegetable oil

2 tbsp honey

1 garlic clove, crushed

¾in (2cm) fresh ginger, finely grated

1 tsp five-spice powder

16 large chicken wings

CALORIES: 240kcals/1007kJ

CARBOHYDRATE: 11g
  sugar: 11g

FAT: 10g
  saturated: 2g

SALT: 1.5g

FIBER: 0g

1 Mix together all the ingredients, except the chicken, in a large bowl.

2 Toss the chicken wings through the marinade, cover, and marinate in the fridge for at least 1 hour. Prepare the grill for cooking.

3 Cook the wings over a hot grill, turning frequently, and basting with the leftover marinade for 10–15 minutes, until they are well cooked and charring slightly at the edges.

COOK IN THE OVEN

These can be cooked on a baking sheet in a preheated oven at 450°F (230°C) for 20-25 mins, turning halfway through.

HOW TO FREEZE

The marinated, uncooked wings can be frozen for up to 3 months. Defrost thoroughly in the fridge before cooking from the start of step 3.

Lemongrass and chile salsa

This salsa transforms grilled fish or skewers of barbecued white meat into an Asian delicacy.

20 mins, plus chilling

SERVES 6

2 lemongrass stalks, outer leaves discarded

2 heaping tbsp chopped Thai basil leaves, plus 6 extra whole leaves

1 tsp finely grated fresh ginger

1 whole red chile, seeded and finely chopped

1 tbsp honey or granulated sugar

3 tbsp soy sauce

2 tsp fish sauce

6 tbsp lime juice

1 Slice off the tops of the lemongrass stalks and discard them. Smash down on the bulb ends with the side of a large knife, or pound using a kitchen mallet. Chop very finely and place in a bowl.

2 Add the basil, ginger, and chile. Pour in the honey or sugar, soy sauce, fish sauce, and lime juice and stir well.

3 Cover and chill for at least 1 hour to give the flavors time to amalgamate and develop.

4 Just before serving, stir in the reserved whole basil leaves, pressing them slightly to release their fragrance.

CALORIES: 15kcals/65kJ
CARBOHYDRATE: 3.5g
sugar: 3.5g
FAT: 0g
saturated: 0g
SALT: 1.7g
FIBER: 0g

Roasted red bell pepper and corn salsa

This chunky salsa is ideal alongside a thick piece of barbecued fish, or a plainly grilled steak.

15 mins   30 mins

SERVES 4

2 large or 3 medium red bell peppers

½ tbsp olive oil, plus extra for rubbing

1 corn cob

1 tbsp chopped flat-leaf parsley leaves

1 tbsp chopped basil leaves

2 tbsp freshly squeezed orange juice

salt and freshly ground black pepper

1 Prepare the grill for cooking. Rub the peppers with a little oil and roast them over a hot barbecue, turning occasionally, until they are just cooked and the skin is charred in places. Cool.

2 Meanwhile, cook the corn in boiling water for 5 minutes until just tender. Drain, transfer it to the hot barbecue, and grill it for another 5 minutes until the kernels are charred in places. Cool.

3 In a bowl, whisk together the herbs, orange juice, and oil and season well. Peel and seed the red bell peppers, being careful of any liquid that will be inside them, as it will be hot. Cut the flesh into ½in (1cm) cubes and add it to the bowl.

4 Hold the cooled corn upright and rest it on a cutting board with one hand. Carefully slice the cooked kernels off with a sharp knife. Add these to the bowl and toss together before serving.

COOK IN THE OVEN

If you do not want to light the grill, roast the peppers and finish the corn under the broiler or in a grill pan.

CALORIES: 83kcals/346kJ
CARBOHYDRATE: 10.5g
sugar: 7g
FAT: 3.5g
saturated: 0.5g
SALT: trace
FIBER: 2.5g

Guacamole

This classic is great with tortilla chips, as a cooling side dish with spicy food, or on a grilled burger.

5 mins

SERVES 4

4 ripe avocados, halved, pitted, and peeled

1 large tomato, peeled, seeded, and finely chopped (see p191)

¼ red onion, very finely chopped

1 red chile, seeded and very finely chopped

1 garlic clove, crushed

handful of cilantro, finely chopped

juice of 1 lime

salt and freshly ground black pepper

1 Place each halved avocado cut-side down on a cutting board. Cut them into small cubes and place in a large, shallow bowl.

2 Take a large fork and gently mash the avocado, leaving it rough and with a few of the cubes still showing. (Cutting the avocado first helps maintain some texture to the finished dish.)

3 Add the remaining ingredients and gently fold them in with the fork. Season to taste and serve immediately, or cover with plastic wrap and chill until needed.

CLEVER WITH LEFTOVERS

Overripe avocados can be turned into this delicious guacamole. Just cut out any discolored parts and use the rest.

CALORIES: 298kcals/1229kJ

CARBOHYDRATE: 5g
  sugar: 2.5g

FAT: 30g
  saturated: 7g

SALT: trace

FIBER: 7.5g

Tzatziki

Traditionally served in Greece as an appetizer with pita bread, this dip can also be served with lamb dishes.

10 mins

SERVES 4

4in (10cm) piece of cucumber, quartered lengthwise and seeded

¾ cup (7oz) Greek yogurt or thick plain yogurt

1 tbsp finely chopped mint leaves

1 tbsp finely chopped dill

1 small garlic clove, crushed

1 tbsp lemon juice

salt and freshly ground black pepper

1 Grate the lengths of cucumber into a sieve, pressing them down to remove most of the excess water.

2 Put the grated cucumber in a clean kitchen towel and squeeze it well to remove the last of the water. Place the squeezed ball of cucumber on a cutting board and chop it up to make it even finer.

3 Mix it together with the remaining ingredients and season to taste. Cover and chill until needed.

Serve this delicious dip with a big pile of crudités including carrots, cucumber, and celery, to encourage fussy eaters to eat more vegetables.

Fussy eaters!

CALORIES: 49kcals/203kJ

CARBOHYDRATE: 3g
  sugar: 3g

FAT: 3g
  saturated: 2g

SALT: 0.2g

FIBER: 0.2g

Grilled pineapple with vanilla ice cream and butterscotch sauce

Another easy grilled dessert, this pineapple looks dramatic and tastes fabulous with cold ice cream.

10 mins   10 mins

SERVES 4

8 slices of pineapple, trimmed well and cut ½–¾in (1–2cm) thick

2 tbsp melted butter

FOR THE SAUCE

5 tbsp unsalted butter

½ cup dark brown sugar

⅔ cup heavy cream

pinch of salt

½ tsp vanilla extract

vanilla ice cream, to serve

1 Prepare the grill for cooking. To make the sauce, melt the butter in a small, heavy-bottomed saucepan. Take it off the heat and whisk in the sugar until it has completely amalgamated. Whisk in the cream, salt, and vanilla extract.

2 Return the sauce to the heat, bring it to a boil, then reduce the heat to a low simmer. Allow it to simmer gently for 10 minutes. Serve warm or cooled—it will thicken as it cools.

3 Meanwhile, grill the pineapple. Brush it on both sides with a little melted butter, then grill it over a hot barbecue for 2–3 minutes on each side, until charred in places and starting to soften.

4 Serve the pineapple with vanilla ice cream and the warm butterscotch sauce to pour overtop.

COOK ON THE STOVE

You can cook the buttered pineapple on a preheated grill pan until it displays black char marks on each side.

CALORIES: 538kcals/2248kJ

CARBOHYDRATE: 39g
  sugar: 40g

FAT: 42g
  saturated: 27g

SALT: 0.4g

FIBER: 2.5g

Baked bananas with chocolate

The simplest of grilled desserts, yet one of the most delicious. Sadly, it's hard to replicate in the oven.

5 mins   10 mins

SERVES 4

4 ripe bananas

3½oz (100g) dark, light, or white chocolate chips, or a combination

vanilla ice cream, to serve

1 Prepare the grill for cooking. Take each banana and cut down, lengthwise, through the skin into the middle of the banana to make a deep slit.

2 Stuff the slit with one-quarter of the chocolate. Push the banana back together and wrap tightly in foil. Repeat to stuff and wrap all the bananas.

3 Cook the bananas over a hot grill for 10 minutes, turning them once. Take off the foil and serve them from their skins, with a spoonful of vanilla ice cream on top.

PREPARE AHEAD

Get the bananas ready for cooking by stuffing them and wrapping them in foil earlier in the day, then toss them on the grill as you serve the main course for a stress-free outdoor dessert.

CALORIES: 225kcals/947kJ

CARBOHYDRATE: 35g
  sugar: 33.5g

FAT: 8g
  saturated: 5g

SALT: trace

FIBER: 1.5g

Unexpected guests

It's usually a pleasure when family or friends turn up unexpectedly, but when it comes around to mealtimes this can be problematic. As a good host you may feel duty bound to invite them to eat, yet worried that you have nothing special to serve. The arrival of another family may double the amount of people to feed, and mass catering can be quite an undertaking. However, with a little ingenuity, a few willing volunteers to set the table or keep guests occupied, and the contents of a well-stocked pantry and fridge, a tasty meal can be conjured up in a matter of minutes.

How to cheat

If you have just one or two extra people at the table, then adding to the carbohydrates you are serving will make the dish go further—potatoes, pasta, or rice are usually on hand. A basket of bread will help fill up your guests too. There are several "cheat" ingredients that are life savers when you have to rustle up a whole meal. Good quality frozen pastry and staples like sausages, individually packed chicken breasts, and fish fillets defrost relatively quickly, or you can make a meal from canned and dried ingredients (see pp14–15).

Snack time treats if you have frozen cookie dough, you can quickly bake some cookies. With frozen puff pastry, you can defrost a sheet in about 30 minutes on the counter and add savory toppings such as olives, anchovies, or slices of eggplant and tomato, or fruit such as apples or canned apricots to make tarts. Bake for 15 minutes.

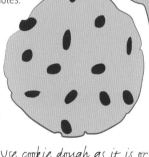

Use cookie dough as it is or add chopped nuts, chocolate chips, or dried fruit.

Make it special

Even if you are serving the simplest of meals, good presentation is the key to good entertaining. A few fresh flowers, attractive tableware, and even a hastily ironed tablecloth will give the meal a celebratory appearance. Then add a few interesting toppings to give even simple meals a sophisticated spin.

Stale bread cut into big chunks and fried makes the best croutons. Add a swirl of cream or crème fraîche too.

Soup with croutons
For a lunchtime treat, start off with an onion sautéed in a little olive oil, then add any combination of root vegetables you have available to make a version of the Harvest vegetable soup (p157). Use a carton of stock from the pantry. For a special treat fry up some croutons and sprinkle them on top.

1

sprinkle some chopped up toasted walnut halves on dishes for added flavor.

Tasty morsels

While your guests are enjoying a pre-dinner glass of wine, rustle up some quick nibbles to stop them getting too peckish. Pitta bread crisps (see p242) can be prepared in minutes and make a delicious light bite.

Use whatever berries you have available. strawberries, raspberries, or blueberries are ideal.

Simple baked goods

If you find you have afternoon guests, then a few speedy baked items will almost certainly go down well.

Scones (p440) are one of the easiest things to prepare, and the quickest things to bake. Bear in mind that they need no further decoration and can be served warm from the oven—they make the perfect last-minute treat.

If you are out of bread but want to serve some homemade soup, then **Soda bread** (p450) is the thing for you. Its rustic appearance and wholesome taste make a perfect match for some warming, wintery soup, and the lack of yeast in the recipe means that you don't have to wait for it to rise.

Using a few simple ingredients you can whip up these delicious **Quick cheese pastries** (p442) in a matter of minutes. Use whatever cheese you have available.

For a brunch treat, try making these tasty **Savory breakfast muffins** (p442) and serving them warm from the oven, with some scrambled eggs. If you don't have ham and cheese, substitute canned sweet corn, seeded and finely diced tomatoes, or briefly sautéed mushrooms.

2 Pasta with nuts

Pasta dishes are easy to put together using whichever dried pasta you have with a sauce you have batch cooked and saved in the freezer. To give it a twist, add some nuts, such as walnuts or pine nuts, and sprinkle on top or mix in.

3 Ice cream with fruit

It's rare for someone to refuse some good quality, homemade ice cream (p329). Jazz up your dessert with some chocolate sauce and some chopped fresh fruit, or a selection of cake sprinkles for younger visitors.

Roast chicken

A simple roast chicken can be a marvelous thing, and should be the backbone of any home cook's repertoire.

5 mins   1¼–1½ hrs, plus resting

SERVES 4–6

1 good-quality chicken, 3lb 3oz–4½lb (1.5–2kg)

1 tbsp butter, softened

salt and freshly ground black pepper

½ lemon

1 Preheat the oven to 450°F (230°C). Wipe the chicken skin dry with paper towels. Undo the string that holds the legs together and work the legs away from the body slightly. This will help the legs to cook more quickly and prevent the breast from drying out.

2 Rub the butter all over the bird, then season it well inside and out. Place it in a roasting pan

and squeeze the lemon over the chicken, putting the squeezed-out lemon shell inside the cavity. Pour water to a depth of ⅛in (3mm) around the chicken; this will help to make the gravy later.

3 Roast the chicken for about 15 minutes, then reduce the oven temperature to 350°F (180°C) and roast it for another 20 minutes per 1lb 2oz (500g), or until the juices run clear when you insert a skewer into the thickest part of the thigh.

4 When the chicken is cooked, remove it from the pan and rest it for 10 minutes, lightly covered with foil, while you make the gravy (see p307).

BATCHING AND FREEZING

The leftover carcass can be frozen in a large freezer bag. Collect 3 or 4 chicken carcasses, then use them to make a triple quantity of chicken stock (see p94). Reduce the stock to intensify the flavors, then freeze in small amounts to add great-tasting richness to sauces, stews, and gravies.

CALORIES: 219kcals/922kJ

CARBOHYDRATE: 0g
  sugar: 0g

FAT: 6g
  saturated: 2.5g

SALT: 0.3g

FIBER: 0g

Herby roast chicken

An herby butter spread under the skin of the chicken keeps the bird moist and succulent during cooking.

10 mins   1¼–1½ hrs, plus resting

SERVES 4–6

1 good-quality chicken, 3lb 3oz–4½lb (1.5–2kg)

3 tbsp butter, softened

1 tbsp finely chopped tarragon leaves

1 tbsp finely chopped flat-leaf parsley leaves

1 tbsp thyme leaves

1 garlic clove, crushed

grated zest and juice of ½ lemon

salt and freshly ground black pepper

1 tbsp olive oil

1 Preheat the oven to 450°F (230°C). Wipe the chicken skin dry with paper towels. Undo the string and work the legs away from the body (see recipe, left).

2 Make an herb butter by mashing together the butter, herbs, garlic, and lemon zest. Season well.

3 Loosen the skin where the breasts begin and slide your fingers gently between skin and breast as far as you can on either side without tearing the skin.

4 Push the herb butter under the skin, patting down to spread the butter out. Put the chicken in a roasting pan.

5 Rub the skin with the oil and season. Squeeze the half lemon over the top, then put the lemon shell in the cavity. Roast for 15 minutes, then reduce the oven temperature to 350°F (180°C) and roast for 20 minutes per 1lb 2oz (500g), or until the juices run clear. Rest for 10 minutes, covered with foil.

PREPARE AHEAD

A perfect picnic dish, cook this up to 2 days ahead, then serve cold with Potato salad (see p158), green salad, and bread.

HOW TO FREEZE

Remove the chicken from the bones in big chunks before freezing for up to 3 months. Smaller pieces may dry out.

CALORIES: 273kcals/1143kJ

CARBOHYDRATE: 0g
  sugar: 0g

FAT: 12g
  saturated: 5g

SALT: 0.4g

FIBER: 0g

Roast chicken and root vegetables

Cooking a whole chicken in a pan of colorful root vegetables will give you a convenient and healthy meal in one.

20 mins   1 hr 15 mins,
             plus resting

SERVES 4–6

1 good-quality chicken,
  3lb 3oz–4½lb (1.5–2kg)

4 large potatoes, peeled and quartered

3 large carrots, cut into 1in (3cm)
  chunks

2 parsnips, cut into 1in (3cm)
  chunks

2 leeks, white part only, cut into
  1in (3cm) chunks

2 tbsp olive oil

salt and freshly ground black pepper

1 tbsp butter, softened

½ lemon

½ cup white wine
  or chicken stock (see p94)

1 Preheat the oven to 400°F (200°C). Wipe the skin of the chicken dry with paper towels. Undo the string and work the legs away from the body slightly (see recipe, far left).

2 Put the vegetables in a large roasting pan, toss them with the oil, and season well. Push them to the sides of the pan to make room for the chicken.

3 Rub the chicken all over with the butter and season it well. Put the chicken into the space you made in the roasting pan, surrounded by the vegetables. (Do not put it on top, or the vegetables may cook unevenly.) Squeeze the half lemon over the breast, then put the squeezed-out lemon shell inside the cavity.

4 Pour the wine or stock around the vegetables and roast in the oven for about 1¼ hours, turning the vegetables occasionally, or until the chicken juices run clear when you insert a skewer into the thickest part of the thigh.

5 Rest the chicken for 10 minutes, lightly covered with foil. Pour any juices that come from the chicken back into the vegetables, then carve the chicken and serve with the vegetables and juices.

COOK'S TIP

Roasting the vegetables with the chicken will soak up a lot of the chicken juices, and not leave much for a gravy. Try serving it with a "wet" vegetable such as slow-cooked Savoy cabbage (see p166), or even with Bread sauce (see p317).

CLEVER WITH LEFTOVERS

Make extra root vegetables when you roast this dish. Then take the cold leftover roasted roots, mix them with leftover gravy and chicken stock (see p94), and purée with an electric hand-held blender for an instant roast chicken and root vegetable soup.

CALORIES: 444kcals/1868kJ

CARBOHYDRATE: 37g
  sugar: 9g

FAT: 11g
  saturated: 3g

SALT: 0.4g

FIBER: 8.5g

Individual mushroom and leek potato pies

This comforting wintry vegetable dish is perfect to serve vegetarian guests alongside a traditional Sunday lunch.

15 mins | 20 mins, plus resting

SPECIAL EQUIPMENT
4 x 3in- (8cm-) wide, 1½in- (4cm-) high metal rings

SERVES 4

4 large Portobello mushrooms

4 tbsp olive oil

2 tbsp butter

2 leeks, cut into ¾in (2cm) chunks

2 tbsp all-purpose flour

⅔ cup whole milk

2½oz (75g) blue cheese, such as Stilton, crumbled

salt and freshly ground black pepper

2 cups mashed potatoes

1 heaping tbsp whole grain mustard

1 Preheat the oven to 400°F (200°C). Brush the mushrooms with half the oil and cook them on a grill pan or under a hot broiler for 3 minutes on each side until they soften.

2 Heat the remaining 2 tbsp of oil and the butter in a small saucepan. Cook the leeks, covered, over low heat for 5–7 minutes, stirring occasionally until they soften. Add the flour to the pan and mix it into the leeks, then gradually stir in the milk.

3 Bring the sauce to a boil, then reduce the heat to a simmer and cook until it thickens. Add the cheese and continue to stir until the cheese has melted. Season with pepper (the cheese is quite salty).

4 Place four 3in- (8cm-) wide, 1½in- (4cm-) high metal rings on a baking sheet. Put a mushroom in the bottom of each ring, gill-side up. It should fit neatly. Cover the mushrooms with the cheesy leek mixture and season well.

5 Reheat the mashed potatoes slightly in a microwave to soften them, then beat in the mustard and taste for seasoning. Divide the potatoes between the metal rings and finish the top nicely.

6 Bake for 15–20 minutes until the top is golden brown and the vegetables cooked through. Let rest for 5 minutes before carefully running a small, sharp knife around the inside of the ring and easing the pies out onto warmed plates to serve.

VARIATION

Try mixing the grilled mushrooms and cheesy leek mixture, omitting the potato, and dividing the mixture between 4 ramekins. Cover each with a disk of store-bought all-butter puff pastry, and bake as in step 6.

PREPARE AHEAD

These pies can be prepared up to 1 day ahead, covered, and chilled. Simply return them to room temperature before cooking as in step 6.

CALORIES: 410kcals/1703kJ

CARBOHYDRATE: 23g
sugar: 4g

FAT: 30g
saturated: 13g

SALT: 0.8g

FIBER: 4.5g

Mediterranean vegetable and goat cheese timbale

This individual tower of summery flavors can be served to vegetarian guests, or used as an appetizer.

15 mins

20 mins, plus resting

SPECIAL EQUIPMENT

4 x 3in- (8cm-) wide, 1½in- (4cm-) high metal rings

SERVES 4

2 large sweet potatoes, cut into 8 x ¾in (2cm) slices

1 large eggplant, cut into 8 x ¾in (2cm) slices

olive oil, for brushing

2 large tomatoes, thinly sliced

¼ cup finely chopped basil leaves

salt and freshly ground black pepper

4½oz (125g) goat cheese, finely sliced

1 Preheat the oven to 400°F (200°C). Brush the sweet potatoes and eggplant with the oil and cook them on a grill pan or under a hot broiler for 3–4 minutes on each side, until they are softened and charred in places.

2 Place a slice of the sweet potatoes in each of four 3in- (8cm-) wide, 1½in- (4cm-) high metal rings on a baking sheet. If the potato does not fit in neatly, break off bits of a bigger slice to fill any gaps. Top each with a slice of tomato, divide over half the basil, and season well. Cover each with a slice of eggplant and divide over half the cheese. Press down well, then repeat the layers, finishing with the goat cheese.

3 Bake for 15–20 minutes, until the top is golden brown and the vegetables are cooked through. Let rest for 5 minutes before carefully running a small, sharp knife around the inside of the ring and easing the vegetable towers out onto warmed plates to serve.

VARIATION

If you have a single guest, you will need ½ sweet potato, 2 slices of eggplant, ½ tomato, and 1oz (30g) goat cheese to make one portion.

PREPARE AHEAD

This timbale can be assembled up to 1 day ahead, covered, and chilled. Return it to room temperature before cooking as in step 3.

COOK'S TIP

If one of your guests is vegetarian, it can be difficult to cook for them and everyone else at the same time. This individual vegetarian dish can be made in advance, then served alongside a summery herby roast chicken to make a great warm-weather meal.

CALORIES: 254kcals/1069kJ

CARBOHYDRATE: 28g
  sugar: 10g

FAT: 12g
  saturated: 6g

SALT: 0.6g

FIBER: 6g

Sage and onion stuffing balls

Cooking the stuffing separately from the meat gives it a deliciously crispy exterior.

15 mins, plus cooling   35 mins

SERVES 4

butter, for greasing

1 tbsp olive oil

1 large onion, very finely chopped

1½ cups fresh white bread crumbs

2 tbsp finely chopped sage leaves

salt and freshly ground black pepper

1 large egg, lightly beaten

1 Preheat the oven to 350°F (180°C). Butter a medium, shallow, ovenproof dish.

2 Heat the oil in a saucepan over medium heat, cover, and gently cook the onion for 10 minutes. Let cool.

3 Stir in the bread crumbs, sage, and a generous amount of seasoning. Add the egg and stir.

4 Using your hands, form the stuffing into 8 equal-sized balls. Place in the buttered dish and bake for 20–25 minutes.

VARIATION

Alternatively, cook the stuffing balls in the roasting pan around a chicken or turkey for the last 30 minutes of roasting time. To cook the stuffing inside a chicken or turkey, make as above up to the end of step 3 and then loosely stuff the neck end of the bird just before roasting.

PREPARE AHEAD

These simple stuffing balls can be prepared ahead. Open-freeze on a baking sheet, then bag up and store in a freezer bag for up to 6 months. Defrost in a single layer on a plate and bake as usual.

CALORIES: 142kcals/597kJ

CARBOHYDRATE: 21g
  sugar: 2.5g

FAT: 5g
  saturated: 1g

SALT: 0.5g

FIBER: 1.5g

Chestnut-cranberry stuffing

Chestnuts, apples, and cranberries turn ground sausage into a suitable accompaniment to a holiday feast.

15 mins   30 mins

SERVES 6

butter, for greasing

4½oz (125g) pork sausage

2 cups fresh brown bread crumbs

1 tsp dried thyme

finely grated zest of 1 lemon

1 red eating apple, unpeeled, cored, and finely chopped

1oz (30g) dried cranberries

7oz (200g) cooked, peeled chestnuts, roughly chopped

1 large egg, lightly beaten

salt and freshly ground black pepper

1 Preheat the oven to 350°F (180°C). Butter a medium ovenproof dish.

2 Place all the ingredients in a medium mixing bowl, season generously, and stir well to combine.

3 Using your hands, form the stuffing into 18 equal-sized balls. Place into the prepared dish and bake for 20 minutes.

VARIATION

To cook the stuffing inside a chicken or turkey, loosely stuff the neck end of the bird just before roasting. Never stuff with a stuffing containing raw egg or meat ahead of time, as that poses a risk of food poisoning.

PREPARE AHEAD

This stuffing can be cooked a day or two ahead, covered and chilled, then covered with foil and reheated when the turkey is out of the oven and resting.

CALORIES: 229kcals/965kJ

CARBOHYDRATE: 34g
  sugar: 9.5g

FAT: 7g
  saturated: 2g

SALT: 0.9g

FIBER: 3g

Herby apricot stuffing

Meat eaters and vegetarians alike will enjoy digging into this fruity apricot stuffing.

15 mins   30 mins

SERVES 4–6

butter, for greasing

3½oz (100g) dried apricots, finely chopped

juice of 1 orange

1 piece crystallized ginger, finely chopped

1 cup fresh white bread crumbs

¾oz (20g) toasted pine nuts

3 tbsp chopped flat-leaf parsley leaves

4 sprigs of rosemary, leaves chopped

¼ cup vegetable shortening vegetable suet

1 large egg, lightly beaten

salt and freshly ground black pepper

1 Preheat the oven to 350°F (180°C). Butter a medium ovenproof dish.

2 Place all the ingredients in a medium mixing bowl, season generously, and stir well to combine.

3 Spoon the stuffing into the prepared dish and bake for 30 minutes.

VARIATION

If you do not have pine nuts, chopped hazelnuts, pecans, or almonds can be substituted instead.

COOK'S TIP

To cook the stuffing in a chicken or turkey, loosely stuff the neck end of the bird just before roasting. This stuffing would also be great inside a boned pork loin.

CALORIES: 323kcals/1354kJ

CARBOHYDRATE: 35g
sugar: 17g

FAT: 17g
saturated: 6g

SALT: 0.6g

FIBER: 3.5g

Classic pan gravy

This is a proper old-fashioned, rich and thick gravy, just like our grandmothers used to make.

5 mins   10 mins

SERVES 4

pan juices from a roast

1 heaping tbsp all-purpose flour

up to 1¼ cups chicken stock (see p94), if needed

2 tbsp sherry or marsala (optional)

1 tbsp redcurrant jelly

salt and freshly ground black pepper

1 When the roast has cooked and is resting, pour off all the cooking juices into a bowl.

2 Add 3 tbsp of the fat, which floats to the top, back into the roasting pan. Place the roasting pan over low heat and add the flour. Cook the flour, whisking constantly, for 2–3 minutes until it bubbles and starts to color.

3 Meanwhile, skim off as much of the remaining fat as possible from the cooking liquid and discard it, then pour the juices into the flour mixture a little at a time, whisking as you go, until you have a thick, rich gravy. Use the chicken stock if you need more liquid. Add the sherry (if using) and the redcurrant jelly and taste for seasoning. Bring it to a boil, making sure the jelly has melted, reduce to a simmer, and cook for 5 minutes before serving.

VARIATION

For a lighter gravy, just add a little white wine to the cooking juices (omit the flour, sherry, and jelly), and whisk over low heat until they reduce to a thinner gravy, then season to taste.

CALORIES: 72kcals/300kJ

CARBOHYDRATE: 5g
sugar: 2.5g

FAT: 3g
saturated: 0.5g

SALT: 0.2g

FIBER: 0g

Sausage and mustard mash canapés

These simple canapés will please young and old alike, and preparing them ahead saves time on the day.

20 mins   45 mins

SPECIAL EQUIPMENT

piping bag fitted with ½in (1cm) star-shaped nozzle

MAKES 40

4 large white potatoes, approx. 1lb 2oz (500g) in total

salt and freshly ground black pepper

2 tbsp butter

1 tbsp Dijon mustard

1 tbsp wholegrain mustard

40 cooked cocktail sausages

handful of chopped flat-leaf parsley leaves, to serve

1 Preheat the oven to 400°F (200°C). Simmer the potatoes in salted water for 20–25 minutes, or until tender. Drain well, then mash to a smooth purée with the butter and mustards, using a potato ricer if possible, for a really smooth result. Season well.

2 Meanwhile, slit each sausage down the middle. They should almost open flat.

3 When the mash has cooled a little, put it into a piping bag fitted with a ½in (1cm) star-shaped nozzle. Pipe into each sausage and lay on a baking sheet.

4 Cook at the top of the hot oven for 15–20 minutes, until the potato is crispy. Allow to cool a little and sprinkle with parsley before serving.

PREPARE AHEAD

These sausages can be prepared to the end of step 3 a day ahead of a party and kept, covered, in the fridge. For a large party, double or triple the quantities and bake in batches, so you can serve hot sausages to guests in 2 or 3 waves.

CALORIES: 62kcals/257kJ

CARBOHYDRATE: 3g
    sugar: 0.5g

FAT: 4g
    saturated: 1.5g

SALT: 0.4g

FIBER: 0g

Roasted asparagus and prosciutto bundles

This easy but elegant dish makes a great appetizer, and each bundle is one perfect serving.

10 mins   15 mins

SERVES 4 (as an appetizer)

24 thin asparagus spears

2 tbsp olive oil

salt and freshly ground black pepper

4 prosciutto slices

1 Preheat the oven to 450°F (230°C). Trim the asparagus spears of their woody ends, put them on a plate, and rub with 1 tbsp of olive oil. Season well.

2 Lay a slice of the prosciutto on a board and put one-quarter of the asparagus spears in the middle. Carefully wrap the prosciutto around the asparagus to make a neat parcel, leaving the tips exposed. Lay it on a baking sheet with the seam of the meat facing down. Repeat to make 4 parcels. Brush the prosciutto with the remaining olive oil.

3 Bake at the top of the hot oven for 15 minutes, until the prosciutto is crispy and the asparagus cooked through. Serve as it is, or with a Hollandaise sauce (see p254), or a poached egg.

COOK'S TIP

As well as an appetizer, this makes a lovely vegetable side dish to serve with salmon fillets or chicken breasts.

CALORIES: 119kcals/492kJ

CARBOHYDRATE: 2g
    sugar: 2g

FAT: 9g
    saturated: 3g

SALT: 0.2g

FIBER: 2.5g

Home-cured gravlax and dill mayonnaise

Gravlax, which means "buried salmon" in Swedish, is delicious, and relatively inexpensive to make at home.

20 mins,
plus 3 days
marinating

SPECIAL EQUIPMENT
food processor or blender

SERVES 6–10

2 tbsp coarse sea salt

3 tbsp granulated sugar

1 tsp freshly ground black pepper

1¾oz (50g) dill, finely chopped, stalks included

1¾lb (800g) piece of very fresh salmon from the center of the fillet (most of a side of salmon)

rye or pumpernickel bread, to serve

FOR THE DILL MAYONNAISE

2 large very fresh egg yolks (see food safety note on raw eggs, p11)

1 tbsp rice wine vinegar, or to taste

2 tbsp Dijon mustard

¼ cup roughly chopped dill stalks

½ tbsp granulated sugar

salt and freshly ground black pepper

2 cups sunflower or vegetable oil

1 In a small bowl, mix the salt, sugar, black pepper, and dill. Cut the salmon across the middle to form 2 equal-sized pieces. Lay 1 piece, skin-side down, on the edge of a roll of plastic wrap. Cover the flesh of the fish with the dill mixture, then put the second piece of salmon on top of the first, skin-side up.

2 Wrap the salmon a few times in the plastic wrap, being careful to wrap both lengthwise and widthwise so it is entirely enclosed in a tight parcel. Place on a trivet in a deep roasting pan. Refrigerate the salmon for 3 days, turning it morning and evening so that each side of the fish gets soaked in the marinade.

3 After 3 days, carefully unwrap the fish—there will be a lot of juice from the marinade. Put the fish, skin-side down, on a cutting board and gently scrape away most of the dill that remains on top of the flesh with a sharp knife.

4 To make the mayonnaise, put the egg yolks, vinegar, mustard, dill, and sugar into the bowl of a food processor or blender, and season well. Add a little of the oil and process to a smooth paste. With the motor running, slowly add the remaining oil in a thin stream, until the mixture thickens and emulsifies. Taste and adjust the acidity with more vinegar, if needed. Refrigerate until needed, and for up to 1 day.

5 The salmon can now be carved from the skin in thin slices at a sharp angle, as you would carve a side of smoked salmon. Serve with the dill mayonnaise and some rye or pumpernickel bread.

VARIATION
Gravlax is very adaptable. Flavor the salt and sugar cure with alcohol, such as vodka, or add grated raw beets for a stunning pink cure.

CALORIES:	206kcals/856kJ
CARBOHYDRATE: 3g	
sugar: 3g	
FAT: 14g	
saturated: 2g	
SALT: 1.3g	
FIBER: 0g	

Summery shrimp towers

Most of these impressive appetizers can be prepared ahead, then it's just a simple assembly job before serving.

30 mins   15 mins

SPECIAL EQUIPMENT
4 x 3in- (8cm-) wide and 1½in- (4cm-) high metal rings

SERVES 4

2 large beefsteak tomatoes

5 tbsp olive oil

salt and freshly ground black pepper

1 large eggplant, cut into 8 x ¾in (2cm) slices

2 avocados, halved and pitted

1 lemon

2 tbsp finely chopped basil leaves

1 tbsp balsamic vinegar

20 raw tiger shrimp, shelled, heads removed, and deveined

1 Trim the tops and bases off the tomatoes (save them for stock) and slice each in half horizontally. Heat 1 tbsp of the oil in a large, non-stick grll pan or frying pan and cook the halves for 4–5 minutes each side, seasoning after turning, until cooked but not collapsing. Set aside. Wipe the pan with paper towels.

2 Add 2 tbsp of the olive oil to the pan and cook the eggplant slices for 8–10 minutes each side, seasoning them after turning, until golden brown and cooked through. Drain them on paper towels.

3 Dice the flesh of the avocados into small cubes and mix with the juice of ½ lemon, the basil, balsamic vinegar, and 1 tbsp of the olive oil.

4 To assemble the towers, put a 3in- (8cm-) wide and 1½in- (4cm-) high metal ring in the middle of a plate and add a tomato half, squishing it in slightly. Add a spoonful of the avocado mix, then 2 slices of the eggplant, and finally another spoonful of avocado. Season every layer lightly as you build the tower.

5 When you are ready to serve, quickly pan-fry the shrimp in the remaining 1 tbsp of olive oil for 2–3 minutes, until they change color to a vivid pink. Season them well and squeeze over the remaining ½ lemon. Top each tower with 5 shrimp, nicely arranged, then carefully remove the ring to serve.

CALORIES: 333kcals/1380kJ
CARBOHYDRATE: 6g
    sugar: 5g
FAT: 29g
    saturated: 6g
SALT: 0.26g
FIBER: 6g

Smoked oyster soup

This sophisticated soup is a great dinner party appetizer. No one will realize it's actually quite simple to make.

10 mins   30 mins

SPECIAL EQUIPMENT
blender

SERVES 4 (as an appetizer)

2 tbsp olive oil

1 onion, finely chopped

2 large white potatoes, approx. 12oz (350g) in total, peeled and roughly chopped

1 x 3oz (85g) can of smoked oysters in sunflower oil, drained and rinsed

3½ cups fish stock

¼ cup whipping cream, plus extra to serve

salt and freshly ground black pepper

1 tbsp dry sherry (optional)

1 Heat the olive oil in a large, heavy-bottomed saucepan. Cook the onion over low heat, covered, for 5–7 minutes until it softens, but is not brown.

2 Add the potatoes, smoked oysters, fish stock, and cream, and season with a little salt and pepper. Bring the soup to a boil, then reduce to a simmer, partially cover, and cook for 20–25 minutes, until the potatoes are soft.

3 Purée the soup until smooth (if you are using a blender, you may have to do this in batches; it is important not to fill the blender more than one-third full with hot liquid). Now pass it through a sieve so that it is completely smooth.

4 Return the soup to the pan and heat it gently. Add the sherry (if using) and serve with a swirl of cream in the center of the bowls and a sprinkling of pepper.

CALORIES: 209kcals/869kJ
CARBOHYDRATE: 17g
    sugar: 2g
FAT: 13g
    saturated: 5g
SALT: 2.5g
FIBER: 2g

Mini naan toasts with roasted vegetables and goat cheese

These pretty little appetizers taste as delicious as they look, and can be prepared well in advance.

30 mins   **35 mins**

SPECIAL EQUIPMENT
1½in (4cm) round cutter

MAKES 40

½ eggplant, approx. 5½oz (150g), cut into ½in (1cm) cubes

½ red bell pepper, approx. 3½oz (100g), cut into ½in (1cm) cubes

1 zucchini, approx. 4¼oz (120g), cut into ½in (1cm) cubes

½ red onion, approx. 3½oz (100g), finely chopped

2 tbsp olive oil, plus extra if needed

salt and freshly ground black pepper

2 plain naan breads

3½oz (100g) soft goat cheese

3½oz (100g) cream cheese, softened

2 tbsp finely chopped basil leaves

1 Preheat the oven to 400°F (200°C). Put the eggplant, red bell pepper, zucchini, and onion in a large roasting pan in a single layer. Toss with the olive oil and season.

2 Cook for 20 minutes, turning after 15 minutes, until soft and charred at the edges. Set aside to cool, adding ½ tbsp of oil if they look dry. Taste for seasoning.

3 Meanwhile, cut the naan breads into small circles using a 1½in (4cm) round cutter and put on a baking sheet. Cook for 10–15 minutes until golden brown and crispy. Set aside to cool.

4 In a bowl, beat the goat cheese, cream cheese, and basil and season well. When ready to serve, spread each piece of bread with a little herby goat cheese and top with 1 tsp of vegetables, pressing down slightly so the vegetables stick to the cheese.

PREPARE AHEAD
The separate parts of this canapé can be made up to 2 days ahead and stored in airtight containers (the vegetables and the cheese should be stored in the fridge).

CALORIES: 45kcals/189kJ

CARBOHYDRATE: 3.5g
sugar: 0.5g

FAT: 3g
saturated: 1g

SALT: 0.15g

FIBER: 0.5g

Roast side of salmon with cucumber and dill salad

A whole side of salmon makes a stunning, popular centerpiece at a party or buffet, and is really simple to prepare.

20 mins, plus draining   25 mins

SPECIAL EQUIPMENT
food processor

SERVES 6-8

1 skinless and boneless side of salmon

1 tbsp olive oil

salt and freshly ground black pepper

2 lemons, cut into wedges, to serve

plain yogurt, to serve

FOR THE SALAD

2 cucumbers, very finely sliced with a food processor

2 tbsp coarse sea salt

2 tbsp granulated sugar

¼ cup rice wine vinegar

handful of dill, finely chopped

1 For the salad, toss the cucumber in the salt, put in a colander, and weigh down with a plate. Leave in the sink for 1 hour to remove the excess water. Rinse briefly, put it into a clean kitchen towel, and squeeze to remove excess water.

2 Preheat the oven to 425°F (220°C). Whisk the sugar and vinegar with 2 tbsp of boiling water to dissolve in a bowl. Toss in the cucumber and dill, cover, and chill for at least 30 minutes.

3 Put the salmon on a very large baking sheet and rub with the oil. Season well and roast at the top of the oven for 20–25 minutes, until cooked, but moist in the middle.

4 Serve the salmon with lemon wedges, the cucumber and dill salad, and a bowl of plain yogurt.

CLEVER WITH LEFTOVERS

Cold roast salmon is perfect to mix into fishcakes (see p85), or with mayonnaise and leftover Cucumber and dill salad (drained well first) to serve with crackers and salad leaves for a light lunch.

CALORIES: 374kcals/1557kJ

CARBOHYDRATE: 5g
    sugar: 5g

FAT: 22g
    saturated: 4g

SALT: 1.4g

FIBER: 0.5g

Catalan seafood zarzuela

This traditional Catalan stew makes an opulent appetizer or summer lunch. Add more mussels if you can't find clams.

15 mins   25 mins

SERVES 4

1 tbsp olive oil

1 onion, finely chopped

2 garlic cloves, finely chopped

1¼ cups dry white wine

1¼ cups fish stock

2 tbsp tomato paste

generous pinch of saffron threads

salt and freshly ground black pepper

12 fresh mussels, scrubbed, and beards removed (discard any that stay open when sharply tapped)

12 fresh clams, scrubbed (discard any that stay open when sharply tapped)

10oz (300g) firm white fish fillets, such as haddock or cod, pin-boned, skinned, and cut into bite-sized pieces

2 squid pouches (approx. 6oz/175g in total), sliced into ¼in- (5mm-) thick rings

8 raw large shrimp, shells on, deveined

3 tbsp chopped flat-leaf parsley leaves

crusty bread, to serve

1 Heat the oil in a deep-sided frying pan over medium heat and cook the onion for 10 minutes, covered. Add the garlic and cook for 1 minute. Add the wine and simmer for 5 minutes. Add the stock, tomato paste, and saffron and season. Return to a simmer, add the clams and mussels, and cook for 3 minutes.

2 Add the white fish, squid, and shrimp and cook for 2 minutes. Cover and cook for 5 minutes more. Discard any mussels or clams that do not open on cooking. Stir in the parsley. Serve with crusty bread.

VARIATION

Saffron is a very expensive spice, and not to everyone's taste. For a less authentic, but still delicious stew with a smoky edge, add 1 tsp of smoked paprika instead.

CALORIES: 314kcals/1319kJ

CARBOHYDRATE: 7g
sugar: 3g

FAT: 6g
saturated: 1g

SALT: 2.3g

FIBER: 0.5g

Roast turkey

Cooked this way, the turkey will be juicy and delicious. Look for a smaller turkey as they are easier to cook correctly.

10 mins   2½–3 hrs, plus resting

SERVES 8–10

8–10lb (4–5kg) turkey

2 tbsp butter

salt and freshly ground black pepper

handful of thyme sprigs

1 Preheat the oven to 325°F (160°C). Remove any giblets from inside the turkey and use them to make a stock.

2 Weigh the turkey so you can calculate its cooking time, then place it in a large roasting pan. Smear the breast with the butter, and season the bird well inside and out. Pop the thyme into the cavity.

3 Place greaseproof paper over the breast of the turkey, then cover it with a large sheet of foil, sealing it to the roasting pan so no steam will escape.

4 Roast the turkey for 15 minutes per 1lb (450g) of weight. Remove the foil for the last 30 minutes and increase the oven temperature to 400°F (200°C), so the skin can brown nicely. Remove the turkey from the oven and rest it, covered in foil, for at least 30 minutes before serving.

VARIATION

Try spreading the butter underneath the skin of the bird, easing the skin gently from the breast, before roasting.

COOK'S TIP

To ensure a turkey is cooked through, use a meat thermometer to test the thickest part of the thigh. It should have a temperature of 160°F (71°C).

CLEVER WITH LEFTOVERS

A turkey yields a lot of meat. The cold leftover meat can be used in place of cooked cold chicken in any of the recipes in this book.

CALORIES: 248kcals/1048kJ

CARBOHYDRATE: 0g
  sugar: 0g

FAT: 5g
  saturated: 2.5g

SALT: 0.3g

FIBER: 0g

Stuffed roast goose

Try roasting a rich goose instead of a turkey at your next holiday gathering.

20 mins | 3¼ hrs, plus resting

SERVES 6–8

9lb (4.5kg) goose with giblets

4 onions, finely chopped

10 sage leaves, chopped

4 tbsp butter, melted and cooled

1 cup fresh bread crumbs

1 large egg yolk

salt and freshly ground black pepper

2 tbsp all-purpose flour

tart applesauce, to serve

1 Preheat the oven to 450°F (230°C). Remove excess fat from inside the goose. Prick the skin all over with a fork. Make a stock with the giblets, reserving the liver.

2 Boil the onions and chopped goose liver in a little water for 5 minutes, then drain. Mix with the sage, butter, bread crumbs, egg, and seasoning. Stuff loosely into the cavity and sew up with a trussing needle and kitchen string, or secure with a skewer. Cover the wings and drumsticks with foil.

3 Place the goose upside down on a rack in a deep roasting pan. Roast for 30 minutes, then turn the goose over and roast for another 30 minutes. Drain off the fat in the roasting pan (reserve it). Cover with foil, reduce the oven temperature to 375°F (190°C), and roast for 1½ hours. Drain off the fat again. Remove the foil and roast for a final 30 minutes. Put on a warm serving dish and rest for 30 minutes.

4 To make the gravy, heat 3 tbsp of goose fat in a pan, stir in the flour, and cook for 5 minutes over low heat. Gradually whisk in enough hot giblet stock to make a gravy. Pour off all the fat from the roasting pan and pour in the gravy, stirring up the brown juices. Strain.

5 Carve the goose and serve with the gravy, stuffing, and a tart applesauce.

COOK'S TIP

The clear fat rendered early in cooking is great saved in the fridge and used to roast potatoes. Discard the cloudy or brown fat rendered in the later stages.

CALORIES: 559kcals/2328kJ

CARBOHYDRATE: 12g
sugar: 8g

FAT: 38g
saturated: 13g

SALT: 0.4g

FIBER: 2g

Bacon-wrapped sausages

Serve these with pancakes and scrambled eggs for a child-friendly Easter brunch.

10 mins   30 mins

SERVES 4

10 slices thick-cut bacon

20 cocktail sausages

1 Preheat the oven to 400°F (200°C). Take a slice of bacon, place it on a cutting board, and scrape the blade of a knife along it, while pulling on its end, so the bacon stretches out. Cut each piece in half to make 20 short, thin slices.

2 Wrap each cocktail sausage in a half-piece of bacon, then put them on a baking sheet with the ends of the bacon facing down.

3 Cook in the hot oven for 20–30 minutes, turning occasionally, until the bacon is crispy and the sausages cooked through.

PREPARE AHEAD

These can be prepared up to 2 days in advance and stored on their baking sheet, well wrapped in plastic wrap, in the fridge. Return to room temperature for 30 minutes before cooking as directed.

HOW TO FREEZE

The cocktail sausages can be wrapped and frozen, uncooked, for up to 8 weeks. Defrost thoroughly before cooking.

CALORIES: 416kcals/1725kJ
CARBOHYDRATE: 5g
  sugar: 1.5g
FAT: 33g
  saturated: 12g
SALT: 3.8g
FIBER: 0g

Brussels sprouts with pancetta and chestnuts

Many die-hard sprout haters will love this sweet and meaty treatment of the vegetables.

10 mins   15 mins

SERVES 4–6

salt and freshly ground black pepper

1lb 2oz (500g) baby Brussels sprouts

1 tbsp butter, plus extra if needed

1 tbsp olive oil

3½oz (100g) chopped pancetta

3½oz (100g) cooked and peeled chestnuts, roughly chopped

1 Bring a large pan of salted water to a boil. Cook the Brussels sprouts for 4–5 minutes, until they are just cooked, then drain well and refresh them under cold water. Drain again and set aside.

2 In a wok, heat the butter and olive oil. When the butter has melted, add the pancetta and cook over medium heat for 3–4 minutes, until it is crispy. Add the chestnuts and cook for another minute.

3 Add the Brussels sprouts and cook for another 2–3 minutes, until heated through, adding a little more butter if necessary and seasoning well with pepper (not salt as the pancetta is quite salty).

CALORIES: 237kcals/990kJ
CARBOHYDRATE: 13g
  sugar: 5.5g
FAT: 16g
  saturated: 6g
SALT: 1g
FIBER: 8g

VARIATION

For an Asian take on sprouts, shred the blanched sprouts. Stir-fry in 2 tbsp of oil over high heat, adding 1 finely chopped chile, 1 finely grated garlic clove, and 1in (2.5cm) finely grated fresh ginger. Finish with a splash each of soy sauce and rice wine.

Cranberry sauce

Fresh cranberries are easy to buy in winter, so try using them to make this delicious, fresh cranberry sauce.

5 mins   10 mins

SERVES 8

12oz (350g) pack of cranberries

¾ cup orange juice

¼ cup tbsp port

⅔ cup granulated sugar

1 Put the cranberries in a small, heavy-bottomed pan and cover them with the orange juice and port. Add the sugar.

2 Bring the liquid to a boil, then reduce to a simmer and cook over low heat for 10 minutes, until the cranberries have softened and burst and the mixture has thickened and reduced.

VARIATION

Adapt the sauce recipe to your family's tastes. For a more tart sauce, reduce the amount of sugar to taste. Cranberry sauce also works well with many winter spices: try adding ½ tsp of allspice, or ground ginger, or freshly ground black pepper to the recipe.

PREPARE AHEAD

You can make this up to 3 days ahead and store, in an airtight container, in the fridge. Either reheat gently to serve, or serve it cold.

COOK'S TIP

For a smoother finish, use a hand-held blender to briefly purée the finished sauce to your desired consistency.

CALORIES: 85kcals/362kJ
CARBOHYDRATE: 19g
   sugar: 19g
FAT: 0g
   saturated: 0g
SALT: trace
FIBER: 1.5g

Bread sauce

A classic British accompaniment to roast turkey, chicken, or pheasant, this subtly spiced sauce is deeply comforting.

5 mins   10 mins
plus resting

SERVES 6–8

2 cups whole milk

1 onion, peeled and halved
   horizontally (across its equator)

6 cloves

2 cups fresh white bread crumbs

salt and freshly ground black pepper

grated nutmeg, to serve (optional)

pat of butter, to serve (optional)

1 Put the milk, onion, and cloves in a small saucepan and bring them to a boil. Turn the heat off and cover the pan, leaving the onion and cloves to infuse for at least 1 hour.

2 When you are ready to cook the bread sauce, remove the onion and cloves from the milk, add the bread crumbs, and season well. Heat the sauce over medium heat until it is warmed through and thickened. Stir in a grating of fresh nutmeg and a pat of butter to serve (if using).

PREPARE AHEAD

To get ahead at Christmas time, infuse and strain the milk a couple of days ahead, cover, and store in the fridge. The bread crumbs can also be made in advance and frozen until needed.

CALORIES: 130kcals/550kJ
CARBOHYDRATE: 21g
   sugar: 3.5g
FAT: 3g
   saturated: 1.5g
SALT: 0.6g
FIBER: 0.5g

Boeuf en croûte

Also known as Beef Wellington, this rich and luxurious dish is simple to finish off and serve; perfect for entertaining.

45 mins   45–60 mins, plus standing

SERVES 6

2¼lb (1kg) filet of beef, cut from the thick end and trimmed of fat

salt and freshly ground black pepper

2 tbsp sunflower or vegetable oil

3 tbsp unsalted butter

2 shallots, finely chopped

1 garlic clove, crushed

9oz (250g) mixed wild mushrooms, finely chopped

1 tbsp brandy or Madeira

1lb 2oz (500g) store-bought all-butter puff pastry

1 large egg, lightly beaten

1 Preheat the oven to 425°F (220°C). Season the meat all over with salt and pepper. Heat the oil in a large frying pan and cook the beef until browned all over. Place in a roasting pan and roast for 10 minutes. Remove and leave it to cool.

2 Melt the butter in a pan. Cook the shallots and garlic for 2–3 minutes, stirring, until softened. Add the mushrooms and cook, stirring, for 4–5 minutes until the juices evaporate. Add the brandy and let it bubble for 30 seconds. Let cool.

3 Roll out one-third of the dough to a rectangle about 2in (5cm) larger than the beef. Place on a baking sheet and prick with a fork.

4 Bake for 12–15 minutes until crisp. Cool, then spread one-third of the mushroom mixture in the center. Place the beef on top and spread over the remaining mushroom mixture. Roll out the remaining dough and place over the beef. Brush the egg around the edges of the raw dough, and press them down on the cooked dough base to seal.

5 Brush the egg all over the dough. Slit the top for steam to escape. Bake for 30 minutes for rare, 35 for medium-rare, or 45 for well done. If the dough starts to become too brown, cover it loosely with foil. Remove from the oven and let it stand for 10 minutes before serving. Slice with a very sharp knife.

VARIATION

This is undoubtedly an expensive dish for a special occasion, but to save a few pennies, substitute ordinary field mushrooms for button mushrooms. For extra flavor, add a handful of dried wild mushrooms, soaked in boiling water for 30 minutes, then drained and chopped, to the fresh mushrooms.

CALORIES: 662kcals/2764kJ

CARBOHYDRATE: 29g
  sugar: 1.5g

FAT: 41g
  saturated: 19g

SALT: 0.9g

FIBER: 8g

Herb-crusted rack of lamb with red wine sauce

Simple but impressive, and a great centerpiece for a special meal. Double the ingredients to serve more people.

15 mins, plus resting

12–22 mins

SPECIAL EQUIPMENT
food processor

SERVES 4

1½ tbsp olive oil

2 x 6-bone racks of lamb, Frenched

¾ cup fresh bread crumbs

1 tbsp chopped rosemary leaves

2 tbsp chopped flat-leaf parsley leaves

1 tbsp thyme leaves

salt and freshly ground black pepper

2 tbsp Dijon mustard

FOR THE SAUCE

⅔ cup red wine

⅔ cup lamb or beef stock

2 tbsp redcurrant jelly

mashed potatoes and thin green beans, to serve

1 Preheat the oven to 400°F (200°C). Heat the oil in a roasting pan over medium heat and cook the lamb racks for 1 minute on each side, until browned all over. Discard any excess oil and set the meat aside.

2 Put the bread crumbs, herbs, and seasoning in the small bowl of a food processor and process them for a minute, until the herbs turn the bread crumbs bright green. Brush the meaty side of each rack with 1 tbsp of the mustard. Firmly pat half the herb mixture onto the mustard-covered side of each rack. Shake off any excess.

3 Roast the lamb for 10 minutes for rare meat, 15 minutes for medium, and 20 minutes for well done. Let rest, loosely covered with foil, for 5 minutes.

4 To make the sauce, put the wine and stock into a heavy-bottomed saucepan and bring to a boil. Stir in the redcurrant jelly until it has melted, reduce to a low simmer, and cook for 10 minutes until reduced. Season with pepper, to taste.

5 Carve the lamb into chops and serve 3 per person with a little of the sauce, mashed potatoes, and thin green beans.

COOK'S TIP
For the best presentation, cover the Frenched bones with foil before roasting and they will maintain their whiteness and not scorch.

CALORIES: 387kcals/1619kJ

CARBOHYDRATE: 14g
sugar: 5.5g

FAT: 19g
saturated: 6g

SALT: 1.2g

FIBER: 0.5g

Whole glazed ham

Buying a pre-cooked ham means that it simply needs to be brought up to a safe temperature to eat.

20 mins   2½ hrs

SERVES 8–10

4½lb (2kg) piece of smoked ham

FOR THE GLAZE

3 heaping tbsp smooth marmalade

2 tbsp pineapple juice

1 tbsp honey

1 heaping tbsp light brown sugar

2 tbsp whole grain mustard

salt and freshly ground black pepper

1 Preheat the oven to 325°F (160°C). Put the ham, skin-side up, on a rack inside a large roasting pan, and pour water to a depth of 1in (3cm) into the pan. Cover tightly with foil, making sure it is well sealed so that no steam escapes. Cook for 2 hours.

2 Meanwhile, in a pan, mix the glaze ingredients and bring to a boil. Reduce to a simmer and cook for 5–7 minutes, until thick.

3 Remove the ham from the oven and increase the temperature to 400°F (200°C).

Cut a criss-cross in the fat. Brush some glaze over the top.

4 Return the ham to the oven for 30 minutes, brushing with glaze every 10 minutes until browned and crispy. Serve hot with mashed potatoes and Slow-cooked red cabbage (see p165).

CLEVER WITH LEFTOVERS

This will give you plenty of leftovers. It is a great standby in the holidays when you can serve it cold for days afterward, with baked potatoes, or in sandwiches and omelets.

COOK'S TIP

To cook a larger ham, simply calculate cooking time as 30 minutes per 1lb 2oz (500g) of meat, increasing the temperature for the final 30 minutes.

CALORIES: 362kcals/1527kJ

CARBOHYDRATE: 6g
  sugar: 6g

FAT: 11g
  saturated: 4g

SALT: 5.7g

FIBER: 0g

Chinese roast duck and pancakes

This recipe is likely to become a favorite with all the family; children love to assemble their own pancake rolls.

20 mins 1 hr 10 mins

SERVES 4

4 duck legs

1 heaping tsp five-spice powder

1 tsp coarse sea salt

freshly ground black pepper

1 cucumber

2 bunches of scallions

2 x 4oz packages of Chinese pancakes

12oz jar of hoisin sauce or plum sauce

1 Preheat the oven to 325°F (160°C). Prick the skin of the duck legs all over with a fork. Mix the five-spice powder, salt, and plenty of pepper and rub it all over the legs.

2 Put the duck legs, skin-side up, on a rack inside a roasting pan and cook them for 45 minutes. Then increase the oven temperature to 425°F (220°C) and cook them for another 25 minutes until the skin is crispy and the duck is cooked through.

3 Meanwhile, prepare the vegetables. Cut the cucumber in quarters, lengthwise, then use a teaspoon to scoop the seeds from each piece. Cut each long piece into 4 chunks, then cut each chunk lengthwise into thin strips, so that you are left with a pile of thin cucumber batons. Cut the scallions into thin strips.

4 When the duck is ready, place it on a cutting board and pull both meat and crispy skin from the bones with 2 forks. Keep it warm.

5 Heat the Chinese pancakes according to the package instructions. Serve the duck with the shredded vegetables, pancakes, and the hoisin or plum sauce.

CALORIES: 497kcals/2082kJ

CARBOHYDRATE: 31g
 sugar: 17.5g

FAT: 16g
 saturated: 3.5g

SALT: 2.3g

FIBER: 3g

Smart with leftovers

In the past, cooking with leftovers would have been a cornerstone of the repertoire of every family cook. For most families, meat products were expensive, and fruits and vegetables available only seasonally, so it made sense to make the most of what you had, when you had it. These days food is much more easily available, and it's easy to feel that we don't have the time or experience to turn the odds and ends in the fridge into another meal. Often we can end up discarding what we cannot easily cook. However, with a few helpful hints you can save time as well as money, and cut back on food waste.

Good things to keep

There are times when it makes sense to deliberately cook more than needed, just for the leftovers. Cold roast meat, a roast chicken carcass with meat left on it, and extra pasta are all worth keeping in the fridge. If cooking extra rice, be sure to cool the leftovers as quickly as possible (ideally within an hour). Only store the leftover rice in the fridge for one day, and make sure it is steaming throughout when reheating. Use leftover meat for salads or sandwiches, and cook up the chicken carcass to make a rich stock (p84). Even leftover vegetables can be added to a soup or stir-fry, and staples like eggs, cheese, and store-bought pastry can help to turn leftovers into delicious dishes in minutes.

Good things to save (and what to turn them into)

⭐ Mashed potatoes (fishcakes, potato pancakes)

⭐ Basmati rice (salads, stir-fries)

⭐ Simple risotto (risotto cakes, involtini)

⭐ Sausages (hearty soups, pasta sauces)

⭐ Cooked bacon (sandwiches, salads)

⭐ Slow-cooked barbecued pork (wraps)

⭐ Croissants, especially the chocolate ones (bread and butter pudding p349)

New dishes from leftovers

Transforming your leftovers into brand new family meals takes only a little effort. Roasts can provide a lot of extra meat to use, and excess rice or potatoes just need the addition of something tasty to produce the next day's supper.

Roast pork

Roast pork If you made a hearty Sunday roast you will probably have lots of leftover meat. With the addition of some pantry essentials, you can produce a very tasty Monday night supper, such as Leftover pork chili (p146).

Risotto

Adult meals to toddler dishes

Turn any roast chicken left over from Sunday dinner into a simple supper for the children. Make a pasta casserole using small pasta shapes, the leftover chicken, some Easy cheesy sauce (p34), and a handful of frozen peas.

Mashed potatoes

Risotto The remaining rice from a simple risotto dish can be turned into crispy involtini, such as Mozzarella-stuffed risotto balls (p221), in a matter of minutes. Spread out the leftover rice in a large container so that it dries out well to make it easier to handle the next day.

Leftovers into lunches

Leftover rice, pasta, or even boiled new potatoes can all form the basis of some wonderful portable food, suitable for a lunch box, such as Jeweled rice salad (p218), Potato salad with celery and capers (p158), or Pasta salad with shrimp and pesto (p188).

Mashed potatoes If you know you will need extra mashed potatoes for a recipe such as Smoked haddock fishcakes (p84), make sure you mash the potatoes with almost no added liquid before removing what you will need for the next day.

Soft fruit bruschetta with mascarpone

A quick and impressive dessert that makes the most of seasonal summer fruits.

10 mins, plus macerating   5 mins

SERVES 4

2 tbsp confectioners' sugar

½ tbsp balsamic vinegar

7oz (200g) strawberries, cut into raspberry-sized chunks

2 ripe peaches, peeled and cut into raspberry-sized chunks

5½oz (150g) raspberries

4 large or 8 small thick slices of brioche or challah bread

2 tbsp butter, softened

7oz (250g) tub of mascarpone

CALORIES: 562kcals/2354kJ

CARBOHYDRATE: 48g
  sugar: 27g

FAT: 37g
  saturated: 24g

SALT: 0.6g

FIBER: 4.5g

1 In a bowl, mix 1 tbsp of the confectioners' sugar with the vinegar until the sugar has dissolved.

2 Add the strawberries and mix through. Leave to macerate at room temperature for about 30 minutes. Stir in the peaches and raspberries.

3 Meanwhile, spread the slices of brioche with a little butter on both sides and toast them on a preheated grill pan, or under a broiler. Spread thickly with the mascarpone (you may not need the whole tub) and top each evenly with the berry mixture. Dust with the remaining confectioners' sugar and serve immediately.

VARIATION

Omit the berries and use 3–4 peaches instead. Once the brioche is toasted and topped, sprinkle with 1 tbsp dark brown sugar and broil under a hot broiler, or blast with a blowtorch, until glazed.

Summer pudding

Make this classic, elegant dessert when summer fruits are at their best, and serve with cream.

15 mins, plus chilling   5 mins

SPECIAL EQUIPMENT
1-quart (900ml) pudding mold or bowl

SERVES 4

1¼lb (550g) prepared mixed berries, such as raspberries, redcurrants, strawberries, blackcurrants, or blueberries, plus extra for serving

½ cup granulated sugar

8 thin slices of white bread, crusts cut off

heavy cream, softly whipped, to serve

CALORIES: 266kcals/1131kJ

CARBOHYDRATE: 57g
  sugar: 34g

FAT: 1g
  saturated: 0.2g

SALT: 0.7g

FIBER: 5g

1 Place the fruit and sugar in a saucepan and add 3 tbsp of water. Heat until simmering and cook for 5 minutes.

2 Line a 1-quart (900ml) pudding mold with 6 slices of the bread. Carefully spoon the fruit and all the juices into the lined bowl and cover with the remaining bread, cutting to fit if necessary. Place a saucer on top and then a 14oz (400g) can to weigh it down. Place in the fridge overnight.

3 Just before serving, remove the saucer and can and place a serving plate over the bowl. Invert the pudding onto the plate and top with a few fresh berries to decorate. Cut into wedges and serve with the heavy cream.

VARIATION

Later in the year, try autumn pudding. Simmer sliced apples for 20 minutes, adding blackberries and the sugar for the last 5 minutes (the total weight of fruit should be 1¼lb/550g).

Raspberry towers

This easy yet impressive dessert is perfect for entertaining and can be assembled at the last minute.

30 mins, plus chilling   35 mins

SPECIAL EQUIPMENT

2¾in (7cm) round cookie cutter

SERVES 4

5 tbsp butter

½ cup granulated sugar

1 large egg yolk

½ tsp vanilla extract

pinch of salt

1 cup all-purpose flour, sifted, plus extra for dusting

¾ cup heavy cream

1 tbsp confectioners' sugar, plus extra for dusting

10oz (300g) raspberries

1 Beat the butter and granulated sugar together until fluffy. Beat in the yolk, vanilla, and salt. Stir in the flour to make a dough. Wrap in plastic wrap and chill for 30 minutes. Preheat the oven to 350°F (180°C).

2 Roll out the dough as thinly as possible on a floured surface and cut out 12 rounds with a 2¾in (7cm) cookie cutter. Any leftover dough can be frozen.

3 Bake for 10 minutes on a baking sheet lined with parchment paper until golden at the edges. Leave on the pan for a couple of minutes, then transfer to a wire rack to cool completely.

4 Whip the cream with the confectioners' sugar until stiff. Spread a spoonful of cream on a cookie and cover with raspberries. Take a second cookie and spread a thin layer of cream underneath. Stick it on top. Repeat, finishing the tower with the nicest-looking cookie. Dust with confectioners' sugar to serve.

CLEVER WITH LEFTOVERS

Purée extra fruit with 1 tbsp confectioners' sugar and pass through a nylon sieve to make a sauce to serve with the Raspberry towers.

HOW TO FREEZE

Any uncooked dough can be wrapped in plastic wrap and frozen for up to 12 weeks. Defrost thoroughly before baking.

CALORIES: 687kcals/2871kJ
CARBOHYDRATE: 65g
   sugar: 40g
FAT: 44g
   saturated: 27g
SALT: 0.6g
FIBER: 4g

Warm winter fruit salad

There's no need to miss out on fresh fruits in fall or winter; try them warm with a sweet syrup.

20 mins   35 mins

⅓ cup granulated sugar

⅔ cup red wine

finely grated zest and juice of 1 orange, plus 2 oranges, peeled and sliced into rounds

1 cinnamon stick

2 ripe pears, quartered, cored, and peeled

4 plums, halved and pitted

1 Place the sugar in a medium, heavy-bottomed pan and add 1¼ cups of water. Place over medium-low heat to dissolve the sugar. When it has all completely dissolved, increase the heat and bring it to a boil, then reduce the heat once more and simmer for 10 minutes.

2 Add the wine, orange zest and juice, and cinnamon stick to the pan and bring to a boil.

3 Reduce the heat and add the pears and plums. Cover and simmer over medium heat for

10 minutes, or until the fruit is tender (test by piercing a big piece with a knife; it should meet no resistance). Stir in the orange slices.

4 Carefully remove the fruit from the pan using a slotted spoon, taking as little liquid as possible with the pieces, and set aside in a serving dish.

5 Boil the syrup over high heat for 10 minutes to reduce it; it should thicken slightly. Remove the cinnamon stick from the syrup and pour it over the fruit. Serve warm or at room temperature.

CALORIES: 193kcals/819kJ
CARBOHYDRATE: 39g
   sugar: 40g
FAT: 0g
   saturated: 0g
SALT: trace
FIBER: 4.5g

Cherry and almond clafoutis

This French classic is easy to rustle up from a few pantry and fridge essentials.

15 mins   30-35 mins

SPECIAL EQUIPMENT

11 x 8 x 2in (28 x 20 x 5cm) ovenproof dish

electric hand-held mixer

SERVES 4

2 tbsp butter, melted, plus extra for greasing

2 large eggs

¼ cup vanilla or granulated sugar

2 tbsp all-purpose flour, sifted

½ cup whole milk

1 x 14oz (440g) can pitted black cherries in syrup, drained

1oz (30g) sliced almonds

sifted confectioners' sugar and whipped cream, to serve

> CALORIES: 267kcals/1122kJ
> CARBOHYDRATE: 29g
>   sugar: 26g
> FAT: 14g
>   saturated: 5g
> SALT: 0.3g
> FIBER: 0.8g

1 Preheat the oven to 350°F (180°C). Butter a 11 x 8 x 2in (28 x 20 x 5cm) ovenproof dish.

2 Place the eggs and vanilla sugar or granulated sugar in a large bowl and whisk with an electric hand-held mixer until light and fluffy, then fold in the flour. Pour in the melted butter and whisk until well combined. Add the milk and stir well.

3 Arrange the cherries in the ovenproof dish and pour the batter over. Sprinkle the almonds on top and place the dish on a baking sheet.

4 Bake for 30–35 minutes, until risen and golden brown. Dust with confectioners' sugar and serve with whipped cream.

VARIATION

In the summer, when fresh berries are cheap and plentiful, use these instead. Try raspberries, blackcurrants, blueberries, or blackberries instead of the canned cherries.

Apricot clafoutis

Canned apricots taste just fine in this French favorite, when fresh are out of season.

10 mins   35 mins, plus cooling

SERVES 4

unsalted butter, for greasing

9oz (250g) ripe apricots, halved and pitted, or 1 x 14oz (400g) can apricot halves, drained

1 large egg, plus 1 large egg yolk

2 tbsp all-purpose flour, sifted

¼ cup granulated sugar

⅔ cup heavy cream

¼ tsp vanilla extract

thick cream or crème fraîche, to serve (optional)

> CALORIES: 322kcals/1342kJ
> CARBOHYDRATE: 21g
>   sugar: 17.5g
> FAT: 24g
>   saturated: 14g
> SALT: 0.1g
> FIBER: 2g

1 Preheat the oven to 400°F (200°C). Lightly grease a baking dish that is big enough to fit the apricots in a single layer. Place the apricots in a single layer in the dish; there should be space between them.

2 In a bowl, whisk together the egg, egg yolk, and the flour. Whisk in the granulated sugar. Finally add the cream and vanilla extract and whisk thoroughly to form a smooth custard.

3 Pour the custard around the apricots, so the tops are just visible. Bake on the top rack of the oven for 35 minutes, until puffed up and lightly golden brown in places. Remove and let cool for at least 15 minutes before eating. It is best served warm with thick cream or crème fraîche.

PREPARE AHEAD

The clafoutis is best when it's freshly baked and served warm, but it can be cooked up to 6 hours ahead and served at room temperature.

Summer fruits with easy "brûlée" topping

This simple little trick can turn a luscious fruit salad into something far more special.

10 mins, plus resting and chilling

SERVES 4–6

14oz (400g) mixed soft summer fruits, such as strawberries, raspberries, peaches, or blueberries

2½ tbsp granulated sugar

¾ cup (7oz) heavy cream

¾ cup (7oz) Greek yogurt

1 tsp vanilla extract

4 heaping tbsp brown sugar, plus extra if needed

1 Make a fruit salad by cutting the fruit into similar-sized chunks, about ½in (1cm), or the same size as your smallest fruit, discarding the peach pits, if using. Mix in 1 tbsp of the granulated sugar and leave to macerate, at room temperature, for 1 hour.

2 Whisk together the cream and remaining granulated sugar until it is thick. Gently fold in the Greek yogurt and vanilla extract until well combined and chill until needed.

3 When the fruit is ready, spread it out in a large shallow bowl and cover it with a thick layer of the whipped cream mixture. Sprinkle in the brown sugar as evenly as possibly, until there is a thin, even layer all over the cream, and you cannot see it underneath. You may need a little more sugar, depending on the diamater of your serving bowl.

4 Chill the fruit salad in the fridge for 30 minutes, until the sugar has dissolved and there are no granules left.

COOK'S TIP

It is often hard to measure thick liquids. As a guide, ¾ cup of Greek yogurt will weigh about 7oz (200g), so weigh the yogurt if you find it easier.

CALORIES: 274kcals/1141kJ
CARBOHYDRATE: 21g
 sugar: 21g
FAT: 20g
 saturated: 13g
SALT: 0.2g
FIBER: 1.5g

Mango kulfi

This Indian-inspired iced dessert can also be made into child-sized popsicles, using a popsicle mold and sticks.

 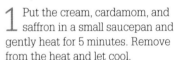

15–20 mins, plus freezing **5 mins**

SPECIAL EQUIPMENT
blender or food processor

4 x 5fl oz (150ml) ramekins or popsicle molds

SERVES 4

⅔ cup whipping cream

6 cardamom pods, crushed

pinch of saffron strands

¾ cup sweetened condensed milk

2 ripe mangoes, flesh only, roughly chopped

1¾oz (50g) pistachio nuts, roughly chopped (optional)

CALORIES: 420kcals/1762kJ
CARBOHYDRATE: 37g
 sugar: 37g
FAT: 26g
 saturated: 13g
SALT: 0.2g
FIBER: 2.5g

1 Put the cream, cardamom, and saffron in a small saucepan and gently heat for 5 minutes. Remove from the heat and let cool.

2 Put the condensed milk and mango into a blender or food processor and strain the cream into it through a sieve or tea strainer. Blend until completely smooth. Press through a sieve if you want to make sure there are no stray lumps, but this is not essential.

3 Scatter the bottom of four 5fl oz (150ml) cup ramekins or popsicle molds with a few chopped pistachios (if using), then pour in the kulfi mixture and freeze at least overnight, or until needed.

4 To serve, fill a bowl with hot water and carefully dip the bottom of each ramekin or popsicle briefly into the water to loosen the kulfi. Be careful not to allow the water to drip onto the kulfi. Run a small knife around the edge of each ramekin, and turn the kulfi onto individual serving plates, or simply remove from the popsicle molds and serve.

Lemon meringue pie

The sharpness of lemon combined with a vanilla meringue topping makes this pie a legendary family favorite.

30 mins   40–50 mins

SPECIAL EQUIPMENT
9in (23cm) loose-bottomed tart pan
baking beans

SERVES 8

3 tbsp butter, cut into cubes,
plus extra for greasing

14oz (400g) store-bought pie dough

3 tbsp all-purpose flour, plus extra
for dusting

6 large eggs, at room temperature,
separated

3 tbsp cornstarch

1½ cups granulated sugar

juice of 3 lemons

1 tbsp finely grated lemon zest

½ tsp cream of tartar

½ tsp vanilla extract

1 Preheat the oven to 400°F (200°C). Lightly grease a 9in (23cm) loose-bottomed tart pan. Roll out the dough on a floured surface and use it to line the pan.

2 Line the dough with parchment paper, then fill with baking beans. Place on a baking sheet and bake for 10–15 minutes or until pale golden. Remove the paper and beans and bake for 5 minutes until golden all over. Reduce the oven temperature to 350°F (180°C). Let the crust cool slightly.

3 Place the egg yolks in a bowl and lightly beat. Combine the cornstarch, flour, and 1 cup of the sugar in a saucepan. Slowly add 1½ cups of water and heat gently, stirring, until the sugar dissolves and there are no lumps. Increase the heat slightly and stir for 3–5 minutes, or until the mixture starts to thicken.

4 Beat several spoonfuls of the hot mixture into the egg yolks. Pour this back into the pan and slowly bring to a boil, stirring. Boil for 3 minutes, then stir in the lemon juice, zest, and butter. Boil for another 2 minutes or until thick and glossy, stirring constantly. Remove the pan from the heat; cover to keep warm.

5 Whisk the egg whites in a large bowl until foamy. Sprinkle in the cream of tartar and whisk, adding the remaining sugar 1 tbsp at a time. Add the vanilla with the last of the sugar, whisking until thick and glossy.

6 Place the crust on a baking sheet, pour in the lemon filling, then top with the meringue, spreading it to cover the filling up to the crust edge. Be careful not to spill it over the dough, or the tart will be hard to remove from the pan.

7 Bake for 12–15 minutes, or until lightly golden. Transfer to a wire rack and cool completely. Turn out of the pan to serve.

COOK'S TIP

If you are not careful, the meringue topping can slide around on top of the lemon filling. Make sure it is touching the crust around the entire pie before baking, to stop it from dislodging.

CALORIES:	578kcals/2431kJ
CARBOHYDRATE:	81g
sugar:	53g
FAT:	24g
saturated:	9g
SALT:	0.7g
FIBER:	1.5g

Tarte aux pommes

This French classic uses both cooking apples that stew down to a purée and dessert apples that keep their shape.

20 mins, plus chilling

50–55 mins

SPECIAL EQUIPMENT

9in (22cm) loose-bottomed tart pan

baking beans

MAKES 8 SLICES

14oz (375g) store-bought pie dough

all-purpose flour, for dusting

4 tbsp unsalted butter

1lb 10oz (750g) Gala apples, peeled, cored, and chopped

½ cup granulated sugar

finely grated zest and juice of ½ lemon

2 tbsp Calvados or brandy

2 Granny Smith apples

2 tbsp apricot jam, sieved, for glazing

1 Roll the dough out on a floured surface to ⅛in (3mm) thick and use it to line a 9in (22cm) loose-bottomed tart pan, leaving an overlap of at least ¾in (2cm). Prick with a fork. Chill for 30 minutes.

2 Preheat the oven to 400°F (200°C). Line the dough with parchment paper and baking beans. Bake for 15 minutes. Remove the paper and beans, then bake for 5 minutes until golden.

3 Meanwhile, melt the butter in a saucepan and add the Gala apples. Cover and cook over low heat, stirring occasionally, for 15 minutes, or until soft and mushy.

4 Push the cooked apple through a nylon sieve to make a smooth purée, then return it to the saucepan.

Reserve 1 tbsp of granulated sugar and add the rest to the apple purée. Stir in the lemon zest and Calvados or brandy. Return it to the heat and simmer, stirring, until it thickens.

5 Spoon the purée into the crust. Peel, core, and thinly slice the Granny Smith apples and arrange in concentric circles on top of the purée. Brush with the lemon juice and sprinkle with the reserved granulated sugar.

6 Bake for 30–35 minutes, or until the apple slices have softened and are turning golden. Use a small, sharp knife to trim the excess dough for a neat edge.

7 Warm the apricot jam and brush it over the top. Cut into slices and serve.

COOK'S TIP

A glaze will make any homemade fruit tart look as appetizing as those in a bake shop. Apricot jam works well for apples and pears, but for a red fruit tart brush with warmed redcurrant jelly. Press jam through a sieve before using as a glaze, to remove any lumps of fruit.

PREPARE AHEAD

The tart will keep in an airtight container for up to 2 days. Reheat at 350°F (180°C) for 15 minutes before serving.

CALORIES: 365kcals/1534kJ

CARBOHYDRATE: 45g
  sugar: 25g

FAT: 18g
  saturated: 7.5g

SALT: 0.5g

FIBER: 2.5g

Tarte Tatin

This tart is named after two French sisters, who earned a living by baking their father's favorite apple tart.

45-50 mins, plus chilling
35-50 mins

SPECIAL EQUIPMENT
food processor with dough hook
9–10in (23–25cm) ovenproof pan

SERVES 8

1¾ cups all-purpose flour, plus extra for dusting

2 large egg yolks

1½ tbsp granulated sugar

pinch of salt

5 tbsp unsalted butter, softened

FOR THE FILLING

8 tbsp butter

1¼ cups granulated sugar

14-16 apples, approx 5½lb (2.4kg) in total

1 lemon

crème fraîche, to serve (optional)

CALORIES: 523kcals/2208kJ

CARBOHYDRATE: 75g
sugar: 60g

FAT: 27g
saturated: 14g

SALT: 0.2g

FIBER: 9g

---

1 For the dough, sift the flour into a food processor fitted with a dough hook and add all the other ingredients with 1 tbsp of water. Work the ingredients together until they form a ball. Wrap in plastic wrap and chill for 30 minutes until firm.

2 For the filling, melt the butter in a 9–10in (23–25cm) ovenproof pan. Stir in the sugar. Cook over medium heat, stirring occasionally, until caramelized to deep golden. Let it cool to tepid.

3 Meanwhile, peel, halve, and core the apples. Cut the lemon in half and rub the apples all over with it, to prevent discoloration. Add the apples, cut-sides down, to the caramel pan. Cook over high heat for 15–25 minutes. Turn once.

4 Remove from the heat. Cool for 15 minutes. Preheat the oven to 375°F (190°C). Roll out the dough on a floured surface to a round, 1in (2.5cm) larger than the pan. Tuck the edges of the dough around the apples. Bake for 20–25 minutes until golden. Cool to tepid, then set a plate on top, hold firmly together, and invert. Spoon some caramel over the apples. Serve with crème fraîche (if using).

Apricot tart

This classic French tart is filled with a delicate custard and juicy apricots and makes a delicious dessert.

30 mins, plus chilling
50 mins-1 hr

SPECIAL EQUIPMENT
food processor (optional)

9in (22cm) loose-bottomed tart pan

baking beans

SERVES 6–8

FOR THE DOUGH

1¼ cups all-purpose flour, plus extra for dusting

1 tbsp granulated sugar

7 tbsp unsalted butter, softened, cut into pieces

1 large egg, separated

FOR THE FILLING

¾ cup heavy cream

¼ cup granulated sugar

2 large eggs, plus 1 large egg yolk

½ tsp vanilla extract

1 x 14oz can apricot halves, drained

confectioners' sugar, for dusting

CALORIES: 382kcals/1598kJ

CARBOHYDRATE: 28g
sugar: 13g

FAT: 27g
saturated: 16g

SALT: 0.1g

FIBER: 1.5g

---

1 To make the dough, rub the flour, sugar, and butter together with your fingertips, or pulse-blend in a food processor, until the mixture resembles fine crumbs. Add the egg yolk and enough water to form a soft dough. Wrap and chill for 30 minutes. Preheat the oven to 350°F (180°C).

2 Roll out the dough on a floured surface to ⅛in (3mm) thick and use to line a 9in (22cm) loose-bottomed tart pan, leaving an overhang of at least ½in (1cm). Prick with a fork, brush with the egg white to seal, line with parchment paper, and fill with baking beans. Bake for 20 minutes. Remove the beans and paper, and bake for another 5 minutes. Trim off the ragged edges while warm.

3 For the filling, whisk the cream, sugar, eggs, yolk, and vanilla in a bowl. Lay the apricots, cut-sides down, over the tart crust. Place on a baking sheet and pour the cream mixture over the fruit. Bake for 30–35 minutes until just set. Allow to cool to room temperature before dusting with confectioners' sugar to serve.

HOW TO FREEZE

This crust can be wrapped well in plastic wrap, then sealed with foil and frozen for up to 12 weeks.

Treacle tart

A classic English tart that remains a favorite. Treacle can be hard to find in the US, but molasses can be used instead.

30 mins, plus chilling   50–55 mins

SPECIAL EQUIPMENT

food processor (optional)

9in (22cm) loose-bottomed tart pan

baking beans

hand-held blender

SERVES 6–8

1 cup all-purpose flour, plus extra for dusting

7 tbsp unsalted butter, chilled and cut into cubes

¼ cup granulated sugar

1 large egg yolk

½ tsp vanilla extract

FOR THE FILLING

¾ cup corn syrup

¾ cup heavy cream

2 large eggs

finely grated zest of 1 orange

1 cup brioche or croissant crumbs

thick cream or ice cream, to serve

1 Using your fingertips, rub together the flour and butter, or pulse-blend in a food processor, to form fine crumbs. Stir in the sugar. Beat together the egg yolk and vanilla extract and mix them into the dry ingredients. Bring the mixture together to form a soft dough, adding a little water if it seems dry. Wrap in plastic wrap and chill for 30 minutes. Preheat the oven to 350°F (180°C).

2 Roll out the dough on a floured surface to 1/8in (3mm) thick. It will be quite fragile, so if it starts to crumble, just bring it together with your hands and gently knead it to get rid of any cracks. Line a 9in (22cm) loose-bottomed tart pan with the rolled-out dough, leaving an overlapping edge of at least ¾in (2cm) all around the rim. Prick the bottom all over with a fork.

3 Line the dough with parchment paper and baking beans. Place it on a baking sheet, and blind-bake for 20 minutes. Remove the

beans and paper, and return it to the oven for 5 minutes. Reduce the oven temperature to 340°F (170°C).

4 For the filling, measure out the corn syrup into a large measuring cup. Measure the cream on top of it (the density of the syrup will keep the two separate, making measuring easy). Add the eggs and orange zest, and process together with a hand-held blender until well combined. Alternatively, transfer to a bowl and whisk. Gently fold in the brioche crumbs.

5 Place the tart crust on a baking sheet, pull out an oven rack from the center of the oven, and put the baking sheet on it. Pour the filling into the crust and carefully slide the rack back into the oven.

6 Bake the tart for 30 minutes until just set, but before the filling starts to bubble up. Trim the crust edge with a small, sharp knife while still warm, then leave to cool in its pan for at least 15 minutes before turning out. Serve warm with thick cream or ice cream.

COOK'S TIP

Try using eggs and cream to lighten the more traditional filling of bread crumbs and syrup. This process incorporates more air and creates a mousse-like effect.

PREPARE AHEAD

The unfilled crust can be stored in an airtight container for up to 3 days, or wrapped well in plastic wrap, sealed with foil, and frozen for up to 12 weeks.

CALORIES: 452kcals/1895kJ

CARBOHYDRATE: 45g
  sugar: 27g

FAT: 28g
  saturated: 16g

SALT: 0.4g

FIBER: 1g

Strawberry tart

Master the basics of this fresh fruit tart and you can adapt it by replacing the strawberries with other soft fruit.

40 mins, plus chilling   25 mins

SERVES 6–8

SPECIAL EQUIPMENT

9in (22cm) loose-bottomed tart pan

baking beans

INGREDIENTS

1 cup all-purpose flour, plus extra for dusting

7 tbsp unsalted butter, chilled and cut into cubes

¼ cup granulated sugar

1 large egg yolk

½ tsp vanilla extract

6 tbsp redcurrant jelly, for glazing

10oz (300g) strawberries, thickly sliced

FOR THE CRÈME PÂTISSIÈRE

½ cup granulated sugar

5 tbsp cornstarch

2 large eggs

1 tsp vanilla extract

1¾ cups whole milk

1 In a bowl, rub the flour and butter together to form fine crumbs. Stir in the sugar. Beat together the egg yolk and vanilla extract, and add them to the flour mixture. Bring together to a dough, adding a little water if needed. Wrap in plastic wrap and chill for 30 minutes.

2 Preheat the oven to 350°F (180°C). Roll out the dough on a floured surface to ⅛in (3mm) thick. Use the rolled-out dough to line a 9in (22cm) loose-bottomed tart pan, leaving an overlapping edge of about ¾in (2cm). Use a pair of scissors to trim any excess dough that hangs down further than this.

3 Prick the dough bottom all over with a fork to prevent air bubbles from forming as it bakes. Carefully line the dough with a piece of parchment paper.

4 Scatter baking beans over the paper. Place on a baking sheet and bake for 20 minutes. Remove the beans and paper and bake for 5 minutes more. Trim the excess dough while it is still warm. Melt

the redcurrant jelly with 1 tbsp of water and brush a little over the crust. Let cool.

5 For the crème pâtissière, beat the sugar, cornstarch, eggs, and vanilla extract in a bowl. In a heavy-bottomed saucepan, bring the milk to a boil and take it off the heat just as it bubbles. Pour the hot milk onto the egg mixture in the bowl, whisking all the time.

6 Return the mixture to a pan and bring to a boil over medium heat, whisking constantly. When it thickens, reduce the heat to low and continue to cook gently, stirring constantly, for 2–3 minutes. Transfer to a bowl, cover with plastic wrap directly on its surface, and let cool completely.

7 Beat the crème pâtissière until smooth and spread it over the crust with a spatula. Top with the strawberries. Heat the jelly glaze again and brush over the strawberries, then leave to set. Remove from the pan to serve.

PREPARE AHEAD

This tart is best eaten on the day it is made, but the components will keep well overnight if properly stored. Wrap the crust well and keep it in an airtight container. Pour the crème pâtissière into a bowl, place plastic wrap directly onto its surface, and also cover the bowl with plastic wrap before storing in the fridge. The next day, scrape the crème pâtissière into the crust, slice the strawberries, and arrange over the top, as in step 7.

CALORIES: 353kcals/1490kJ

CARBOHYDRATE: 48g
    sugar: 30g

FAT: 15g
    saturated: 9g

SALT: 0.1g

FIBER: 1g

Raspberry tart with chocolate cream

A fruit tart with a twist, here the crème pâtissière is enriched with chocolate—a perfect partner for fresh raspberries.

40 mins,
plus chilling

20-25 mins

SERVES 6-8

SPECIAL EQUIPMENT

9in (22cm) loose-bottomed tart pan

baking beans

INGREDIENTS

1 cup all-purpose flour, plus extra for dusting

3 tbsp cocoa powder

7 tbsp unsalted butter, chilled and cut into cubes

¾ cup granulated sugar

1 large egg yolk, plus 2 large eggs

1½ tsp vanilla extract

5 tbsp cornstarch, sifted

2 cups whole milk

6oz (175g) good-quality dark chocolate, broken into pieces

14oz (400g) raspberries

confectioners' sugar, for dusting

1 Rub together the flour, cocoa, and butter, until they resemble fine crumbs. Stir in ¼ cup of the sugar. Beat the egg yolk with ½ tsp of vanilla extract and add to the flour mixture to form a soft dough. Add a little cold water if it seems too stiff. Wrap in plastic wrap and chill for 30 minutes.

2 Preheat the oven to 350°F (180°C). Roll the dough out on a floured surface to ⅛in (3mm) thick. Use it to line a 9in (22cm) loose-bottomed tart pan, leaving an overlapping edge of ¾in (2cm), trimming the excess with scissors. Prick the bottom with a fork.

3 Line the dough with parchment paper and weigh down with baking beans. Place on a baking sheet and bake for 20 minutes. Remove the beans and paper and return it to the oven for another 5 minutes. Trim off the excess dough with a sharp knife while still warm.

4 For the crème pâtissière, beat together the remaining ¼ cup of sugar, the cornstarch, whole eggs, and the remaining 1 tsp of vanilla extract. In a pan, bring the milk and 3½oz (100g) of the chocolate to a boil, whisking all the time. Take it off the heat just as it starts to bubble up. Pour the milk onto the egg mixture, whisking all the time as you do.

5 Return the chocolate mixture to the cleaned-out pan and bring to a boil over medium heat, whisking constantly. When it bubbles and begins to thicken, reduce the heat to its lowest setting and cook for 2–3 minutes, again whisking all the time. Pour into a bowl, cover the surface with plastic wrap to prevent a skin from forming, and let cool.

6 Melt the remaining chocolate in a bowl set over a pan of simmering water (make sure the bowl does not touch the water),

and brush around the inside of the tart crust to seal and add a new layer of texture. Let set. Beat the cold chocolate crème pâtissière with a wooden spoon and pour into the crust, smoothing it down evenly with a spatula or palette knife.

7 Arrange the raspberries over the chocolate crème pâtissière, remove the tart from the pan, and serve dusted with the confectioners' sugar.

PREPARE AHEAD

This tart is best eaten on the day it is made, but can be stored, without the berries, in the fridge overnight. Add the raspberries and confectioners' sugar to serve.

CALORIES:	443kcals/1867kJ
CARBOHYDRATE:	53g
sugar:	37g
FAT:	22g
saturated:	13g
SALT:	0.2g
FIBER:	3.5g

Tarte au citron

This French classic is both rich and refreshing, with melt-in-the-mouth dough and a tangy, smooth, creamy filling.

35 mins, plus chilling 45 mins

SPECIAL EQUIPMENT
food processor (optional)

9½in (24cm) loose-bottomed tart pan

baking beans

SERVES 6–8

1¼ cups all-purpose flour, plus extra for dusting

6 tbsp butter, chilled

3 tbsp granulated sugar

1 large egg, lightly beaten

FOR THE FILLING

5 large eggs

¾ cup granulated sugar

finely grated zest and juice of 4 lemons, plus extra zest to serve

1 cup heavy cream

confectioners' sugar, to serve

1 To make the dough, rub together the flour and butter with your fingertips, or pulse them in a food processor until the mixture looks like fine crumbs. Stir in the sugar until well combined. Add the egg and draw the mixture together, first with a fork and then with your hands, to form a ball of dough. If it is too dry and crumbly to come together, carefully add water, 1 tbsp at a time, until it does.

2 On a lightly floured surface, roll out the dough into a large circle of even thickness, and use it carefully to line a 9½in (24cm) loose-bottomed tart pan, pushing it well into the contours. Cover and chill for at least 30 minutes.

3 For the filling, beat the eggs and sugar. Whisk in the lemon zest and juice and then the cream until evenly blended. Transfer to a bowl, cover, and chill for 1 hour.

4 Preheat the oven to 375°F (190°C) and put in a baking sheet. Line the crust with parchment paper, fill with baking beans, and bake blind on the hot sheet for 10 minutes. Remove the paper and beans and bake for another 5 minutes on the pan, or until the dough bottom is crisp with no sign of damp or raw dough.

5 Reduce the oven temperature to 275°F (140°C). With the tart pan still on the baking sheet, pull out the oven rack, pour in the lemon filling, being careful not to allow it to spill over the edges, and slide the rack back in. Bake for 30 minutes, or until the filling has just set but retains a slight wobble.

6 Remove the tart from the oven and let cool on a wire rack. Turn out of the pan and serve, dusted with confectioners' sugar and sprinkled with lemon zest.

PREPARE AHEAD
The unfilled crust can be prepared ahead and stored in an airtight container for up to 3 days, or well wrapped in plastic wrap, sealed with foil, and frozen for up to 12 weeks.

COOK'S TIP
Try to choose unwaxed lemons, especially if a recipe calls for lemon zest. If these are unavailable, scrub the fruits to remove the wax coating. Pick lemons that are heavy for their size, indicating that they have lots of juice.

CALORIES: 496kcals/2075kJ

CARBOHYDRATE: 47g
  sugar: 32g

FAT: 31g
  saturated: 17g

SALT: 0.4g

FIBER: 1g

Plum tart

The perfect use for plums that are a little tart to eat on their own; baking brings out their sweetness.

40 mins, plus chilling and resting

25-30 mins

SPECIAL EQUIPMENT

electric hand-held mixer

8in (20cm) loose-bottomed tart pan

SERVES 4

FOR THE DOUGH

1 cup all-purpose flour, plus extra for dusting

6 tbsp unsalted butter, chilled and cut into cubes

¼ cup granulated sugar

1 large egg yolk

FOR THE FILLING

6 tbsp unsalted butter, softened

⅓ cup granulated sugar

2 large eggs, lightly beaten

2 tbsp all-purpose flour

1 cup ground almonds

3 plums, quartered and pitted

¼oz (10g) sliced almonds

confectioners' sugar, to serve

crème fraîche, to serve

1 To make the dough, rub the flour and butter together to form fine crumbs. Stir in the sugar. Add the egg yolk to the flour mixture and bring together to form a smooth dough, adding 1–2 tbsp of cold water if necessary. Wrap in plastic wrap and chill for 1 hour. Preheat the oven to 350°F (180°C).

2 For the filling, place the butter and sugar in a bowl and whisk with an electric hand-held mixer until pale and fluffy. Whisk in the eggs, flour, and ground almonds to form a smooth paste.

3 On a floured work surface, roll the dough out into a circle large enough to line an 8in (20cm) loose-bottomed tart pan. Place the dough in the pan, pressing down well into the bottom and around the edges. Trim any excess dough and prick the bottom of the tart with a fork. Place the pan on a baking sheet.

4 Spoon the almond paste into the crust and, using the back of a spoon, spread it out to form an even layer. Arrange the plum quarters, skin-side up, in the almond paste and sprinkle in the sliced almonds.

5 Bake the tart for 25–30 minutes, or until golden and set. Let the tart cool slightly in the pan for 5 minutes, then carefully remove it. Sift confectioners' sugar overtop and serve warm with crème fraîche.

VARIATION

Peeled, halved, quartered, and cored pears, or quartered and pitted apricots, can be used as an alternative to the plums. Slightly underripe or tart fruits will work well.

PREPARE AHEAD

Make the dough up to 24 hours in advance, wrap in plastic wrap, and keep in the fridge until ready to use.

CALORIES: 841kcals/3533kJ

CARBOHYDRATE: 69g
    sugar: 40g

FAT: 57g
    saturated: 27g

SALT: 0.2g

FIBER: 2.5g

Lemon meringue roulade

The traditional filling for a Lemon meringue pie (see p336) is given a new twist in this incredibly light dessert.

30 mins   15 mins

SPECIAL EQUIPMENT

10 x 14in (25 x 35cm) Swiss roll pan

electric hand-held mixer

SERVES 8

5 large egg whites, at room temperature

1 cup granulated sugar

½ tsp white wine vinegar

1 tsp cornstarch

½ tsp vanilla extract

1 cup heavy cream

4 tbsp good-quality lemon curd

confectioners' sugar, for dusting

1 Preheat the oven to 350°F (180°C) and line a 10 x 14in (25 x 35cm) Swiss roll pan with parchment paper. Whisk the egg whites with an electric hand-held mixer on high speed, until stiff peaks form. Reduce the speed and whisk in the sugar, a little at a time, until thick and glossy.

2 Mix the vinegar, cornstarch, and vanilla extract and fold them in, trying to keep the mixture as well aerated as possible. Spread the mixture into the pan and bake in the center of the oven for 15 minutes. Remove from the oven and set it aside. Allow it to cool to room temperature.

3 Meanwhile, whisk the cream until thick but not stiff; it should remain unctuous. Fold in the lemon curd roughly until just mixed; a few ripples will enhance the roulade. Sprinkle confectioners' sugar over a fresh sheet of parchment paper.

4 Carefully turn the cooled roulade out of the pan onto the sugared parchment. Spread the lemon cream over the unbaked side of the roulade with a palette knife. Use the parchment to roll up the meringue firmly, but without squeezing out the cream. Place seam-side down on a serving plate, cover, and chill until needed. Sift over confectioners' sugar to serve.

PREPARE AHEAD

The meringue can be made up to 3 days in advance and stored, unfilled, in an airtight container. If you want to store it this way, it helps to roll it up loosely, using a clean sheet of parchment paper, and store it in the roll. If you store it flat, it may crack when you try to roll it.

CALORIES: 275kcals/1149kJ

CARBOHYDRATE: 28g
  sugar: 28g

FAT: 17g
  saturated: 10g

SALT: 0.1g

FIBER: 0g

Strawberry pavlova

Freeze your leftover egg whites, one at a time if necessary, until you have enough to make this well-loved dessert.

15 mins 1 hr 15 mins

SPECIAL EQUIPMENT
electric hand-held mixer

SERVES 8

6 large egg whites, at room temperature

pinch of salt

approx. 1½ cups granulated sugar

2 tsp cornstarch

1 tsp vinegar

1¼ cups heavy cream

strawberries, to decorate

1 Preheat the oven to 350°F (180°C). Line a baking sheet with parchment paper. Draw an 8in (20cm) diameter circle on the parchment paper with a pencil. Reverse the parchment, so the pencil mark is underneath and won't transfer to the meringue.

2 Put the egg whites in a large, clean, grease-free bowl with the salt. Using an electric hand-held mixer, whip the egg whites until stiff peaks form. Start whisking in the sugar 1 tbsp at a time, whisking well after each addition. Continue whisking until the whites are stiff and glossy. Mix the cornstarch and vinegar and whisk them in. Spoon into a mound inside the circle on the parchment, spreading it to the edges of the circle. Form neat swirls, using a palette knife, as you spread out the meringue.

3 Bake for 5 minutes, then reduce the oven temperature to 250°F (120°C) and cook for 1¼ hours. Let cool completely in the oven. Whip the cream until it holds its shape. Spoon onto the meringue base and decorate with the strawberries, hulled, and halved or sliced. Serve in wedges.

PREPARE AHEAD

The meringue base will keep in a dry, airtight container for up to 3 days; keep it away from extremes of heat or cold. Whip and add the cream, and add the berries, just before serving.

CALORIES: 377kcals/1578kJ

CARBOHYDRATE: 46g
  sugar: 46g

FAT: 20g
  saturated: 12.5g

SALT: 0.3g

FIBER: 0g

Eton mess

This is a crowd-pleasing dessert that's quick to make, and even quicker if you use store-bought meringues.

10 mins, plus chilling

SERVES 6

2 cups heavy cream

1 tsp vanilla extract

2 tbsp granulated sugar

5½oz (150g) meringues

10oz (300g) strawberries, chopped quite small

5½oz (150g) raspberries

CALORIES: 548kcals/2275kJ

CARBOHYDRATE: 33g
sugar: 33g

FAT: 45g
saturated: 28g

SALT: 0.1g

FIBER: 1.5g

1 Whip the cream until it is very stiff, then whisk in the vanilla extract and fold in the sugar.

2 Place the meringues in a freezer bag and smash with a rolling pin to break into uneven pebble-sized pieces. It's nice to have a mixture of large pieces and smaller crumbs for the best texture.

3 Fold together the cream mixture, the meringues, and the fruit. Cover and chill for at least 1 hour before serving.

VARIATION

Try replacing half the heavy cream with Greek yogurt for a lighter taste.

CLEVER WITH LEFTOVERS

This is a dish that is easy to adapt to include any berries that need to be used up quickly. Their ripe juices will enhance the dessert.

Chocolate amaretti roulade

An irresistible combination of crunchy cookie, soft cream, and yielding chocolate cake.

30 mins **20 mins**

SPECIAL EQUIPMENT

9 x 13in (23 x 33cm) Swiss roll pan

electric hand-held mixer

SERVES 4

6 large eggs, separated

¾ cup granulated sugar

½ cup cocoa powder

confectioners' sugar, for dusting

1¼ cups heavy cream
or whipping cream

2–3 tbsp Amaretto or brandy

20 amaretti cookies, crushed, plus 2 extra, to serve

1¾oz (50g) dark chocolate, grated

CALORIES: 863kcals/3594kJ

CARBOHYDRATE: 55g
sugar: 55g

FAT: 61g
saturated: 32g

SALT: 0.7g

FIBER: 2.5g

1 Preheat the oven to 350°F (180°C). Line a 9 x 13in (23 x 33cm) Swiss roll pan with parchment paper. Put the egg yolks and granulated sugar in a heatproof bowl set over simmering water and whisk for 10 minutes until pale, thick, and creamy. Remove from the heat. Whisk the egg whites to soft peaks.

2 Sift the cocoa into the egg yolk mixture and gently fold in with the egg whites. Pour into the pan. Bake for 20 minutes, until just firm.

3 Turn onto a sheet of parchment paper dusted with confectioners' sugar. Remove the pan, leave the top paper, and cool for 30 minutes.

4 Whip the cream until soft peaks form. Peel the paper from the cake, trim the edges, then drizzle with Amaretto. Spread with the cream and scatter with most of the amaretti and chocolate.

5 Starting from a short side, roll it up. Sprinkle over the remaining amaretti and chocolate and dust with confectioners' sugar.

Sticky toffee pudding

A modern classic that never fails to please. A fabulous dessert to serve to guests on a cold day.

20 mins | 35–40 mins, plus resting

SPECIAL EQUIPMENT
1-quart (1-liter) deep, ovenproof dish

electric hand-held mixer

SERVES 4–6

8 tbsp butter, plus extra for greasing

3½oz (100g) chopped dates

½ tsp baking soda

1 cup light brown sugar

1¼ cups heavy cream

1 large egg, lightly beaten

1 cup self-rising flour, sifted

whipped cream or custard, to serve

1 Preheat the oven to 350°F (180°C). Butter a 1-quart (1-liter) deep, ovenproof dish.

2 Place the dates and baking soda in a heatproof bowl. Pour in ½ cup of boiling water, stir well, and set aside for 10 minutes.

3 Place 5 tbsp of the butter, ½ cup of the sugar, and the cream in a non-stick pan. Heat gently until the sugar dissolves, then bring to a boil for 3 minutes. Pour half the sauce into the dish.

4 Put the remaining sugar and butter in a bowl and beat with an electric hand-held mixer. Whisk in the egg and the date mixture. Fold in the flour and pour into the dish, on top of the sauce. Bake for 35–40 minutes, or until a skewer comes out clean. Leave for 5 minutes, then invert onto a dish. Serve with whipped cream or custard and the reserved sauce.

VARIATION

For a sticky toffee and walnut pudding, fold in 2½oz (75g) chopped walnuts at the same time as the flour.

CALORIES: 637kcals/2654kJ
CARBOHYDRATE: 54g
   sugar: 40g
FAT: 45g
   saturated: 28g
SALT: 0.8g
FIBER: 2g

Chocolate brownie pudding

This decadent dessert is delicious, but very rich, and a little goes a long way.

15 mins | 45–50 mins

SPECIAL EQUIPMENT
electric hand-held mixer

12 x 8in (30 x 20cm) ovenproof dish

SERVES 6–8

½ cup all-purpose flour

½ cup cocoa powder

4 large eggs

1 cup light brown sugar

¾ cup granulated sugar

1 tsp vanilla extract

14 tbsp butter, melted and cooled, plus extra for greasing

vanilla ice cream, to serve

1 Preheat the oven to 325°F (160°C). Sift the flour and cocoa powder together.

2 Put the eggs, sugars, and vanilla extract into a large bowl and whisk with an electric hand-held mixer for 3–4 minutes until the mixture is light and fluffy.

3 Fold in the flour mixture until it is well-combined. Finally, mix in the melted butter.

4 Pour the batter into a greased 12 x 8in (30 x 20cm) ovenproof dish and place it inside a large roasting pan. Carefully pour hot water into the pan until it is halfway up the sides of the ovenproof dish.

5 Transfer the pan carefully to the oven and bake for 45–50 minutes until it is cooked at the edges, but still a little wobbly in the center. Serve warm with vanilla ice cream.

PREPARE AHEAD

Make this to the end of step 3 up to 1 day ahead, cover, and keep in the fridge until needed. Return to room temperature before cooking as in steps 4 and 5.

CALORIES: 447kcals/1872kJ
CARBOHYDRATE: 50g
   sugar: 46g
FAT: 25g
   saturated: 15g
SALT: 0.7g
FIBER: 1.5g

Classic bread and butter pudding

A favorite for generations, this is also an economical dish for the whole family.

15 mins, plus soaking **25–35 mins, plus resting**

SERVES 4

2 tbsp butter, softened, plus extra for greasing

6 slices of day-old white bread, crusts cut off

1¾oz (50g) golden raisins

2 cups whole milk

2 large eggs, lightly beaten

½ tsp ground cinnamon

finely grated zest of 1 lemon

3 tbsp granulated sugar

custard, to serve

1 Grease a medium ovenproof dish. Butter the bread and cut each slice into 4 triangles.

2 Arrange half the bread in the bottom of the dish. Sprinkle in half the golden raisins. Top with the remaining bread, in neat rows, and the remaining golden raisins.

3 Place the milk, eggs, cinnamon, lemon zest, and 2 tbsp of the sugar in a bowl and whisk together with a fork until well combined. Pour the mixture over the bread. Set aside for at least 15 minutes, for the custard to soak into the bread, then push the golden raisins under the custard so they don't burn in the oven. When ready to bake, preheat the oven to 350°F (180°C).

4 Sprinkle the remaining sugar over the top of the pudding and bake for 25–35 minutes, or until golden brown. Remove from the oven and set aside for 10–15 minutes. Serve warm, with custard.

CALORIES: 376kcals/1596kJ
CARBOHYDRATE: 47g
  sugar: 26g
FAT: 16g
  saturated: 8g
SALT: 1g
FIBER: 1.5g

PREPARE AHEAD

Make up to the end of step 3 (but don't preheat the oven), cover, and chill for up to 1 day, before baking as in step 4.

Panettone and marmalade bread and butter pudding

The sophisticated and subtle flavor of panettone and the tang of marmalade add interest to this dessert.

20 mins, plus soaking **30 mins, plus resting**

SERVES 4

butter, for greasing

9oz (250g) panettone, sliced

½ cup marmalade

¾ cup whole milk

3 large eggs, lightly beaten

finely grated zest and juice of 1 orange

3 tbsp heavy cream

¼ cup light brown sugar

½ tsp pumpkin pie spice

whipped cream, to serve

1 Butter a medium ovenproof dish. Spread each slice of panettone with marmalade. Arrange the slices neatly in the buttered dish.

2 In a bowl, combine the milk, eggs, orange zest and juice, cream, sugar, and pumpkin pie spice. Whisk together with a fork until well combined.

3 Pour the mixture over the panettone, gently re-submerge the bread under the mixture with the back of a fork, and set aside for 15 minutes. Preheat the oven to 325°F (160°C).

4 Place the dish on a baking sheet and bake for 30 minutes. Serve warm or at room temperature, with whipped cream.

CALORIES: 537kcals/2255kJ
CARBOHYDRATE: 75g
  sugar: 50g
FAT: 21g
  saturated: 11g
SALT: 0.8g
FIBER: 1.5g

VARIATION

For a festive version, add 2–3 tbsp of crystallized and candied fruits and ginger to this recipe, chopping them finely and adding them under the top layer of panettone.

Chocolate croissant bread and butter pudding

An unapologetically indulgent dessert, this is one to save for a special occasion.

15 mins, plus soaking

30 mins, plus resting

SPECIAL EQUIPMENT
electric hand-held mixer

SERVES 4

butter, for greasing

4 pains au chocolat, thinly sliced

¾ cup heavy cream

¾ cup whole milk

1 vanilla bean, split, seeds scraped out and reserved

2 tbsp granulated sugar

3 large egg yolks

1¾oz (50g) white chocolate chips or buttons

confectioners' sugar, to serve

half-and-half, to serve

CALORIES: 716kcals/2978kJ

CARBOHYDRATE: 47g
    sugar: 26g

FAT: 55g
    saturated: 30g

SALT: 0.8g

FIBER: 2g

1 Preheat the oven to 400°F (200°C). Butter a medium ovenproof dish and arrange the sliced pastries in the dish.

2 Place the cream, milk, vanilla bean, and scraped-out seeds in a small, non-stick pan over medium heat. Gently heat to a simmer.

3 Meanwhile, put the sugar and yolks in a heatproof bowl and whisk with an electric hand-held mixer until pale and creamy.

4 Stir the white chocolate into the milk mixture and stir constantly until melted. Remove the vanilla bean from the milk mixture. Pour the milk mixture over the egg mixture, whisking constantly.

5 Pour the mixture back into the rinsed-out pan, and heat gently until thickened, stirring constantly with a wooden spoon. Pour the thickened custard over the pastry slices and set aside for 15 minutes. Bake in the oven for 20 minutes, then leave to rest for at least 10 minutes. Sift over confectioners' sugar and serve with half-and-half.

Creamy rice pudding

The comforting taste of childhood. Serve with a spoonful of fruity strawberry jam for added nostalgia.

5 mins

2 hrs 10 mins, plus resting

SPECIAL EQUIPMENT
medium Dutch oven

SERVES 4

2 tbsp butter

3½oz (100g) short-grain pudding rice

¼ cup vanilla or golden granulated sugar

3½ cups whole milk

⅔ cup heavy cream

grated nutmeg, to taste

CALORIES: 585kcals/2439kJ

CARBOHYDRATE: 49g
    sugar: 30g

FAT: 38g
    saturated: 24g

SALT: 0.5g

FIBER: 0.2g

1 Preheat the oven to 275°F (140°C). Melt the butter in a medium Dutch oven over low heat.

2 Add the rice to the dish and stir well to coat in the butter. Stir the sugar into the rice and pour in the milk and cream. Stir well to combine.

3 Over medium heat, stirring constantly, gradually bring to a simmer. Sprinkle in the nutmeg, cover, and bake in the oven for 2 hours. Set aside to rest for 20 minutes before serving.

VARIATIONS

For an extra treat, stir in a handful of dark, white, or milk chocolate chips. For added flavor and texture, stir in 1¾oz (50g) dried fruit, such as golden raisins, chopped apricots, figs, or prunes, and ½ tsp ground cinnamon, just before resting in step 3.

Chocolate lava cakes

Usually thought of as a restaurant dessert, chocolate lava cakes are surprisingly easy to prepare at home.

20 mins, plus chilling   12–15 mins

SPECIAL EQUIPMENT
4 x 4in (10cm) ramekins

SERVES 4

11 tbsp unsalted butter, cut into cubes, plus extra for greasing

1 heaping tbsp all-purpose flour, sifted, plus extra for dusting

5½oz (150g) good-quality dark chocolate, broken into pieces

3 large eggs

¼ cups granulated sugar

cocoa powder or confectioners' sugar, for dusting (optional)

ice cream, to serve (optional)

CALORIES: 633kcals/2655kJ
CARBOHYDRATE: 43g
    sugar: 41g
FAT: 47g
    saturated: 28g
SALT: 0.2g
FIBER: 1.5g

1 Preheat the oven to 400°F (200°C). Grease the sides and bottoms of four 4in (10cm) ramekins. Sprinkle with a little flour, pouring out any excess. Line the bottoms with parchment paper.

2 Gently melt the chocolate and butter in a heatproof bowl over simmering water (the bowl must not touch the water). Cool slightly.

3 In a separate bowl, whisk the eggs and sugar. Beat in the chocolate mixture. Fold in the flour. Divide between the ramekins.

4 Cook in the middle of the oven for 12–15 minutes. The middles should still be soft to the touch. Run a knife around the edges. Turn the fondants onto serving plates and peel off the parchment.

5 Dust with cocoa powder or confectioners' sugar, if desired, and serve with ice cream.

PREPARE AHEAD

The raw mixture in the ramekins can be covered and refrigerated overnight, or frozen for up to 1 week. Return to room temperature before cooking.

Berry and banana crumble

An unusual mixture, this sweet dish with its soft, unctuous texture makes a great family dessert.

10–15 mins   30–40 mins

SERVES 4–6

14oz (400g) frozen mixed berries, such as blackberries, blackcurrants, redcurrants, strawberries, and raspberries

2 bananas, thickly sliced

⅔ cup all-purpose flour, sifted

7 tbsp butter, chilled and cut into cubes

½ cup oats

¼ cup vanilla or granulated sugar

1¼oz (40g) toasted sliced almonds

custard, to serve

CALORIES: 328kcals/1370kJ
CARBOHYDRATE: 36g
    sugar: 19g
FAT: 18g
    saturated: 9g
SALT: 0.3g
FIBER: 4.5g

1 Preheat the oven to 350°F (180°C). Place all the fruit in a medium baking dish.

2 Put the flour in a large mixing bowl and rub in the butter with your fingertips until the mixture resembles coarse bread crumbs. Stir in the oats, sugar, and almonds.

3 Sprinkle the crumble mixture over the fruit and use the back of a metal spoon to smooth it into an even layer.

4 Place the dish on a baking sheet and bake for 30–40 minutes, or until golden brown. Serve hot with custard.

VARIATION

Try adding 3 tbsp of chopped pecans or walnuts to this topping, or stir in ½ tsp of ground cinnamon.

Plum crumble

Orange and ginger add flavor to the plums, and walnuts add crunch to the topping, in this twist on a classic.

15 mins   35 mins

SERVES 4–6

14oz (400g) plums, halved and pitted

finely grated zest and juice of 1 orange

2 tbsp granulated sugar

½ tsp ground ginger

¾ cup whole wheat flour, sifted

¾ cup all-purpose flour, sifted

14 tbsp butter, chilled and cut into cubes

¾ cup light brown sugar

1¾oz (50g) walnuts, roughly chopped

heavy cream, to serve

1 Preheat the oven to 400°F (200°C). Place the halved plums, orange zest and juice, granulated sugar, and ginger in a medium ovenproof dish. Stir well to coat the plums.

2 Place the flours into a mixing bowl. Rub in the butter until the mixture resembles coarse bread crumbs. Stir in the brown sugar and walnuts.

3 Spoon the crumble mixture over the plums, pressing it down with the back of a metal spoon to form an even layer.

4 Place the dish on a baking sheet and bake for 35 minutes. Serve hot or warm with heavy cream.

PREPARE AHEAD

The topping can be prepared up to 2 days in advance and kept in an airtight container in the fridge until needed.

CALORIES: 553kcals/2311kJ

CARBOHYDRATE: 56g
  sugar: 36g

FAT: 34g
  saturated: 18g

SALT: 0.5g

FIBER: 4.5g

Apple and cinnamon crumble

The spice makes all the difference to this dessert, making the crumble even more appetizing.

20 mins   35 mins

SERVES 4–6

1lb 10oz (750g) apples, peeled, cored, and thinly sliced

½ cup granulated sugar

2 tsp ground cinnamon

1¼ cups all-purpose flour

6 tbsp butter, cut into cubes

vanilla ice cream, to serve

1 Preheat the oven to 400°F (200°C). Place the apple slices, scant 2 tbsp of the granulated sugar, and 1 tsp of the cinnamon in a medium ovenproof dish. Stir well to coat the apple slices.

2 Sift the all-purpose flour and remaining ground cinnamon into a mixing bowl. Rub in the butter until the mixture resembles coarse bread crumbs. Stir in ¼ cup of the granulated sugar.

3 Spoon the mixture over the fruit, pressing it down with the back of a metal spoon to form an even layer. Sprinkle the remaining 2 tbsp of sugar over the top. Place the dish on a baking sheet and bake for 35 minutes. Serve hot with vanilla ice cream.

VARIATION

Use 13oz (375g) blackberries and 13oz (375g) apples to make a blackberry and apple crumble. In this case, omit the ground cinnamon.

CALORIES: 314kcals/1325kJ

CARBOHYDRATE: 48g
  sugar: 28g

FAT: 12g
  saturated: 7.5g

SALT: 0.3g

FIBER: 4g

Cinnamon apple cake

This recipe is delicious either warm as a dessert with cream or cold with a cup of coffee.

30 mins **25-30 mins**

SPECIAL EQUIPMENT
9½in (24cm) square baking pan

SERVES 8–12

8 tbsp butter, cut into cubes, plus extra for greasing

1⅔ cups all-purpose flour, sifted, plus extra for dusting

3-4 apples (depending on size)

1 tbsp lemon juice

3 large eggs

1 cup, plus 1 tbsp granulated sugar

6 tbsp milk

¼ cup half-and-half

1 tbsp baking powder

2 tsp ground cinnamon

1 Preheat the oven to 400°F (200°C). Grease a 9½in (24cm) square baking pan with butter and dust with flour.

2 Peel, core, quarter, and slice the apples, and put in a bowl of water with the lemon juice to prevent browning.

3 Whisk the eggs and 1 cup of the sugar until thick and pale, and the whisk leaves a trail when lifted out of the mixture.

4 Put the butter, milk, and half-and-half in a pan and melt gently, then bring to a boil. Let cool briefly, then stir into the egg mixture. Fold in the flour and baking powder. Pour into the pan.

5 Drain the apples and arrange over the batter. Mix the remaining sugar with the cinnamon and sprinkle over. Bake for 25–30 minutes until golden. Let cool in the pan, then cut into squares.

VARIATION

This cake can be adapted for many other autumn fruits. Try it with pitted plums or apricots, or even pears.

CALORIES: 523kcals/2207kJ
CARBOHYDRATE: 52g
  sugar: 28g
FAT: 32g
  saturated: 19g
SALT: 0.3g
FIBER: 2g

Rhubarb crumble cake

This cake has a rich, almond-scented crumble topping covering sharp, sweet rhubarb.

20 mins **50 mins-1 hr, plus resting**

SPECIAL EQUIPMENT
8in (20cm) springform cake pan
electric hand-held mixer

SERVES 6–8

FOR THE CAKE

14 tbsp unsalted butter, softened, plus extra for greasing

¾ cup granulated sugar

2 large eggs, lightly beaten

1⅔ cups self-rising flour, sifted

½ tsp ground ginger

2 tbsp milk

5½oz (150g) rhubarb, trimmed and chopped into bite-sized pieces

FOR THE TOPPING

⅓ cup all-purpose flour

5 tbsp unsalted butter, chilled and cut into cubes

½ tsp ground cinnamon

2 tbsp demerara sugar

2 tbsp ground almonds

custard or whipped cream, to serve

1 Preheat the oven to 325°F (160°C). Grease an 8in (20cm) springform cake pan and line with parchment paper.

2 Place the butter and sugar in a bowl. Beat with an electric hand-held mixer until light.

3 Add the eggs and beat until well combined. Fold in the flour and ginger, then the milk.

4 Spoon the mixture into the pan. Push the rhubarb pieces into the batter, spreading them evenly.

5 In a bowl, rub the flour and butter to coarse crumbs. Stir in the cinnamon, sugar, and almonds. Sprinkle over the cake and press down lightly. Bake for 50 minutes to 1 hour until a skewer emerges clean. Leaving it in the pan, cool for 20 minutes.

6 Remove from the pan. Serve warm with custard, or at room temperature with whipped cream.

CALORIES: 523kcals/2207kJ
CARBOHYDRATE: 52g
  sugar: 28g
FAT: 32g
  saturated: 19g
SALT: 0.3g
FIBER: 2g

Easy treacle spongecake

A great last-minute family dessert with ingredients all from the pantry and fridge.

10-15 mins   7-10 mins

SPECIAL EQUIPMENT

1-quart (1-liter) microwaveable pudding bowl

electric hand-held mixer

SERVES 4–6

5 tbsp butter, softened, plus extra for greasing

¼ cup corn syrup

⅓ cup granulated sugar

2 large eggs, lightly beaten

1¼ cups self-rising flour, sifted

3-4 tbsp milk

custard, heavy cream, or vanilla ice cream, to serve

1 Grease a 1-quart (1-liter) microwaveable pudding bowl and spoon the corn syrup into it.

2 Place the butter and sugar into a mixing bowl and cream them together using an electric hand-held mixer. Add the eggs, a little at a time, beating well between each addition.

3 Add the flour to the mixture and beat until a smooth mixture is formed. Add enough milk to give a soft dropping consistency. Spoon the mixture over the syrup in the bowl and level the surface.

4 Microwave the pudding on low (at about 600 watts, if possible) for 7 minutes, or until the cake is just slightly moist and a skewer comes out clean. If the pudding is not cooked, continue to cook it for 1 minute intervals on low, testing after each minute, for up to a total of 10 minutes.

5 Let stand for 5 minutes, before carefully inverting onto a serving dish. Serve immediately with custard, heavy cream, or vanilla ice cream.

CALORIES: 290kcals/1213kJ

CARBOHYDRATE: 37g
  sugar: 21g

FAT: 13g
  saturated: 7g

SALT: 0.6g

FIBER: 1g

Blueberry cobbler

A classic American summer fruit dessert, easy to make, and great for a hungry family.

15 mins   30 mins

SERVES 6–8

FOR THE FILLING

1lb (450g) blueberries

2 apples, or 2 large peaches, sliced

2 tbsp granulated sugar

finely grated zest of ½ lemon

FOR THE COBBLER

2 cups self-rising flour

2 tsp baking powder

⅓ cup granulated sugar, plus 1 tbsp for sprinkling

pinch of salt

5 tbsp unsalted butter, chilled and cut into cubes

½ cup buttermilk

1 large egg, lightly beaten

handful of sliced almonds

custard, or heavy cream, to serve (optional)

1 Preheat the oven to 375°F (190°C). Put the fruit in a shallow ovenproof dish and stir in the sugar and zest. For the cobbler, sift the flour, baking powder, granulated sugar, and salt into a bowl. Add the butter and rub with your fingers, until the mixture resembles crumbs.

2 Beat together the buttermilk and egg, add to the flour mixture, and mix to form a dough. Place walnut-sized spoonfuls over the fruit, leaving space for the mix to spread. Lightly press down to help them combine with the fruit.

3 Evenly sprinkle in the almonds and remaining sugar. Bake for 30 minutes until bubbling. If it browns quickly, cover with foil. Insert a skewer into the middle of the center "cobble": it should emerge clean. If not, return to the oven for 5 minutes, then test again. Let cool briefly before serving straight from the dish, with plenty of custard or heavy cream. This is best eaten on the same day.

PREPARE AHEAD

If you have time earlier in the day to prepare the fruit filling and the dry ingredients for the cobbler, this dessert can be assembled in 5 minutes.

CALORIES: 225kcals/946kJ

CARBOHYDRATE: 30g
  sugar: 25g

FAT: 10g
  saturated: 5.5g

SALT: 0.5g

FIBER: 2g

Lemon cheesecake

This cold-set cheesecake needs no baking, and thus produces a lighter, more delicate result.

30 mins, plus chilling **5 mins**

SPECIAL EQUIPMENT
9in (22cm) round springform cake pan

SERVES 8

9oz (250g) vanilla wafers

7 tbsp unsalted butter, in cubes

juice and finely grated zest of 2 lemons

1 tbsp (10g) powdered gelatin

12oz (350g) cream cheese, at room temperature

¾ cup granulated sugar

1¼ cups heavy cream

1 Line a 9in (22cm) round springform cake pan with parchment paper. Put the wafers in a bag and crush to crumbs with a rolling pin. Melt the butter and pour over the crushed wafers, mixing well to combine. Press the wafer mixture firmly into the bottom of the pan using a wooden spoon.

2 Place the lemon juice in a small heatproof bowl. Sprinkle the gelatin over the surface of the lemon juice and let stand for 5 minutes to soften. Place the bowl over a pan of hot water and stir until all the granules are dissolved. Set aside to cool. Beat together the cream cheese, granulated sugar, and lemon zest until smooth.

3 In a separate bowl, whisk the heavy cream to soft peaks. Make sure it is not stiff. Beat the gelatin mixture into the cream cheese mixture, stirring well to combine. Gently fold the whisked cream into the cheese mixture. Be careful not to lose volume.

4 Pour the cheese mixture onto the chilled wafer base and spread evenly. Smooth the top with a damp palette knife or the back of a damp spoon. Chill for at least 4 hours or overnight. Run a sharp, thin knife around the inside of the pan. Gently turn the cheesecake onto a plate, making sure you remove the parchment paper before cutting into slices.

CALORIES: 655kcals/2732kJ

CARBOHYDRATE: 45g
  sugar: 30g

FAT: 51g
  saturated: 31g

SALT: 0.8g

FIBER: 0.5g

Amaretti and apricot trifle

A sophisticated new twist on an old classic that takes minutes to prepare with items from the pantry.

15 mins, plus chilling

SERVES 4–6

5¾oz (160g) amaretti cookies

2 tbsp sherry (optional)

1 x 14oz (410g) can apricot halves, drained (juice reserved) and roughly chopped

1lb 2oz (500g) fresh custard

1¼ cups heavy cream, whipped

1 Place all but 3 of the amaretti cookies in a glass serving dish. Sprinkle the sherry (if using) or 2 tbsp of the reserved apricot juice over the cookies.

2 Evenly spread all but 2 tbsp of the apricots over the cookies. Pour the custard over the fruit. Top with the cream and spread out in an even layer.

3 Crumble the reserved cookies. Decorate the trifle with them, and the reserved apricots. Cover and chill for 2 hours before serving, but serve on the day of making.

VARIATION
This trifle is also delicious (and looks dramatic) made with canned, drained morello cherries, and sprinkled with sliced almonds as well as amaretti.

CLEVER WITH LEFTOVERS
Slightly stale amaretti cookies will give a welcome crunch to this trifle.

CALORIES: 515kcals/2140kJ

CARBOHYDRATE: 35g
  sugar: 30g

FAT: 37g
  saturated: 19g

SALT: 0.2g

FIBER: 0.7g

Tiramisu

Irresistible to everyone, this version omits the usual alcohol for a more family-friendly dessert.

20 mins,
plus chilling

SERVES 4–6

1lb 2oz (500g) mascarpone cheese

½ cup confectioners' sugar, sifted

3 tbsp fromage frais or crème fraîche

1¼ cups strong cold coffee

6oz (175g) ladyfingers

1 tbsp cocoa powder

1 Place the mascarpone, confectioners' sugar, and fromage frais in a bowl and beat until soft and well combined.

2 Pour the coffee into a shallow bowl and dip the ladyfingers into it, one at a time, to moisten.

3 Arrange one-third of the fingers in a glass serving bowl. Top with one-third of the mascarpone mixture, spreading it out in an even layer to cover the ladyfingers. Repeat this layering twice more, finishing with a layer of mascarpone.

4 Sift over the cocoa powder. Cover with plastic wrap and chill for at least 1 hour, or overnight, before serving.

VARIATION

Top the tiramisu with finely grated chocolate instead of the cocoa powder. White, dark, or milk chocolate, or a combination of the three, will all work well. For an even more chocolatey tiramisu, melt 5½oz (150g) of chocolate and layer it in, along with the mascarpone and ladyfingers.

CALORIES: 486kcals/2035kJ

CARBOHYDRATE: 32g
sugar: 25g

FAT: 36g
saturated: 24g

SALT: 0.3g

FIBER: 0.8g

Profiteroles

These cream-filled choux pastry buns, drizzled with chocolate sauce, make a deliciously decadent dessert.

 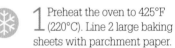

30 mins   22 mins

SPECIAL EQUIPMENT

2 piping bags with a ½in (1cm) plain nozzle and ¼in (5mm) star nozzle

SERVES 4

4 tbsp unsalted butter

½ cup all-purpose flour, sifted

2 large eggs, lightly beaten

FOR THE FILLING AND TOPPING

1½ cups heavy cream

7oz (200g) good-quality dark chocolate, broken into pieces

2 tbsp butter

2 tbsp corn syrup

1 Preheat the oven to 425°F (220°C). Line 2 large baking sheets with parchment paper.

2 Put the butter and ⅔ cup of water into a pan and melt. Bring to a boil, remove from the heat, and pour in the flour. Beat until it forms a ball. Cool for 10 minutes.

3 Gradually beat in the eggs to form a stiff, smooth, shiny paste. Spoon into a piping bag with a ½in (1cm) plain nozzle. Pipe walnut-sized rounds and bake for 20 minutes, until golden. Slit the side of each and bake for 2 minutes to crisp, then transfer to a wire rack to cool.

4 For the filling and topping, pour ½ cup cream into a pan and whip the rest to soft peaks. Add the chocolate, butter, and syrup to the cream in the pan and heat gently. Pile the whipped cream into a piping bag fitted with a ¼in (5mm) star nozzle and pipe into the buns. Serve with the sauce.

HOW TO FREEZE

The unfilled buns can be open-frozen, then transferred to a freezer bag and frozen for up to 12 weeks.

CALORIES: 1008kcals/4185kJ

CARBOHYDRATE: 47g
sugar: 37g

FAT: 87g
saturated: 53g

SALT: 0.3g

FIBER: 2.5g

Quick chocolate mousse

Truly the easiest mousse in the world. It is made with raw egg whites, so the usual advice applies (see p11).

20 mins,
plus chilling

SERVES 4

7oz (200g) good-quality dark chocolate, about 70 percent cocoa solids, broken into pieces

4 large eggs, separated

1 tbsp liqueur, such as blackcurrant or orange (optional)

1 Put the chocolate in a heatproof bowl over a pot of simmering water. The bowl should not touch the water. Melt the chocolate gently over the heat, stirring occasionally. Remove from the heat and allow it to cool completely, but not to solidify again. Whisk the egg whites to stiff peaks.

2 When the chocolate is cool enough, beat in the egg yolks, and then the liqueur (if using). The mixture will stiffen slightly. Take one-third of the egg whites and beat them into the melted chocolate mixture. This will loosen the chocolate up enough to be able to fold in the remaining egg whites.

3 Gently fold the remaining egg whites into the chocolate, making sure they are completely combined, but trying to keep in as much air as possible.

4 Pour the mousse into 1 large or 4 small serving bowls. Chill until firm before serving.

This is very rich, and if you have younger children, they might like it made with a milk chocolate with lower cocoa solids.

Fussy eaters!

CALORIES: 354kcals/1481kJ

CARBOHYDRATE: 31g
  sugar: 31g

FAT: 21g
  saturated: 10g

SALT: 0.2g

FIBER: 1.5g

Creamy custard

The secret to any custard is to heat it gently, so that the eggs do not scramble.

5 mins   10 mins

SERVES 4

1¼ cups whole milk

2 large egg yolks

1 tbsp granulated sugar

¼ tsp vanilla extract

1 tsp cornstarch

1 Heat the milk until it is hot, but not boiling. In a bowl, whisk together the egg yolks, sugar, vanilla extract, and cornstarch.

2 Gradually pour the hot milk into the eggs in a thin stream, whisking it continuously. Return the mixture to the rinsed-out saucepan and place over medium heat, whisking constantly, until it starts to bubble.

3 Reduce the heat to a low simmer and cook for another 5 minutes, until the mixture thickens and coats the back of a wooden spoon.

CALORIES: 99kcals/414kJ

CARBOHYDRATE: 8g
  sugar: 7g

FAT: 6g
  saturated: 3g

SALT: trace

FIBER: 0g

VARIATION

To make a chocolate custard, which is especially appealing to children, add 1 tbsp cocoa powder with the cornstarch. For a more grown-up custard, stir in 1–2 tbsp of Irish cream liqueur when the custard is ready to be served.

French crêpes

Even if you only make crêpes once a year, a good, stress-free recipe will help you cook them with style!

10 mins, plus resting   15–20 mins

SPECIAL EQUIPMENT

electric hand-held mixer

7in (18cm) non-stick frying pan

MAKES 8

¾ cup all-purpose flour

2 large eggs, lightly beaten

¾ cup whole milk

2 tbsp butter, melted

sunflower or vegetable oil, for cooking

FOR THE FILLING

sliced bananas and chocolate spread

stewed apple and ground cinnamon

maple syrup and walnuts

1 Sift the flour into a large bowl. Add the eggs and ¼ cup of the milk and, using an electric hand-held mixer, whisk well to combine.

2 Gradually add the remaining milk, whisking constantly. Stir in both the melted butter and ¼ cup of cold water. Whisk well to give a thin, smooth batter. Set aside to rest for 30 minutes, covered with a clean kitchen towel.

3 Brush the bottom of a 7in (18cm) non-stick frying pan with a little oil. Heat over high temperature on the stovetop.

4 Carefully pour in just enough batter to coat the bottom of the pan and swirl the pan to give an even layer of batter. Cook for 40–60 seconds or until the crêpe is set.

Flip over using a palette knife and cook the other side; reducing the burner temperature if the crêpe is browning too quickly.

5 Remove from the pan and place on a warmed plate. Repeat to cook 7 more crêpes, occasionally brushing the pan with more oil. Stack the crêpes up with a sheet of waxed paper between each, and cover the stack with foil to keep them all warm. Serve the crêpes with bowls containing the banana, apple, and walnut fillings.

PREPARE AHEAD

The crêpe batter can be made up to 2 hours in advance. It is best to cover and chill it after 30 minutes to avoid any risk of taint or fermentation, especially in hot weather.

Slice bananas, oranges, or strawberries, mix with chocolate spread, and use this as a filling to introduce fruit into the diet of children who say they don't like fruit.

Fussy eaters!

CALORIES: 124kcals/519kJ

CARBOHYDRATE: 10g
  sugar: 1.5g

FAT: 7g
  saturated: 3g

SALT: 0.1g

FIBER: 0.5g

Honey and mustard roasted sausages

These are a favorite at both children's and adults' parties. Make more than you think you'll need...

5 mins | 25 mins, plus resting

MAKES 20

20 good-quality cocktail sausages

1 tbsp sunflower or vegetable oil

2 tbsp honey

2 tbsp grain mustard

1 Preheat the oven to 400°F (200°C). Prick the sausages all over with a small fork and put them in a roasting pan. Toss them in the oil so that they are all well covered, then roast at the top of the oven for 20 minutes, turning occasionally, until they are browned and cooked through.

2 In a small bowl, whisk together the honey and mustard. Remove the cooked sausages from the oven, toss them in the honey mixture, and return them to the oven for 5 minutes, turning once, until they are glazed with the honey mixture and sticky.

3 Remove from the oven and let rest for 5 minutes before serving.

PREPARE AHEAD

The sausages can be precooked up to the end of step 1, up to 2 days ahead, covered, and refrigerated. Finish them in the oven with the honey glaze just before serving.

CALORIES: 61kcals/256kJ
CARBOHYDRATE: 2.5g
  sugar: 2g
FAT: 4.5g
  saturated: 1.5g
SALT: 0.4g
FIBER: 0g

Oven-baked potato skins with sour cream dip

These crispy potato skins are a real hit at a party and are a reasonably healthy option, as well as fun to eat.

10 mins | 10 mins

SERVES 4

4 large baking potatoes

2 tbsp sunflower or vegetable oil

salt and freshly ground black pepper

⅔ cup sour cream

4 scallions, finely sliced

1 Preheat the oven to 400°F (200°C). Bake the potatoes in the oven for up to 1 hour, until they are cooked through. Set aside to cool; this will make cutting them more manageable.

2 Cut each potato in half and scoop out all but ¼ in (5mm) of the potato from the skins. Set this aside for another time, perhaps to make mashed potato or fishcakes. Cut each halved potato skin into 4 long, thin slices. Brush on all sides with oil and place, skin-side down, on a baking sheet. Sprinkle them with salt and return to the oven for 20 minutes, until crispy and golden brown on top.

3 Mix together the sour cream and scallions and season well. Serve the potato skins with the sour cream dip.

PREPARE AHEAD

The potatoes can be baked up to 2 days in advance, so try to cook them when you are using the oven for something else anyway. The potato flesh can be used to make the Sausage and mustard mash canapés (see p308), if you are serving them at the party as well.

CALORIES: 317kcals/1330kJ
CARBOHYDRATE: 42g
  sugar: 4g
FAT: 13g
  saturated: 5g
SALT: trace
FIBER: 4.5g

Mini-pizzas

These individual pizzas are perfect party-sized children's snacks, and can be topped and cooked at the last minute.

20 mins,
plus rising

10 mins

SPECIAL EQUIPMENT

food processor with dough hook
(optional)

MAKES 10

FOR THE CRUSTS

2 cups bread flour, plus extra for
dusting

¼ tsp salt

1½ tsp dried yeast

1 tbsp olive oil, plus extra for
greasing

FOR THE TOPPING

1 x 14oz (400g) can crushed tomatoes,
or 1½ cups tomato sauce

2 garlic cloves, crushed

1 tbsp olive oil

freshly ground black pepper

selection of prepared pizza toppings

5½oz (150g) finely sliced mozzarella

1 Put the flour and salt into a large bowl, or the bowl of a food processor fitted with a dough hook. Dissolve the yeast in ⅔ cup of warm water, then add the oil.

2 If making by hand, make a well in the center of the flour. Gradually pour in the liquid, stirring to form a rough dough. Use your hands to bring it together. Turn the dough out onto a floured work surface. Knead for up to 10 minutes, until smooth, glossy, and elastic.

3 If making in a food processor, turn the machine on to a low speed. Pour in the liquid a little at a time, until the mixture begins to come together. You may need to turn off the machine and scrape down the sides once or twice to ensure that all the flour is incorporated. Increase the speed to medium and continue to knead for 5–7 minutes, until smooth, glossy, and elastic.

4 Put the dough in an oiled bowl and cover loosely with plastic wrap. Let rise in a warm place for 2 hours, or until doubled in size.

5 Meanwhile, make the tomato sauce. Put the tomatoes, garlic, and olive oil into a small saucepan and season well with pepper. Bring to a boil, reduce the heat to a low simmer, and cook for 45 minutes to 1 hour, until you have a rich, thick sauce. Taste for seasoning.

6 When ready to cook, preheat the oven to 450°F (230°C). When the dough has risen, turn it onto a lightly floured work surface and knead it briefly. Divide it into 10 equal-sized pieces and roll each one out to a diameter of 5–6in (12–15cm). Lay them on several baking sheets.

7 Top the mini-pizzas with 1 tbsp of the tomato sauce, spread thinly, and any toppings you would like. Finish with a thin layer of mozzarella cheese, and cook at the top of the hot oven for 10 minutes, until golden brown and crispy.

PREPARE AHEAD

The dough can be made the day before up to step 4 and left to rise slowly in the fridge overnight. Just before the party, roll the crusts out and have them ready to top and cook at the last minute.

Put out bowls of toppings and encourage children to build their own pizzas. This way they are more likely to eat them. Try ham, black olives, mushrooms, peppers, or pineapple.

Fussy eaters!

CALORIES:	151kcals/673kJ
CARBOHYDRATE: 19g	
sugar: 1.5g	
FAT: 5.5g	
saturated: 2.5g	
SALT: 0.4g	
FIBER: 1.5g	

Triple decker sandwiches

Getting children to eat anything healthy at a party is not easy; making the savory choices attractive helps.

10 mins

MAKES 36 (bite-sized sandwiches)

8 slices of thin-cut whole wheat bread

4 slices of thin-cut white bread

softened butter or margarine, for spreading

4 slices of ham

16 thin slices of cucumber

¼ cup cream cheese, softened

1 Spread all the slices of bread on one side only with softened butter or margarine.

2 Place 4 of the whole wheat bread slices, buttered-side up, on a cutting board, and lay a piece of ham on each.

3 Top the ham with a white slice of bread, buttered-side down. Butter the top of the bread, then put 4 pieces of cucumber on top of each.

4 Finally, spread the buttered side of the remaining whole wheat bread with 1 tbsp of cream cheese spread per slice and put it, cheese-side down, on the cucumber to make a three-tiered sandwich. Press down well.

5 Trim the sandwiches of their crusts, then cut each sandwich into 9 small squares to serve.

PREPARE AHEAD

These sandwiches can be made with frozen bread slices and left to defrost for 1 day in the fridge, packed in an airtight container or wrapped in foil. Trim them of their crusts, but do not cut them until the last minute to keep them from drying out.

CALORIES: 37kcals/157kJ	
CARBOHYDRATE: 4g	
sugar: 0.3g	
FAT: 2g	
saturated: 1g	
SALT: 0.2g	
FIBER: 0.6g	

Sushi sandwiches

Turn party sandwiches into something special with these easy-to-make sushi versions.

20 mins

MAKES 24 (bite-sized sandwiches)

6 large slices of white or whole wheat bread, crusts removed

1 x 7oz (185g) can of tuna, drained

¼ cup good-quality mayonnaise, plus 1 tbsp

2 scallions, finely chopped

salt and freshly ground black pepper

½ large red bell pepper, finely sliced

½ cucumber, seeded and finely sliced

1 Roll each slice of bread out as thinly as you can with a rolling pin. Mash together the tuna, ¼ cup of mayonnaise, and scallions and season well. Make sure the resulting paste is smooth.

2 Lay a slice of bread out widthwise. Spread a little extra mayonnaise in a ½in (1cm) line at one long edge of the piece of bread farthest from you (to help the sandwich stick together).

Spread a thin layer of tuna over the bread, stopping where the line of mayonnaise starts. Lay a line of red bell pepper at the long edge of the bread nearest to you, and top it with a thin line of cucumber.

3 Pick up the edge nearest you, fold it over the vegetables, then roll until it sticks itself together with the mayonnaise. Trim the edges and cut into 4 pieces, using a sawing action so the shape does not get spoiled. Serve upright.

VARIATION

A vegetarian version can be made with cream cheese, carrot sticks, and a layer of arugula or watercress.

CALORIES: 56kcals/235kJ	
CARBOHYDRATE: 4.5g	
sugar: 0.5g	
FAT: 3g	
saturated: 0.5g	
SALT: 0.2g	
FIBER: 0.5g	

Cheesy chicken meatballs

These chicken meatballs are easy-to-handle finger food and an ideal choice for a children's party.

10 mins, plus chilling | 10 mins

MAKES 20

10oz (300g) ground chicken

½ cup fresh white bread crumbs

¾oz (20g) finely grated Parmesan cheese

2 tbsp finely chopped flat-leaf parsley

salt and freshly ground black pepper

1 tbsp olive oil

1 tbsp butter

1 In a bowl, mix all the ingredients together, apart from the oil and butter, and season well. You may need to use your hands to really get them well combined.

2 Form the mixture into walnut-sized balls and roll them between damp hands to firm them up. Place on a plate, cover, and refrigerate for at least 30 minutes before use.

3 Heat the oil and butter in a large, non-stick frying pan and cook the chicken balls over medium heat for 5–7 minutes, turning occasionally, until they are golden brown and springy to the touch.

VARIATION

Add mushrooms or red bell peppers to the meatballs, ground in a mini food processor, for extra goodness.

HOW TO FREEZE

The cooked meatballs can be cooled and open-frozen on a baking sheet, then transferred into freezer bags for easy storage. Defrost and reheat thoroughly before serving. Use up within 8 weeks.

CALORIES: 39kcals/166kJ

CARBOHYDRATE: 2g
  sugar: 0.1g

FAT: 2g
  saturated: 1g

SALT: 0.1g

FIBER: 0.1g

Tuna and corn melts

A few hot snacks are welcome at a children's party, and these melts are always popular.

5 mins | 10-15 mins

MAKES 8

8 x ½in- (1.5cm-) thick slices of baguette

2 tbsp olive oil

7oz (185g) can of tuna, drained

¼ cup canned corn, drained

2 scallions, finely chopped (optional)

2 tbsp mayonnaise

2½oz (75g) grated cheese, such as Cheddar

salt and freshly ground black pepper

1 Preheat the oven to 425°F (220°C). Place the slices of baguette on a baking sheet and brush both sides with a little oil. Bake at the top of the oven for 5–7 minutes, turning once, until lightly browned on both sides. Set aside.

2 In a bowl, mash together the tuna, corn, scallions (if using), mayonnaise, and half the cheese and season well.

3 Divide the topping equally between the baguette slices, and top each piece with some of the remaining cheese. Bake the slices in the hot oven for another 5–7 minutes, until they are hot and the cheese has melted to a nice golden brown. Remove from the oven and allow to cool for at least 5 minutes before serving.

PREPARE AHEAD

These can be prepared up to the point of baking, covered, then stored in the fridge for up to 1 day. Remove from the fridge and bake in the hot oven as in step 3.

CALORIES: 243kcals/1022kJ

CARBOHYDRATE: 23g
  sugar: 2g

FAT: 11.5g
  saturated: 3.5g

SALT: 1g

FIBER: 1.5g

Kids' parties

The first birthday party you throw for your child can be a nerve-wracking experience, but do take comfort in the fact that when children are very young they may not remember much of it! Even so, the pressure from your child and other parents to produce a marvelous party can be intense. A house full of children, high on sugar and each others' company, needs to be managed well, so plan to spend most of your time with the children, not in the kitchen. Prepare as much as you can ahead of time including checking for any food allergies or vegetarian guests. Finally, don't feel everything must be picture-perfect.

The perfectly balanced party

When you're planning a party meal for young children, remember that they probably will not eat a great deal. Inevitably they will be over-excited and less interested in the food than the party itself, so it makes sense to produce a number of small, bite-sized choices that will cover a variety of tastes. Try to balance hot with cold; sweet with savory, so that there is a bit of everything.

savory first

A good trick is to lay the table with a variety of savory items first and hold back the sweet treats until these healthier foods have been eaten.

Chips later

Try keeping back the chips for a while, and then "remembering" to get them from the kitchen. By this time, hopefully, your guests will have eaten at least one sandwich!

What to serve

It's a party, so the children will want a few classic treats sugar-coated with frosting and sprinkles, but tempt them with healthy options too by making them look appealing with flags, colorful accompaniments, and fun serving dishes.

Hot options You may want to include some hot food items, such as these Mini burgers (p366), especially if the weather is cold. Keep the portions bite-sized and easy to handle and get everyone to dive into them while they're still warm.

For a bit of extra indulgence, decorate these jellies with sprinkles or a dollop of whipped cream.

Sweet treats Colorful food always gets the tastebuds tingling, such as these vibrantly colored Traffic-light jellies (p371). Add these to a well-decorated table, maybe one with a theme, alongside bright and cheery plates and party hats.

Give your frosting texture by making gentle grooves with a small palette knife.

Serving the cake This Butterfly cake (p375) is easy to make and can be decorated with pretty pastel-colored frosting shapes and sparkles. Both this and the Caterpillar cake (p377) can be baked and then frozen uniced for up to three months.

Bite-sized sushi-roll sandwiches look unusual and very appealing.

Savory eats Serve up sandwiches that are the right size for little fingers and make them as attractive as possible. This is a particularly good idea for any "healthy" savory options, such as these pinwheel Sushi sandwiches (p364).

Drinks If you want to reduce the sugar rush, try serving some fresh fruit-based cordials or chilled flavored milkshakes instead of sugary soft drinks and juices. Make them look grown-up adding straws or cocktail umbrellas.

Healthy party choices

Here are some healthy or less sugary choices for party food.

⭐ Small sandwiches with plain fillings and the crusts removed

⭐ Cocktail sausages, hot or cold (p362)

⭐ Cherry tomatoes and cucumber slices

⭐ Grapes and strawberries

⭐ Fruit kebabs (snip off the sharp end of the wooden skewer before serving)

⭐ Rainbow popcorn (p367)

⭐ Mini muffins, such as Banana and date mini muffins (p58)

⭐ Small squares of Oatmeal bars or homemade Granola breakfast bars (p474)

⭐ Mini pizzas (p460)

⭐ Fruit juice "cocktails"

⭐ Fruity ice pops (p59)

Party bags

Children probably won't be hungry enough to eat the birthday cake at the party, so wrap slices in a napkin and put them in the party bags to take home. Depending on the age of the children (and the views of their parents) sweets may not always be appropriate in the party bags. Try giving little toys instead.

Frozen fruity yogurt popsicles

These summery treats are packed full of vitamin-rich blueberries and have a lovely vivid color.

5 mins,
plus freezing

SPECIAL EQUIPMENT

blender or hand-held blender

popsicle molds

MAKES 6–8

16oz (2 cups) plain yogurt

7oz (200g) blueberries

⅔ cup confectioners' sugar

1 Simply blend all the ingredients together in a blender, or using a hand-held blender, until they are smooth, then freeze in popsicle molds for up to 8 weeks.

2 Put the molds carefully under running hot water for a minute to help release the popsicles when you are ready to serve them.

VARIATION

Try making these with other soft fruits, such as strawberries, peaches, or raspberries, and serve all at once for a range of flavors and colors. Just keep the weight of fruit for each batch to 7oz (200g).

CLEVER WITH LEFTOVERS

If you have a few leftover berries or other summer soft fruit that need to be used up quickly, scale this recipe down to make just 1 or 2 popsicles at a time. That way, you will soon build up a rainbow of different colors.

CALORIES: 100kcals/425kJ

CARBOHYDRATE: 16g
   sugar: 16g

FAT: 2g
   saturated: 1g

SALT: 0.1g

FIBER: 0.3g

Chocolate-dipped strawberries

A simple fruity snack is all the better after being dipped in rich, dark chocolate.

15 mins   5 mins

SERVES 8

14oz (400g) strawberries, not too ripe

3½oz (100g) good-quality dark chocolate, more than 60 percent cocoa solids, broken into pieces

1 Wash and dry the strawberries well. Try to leave the hulls in, as this makes the finished fruit easier to pick up.

2 Put the chocolate in a small heatproof bowl and place over a saucepan of simmering water, making sure the bowl does not touch the water. Stir frequently and remove it as soon as it melts.

3 Line a large baking sheet with waxed paper. Hold each strawberry by its leaves and dip the end in the chocolate, so half of the fruit is covered in chocolate.

Allow any excess chocolate to drip off back into the bowl, then place the strawberries on the baking sheet, making sure they do not touch each other.

4 Put in a cool place to set. These should be served the same day, as the chocolate will soften if the strawberries are overripe, or if they are kept in the fridge for too long.

VARIATION

Dip orange segments, pineapple pieces, or even large grapes, for a chocolatey fruit platter.

CALORIES: 77kcals/324kJ

CARBOHYDRATE: 10g
   sugar: 10g

FAT: 3.5g
   saturated: 2g

SALT: 0g

FIBER: 1g

Chocolate cake pops

These create a fabulous centerpiece, and you can customize the chocolate color and sprinkles to suit your party.

45 mins | 20–25 mins, plus chilling

SPECIAL EQUIPMENT
electric hand-held mixer
7in (18cm) round cake pan
food processor
25 popsicle sticks or wooden skewers (sharp ends removed)

MAKES 25

7 tbsp unsalted butter, softened
½ cup granulated sugar
2 large eggs
¾ cup self-rising flour
3 tbsp cocoa powder
1 tsp baking powder
½ cup store-bought chocolate fudge frosting
9oz (250g) white chocolate
assorted bright cake sprinkles

1 Preheat the oven to 350°F (180°C). Place the butter and sugar in a large bowl and cream it with an electric hand-held mixer until light and fluffy. Whisk in the eggs one at a time. Sift together the flour, cocoa, and baking powder and fold into the batter.

2 Pour the batter into a greased and lined 7in (18cm) round cake pan, then level the surface and bake for 20–25 minutes until a skewer comes out clean. Turn onto a wire rack. When the cake is cool, process it in a food processor until it resembles fine crumbs.

3 Weigh out 10oz (300g) of cake crumbs and put them into a mixing bowl. Mix in the chocolate fudge frosting. Using dry hands, roll into balls, each the size of a walnut. You should get about 25 balls. Put them on a plate, cover, and refrigerate for several hours or freeze for up to 30 minutes until they are quite firm, but not frozen.

4 Line 2 baking sheets with waxed paper. Melt the cake covering according to the package instructions. Dip the ends of 25 popsicle sticks in it, one at a time, then push into the cake balls.

5 Dip the cake pops, one at a time, into the molten chocolate mixture, tilting the bowl to help, and lift them out without moving them around. Make sure the chocolate covers the balls up to the stick, as this helps them stay stuck. Allow excess chocolate to drip back into the bowl.

6 Over a bowl, to catch the stray pieces, sprinkle each cake pop with brightly colored sprinkles and transfer them to the lined baking sheets to dry. (To ensure a smooth, round finish, you can stick the lollipop sticks into an apple that has first been cut in half and placed cut-side down. This will help the cake pops dry without any marks to the surface, but can be a rather delicate business.) Continue until all the balls are coated. You will have to work fast at this stage, as the chocolate can harden quickly. These should be eaten the same day they are made, and kept fairly cool, but not cold, for storage purposes.

HOW TO FREEZE
Open-freeze the chilled, undipped cake balls on a baking sheet, then transfer to freezer bags for up to 1 month. Defrost almost completely, but keep them cold and firm before coating and finishing with sprinkles.

CALORIES: 147kcals/615kJ
CARBOHYDRATE: 15g
  sugar: 13g
FAT: 8.5g
  saturated: 5g
SALT: 0.2g
FIBER: 0.3g

Flowery cupcakes

Make these pretty spring-like cupcakes for a girl's birthday party treat.

25 mins | 16-18 mins

SPECIAL EQUIPMENT

electric hand-held mixer

12 cupcake liners

deep 12-hole muffin pan

MAKES 12

7 tbsp butter, softened

⅔ cup granulated sugar

3 large eggs, lightly beaten

1 tsp vanilla extract

1½ cups self-rising flour

1 tsp baking powder

3½ tbsp milk

FOR THE BUTTERCREAM

7 tbsp butter, softened

1⅔ cups confectioners' sugar

½–1 tsp green food coloring

store-bought sugar flowers, or store-bought colored icing, to decorate

---

CALORIES: 319kcals/1340kJ

CARBOHYDRATE: 41g
  sugar: 29g

FAT: 16g
  saturated: 9g

SALT: 0.6g

FIBER: 0.7g

---

1 Preheat the oven to 350°F (180°C). Place the butter and sugar in a bowl and use an electric hand-held mixer to beat them until light and fluffy. Whisk in the eggs and vanilla extract.

2 Sift together the flour and baking powder. Whisk the flour mixture and the milk into the batter alternately. Place 12 cupcake liners in a deep 12-hole muffin pan (this will help them keep their shape).

3 Spoon the cake batter into the liners, filling each two-thirds full. Bake for 16–18 minutes until springy to the touch. Transfer to a wire rack to cool.

4 To make the buttercream, beat the butter, confectioners' sugar, and food coloring until smooth and creamy.

5 When the cakes are cold, cover them in buttercream, using the back of a spoon dipped in warm water to smooth the surface. Decorate with store-bought sugar flowers, or cut your own using store-bought colored icing.

PREPARE AHEAD

The cakes can be made 1 day ahead and stored, un-iced, in an airtight container. Ice them on the day they are to be eaten.

Rocky road squares

These chocolatey treats are very rich, so be sure to cut them into small party-sized pieces.

15-20 mins, plus chilling

SPECIAL EQUIPMENT

7in (18cm) square baking pan

MAKES 36

9oz (250g) dark chocolate, broken into squares

11 tbsp unsalted butter, plus extra for the pan

2 tbsp corn syrup

7oz (200g) shortbread cookies

1¾oz (50g) raisins

1¾oz (50g) dried cranberries

3½oz (100g) mini-marshmallows

CALORIES: 110kcals/460kJ

CARBOHYDRATE: 13g
  sugar: 10g

FAT: 6g
  saturated: 4g

SALT: 0.1g

FIBER: 0.3g

---

1 Put the chocolate, butter, and syrup in a large, heatproof bowl and melt it over a saucepan of simmering water, making sure the bowl does not touch the water. When it has melted, cool slightly.

2 Put the cookies into a plastic bag and smash with a rolling pin until you have small, broken pieces.

3 Mix the cookies into the chocolate mixture. Next mix in the dried fruit and marshmallows.

4 Grease a 7in (18cm) square baking pan with butter and line with parchment paper. Pour in the mixture and press it down firmly with the back of a spoon.

5 Cover and refrigerate for 2 hours, before removing from the pan and cutting into 36 squares with a sharp knife. In warm weather, store these in the fridge.

VARIATION

You can use milk chocolate if you prefer, which will be less rich for young children. Also try varying the type of dried fruit or cookies used.

Butterfly cake

You can decorate this pretty cake any way you like, with bright colored sprinkles, flowers, or even small sweets.

40 mins | 35–40 mins, plus cooling

SPECIAL EQUIPMENT

9½in (24cm) round cake pan
electric hand-held mixer
ruler
cake board (optional)

SERVES 15

14 tbsp unsalted butter, softened, plus extra for greasing

¾ cup granulated sugar

1 tsp vanilla extract

4 large eggs

1½ cups all-purpose flour, sifted

1 tsp baking powder

2 tbsp milk, if needed

FOR THE ICING

2 cups confectioners' sugar

8 tbsp butter, softened

red food coloring

cake decorations, such as sprinkles and sweets, to decorate

1 Preheat the oven to 325°F (160°C). Grease a 9½in (24cm) cake pan and line the bottom with parchment paper.

2 In a large bowl, whisk the butter and sugar with an electric hand-held mixer for at least 5 minutes, until light and fluffy. Whisk in the vanilla.

3 Whisk in the eggs one at a time, making sure to incorporate as much air as possible. Fold in the flour and baking powder until just blended. If it seems stiff, add the milk. Pour the batter into the pan.

4 Bake in the center of the hot oven for 35–40 minutes, until a skewer comes out clean. Cool in the pan for 5 minutes, then turn it out to cool completely on a wire rack.

5 For the icing, beat together the confectioners' sugar and butter until smooth and creamy. Add drops of food coloring until you reach your desired shade of pink. Add a splash of boiling water if it is too stiff.

6 To make the butterfly shape, place the cake on a cutting board and use a bread knife to cut off any rise on the top, so it is completely flat. Turn it over, so the cut side is underneath. Now take a ruler and use it to measure a ¾in- (2cm-) wide strip in the center of the cake. Cut this out and you will be left with 1 long, thin strip of cake and 2 semi-circular pieces. Set the thin strip aside. Now reverse the semi-circles so they are back to back. Cut each semi-circle into 2, roughly two-thirds and one-third each, using the finished picture as a guide. When the pieces are cut and you separate them, they should look like butterfly wings.

7 Ice and decorate the thin cake strip (the body of the butterfly) and place it in the middle of a serving plate or cake board (if using). Ice each wing piece individually, put it in place using a long palette knife or spatula, and use a small palette knife to touch up any areas that have been smeared.

Decorate each before you go on to the next, so the icing does not harden before you begin to press your chosen decorations into it.

COOK'S TIP

Use a paper template to work out the shape. The best cake to use is one with a slightly firmer texture such as this pound cake, as it will be easier to ice, but use an electric hand-held mixer to lighten the texture.

HOW TO FREEZE

The cooked cake, un-iced, can be wrapped well in plastic wrap, sealed with foil, then frozen for up to 12 weeks. Defrost the cake thoroughly before cutting it to shape and icing.

CALORIES: 350kcals/1478kJ
CARBOHYDRATE: 39g
  sugar: 30g
FAT: 20g
  saturated: 12g
SALT: 0.2g
FIBER: 0.5g

Chocolate cake

This is a light, chocolate layer cake and sometimes only chocolate cake will do—especially at party time.

30-40 mins   25-30 mins

SPECIAL EQUIPMENT

2 x 8in (20cm) round, non-stick
   cake pans

electric hand-held mixer

SERVES 4

12 tbsp unsalted butter, softened, plus
   extra for greasing

⅔ cup granulated sugar

3 large eggs, lightly beaten

1¼ cups self-rising flour

3 tbsp cocoa powder

½ tsp of baking powder

FOR THE TOPPING

3½oz (100g) plain chocolate

3½oz (100g) milk chocolate

¾ cup heavy cream,
   at room temperature

1 Grease two 8in (20cm) round,
   non-stick cake pans and line
the bottoms with parchment paper.
Cream the butter and sugar together
in a bowl until they are light and
fluffy. Gradually beat in the egg.

2 Preheat the oven to 350°F
   (180°C). Sift the flour, cocoa
powder, and baking powder into
the bowl and fold them into the
creamed mixture. Divide this
between the pans, smoothing

the tops with a palette knife. Bake
for 20–25 minutes, or until firm,
then turn onto a wire rack.

3 Break both the chocolate bars
   into a bowl and gently melt
them over a pan of simmering
water. Remove the bowl from the
pan. Let cool for 5 minutes, then
stir in the cream and let thicken
for a few minutes.

4 Make sure the cakes are cool
   before putting on the topping.
Put one cake on a serving plate and
spread one-quarter of the topping
over it. Put the other cake on top
and spread the rest of the topping
over the top and sides until the
cake is evenly coated. Let set.

VARIATION

Melt 3½ oz (100g) white chocolate and
pour it into a parchment paper-lined
sheet. Let it set. Break it into small
pieces and use it to decorate the cake.

COOK'S TIP

The eggs should be at room temperature
and added slowly, or the mixture may
curdle. If it does, mix in a little flour.

CALORIES:	410kcals/1717kJ
CARBOHYDRATE:	33g
sugar:	24g
FAT:	29g
saturated:	17g
SALT:	0.3g
FIBER:	1.5g

Caterpillar cake

This classic caterpillar is fun, but the basic body shape could be adapted to make a snake cake, if you prefer.

40 mins **30–35 mins**

SPECIAL EQUIPMENT
10in (25cm) bundt cake pan (optional)
electric hand-held mixer
rectangular cake board, or similar,
  at least 12 x 8in (30 x 20cm)

SERVES 15

14 tbsp unsalted butter, softened, plus
  extra for greasing
¾ cup granulated sugar
1 tsp vanilla extract
4 large eggs
1¼ cups all-purpose flour
½ cup cocoa powder
1 tsp baking powder
2 tbsp whole milk, if needed

FOR THE ICING
1⅔ cups confectioners' sugar
7 tbsp unsalted butter, softened
green food coloring

TO DECORATE
1oz (30g) dark chocolate chips
2 white chocolate chips
2 chocolate buttons
dark green and brown icing pens
sprinkles (optional)
2 green drinking straws (optional)

1 Preheat the oven to 325°F (160°C). Grease a 10in (25cm) bundt pan. Sprinkle a little flour into the pan, then shake to form a fine layer all over. Pour out excess flour and set aside. (If you do not have a bundt pan, see the Cook's Tip.)

2 Beat the butter and sugar with an electric hand-held mixer for 5 minutes, until fluffy. Add the vanilla, then the eggs, beating in as much air as possible.

3 Sift the flour, cocoa powder, and baking powder together, then fold it in. If it seems too stiff, add the milk. Pour into the pan.

4 Bake for 30–35 minutes, until the cake has risen. Cool in the pan for 5 minutes, then turn onto a rack.

5 To make the icing, beat the confectioners' sugar and butter until light and creamy. Add the green food coloring a little at a time until you reach a light green for the face. Set aside ¼ cup, then continue to add food coloring until you reach a dark green for the body.

6 Place the cake on a board and use a bread knife to cut off any rise, so it is flat. Cut in half, to give 2 "C"-shaped pieces. Now cut one-quarter off one of the pieces—this will become the head. Use the picture (below) as a guide to put the body together. Trim the head and tail into a rounded shape.

7 Ice each piece, place it on the cake board, and use a small palette knife to touch up any areas that have been smeared. Use the lighter colored icing for the head.

8 Smooth over any cracks in the icing and place dark chocolate chips along the body, on both sides, for legs. Use icing to stick the white chocolate chips to the chocolate buttons, then fix them on as "eyes." Leave for 1 hour. Use the icing pens to draw on body sections and a smiley mouth. Add sprinkles and drinking straw antennae, if you like.

COOK'S TIP

If you do not have a bundt pan you can use a 9½in (24cm) round cake pan. Prepare as above both the pan and a small (2½in/6.5cm) ovenproof ramekin. Place the ramekin upside down in the pan before pouring the batter around.

CALORIES: 334kcals/1408kJ	
CARBOHYDRATE: 35g	
sugar: 28g	
FAT: 20g	
saturated: 12g	
SALT: 0.3g	
FIBER: 1g	

Food to go

Food to go

Whether you're planning a picnic, packing children's lunch boxes, or trying to save a little money by taking your lunch to work, here are a range of ideas to eat healthily on the go. Beyond the ordinary sandwich, there is a wealth of possibilities from wraps to hearty salads, protein-packed frittatas to mini pies and pastries. Homemade healthy snacks help you and your family avoid eating processed packaged foods when you're hungry out and about.

Pantry essentials

Keeping a few basics in the fridge as well as some pantry essentials means a sudden sunny day can be the excuse for an impromptu picnic. Cans of tuna, salmon, and beans can be the basis of an array of salads and sandwiches. Refrigerator staples such as a good-quality mayonnaise, mustard, pickles, and cheeses make it easy to put together a tasty, portable lunch.

Be creative with bread

Don't get stuck in the habit of using sliced bread for everything. Experiment by making wraps using tortillas, stuffing pita pockets, or even making savory muffins. For a family picnic try cooking mini frittatas with different fillings or put together a Whole stuffed ciabatta (p387)—it's one of the easiest things to transport, as it's meant to be squashed, and can be cut into chunks when you need to eat.

Homemade hummus and crudités (p388), is easy to make and always popular. Crudités could be carrots, celery, or broccoli; or take breadsticks.

Stuffed ciabatta (p387) makes an ideal picnic food. Tasty and easy to carry, it can be sliced when you arrive and served with salad.

Lunch boxes for all

It's very easy to pack the same few items in a child's lunch box day after day, once you know what they like—sandwiches, fruit, something sweet—but no wonder they get bored! On a cold winter's day send them off with warming Harvest Vegetable soup and crusty bread (p157), or when it's warm outside pack some crunchy vegetables and homemade Hummus (p388). Bake a batch of Tuna empanadas (p397), which are robust enough to transport and perfect for small appetites. Packed lunches aren't just for children—you can save time and money taking your lunch to work, too. Try a slice of Red bell pepper and tomato frittata (p236) and salad or why not roast a pan of vegetables (see Oven-roasted ratatouille p175) on a Sunday, and use them over the following two or three days. Eat in a salad, a wrap, or as the filling of a sandwich in a crusty roll spread with a little Herby goat cheese spread (p241). You can add a little stock or water and purée them into a hearty soup, if the weather is cold.

Picnic ideas

The prospect of a picnic on a warm day means you need to think of some tasty portable foods. Lightly grilled vegetables, chunky salads, and overstuffed wraps all seem to taste better eaten outside. Think beyond the usual sandwiches, and try planning ahead by baking Individual pork pies (p399) for a special occasion. Take salads that won't wilt or get squashed such as Cannellini bean, tuna, and red onion (p390), or assemble items such as Chicken Caesar wraps (p386) when you get there.

Proper packaging

The proper packaging can make carrying and eating a meal on the go fuss free. Make sure you choose sturdy containers with tight-fitting lids, or bento boxes with compartments, to separate different courses. Wide-mouthed thermal containers with spoons that fit into the lid can be used to carry hot soups or stews for a warm midday meal.

Snacks on the run

Reuse small plastic containers, well washed, to transport snacks on the go. A handful of dried fruit, nuts, and seeds makes a healthy snack to keep on your desk. Young children will happily snack on a few fistfuls of their favorite cereal or raisins, stashed in a small container. Even teenagers are more likely to grab a healthy snack when presented with some

homemade Granola breakfast bars (p474) or Savory breakfast muffins (p442) as they rush out of the door. To avoid the temptation of unnecessary junk food or snacks, why not bake a batch of the Banana and date mini muffins (p58), which are as good for adults as they are for children? Freeze them the day they are made, then take one or two straight from the freezer to have as a healthy mid-morning snack, along with some freshly chopped fruit packed in an airtight container.

Granola breakfast bars (p474), are a nutritious snack for hungry teens on the run, adults' packed lunches, or after-school snacks for kids.

Sweet potato and goat cheese mini frittatas (p396) make an ideal lunch box item for adults or children, just add some green salad.

Keep it fresh

To keep things fresh and cool in the warmer months, try freezing children's juice boxes or even water bottles before packing their lunch. The frozen liquid will keep everything in the lunchbox cool, and defrost perfectly in time for lunch, ensuring that they'll have a cool drink on a hot day.

Roll wraps up tightly in foil or plastic wrap to keep them fresh or pack the wraps and filling separately for older children to compile themselves.

Double-decker turkey and avocado sandwiches

Serving layered sandwiches is an easy way to make a simple sandwich more attractive.

10 mins

SERVES 4

3 heaping tbsp good-quality mayonnaise

1 heaping tsp Dijon mustard

salt and freshly ground black pepper

butter, softened, for spreading

12 large slices of multigrain bread

2 handfuls of salad leaves

5½oz (150g) thinly sliced turkey breast

2 avocados, thinly sliced

½ lemon

1 Mix the mayonnaise and mustard together and season well. Butter 8 slices of bread on one side only, and 4 slices carefully on both sides.

2 Lay 4 of the single side-buttered slices on a cutting board, buttered-sides up. Top each slice with one-quarter of the salad leaves, pressing them into the bread gently. Lay one-quarter of the turkey on top of each and spread with a thin layer of the mayonnaise.

3 Put a double-side-buttered slice of bread on each sandwich, then layer one-quarter of the avocado over each, drizzle with a little lemon juice, and season well.

4 Top each with a final slice of bread, buttered-side down, and press down well to hold everything together. Carefully trim the crusts off the bread and cut into halves on a diagonal to serve, or pack into a container for transportation.

CALORIES: 614kcals/2572kJ	
CARBOHYDRATE: 55g	
sugar: 4g	
FAT: 32g	
saturated: 9g	
SALT: 2g	
FIBER: 10g	

Herby goat cheese pinwheel sandwiches

These little sandwich bites make a very appealing addition to a picnic spread.

15 mins

MAKES 16

3½oz (100g) soft goat cheese, softened

3½oz (100g) cream cheese, softened

1 heaping tbsp finely chopped basil leaves

1 heaping tbsp finely chopped chives

finely grated zest of ½ lemon

salt and freshly ground black pepper

4 large slices of soft whole wheat bread

butter, softened, for spreading

1 Put the 2 cheeses in a large bowl with the herbs and lemon zest and beat with a wooden spoon until combined. Season well with pepper and a little salt (be careful as goat cheese can be quite salty).

2 Trim the crusts off the bread and roll each slice out with a rolling pin until it is as flat as possible. Spread each slice with butter on one side only.

3 Spread each slice of bread with one-quarter of the cheese mixture and roll it up, starting from a short edge. Trim the edges neatly with a serrated knife and cut each roll in half, then in half again, to make 4 pieces per sandwich. Serve cut-sides up to show the swirled effect, or pack into a container for transportation.

Pinwheels are fun for children to help make and eat. Try using slices of ham as well as the cheese, or use plain or flavored cream cheese.

Fussy eaters!

CALORIES: 78kcals/326kJ	
CARBOHYDRATE: 4g	
sugar: 0.2g	
FAT: 6g	
saturated: 3.5g	
SALT: 0.3g	
FIBER: 0.8g	

Roast beef, watercress, and horseradish mayo sandwiches

Sandwiches can be easily enlivened by flavoring some good, store-bought mayonnaise.

10 mins

SERVES 4

3 heaping tbsp good-quality mayonnaise

1 heaping tsp horseradish sauce

salt and freshly ground black pepper

butter, softened, for spreading

8 large slices of sourdough or rye bread

2 handfuls of watercress

7oz (200g) rare roast beef, thinly sliced

CALORIES: 408kcals/1717kJ

CARBOHYDRATE: 37g
   sugar: 2.5g

FAT: 18g
   saturated: 4g

SALT: 1.4g

FIBER: 2.5g

1 Mix the mayonnaise and horseradish together and season well. Butter each slice of bread on one side only.

2 Lay 4 of the buttered slices on a cutting board, buttered-sides up. Top each slice with a layer of the watercress, pressing it into the bread gently. Then layer one-quarter of the beef on each slice, and spread with a thin layer of the mayonnaise.

3 Top with the final slice of bread, buttered-side down, and press down well to hold everything together. Cut into halves to serve, or pack into a container for transportation.

CLEVER WITH LEFTOVERS

These sandwiches are a cunning and delicious way to use up leftovers from a Sunday roast. Just make sure the slices of beef are rare and carved very thinly.

Roast beet, goat cheese, and arugula sandwiches

These are fabulous for a picnic or packed lunch, or try them at home with toasted bread instead.

10 mins   45 mins

SERVES 4

4 small beets, approx. 2½oz (75g) each, peeled and sliced ¼in (5mm) thick

1 tbsp olive oil

salt and freshly ground black pepper

8 large slices sourdough or other rustic bread

butter, softened, for spreading

7oz (200g) soft goat cheese

2 handfuls of arugula leaves

CALORIES: 436kcals/1832kJ

CARBOHYDRATE: 41g
   sugar: 8g

FAT: 22g
   saturated: 12g

SALT: 2g

FIBER: 4.5g

1 Preheat the oven to 400°F (200°C). Place the beet slices on a baking sheet, brush them with the olive oil, and season them well. Bake them at the top of the oven for 20 minutes, turning once, until they are lightly browned and cooked through. Remove them from the oven and set aside to cool.

2 Spread the slices of bread with butter on one side only. Spread 4 slices with one-quarter each of the goat cheese, season with a little pepper, then add a layer of the cooled beet slices.

3 Top the beets with a layer of the arugula and finish the sandwich with a final slice of bread, buttered-side down. Cut in half to serve, or pack into a container for transportation.

White bean purée, alfalfa, and carrot pita pockets

A delicious mix of moist softness and crunch makes these portable pockets ideal to pack for lunch or a picnic.

15 mins

SPECIAL EQUIPMENT
food processer

SERVES 4

1 x 14oz (400g) can of cannellini beans, drained and rinsed (reserve 2 tbsp of the liquid)

2 large garlic cloves, crushed

2 heaping tbsp finely chopped flat-leaf parsley leaves

1 tbsp olive oil

¼ tsp salt

freshly ground black pepper

2 tbsp lemon juice

4 whole wheat pita breads

1 large carrot, coarsely grated

1¾oz (50g) alfalfa shoots or other shoots

1 To make the bean purée, put the beans, garlic, parsley, olive oil, salt, pepper, lemon juice, and 1 tbsp of the bean liquid into a food processer and process to a rough paste. If it is too thick add another 1 tbsp of the liquid (but remember this needs to be a thick paste to hold up well in the pita bread).

2 Cut each pita in half and open to make 8 small pockets. Spread a layer of bean purée on both inside faces of the pockets.

3 Sprinkle a little carrot and alfalfa into each. Serve layered on top of each other with the stuffing showing, or pack into a container for transportation.

VARIATION

It is easy to adapt this bean purée to your taste. Add roasted red bell peppers for a sweet, red-tinged purée, or roasted garlic for a mellow version (omit the crushed garlic in the latter case).

CALORIES: 287kcals/1203kJ

CARBOHYDRATE: 45g
  sugar: 6.5g

FAT: 5g
  saturated: 0.7g

SALT: 1.8g

FIBER: 12g

Pulled pork wraps

This is a great way to use up any leftover Slow-cooked shoulder of pork (see p281), in an instantly portable meal.

10 mins

SERVES 4

12oz (350g) cooked pulled pork, such as leftover Slow-cooked shoulder of pork (see p281)

2 heaping tbsp good-quality barbecue sauce

4 large wraps

4 large Romaine lettuce leaves

½ cucumber, halved, seeded, and finely sliced

3 tbsp sour cream

1 Shred the pork finely and mix it with the barbecue sauce. Lay the wraps on a work surface. Flatten the lettuce leaves by pressing down on the central rib, and put a large lettuce leaf onto each wrap, with the leaf starting at the edge nearest you. Layer a line of the sliced cucumber along the lettuce leaf, about 1in (3cm) thick, and top each line of cucumber with ½ tbsp of the sour cream.

2 Lay one-quarter of the pork along each line of sour cream. Now take the remaining sour cream and smear a little, with the back of a spoon, all over the piece of wrap furthest from you (it should cover one-third of the wrap). This helps it stick together.

3 Carefully roll up the wrap by picking up the side nearest to you and folding it over the filling. Continue to roll it away from you until the wrap meets itself and sticks together with the sour cream. Slice each end off carefully and cut the wraps in half on a diagonal to serve, or wrap and pack into a container for transportation.

CALORIES: 380kcals/1599kJ	
CARBOHYDRATE: 42g	
sugar: 4g	
FAT: 9g	
saturated: 3.6g	
SALT: 0.9g	
FIBER: 3g	

Shrimp, sweet chili, and Greek yogurt wraps

Sweet, fresh-tasting pea shoots, juicy shrimp, and sharp yogurt make a wonderful combination.

10 mins

SERVES 4

4 large wraps

1¾oz (50g) pea shoots, mixed baby salad leaves, or arugula

½ cucumber, halved, seeded, and finely sliced

6oz (175g) package of cooked, shelled large shrimp, sliced in half horizontally and deveined

3 heaping tbsp Greek yogurt

4 tsp Thai sweet chili sauce

salt and freshly ground black pepper

1 Lay the wraps on a work surface and divide the pea shoots between them, starting at the edge nearest you and covering about one-third of the wrap. Layer one-quarter of the cucumber, then the shrimp, along the pea shoots, and top each with ½ tbsp of yogurt and 1 tsp of chili sauce. Season.

2 Take the remaining yogurt and smear a little, with the back of a spoon, all over the piece of each wrap furthest from you (it should cover one-third of the wrap). This helps it stick together.

3 Fold the side nearest to you over the filling. Roll it away from you until it sticks together with the yogurt. Slice each end off and halve on a diagonal to serve, or pack for transportation.

CLEVER WITH LEFTOVERS

These wraps can easily be adapted to contain any leftover cooked fish (but avoid smoked fish for this recipe).

CALORIES: 249kcals/1054kJ	
CARBOHYDRATE: 43g	
sugar: 5g	
FAT: 2g	
saturated: 1g	
SALT: 1.2g	
FIBER: 3g	

Chicken Caesar wraps

This delicious wrap, with its piquant dressing, has all the flavors of a chicken Caesar salad in a portable form.

10 mins, plus cooking   15–20 mins

SERVES 4

1 tbsp olive oil

salt and freshly ground black pepper

2 boneless, skinless chicken breasts

FOR THE SAUCE

4 anchovy fillets

2 tsp lemon juice

2 tsp Dijon mustard

½ cup good-quality mayonnaise

¼ cup finely grated Parmesan cheese

½ tsp Worcestershire sauce

4 large wraps

4 large Romaine lettuce leaves

1 Preheat a grill pan. Brush it with olive oil and season the chicken breasts on both sides. Grill the chicken over medium heat for 5–10 minutes on each side (depending on size), until charred in places on the outside and cooked through. Let cool. If you are in a hurry, slice it now into thin strips, as it will cool more quickly.

2 While the chicken is cooling, make the Caesar sauce. Put the anchovies and lemon juice in a bowl and mash them with the back of a spoon until the anchovy has turned to paste. (Alternatively, use a mortar and pestle.) Add the mustard, mayonnaise, Parmesan cheese, and Worcestershire sauce, and mix well. Check the seasoning and add some pepper.

3 To assemble the wraps, lay them out on a work surface. Flatten the lettuce leaves by pressing down on the central rib, and put a leaf onto each wrap, with the leaf starting at the edge nearest you. Layer one-quarter of the sliced chicken along the lettuce leaf, and top each line with a good smear of the Caesar sauce, reserving a little to seal the wraps.

4 Take the remaining Caesar sauce and smear a little, with the back of a spoon, all over each piece of wrap farthest away from you (it should cover about one-third of the wrap). This will help the wrap stick together. Then carefully roll up the wrap by picking up the side nearest to you and folding it over the filling. Continue to roll it away from you until the wrap bread meets itself and sticks together with the Caesar sauce.

5 Slice each end off carefully and cut the wraps in half on a diagonal to serve.

CLEVER WITH LEFTOVERS

If you have cold, leftover roast chicken or turkey, use it here instead of grilling fresh chicken breast. You'll need about 10oz (300g) of meat in total.

CALORIES: 575kcals/2406kJ

CARBOHYDRATE: 40g
    sugar: 1.5g

FAT: 33g
    saturated: 7g

SALT: 1.7g

FIBER: 2g

Whole stuffed ciabatta with mozzarella and grilled vegetables

This is incredibly tasty and simple to transport, and will easily feed a family of four.

10 mins, plus chilling   15 mins, plus cooling

SERVES 4

½ eggplant, cut into ½in (1cm) slices

2 zucchini, cut into ½in (1cm) slices

4–6 tbsp olive oil

salt and freshly ground black pepper

1 large beefsteak tomato

1 ciabatta loaf

2 roasted red bell peppers from a jar, drained, and sliced

ball of mozzarella, approx. 4½oz (125g), thinly sliced

handful of basil leaves

1 Preheat a large grill pan or a broiler to its highest setting. Brush the slices of eggplant and zucchini on both sides with olive oil and season them well. Either grill or broil them for 2–4 minutes each side, until they are charred in places and cooked through. Put them on a large plate in a single layer to cool.

2 Slice about ½in (1cm) off each end of the tomato, reserving these pieces. Slice the remaining tomato as thinly as possible.

3 Cut the ciabatta in half, leaving a hinge so you can open it out flat. Drizzle both sides with a little olive oil. Take the ends of the tomato and rub both sides of the bread with the cut side, to soften and flavor the bread, then discard the ends.

4 Cover one side of the loaf with the eggplant, zucchini, and red bell peppers, then top with mozzarella. Sprinkle with the basil, season, then add the tomato.

5 Close the loaf and press down on it hard. Wrap it very tightly in plastic wrap, going around it a few times until it is completely covered and compressed. Leave in the fridge with a weight (such as a cutting board and some cans) on top for at least 4 hours, turning once. Unwrap and slice to serve, or transport in the wrapping and slice at a picnic.

CALORIES: 435kcals/1812kJ

CARBOHYDRATE: 36g
  sugar: 4g

FAT: 25g
  saturated: 6.5g

SALT: 1.2g

FIBER: 8g

Baked Parmesan and rosemary crisps

These easy home-baked crisps transform a simple wrap into a gourmet snack.

5 mins   5–7 mins

SERVES 4

4 large wraps

2 tbsp olive oil

2 tsp rosemary leaves, finely chopped

¼ cup finely grated Parmesan cheese

freshly ground black pepper

Hummus or Baba ghanoush, to serve (see p388)

1 Preheat the oven to 400°F (200°C). Lay the wraps on a work surface and brush all over on both sides with the olive oil.

2 Scatter them with the rosemary and Parmesan and season well with pepper. Place on a baking sheet.

3 Bake them at the top of the oven for 5–7 minutes until golden brown, puffed up, and crispy. Watch them carefully for the last minute, as they burn quickly.

4 Remove them from the oven, then transfer to a wire rack to cool. When they are cool, break them into jagged, irregular pieces and serve with Hummus or Baba ghanoush (see p388).

VARIATION

While it is best to stick with Parmesan cheese for these crisps, you can vary the woody herbs to suit your personal preference. Try the same amount of thyme leaves, or chopped oregano leaves. Soft herbs, such as basil, should not be used here, because they will burn in the oven.

CALORIES: 295kcals/1242kJ

CARBOHYDRATE: 39g
  sugar: 1g

FAT: 10.5g
  saturated: 4g

SALT: 0.8g

FIBER: 2.2g

Hummus

This simple hummus can be adjusted with more garlic or lemon juice, or additional spices, if desired.

5 mins

SPECIAL EQUIPMENT
blender or food processor

SERVES 4 (as part of a mezze)

1 x 14oz (400g) can of chickpeas, drained and rinsed (reserve ¼ cup of liquid)

2 tbsp tahini

2 tbsp olive oil, plus extra to serve

2 tbsp lemon juice, or to taste

1 large garlic clove, crushed, or to taste

¼ tsp ground cumin

¼ tsp salt

freshly ground black pepper

spinkling of paprika

crudités, to serve

1 Put all the ingredients, except the paprika, into a blender or food processor, and process until completely smooth.

2 Taste and adjust the seasoning, or the amount of garlic or lemon juice, as desired.

3 Serve the hummus in a bowl with a swirl of olive oil and a sprinkling of paprika, and some crudités on the side.

VARIATION

Hummus can be flavored to suit your family. Add a handful of pitted black olives, or roasted red bell pepper strips, to the mix before blending, or sprinkle with smoked paprika instead of plain for a more subtle twist.

CLEVER WITH LEFTOVERS

Because it is so adaptable, hummus is an excellent way to use up all kinds of odds and ends. Add any leftover plain beans or lentils (as long as the total weight remains the same), or try a small handful of leftover soft herb leaves.

CALORIES: 167kcals/698kJ	
CARBOHYDRATE: 9.5g	
sugar: 0.5g	
FAT: 12g	
saturated: 1.5g	
SALT: 0.6g	
FIBER: 4g	

Baba ghanoush

Try this delicious smoky Middle Eastern dip with Pita chips (see p242), or just scooped up with fresh bread.

10 mins   30 mins, plus cooling

SPECIAL EQUIPMENT
food processor or blender

SERVES 4 (as part of a mezze)

1 large eggplant

2 tbsp olive oil

1 tbsp lemon juice

3 tbsp tahini

1 garlic clove, crushed

1 tsp smoked paprika

salt and freshly ground black pepper

crudités, or Pita chips (see p242), to serve

1 Preheat the oven to 450°F (230°C). Prick the eggplant all over with a fork, then rub it with 1 tbsp of the olive oil. Place on a baking sheet and bake at the top of the hot oven for 25–30 minutes, turning once, until the skin has completely blackened and the interior is very soft.

2 Remove the eggplant from the oven and let cool. When it is cold, cut it in half and scoop out the flesh into the bowl of a food processor or blender. Add the remaining ingredients and purée the mixture to a rough paste. Taste and adjust the seasoning. Serve with some crudités or Pita chips (see p242).

CALORIES: 129kcals/535kJ	
CARBOHYDRATE: 2g	
sugar: 1.5g	
FAT: 12.5g	
saturated: 2g	
SALT: trace	
FIBER: 3g	

Baba ghanoush tends to be a favorite with everyone who tastes it, so it's worth trying out with children who claim to dislike eggplant.

Fussy eaters!

Artichoke and scallion dip

A pantry recipe that has sophisticated and subtle flavors, but takes just minutes to make.

5 mins

SPECIAL EQUIPMENT
food processor or blender

SERVES 6 (as part of a mezze)

1 x 14oz (390g) can of artichoke hearts, drained

1 garlic clove, halved

3 scallions, coarsely chopped

2 tbsp good-quality mayonnaise

salt and freshly ground black pepper

1 Place the artichokes, garlic, scallions, and mayonnaise in a food processor or blender and process to form a smooth purée.

2 Season to taste with salt and pepper, then spoon into a serving bowl, cover, and refrigerate until ready to use.

VARIATION

If you can find jarred, grilled artichokes, use the same amount to add an agreeably smoky edge to this dip, and sprinkle the finished dip with smoked paprika, too.

PREPARE AHEAD

The dip can be made up to 24 hours in advance, covered with plastic wrap, and chilled until ready to serve.

COOK'S TIP

Good with pita bread, vegetable crudités, or breadsticks. Alternatively, spread on to chunks of French bread.

CALORIES: 48kcals/199kJ
CARBOHYDRATE: 2.5g
  sugar: 2.5g
FAT: 4g
  saturated: 0.5g
SALT: 0.2g
FIBER: 1g

Red bell pepper salad

In Spanish, this dish is called *ensaladilla de pimientos*. Sweet red bell peppers are stewed, then served cold.

10 mins   25 mins

SERVES 4
(as part of a mezze)

3 tbsp olive oil

6 red bell peppers, cut into broad strips

2 garlic cloves, finely chopped

9oz (250g) ripe tomatoes, peeled, seeded, and chopped (see p191)

2 tbsp chopped flat-leaf parsley leaves

salt and freshly ground black pepper

1 tbsp sherry vinegar

1 Heat the oil in a large frying pan, add the peppers and garlic, and cook over low heat for 5 minutes, stirring. Add the tomatoes, increase the heat, and bring to simmering point, then reduce the heat to low, cover, and cook for 12–15 minutes.

2 Stir in the parsley, season well with salt and pepper, and cook for another 2 minutes.

3 Using a slotted spoon, remove the peppers and arrange them in a serving dish.

4 Add the vinegar to the juices in the pan, increase the heat, and simmer the sauce for 5–7 minutes, or until reduced and thickened. Pour the sauce over the peppers and allow the salad to cool.

CALORIES: 158kcals/655kJ
CARBOHYDRATE: 15g
  sugar: 15g
FAT: 9g
  saturated: 1.5g
SALT: trace
FIBER: 5.5g

CLEVER WITH LEFTOVERS

Process any leftover salad in a food processor until smooth. Whisk in enough olive oil to make the mixture into the consistency of a salad dressing and use to coat the salad leaves or roasted vegetables.

Mediterranean vegetable couscous

This lovely summer salad can be adapted to include any vegetables you have available and that are in season.

20 mins, plus cooling   30–40 mins

SERVES 4–6

1 small or ½ large eggplant, cut into ½in (1cm) cubes

1 red bell pepper, cut into ½in (1cm) cubes

1 zucchini, cut into ½in (1cm) cubes

1 red onion, cut into ½in (1cm) cubes

¼ cup olive oil

salt and freshly ground black pepper

2 cups couscous

1 tbsp powdered vegetable stock

2½ tbsp extra virgin olive oil

juice of 1 large lemon

handful of basil leaves, roughly chopped

handful of flat-leaf parsley leaves, roughly chopped

1 Preheat the oven to 400°F (200°C). Put the eggplant, red bell pepper, zucchini, and red onion in a roasting pan and toss them with 2 tbsp of the olive oil. Season them well, spread them out in a single layer, and cook them at the top of the oven for 30–40 minutes, turning them once, until they are well cooked and browned at the edges. Remove them from the oven and allow to cool.

2 Put the couscous into a large, shallow bowl and drizzle in the remaining 1½ tbsp of the olive oil. Rub the olive oil into the couscous with your hands to ensure that all the grains have a covering of oil (this will help to keep them from sticking together). Scatter in the powdered vegetable stock and mix it in with a fork.

3 Pour 2 cups of boiling water over the couscous and stir it in briefly with a fork. The water should just cover the couscous (if it does not, add a little more). Immediately cover the bowl with a tight layer of plastic wrap, sealing it well to ensure that no steam escapes. Let steam for 5 minutes, then remove the plastic wrap and test the grains, which should be nearly soft, and all the water soaked in. Fluff the couscous with a fork and let cool, fluffing it again occasionally to make sure it does not stick together.

4 When the vegetables and the couscous have cooled, assemble the salad by tossing them together in a large bowl along with the extra virgin olive oil, the lemon juice, and herbs. Season to taste and serve.

VARIATION

Try this recipe with green summer vegetables and arugula dressing. Make the dressing by processing together ¼ cup extra virgin olive oil, scant 1 cup roughly chopped arugula leaves, ¼ cup lemon juice, and salt and pepper until it is a thick, dark green liquid. Add the dressing to the cooked couscous, then toss in ¾ cup each of frozen fava beans and petit pois, cooked, drained, and cooled, with a handful of roughly chopped mint leaves. Crumble 3½oz (100g) feta cheese over the top to serve.

CALORIES: 361kcals/1500kJ
CARBOHYDRATE: 42g
  sugar: 5g
FAT: 18g
  saturated: 2.5g
SALT: 1.6g
FIBER: 3g

Apricot, pine nut, and cilantro couscous

This Middle Eastern-inspired salad is equally good with dishes such as Slow-cooked Moroccan lamb (see p132).

12 mins, plus cooling

SERVES 4-6

2 cups couscous

1½ tbsp olive oil

1 tbsp powdered vegetable stock

1¾oz (50g) pine nuts

3½oz (100g) dried apricots, finely chopped

large handful of cilantro leaves, finely chopped

4½ tbsp extra virgin olive oil

juice of 1 large lemon

salt and freshly ground black pepper

1 Put the couscous in a bowl and drizzle in the 1½ tbsp of olive oil. Rub it into the couscous, scatter in the powdered vegetable stock, and mix it in.

2 Measure 2 cups of boiling water into a liquid measuring cup. Pour it over the couscous and stir briefly. The water should just cover the couscous. Immediately seal with plastic wrap.

3 Leave for 5 minutes, then test the grains, which should be nearly soft, and all the water soaked in. Fluff the couscous and let cool, fluffing it occasionally to separate the grains.

4 Meanwhile, dry-fry the pine nuts in a non-stick frying pan over medium heat, stirring, until they color. Be careful, as they can burn quickly. Set aside to cool.

5 Toss together the cooled couscous, pine nuts, apricots, and cilantro. Mix in the extra virgin olive oil and lemon juice and season to taste.

CALORIES: 461kcals/1917kJ

CARBOHYDRATE: 47g
  sugar: 11g

FAT: 27g
  saturated: 3g

SALT: 1.6g

FIBER: 3g

Panzanella

Good-quality bread is a joy, and even when it is past its best it can be used in this delectable Italian salad.

15 mins, plus standing

SERVES 4-6

12oz (350g) unsliced stale dense-textured white bread, such as ciabatta or sourdough, roughly torn into bite-sized pieces

1lb 5oz (600g) mixed tomatoes, at room temperature, such as red, yellow, green, purple baby plum, cherry, or beefsteak, all roughly chopped into bite-sized chunks

1 red onion, finely chopped

2 garlic cloves, finely chopped

2 tbsp capers in brine, drained

salt and freshly ground black pepper

leaves from 1 bunch of basil, roughly torn

FOR THE DRESSING

6 tbsp extra virgin olive oil

3 tbsp red wine vinegar

½ tsp ground mustard

½ tsp granulated sugar

1 Place the bread, tomatoes, onion, garlic, and capers in a large serving bowl. Season well and stir to combine.

2 Place the dressing ingredients in a small bowl, season, and stir well. Pour over the bread and tomato mixture and stir to coat.

3 Set aside for at least 10 minutes and up to 2 hours, at room temperature, to allow the flavors to mingle. Stir the basil leaves into the salad just before serving.

VARIATION

Add pitted black olives and drained anchovies for a salad with more robust and piquant flavors.

CALORIES: 396kcals/1664kJ

CARBOHYDRATE: 47g
  sugar: 8.5g

FAT: 19g
  saturated: 3g

SALT: 1.7g

FIBER: 4.5g

Quick pink pickled onions

These quick pickles make a great addition to a picnic to serve with cold meats or Individual pork pies (see p399).

5 mins, plus chilling

SERVES 4–8

2 tbsp granulated sugar

2 tsp salt

¾ cup cider vinegar

2 red onions, halved and very finely sliced

1 Put the sugar and salt in a bowl and add a little of the vinegar. Whisk until the salt and sugar crystals have dissolved, then add the rest of the vinegar.

2 Toss through the onions and cover. Leave at room temperature for 1 hour before serving, or packing into a sterilized jam jar (see Cucumber and dill pickles, right) for transportation.

VARIATION

For even pinker onions, add a small chunk of raw beet to the vinegar mixture before adding the onion. Stir it once or twice, to distribute the vibrant color, before serving or storing.

PREPARE AHEAD

These pickled onions will keep in the fridge for up to 1 week, packed in a sterilized, sealed jar. Make sure they are always covered with vinegar.

CALORIES: 34kcals/142kJ
CARBOHYDRATE: 7g
    sugar: 6g
FAT: 0g
    saturated: 0g
SALT: 1g
FIBER: 0.7g

Cucumber and dill pickles

These "refrigerator pickles" are almost instant, so try out making your own portable pickles.

10 mins, plus sterilizing, and chilling

SPECIAL EQUIPMENT

2 x 7fl oz (200ml) jam jars with lids

MAKES 2 JARS

¼ cup granulated sugar

2 tsp salt

¾ cup white wine vinegar or rice wine vinegar

freshly ground black pepper

4–5 pickling (small) cucumbers, thinly sliced

1 tbsp finely chopped dill fronds

½ tsp dill seeds, lightly crushed

1 Preheat the oven to 275°F (140°C). Wash two 7fl oz (200ml) jam jars, place upside-down on a baking sheet, and put in the oven for at least 15 minutes. This will sterilize them. Put the lids in a metal bowl and pour a kettleful of boiling water over. Leave for 5 minutes, then remove and let drain. Dry well with paper towels.

2 Put the sugar and salt in a bowl and add a little vinegar. Whisk until the salt and sugar dissolve, then add the rest of the vinegar and a good grinding of pepper.

3 Once the jars are cold, layer the cucumbers into the jars, adding a sprinkling of chopped dill and a few dill seeds between each layer.

4 When the jars are full, pour in the vinegar mixture and seal. Shake them to disperse the liquid evenly and refrigerate overnight for them to get really crispy.

PREPARE AHEAD

These pickles will keep in the fridge for up to 1 month, packed in a sterilized, sealed jar (see above). Make sure they are always covered with vinegar.

CALORIES: 156kcals/649kJ
CARBOHYDRATE: 30g
    sugar: 30g
FAT: 0g
    saturated: 0g
SALT: 4g
FIBER: 3g

Homemade mayonnaise

There is nothing difficult about making mayonnaise, and a food processer makes it even easier.

10 mins

SPECIAL EQUIPMENT
food processor

MAKES 1 CUP

2 large egg yolks

¼ tsp salt

2 tsp lemon juice

1 cup sunflower or vegetable oil

1 tsp Dijon mustard, or more, to taste

1 tsp white wine vinegar, or more, to taste

1 Put the egg yolks, salt, lemon juice, and 2 tsp of water in a food processor. Blend for a minute.

2 Add the oil in a very slow, thin stream, really little more than a few drops at a time to begin with, with the motor running all the time.

3 As the mixture starts to thicken, continue to add the oil in a thin, steady stream. Once it emulsifies to a thick mayonnaise, add the mustard and vinegar, taste, and add more of either if desired. Refrigerate until needed.

VARIATION

After the mayonnaise is made, chopped herbs, crushed garlic, or spices can be added as you like.

PREPARE AHEAD

The mayonnaise will keep, covered, in the fridge for up to 3 days. Be aware that it contains raw eggs, so the usual food safety rules apply (see p11).

CALORIES: 89kcals/368kJ
CARBOHYDRATE: 0g
 sugar: 0g
FAT: 10g
 saturated: 1g
SALT: 0.1g
FIBER: 0g

Potted shrimp

These individual servings make a lovely picnic treat, served simply spread on crusty whole wheat bread.

15 mins, plus chilling   10 mins

SPECIAL EQUIPMENT
4 x 4½fl oz (125ml) ramekins

SERVES 4

20 tbsp unsalted butter

2 tsp lemon juice

pinch of grated nutmeg

salt and freshly ground black pepper

12oz (350g) cooked and peeled small shrimp, or brown shrimp

1 First, clarify the butter. Put it into a small saucepan over low heat. As it melts, foam will come to the surface; pour the pan and skim it off. Gently pour the butter into a bowl, through a strainer. Stop pouring before the whitish milk solids in the pan come out; discard the solids. You should have a bowl of golden, clear butter.

2 Clean the saucepan and return to the heat with three-quarters of the butter and the remaining ingredients. Simmer for 5 minutes.

3 Remove the shrimp with a slotted spoon and pack them into four 4½fl oz (125ml) ramekins, pressing down with a spoon. Now strain the butter from the pan over the shrimp, stopping when you see the residue is about to come out.

4 Cover and chill until set (at least 2 hours). Melt the remaining butter and pour over the shrimp to create a thin seal. Cover and chill once more until set. Remove from the fridge 15–20 minutes before serving, for the butter to soften.

VARIATION

Try using the same amount of white crab, or diced salmon, instead of shrimp, adding 1 tbsp of chopped dill to the salmon at the point of potting.

CALORIES: 625kcals/2612kJ
CARBOHYDRATE: 0g
 sugar: 0g
FAT: 62g
 saturated: 41g
SALT: 1.2g
FIBER: 0g

Salmon rillettes

This piquant pâté from France should be prepared with a fairly rough texture.

15 mins

SERVES 4

4 tbsp butter, softened

9oz (250g) hot-smoked salmon, skinned

¼ cup (2oz) Greek yogurt

finely grated zest and juice of ½ lemon

2 tbsp snipped chives

1 x 2½oz (50g) jar of salmon caviar

handful of watercress and lemon wedges, to serve

1 Put the butter in a bowl and beat with a wooden spoon until smooth. Break up the salmon into small pieces, add to the bowl, and mash with a fork.

2 Add the yogurt, lemon zest and juice, and chives, and stir until evenly combined.

3 Spoon on to serving plates and top with caviar. Serve with watercress sprigs and lemon wedges to squeeze over.

VARIATION

Use the same quantity of poached fresh salmon fillet to make poached salmon rillettes, removing the skin after the fish has been cooked.

PREPARE AHEAD

The rillettes can be made up to 24 hours in advance, covered, and stored in the fridge, or frozen for up to 8 weeks.

COOK'S TIP

For attractive canapés, spread the rillettes, 1 tsp of caviar, and a sprig of watercress onto small rounds of pumpernickel, cut with a round cutter.

CALORIES: 252kcals/1047kJ
CARBOHYDRATE: 1g
 sugar: 1g
FAT: 20g
 saturated: 10g
SALT: 3.1g
FIBER: 0.3g

Sweet potato and goat cheese mini frittatas

These pocket-sized frittatas with their sweet, rich flavors make great portable snacks.

10 mins   35-40 mins

SPECIAL EQUIPMENT

6-hole muffin pan

6 paper liners (optional)

MAKES 6

9oz (250g) sweet potato, cut into ½in (1cm) cubes

1 tbsp olive oil, plus extra for greasing (optional)

salt and freshly ground black pepper

1 tbsp thyme leaves

1¾oz (50g) goat cheese, cut into small cubes

4 large eggs

2 tbsp heavy cream

CALORIES: 162kcals/678kJ
CARBOHYDRATE: 8.5g
 sugar: 2.5g
FAT: 11g
 saturated: 4.5g
SALT: 0.3g
FIBER: 1.3g

1 Preheat the oven to 400°F (200°C). Toss the sweet potato in the oil and spread in a single layer on a baking sheet. Season well and roast at the top of the oven for 20 minutes, turning halfway, until browned in places and cooked. Let cool. Reduce the oven temperature to 350°F (180°C).

2 In a bowl, toss the cooled sweet potatoes, thyme, and goat cheese, and season. Grease a 6-hole muffin pan well with a little oil, or line it with paper liners, and divide the mixture between them.

3 Whisk the eggs and cream, season, and divide equally over the sweet potato. Use a teaspoon to mix the egg into the filling.

4 Bake in the top of the hot oven for 15–20 minutes, until puffed up and golden brown. If you have just greased the pan, allow to cool in the pan until barely warm before removing to a wire rack. If you are using liners, allow to cool in the pan for 5 minutes before removing and cooling completely on a wire rack.

Tuna empanadas

Originally from Spain and Portugal, these savory pastries called empanadas translate as "wrapped in bread."

45 mins, plus chilling   40-50 mins

SPECIAL EQUIPMENT
3½in (9cm) round cutter

MAKES 24

2½ cups all-purpose flour, plus extra for dusting

sea salt

6 tbsp unsalted butter, cut in cubes

2 large eggs, lightly beaten, plus extra for glazing

FOR THE FILLING

1 tbsp olive oil, plus extra for greasing

1 onion, finely chopped

½ cup canned tomatoes, drained weight

2 tsp tomato paste

1 x 5oz (140g) can of tuna, drained

2 tbsp finely chopped parsley

freshly ground black pepper

1 To make the dough, sift the flour into a bowl with ½ tsp salt. Add the butter and rub it in. Mix in the eggs with 4–6 tbsp of water. Wrap in plastic wrap and chill for 30 minutes.

2 Heat the oil in a frying pan, add the onion, and cook over medium heat for 5 minutes. Add the tomatoes, tomato paste, tuna, and parsley, and season with pepper. Reduce the heat and simmer for 10–12 minutes, stirring occasionally. Allow to cool.

3 Preheat the oven to 375°F (190°C). Roll out the pastry to ⅛in (3mm) thick. Cut out 24 rounds with a 3½in (9cm) round cutter. Put 1 tsp of the filling on each. Brush the edges with water, fold over, and pinch together.

4 Place on an oiled baking sheet and brush with egg. Bake for 25–30 minutes. Serve warm.

PREPARE AHEAD
These keep in the fridge for 2 days. Reheat in an oven at 325°F (160°C) for 10 minutes before serving.

CALORIES: 115kcals/484kJ

CARBOHYDRATE: 14g
 sugar: 0.7g

FAT: 4.5g
 saturated: 2g

SALT: 0.15g

FIBER: 1g

Sausage rolls

Classic finger food for picnics and parties, these are so easy to make you may never go back to store-bought.

30 mins, plus chilling

10–12 mins, plus cooling

MAKES 24

9oz (250g) store-bought puff pastry

all-purpose flour, for dusting

1½lb (675g) ground sausage

1 small onion, finely chopped

1 tbsp thyme leaves

1 tbsp finely grated lemon zest

1 tsp Dijon mustard

1 large egg yolk

sea salt and freshly ground black pepper

1 large egg, lightly beaten, for glazing

CALORIES: 114kcals/477kJ

CARBOHYDRATE: 5g
sugar: 0.7g

FAT: 8g
saturated: 3g

SALT: 0.6g

FIBER: 0g

1 Preheat the oven to 400°F (200°C). Line a baking sheet with parchment paper and chill. Cut the pastry in half. Roll each piece out on a floured surface to a 12 x 6in (30 x 15cm) rectangle, then cover and chill for 30 minutes. Mix the sausage with the onion, thyme, lemon zest, mustard, and egg yolk. Season.

2 Lay the pastry on a flat surface. Form the sausage mixture into 2 logs and place a log in the center of each piece of pastry. Brush the pastry with the egg, roll it over, and press to seal. Cut each roll into 12.

3 Place on the chilled pan, make 2 snips at the top of each roll with scissors, then brush with egg. Bake for 10–12 minutes or until golden and flaky. Serve warm, or transfer to a wire rack to cool.

PREPARE AHEAD

These can be stored in an airtight container in the fridge for 2 days, or frozen, uncooked, for up to 8 weeks.

Cornish pasties

Although not traditional, a splash of Worcestershire sauce adds a depth of flavor to the pasty filling.

20 mins, plus chilling

40–45 mins, plus cooling

MAKES 4

7 tbsp lard, chilled and cut into cubes

4 tbsp unsalted butter, chilled and cut into cubes

1½ cups all-purpose flour, plus extra for dusting

½ tsp salt

1 large egg, lightly beaten, for glazing

FOR THE FILLING

9oz (250g) beef skirt steak, trimmed and cut into ½in (1cm) cubes

2¾oz (80g) rutabaga , peeled and cut into ¼in (5mm) cubes

3½oz (100g) waxy potatoes, peeled and cut into ¼in (5mm) cubes

1 large onion, finely chopped

splash of Worcestershire sauce

1 tsp all-purpose flour

salt and freshly ground black pepper

CALORIES: 700kcals/3091kJ

CARBOHYDRATE: 62g
sugar: 4g

FAT: 44g
saturated: 20g

SALT: 0.8g

FIBER: 5g

1 Rub the lard and butter into the flour until it resembles fine crumbs. Add the salt and enough water to form a soft dough. Knead briefly on a floured surface. Wrap in plastic wrap and chill for 1 hour.

2 Preheat the oven to 375°F (190°C). Mix all the filling ingredients and season well. On a well-floured work surface, roll the dough out to ¼in (5mm) thick. Using a saucer, cut 4 circles from the dough. Re-roll the scraps.

3 Fold the circles in half, then flatten them out again, leaving a slight mark down the center. Pile one-quarter of the filling into each circle, leaving a ¾in (2cm) border all around. Brush the border of the dough with a little beaten egg.

4 Pull both edges up over the filling and press to seal. Crimp the seal with your fingers. Brush a little beaten egg all over the pasties. Bake in the center of the oven for 40–45 minutes until golden brown. Allow to cool for at least 15 minutes before eating warm or cold.

PREPARE AHEAD

These will keep, covered, in the fridge for 2 days—reheat at 350°F (180°C) for 20 minutes; or freeze the assembled pasties, uncooked, for up to 8 weeks.

Individual pork pies

Try making these bite-sized pork pies for a special picnic treat. Remember to pack a jar of mustard, too.

40 mins, plus chilling   1 hr

SPECIAL EQUIPMENT
food processor (optional)

12-hole muffin pan

small funnel (optional)

MAKES 12

FOR THE FILLING
7oz (200g) pork belly, trimmed of fat and skin and cut into cubes

7oz (200g) pork shoulder, trimmed and cut into cubes

1¾oz (50g) bacon, trimmed and cut into cubes

10 sage leaves, finely chopped

sea salt and freshly ground black pepper

¼ tsp nutmeg

¼ tsp allspice

FOR THE HOT WATER PASTRY
3 cups all-purpose flour, plus extra for dusting

½ tsp fine salt

⅔ cup lard or beef dripping, cut into cubes

1 large egg, lightly beaten, for glazing

FOR THE JELLY (OPTIONAL)
½ tbsp unflavored powdered gelatin

1 cup chicken stock (see p94)

1 Preheat the oven to 400°F (200°C). Put all the ingredients for the filling into a food processor and pulse until the meat is chopped, but not mushy.

2 To make the hot water pastry, place the flour and salt in a bowl and make a well in the middle. Combine lard or dripping with ⅔ cup boiling water in a bowl and stir until the fat melts.

3 Pour the liquid into the flour and mix. You will need to use your hands to bring it into a soft dough. Be careful, as it will be hot. Cut off one-quarter of the dough, wrap it in a clean kitchen towel, and set it aside somewhere warm.

4 You need to work quickly as the dough hardens as it cools. Turn the dough onto a well-floured work surface and roll it out to ¼in (5mm) thick. Cut out 12 circles big enough to line a 12-hole muffin pan, allowing them to overlap the edges. Pack the filling into each and brush egg around the edges.

5 Roll out the set-aside dough. Cut out 12 lids to fit the crusts. Top the filling with the lids and press down the sides to seal. Brush with egg. Use a chopstick to make a hole in each pie if you wish to fill it with jelly later, or cut 2 slits to allow the steam to escape if you don't.

6 Bake for 30 minutes, then reduce the oven temperature to 325°F (160°C) and cook for 30 minutes. Let cool for 10 minutes before turning out.

7 To make the jelly, pour ¼ cup of chicken stock into a bowl. Sprinkle in the gelatin and let sit 5 minutes. Heat the remaining stock and add the gelatin, stirring until it dissolves. Cool. Once the liquid starts to thicken, use a small funnel to pour it into each pie. Refrigerate to set overnight. These will keep, covered and chilled, for up to 3 days.

CALORIES: 312kcals/1303kJ

CARBOHYDRATE: 24g
  sugar: 0.5g

FAT: 18g
  saturated: 7g

SALT: 0.4g

FIBER: 1.4g

Baking

Baking

If you follow a few basic rules, baking can be quite straightforward, and even novice bakers can achieve great results. Follow the recipe carefully, measure out ingredients accurately, be patient, and with the clever tips on this page you should do well. Baking is a great way to get kids interested in cooking—cookies, scones, and cakes are always popular treats to start with. Some store-bought baked goods are made with unhealthy amounts of sugar, salt, and fat, so by making your own you will know exactly what your family is eating. Baked goods are perfect for snacks, picnics, and parties, as well as everyday treats, and nothing beats the smell of bread or cookies baking in the oven.

Get organized

The most important thing to do before you start is to read all the way through the recipe before attempting it for the first time. You may be overwhelmed with the desire to get started, but you need to be sure that you have enough time to see all the stages of a recipe through, especially if it involves pauses for rising or proofing. It's important to make sure ingredients are at the temperature stated in the recipe, too. Using cake pans of the correct size is also vital to the success of a recipe, so make sure they are the size stipulated. Finally, adjust your oven shelves to the desired height before you heat the oven, and make sure the oven reaches the correct temperature well before you are due to start baking.

Master the basics first, such as a classic sponge cake with an easy filling, like this Victoria sponge cake (p423). As your confidence grows you can get more ambitious with the recipes you tackle.

Useful baking equipment

Essentials	Good to have
Digital scales	Spatula
Wooden spoons	Silicone paper
Balloon whisk	Baking spray
Mixing bowls	Electric hand-held mixer
Fine metal sieve	Food processor or standing mixer
Good-quality, heavy baking pans and sheets in various sizes	Cookie cutters
	Piping set
Waxed paper	Oven thermometer
Measuring spoons	

Know your chemistry

Cooking may be an art, but baking is a science. The artistry can come after the science, by all means, but there is a basic chemistry involved in turning simple ingredients into light baked goods. The essential component of many recipes is air—this is introduced through the fermentation of yeast, the leavening of rising agents such as baking powder, or the simple addition of stiffly whisked egg whites. A light touch when folding in dry ingredients, egg whites, or bringing together pastry or scones, is essential, so try not to be heavy handed or overmix ingredients. When transferring cake mix to a pan, smooth the top gently, but try to avoid pressing down and expelling all the air. When baking bread, make sure you allow time for the yeast to become active and aerate the dough, which will help it rise and give it a light texture.

Savory bakes, such as this moist Zucchini and feta loaf (p453) are well worth the effort. Home-baked loaves and bakes are versatile and ideal for packed lunches, picnics, and afternoon snacks.

Rise to the occasion

There are so many mouthwatering treats here that it's going to be hard to know where to start. Cookies are easy to tackle, and the supremely useful Slice and bake butter cookies (p407) use a cookie dough you can make and store in the fridge or freezer until you need it. If you have guests and want to impress, choose a Lemon drizzle cake (p421) or Coffee and Walnut cake (p429), or wow your dinner guests with an irresistible Genoise cake with raspberries and cream (p422). For a party, choose from Red velvet cupcakes with cream cheese icing (p415) or an Angel food cake (p418), or frost the delicious Rich fruit cake (p419) for a special celebration.

Try something different

Don't forget the savory bakes! For some easy savory treats, start with some store-bought puff pastry for Quick cheese pastries (p442) or mix up some Savory breakfast muffins (p442) for a weekend treat. Home-baked bread is also wonderful. If you don't have time to allow for rising and proofing, start by trying some quick breads such as Brown soda bread (p450) or Sweet potato and rosemary rolls (p452), and build up your confidence before tackling a Rosemary foccacia (p447) or some delicious home-baked Pretzels (p445).

Tips for success

There's no mystery to making your own delicious and nutritious baked goods. These few tricks of the trade will show you how easy it can be.

Look after your ingredients

Store flours and sugars in airtight containers to keep them fresh, dry, and moisture free.

Weigh

Invest in some digital scales to ensure that you are accurate with your measurements.

Spray

Baking sprays help to distribute a thin, even layer of fat around the pan, which helps to stop cakes from sticking.

Line

Cut reusable silicone baking sheets to the size of your cake pans for a perfect, non-stick result every time.

Test

Many ovens, especially older ones, do not always heat up accurately to the temperature the recipe requires; they may run hotter, or colder. A simple in-oven thermometer that hangs from the shelves will help you get to and maintain the correct temperature for a successful bake.

Rest

If a recipe says to rest something, there is usually a reason. Most cookies, for example, will need a few minutes resting on their baking sheets to firm up before you move them, or they will break. It may be tempting to cut into warm bread, but if you do it straight from the oven, the result will be stodgy, rather than light, moist bread.

Store

Home-baked goods keep fresher for longer if you store them correctly. Have plenty of different-sized airtight containers for cookies and cakes, and wrap fruit cakes in foil to stop the moisture from escaping, before putting them in a pan. Covering the top of a delicately iced cake in waxed paper helps preserve the decorations.

Fats

For sweet pastry, use a good quality, unsalted butter to give a perfectly crisp texture. Savory pastry can be made with half butter, half lard for an old-fashioned, crumbly pastry. Cooking margarine gives an airy texture to cakes.

Oat and raisin cookies

These crisp, crumbly cookies are packed full of fiber-filled oats and sweet raisins for a healthier treat.

10 mins   15 mins

MAKES 15

11 tbsp butter

½ cup granulated sugar

1 cup self-rising flour, sifted

1 cup oats

1¾oz (50g) raisins

1 tsp baking soda

1 Preheat the oven to 350°F (180°C). Melt the butter in a large saucepan over low heat. Allow it to cool while you measure out the other ingredients.

2 Mix the sugar, flour, oats, and raisins into the cooled, melted butter and stir well.

3 In a cup, mix the baking soda with 1 tbsp boiling water until it dissolves, then mix it well into the cookie mixture.

4 Take 1 tbsp of the mixture and roll it into a ball between your hands. Flatten it slightly and put it on a baking sheet. Repeat to use up all the dough, spacing them well apart on the pan, as they will spread.

5 Bake in the center of the oven for 12–15 minutes until they turn golden brown. Remove the cookies from the oven and let cool on their baking sheets for 5 minutes (they will break if you do not), then transfer them to a wire rack to cool completely.

CALORIES: 164kcals/687kJ

CARBOHYDRATE: 19g
 sugar: 9g

FAT: 9g
 saturated: 5g

SALT: 0.4g

FIBER: 1g

Double chocolate chip cookies

The ultimate chocolate treat—try these freshly baked and still warm with a cold glass of milk.

10 mins   15 mins

SPECIAL EQUIPMENT
electric hand-held mixer

MAKES 15

7 tbsp butter, softened

½ cup granulated sugar

½ cup light brown sugar

1 large egg, lightly beaten

1 tsp vanilla extract

1¼ cups all-purpose flour

¼ cup cocoa powder

½ tsp baking powder

¼ tsp salt

1 tbsp whole milk

3½oz (100g) chocolate chips

1 Preheat the oven to 180°C (350°F). In a large bowl, cream together the butter and sugars until light and fluffy, then beat in the egg and vanilla extract.

2 Sift the flour, cocoa powder, baking powder, and salt together, and mix it in to the cookie mixture, until it is well combined. Mix in the milk.

3 Fold in the chocolate chips. Place tablespoons of the cookie mixture onto several baking sheets, spaced well apart as they will spread on cooking.

4 Bake the cookies in the center of the oven for 15 minutes, until just cooked. Let cool on the baking sheets for 5 minutes before transferring them to a wire rack to cool completely.

HOW TO FREEZE

The baked cookies can be frozen in an airtight container for up to 6 months. Defrost thoroughly before eating.

CALORIES: 180kcals/758kJ

CARBOHYDRATE: 25g
 sugar: 17g

FAT: 8g
 saturated: 5g

SALT: 0.2g

FIBER: 0.6g

Pistachio and cranberry oat cookies

Using pistachios and cranberries brings a healthy, chewy bite to these easy-to-make cookies.

20 mins   10–15 mins

SPECIAL EQUIPMENT
electric hand-held mixer

MAKES 24

7 tbsp unsalted butter, softened

1 cup light brown sugar

1 large egg, lightly beaten

1 tsp vanilla extract

1 tbsp honey

1 cup self-rising flour, sifted

1 cup oats

pinch of salt

3½oz (100g) pistachios, lightly toasted and roughly chopped

3½oz (100g) dried cranberries, roughly chopped

a little milk, if needed

1 Preheat the oven to 375°F (190°C). Put the butter and sugar in a bowl and cream with an electric hand-held mixer until smooth. Add the egg, vanilla extract, and honey and beat well.

2 Add the flour, oats, and salt, stirring with a wooden spoon to combine. Add the chopped nuts and cranberries, and mix until thoroughly combined. If the mixture is too stiff, add a little milk until it becomes pliable.

3 Take walnut-sized pieces and roll them into balls between your palms. Place on 2 or 3 baking sheets lined with parchment and flatten slightly, spacing them well apart on the pan.

4 Bake for 10–15 minutes until golden brown (you may need to do this in batches). Leave on the pan to cool, then transfer to a wire rack. These will keep in an airtight container for up to 5 days.

VARIATION

Once you have mastered this recipe for oat cookies, try experimenting with different combinations of fresh or dried fruit and nuts, or adding seeds such as sunflower seeds and pumpkin seeds into the cookie dough mixture.

CALORIES: 145kcals/611kJ

CARBOHYDRATE: 19g
  sugar: 12g

FAT: 6g
  saturated: 2.5g

SALT: 0.1g

FIBER: 1g

Pistachio, cranberry, and orange biscotti

Try baking these colorful Italian cookies as a festive treat or gift, packaging them in a colorful jar or tin.

15 mins   45–50 mins

MAKES 25–30

2 cups self-rising flour, plus extra for dusting

½ cup granulated sugar

3½oz (100g) shelled unsalted pistachios, toasted and chopped

1¾oz (50g) dried cranberries, roughly chopped

finely grated zest of 1 orange

2 large eggs

1 tsp vanilla extract

4 tbsp unsalted butter, melted and cooled

CALORIES: 80kcals/338kJ
CARBOHYDRATE: 10g
  sugar: 5g
FAT: 3.5g
  saturated: 1g
SALT: 0.1g
FIBER: 0.5g

1 Preheat the oven to 350°F (180°C). Line 1 or 2 baking sheets with parchment paper. Sift the flour into a large bowl. Stir in the sugar, pistachios, and cranberries. Whisk together the orange zest, eggs, vanilla extract, and butter. Gradually stir into the flour.

2 Turn the dough onto a floured work surface. With your hands, form it into two 8in (20cm) logs. Place on a lined baking sheet and bake for 25 minutes in the middle of the oven. Cool slightly.

3 With a serrated knife, cut the logs on a slant into 1½–2in- (3–5cm-) thick slices. Put the biscotti on 1 or 2 baking sheets, as needed, and return to the oven for 20 minutes to dry even more, turning halfway through with a palette knife. Cool the biscotti on a wire rack to harden them and allow any moisture to escape. These will keep in an airtight container for up to 1 week.

Pecan sandies

These addictive cookies are so-called because they have the texture (though not the taste!) of fine sand.

15 mins,   15 mins
plus chilling

SPECIAL EQUIPMENT
electric hand-held mixer

MAKES 18–20

7 tbsp unsalted butter, softened

⅓ cup light brown sugar

¼ cup granulated sugar

½ tsp vanilla extract

1 large egg yolk

1¼ cups all-purpose flour, sifted, plus extra for dusting

2½oz (75g) pecans, chopped

CALORIES: 111kcals/468kJ
CARBOHYDRATE: 10g
  sugar: 5g
FAT: 7g
  saturated: 3g
SALT: 0g
FIBER: 0.5g

1 Preheat the oven to 350°F (180°C). In a large bowl, cream together the butter and sugars with an electric hand-held mixer until light and fluffy. Add the vanilla extract and the egg yolk and mix well to combine. Fold in the flour and then the pecans. Bring it together to form a rough dough.

2 Turn the dough onto a lightly floured work surface and knead it to form a smooth dough. Roll into a log about 8in (20cm) long. If the dough seems too soft to cut, chill it for 30 minutes to allow it to firm up.

3 Slice ½in (1cm) disks from the log, and place them spaced apart on 2 baking sheets lined with parchment paper. Bake in the top of the oven for 15 minutes, until golden at the edges. Leave on the sheets for a few minutes, then transfer to a wire rack to cool.

HOW TO FREEZE

There's nothing better than the aroma and flavor of just-baked cookies. At the end of step 2, freeze the dough for up to 12 weeks. Now you can have fresh-baked cookies at any time.

Strawberry shortcakes

These make a perfect summer dessert. A classic when strawberries are juicy and sweet.

15 mins   15–17 mins

SPECIAL EQUIPMENT
3in (8cm) cookie cutter

SERVES 4

9oz (250g) strawberries

2 tbsp confectioners' sugar

2¼ cups self-rising flour, sifted, plus extra for dusting

1 tsp baking powder

2 tbsp granulated sugar

7 tbsp butter, cut into cubes

1 egg, beaten, plus extra for glazing

½ cup whole milk

⅔ cup heavy cream

1 Preheat the oven to 375°F (190°C). Prepare the strawberries by slicing them ¼in (5mm) thick and tossing them in 1 tbsp of the confectioners' sugar. Let them macerate at room temperature.

2 Rub the flour, baking powder, granulated sugar, and butter together until the mixture resembles fine bread crumbs.

3 Beat the egg and milk together. Make a well in the center of the flour mixture and pour the liquid into the center. Slowly incorporate the flour to make a soft dough, using a fork first and then your fingertips, but do not over-mix, or the mixture will become tough.

4 Turn the dough onto a floured work surface and knead it just long enough to bring it together. Pat it into a 1in- (3cm-) thick piece and cut out 4 rounds with an 3in (8cm) cookie cutter.

5 Place the shortcakes onto a baking sheet lined with parchment paper, and brush them with a little beaten egg. Bake them in the center of the hot oven for 15–17 minutes until well-risen and golden brown.

6 Remove from the oven and cool on a wire rack. Meanwhile, whisk the cream until billowing.

7 To serve the shortcakes, split them in half. Fill each with the cream, dividing it evenly, then top with some sliced strawberries, including some juice. Put the tops on and dust with the remaining 1 tbsp of confectioners' sugar to serve.

HOW TO FREEZE
The cooked shortcakes can be open-frozen on the day they are made, then transferred to a freezer bag for up to 12 weeks. Defrost thoroughly, fill, and eat within 1 day.

CALORIES: 740kcals/3096kJ

CARBOHYDRATE: 73g
sugar: 21g

FAT: 45g
saturated: 27g

SALT: 1.5g

FIBER: 4g

Madeleines

Light and incredibly addictive, buttery madeleines make an elegant afternoon treat.

15–20 mins   10 mins

SPECIAL EQUIPMENT
madeleine pan, or small 12-hole mini-muffin pan
electric hand-held mixer

MAKES 12

4 tbsp unsalted butter, melted and cooled, plus extra for greasing
½ cup self-rising flour, sifted, plus extra for dusting
¼ cup granulated sugar
2 large eggs, lightly beaten
1 tsp vanilla extract
confectioners' sugar, for dusting

CALORIES: 88kcals/371kJ
CARBOHYDRATE: 8.5g
  sugar: 5g
FAT: 5g
  saturated: 3g
SALT: trace
FIBER: 0.2g

1 Preheat the oven to 350°F (180°C). Carefully brush a madeleine pan, or small 12-hole bun pan, with melted butter and dust with a little flour. Invert the pan and tap to remove excess flour.

2 Put the sugar, eggs, and vanilla into a mixing bowl. Using an electric hand-held mixer, mix for 5 minutes until the mixture is pale, thick, and holds a trail (this is known as the "ribbon stage").

3 Sift the flour over the top and pour the melted butter down the side of the mixture. Using a large rubber spatula, fold them in carefully and quickly, being careful not to knock out too much air.

4 Fill the hollows in the pans evenly with the batter and bake for 10 minutes. Remove from the oven and transfer to a wire rack to cool. Dust with confectioners' sugar to serve.

Blueberry muffins with streusel topping

These muffins make a quick and easy anytime treat. Use frozen blueberries if you have them.

20 mins   15–20 mins

SPECIAL EQUIPMENT
12-hole muffin pan
12 paper muffin liners

MAKES 12

FOR THE STREUSEL TOPPING
⅓ cup light brown sugar
½ cup all-purpose flour
1 tsp ground cinnamon
2 tbsp butter

FOR THE MUFFINS
2 cups self-rising flour
1 tsp baking powder
¼ tsp salt
½ cup granulated sugar
½ cup whole milk
½ cup (4oz) plain yogurt
¼ cup sunflower or vegetable oil
1 large egg, lightly beaten
1 tsp vanilla extract
3½oz (100g) blueberries

1 Preheat the oven to 400°F (200°C) and line a 12-hole muffin pan with paper muffin liners. Make the topping: rub together the sugar, flour, cinnamon, and butter.

2 Sift the flour, baking powder, and salt into a bowl. Add the sugar. Measure the milk, yogurt, and oil into a bowl and beat in the egg and vanilla. Stir the wet ingredients into the dry, then mix in the berries. Spoon into the cups and top evenly with the streusel.

3 Bake for 15–20 minutes, cool in the pan for 5 minutes, then transfer to a wire rack to cool.

HOW TO FREEZE

The cooked muffins can be frozen in an airtight container for up to 6 months. Defrost thoroughly before serving.

CALORIES: 224kcals/945kJ
CARBOHYDRATE: 36g
  sugar: 19g
FAT: 6.5g
  saturated: 2g
SALT: 0.4g
FIBER: 1g

Lemon and poppy seed muffins

These light and lemony muffins make a pleasant, refreshing change when baked for weekend breakfast or brunch.

10 mins   15 mins

SPECIAL EQUIPMENT

12-hole muffin pan

12 paper muffin liners

MAKES 12

2 cups self-rising flour

1 tsp baking powder

¼ tsp salt

½ cup granulated sugar

finely grated zest of 1 lemon

1 heaping tsp poppy seeds

½ cup whole milk

½ cup (4oz) plain yogurt

¼ cup sunflower or vegetable oil

1 large egg, lightly beaten

2 tbsp lemon juice

FOR THE GLAZE

2 tbsp lemon juice

1¼ cups confectioners' sugar

finely grated zest of 1 lemon

1 Preheat the oven to 400°F (200°C) and line a 12-hole muffin pan with paper muffin liners. Sift the flour, baking powder, and salt into a large bowl. Use a balloon whisk to mix through the sugar, lemon zest, and poppy seeds.

2 Measure the milk, yogurt, and oil into a bowl, then add the egg and lemon juice and beat it all together thoroughly. Pour the liquid into the center of the dry ingredients and mix with a wooden spoon until just combined. Be careful not to over-mix.

3 Divide the mixture equally between the muffin liners and bake in the middle of the preheated oven for 15 minutes until the muffins are lightly brown and well risen. Remove from the oven and let cool in the pan for 5 minutes before transferring to a wire rack to cool completely.

4 For the glaze, mix the lemon juice and confectioners' sugar to a thin icing, drizzle it over the muffins, and sprinkle them with lemon zest.

HOW TO FREEZE

The cooked muffins can be frozen in an airtight container for up to 6 months. Defrost thoroughly before serving.

CALORIES: 209kcals/886kJ

CARBOHYDRATE: 38g
  sugar: 24g

FAT: 5g
  saturated: 1g

SALT: 0.4g

FIBER: 1g

Vanilla cupcakes with vanilla frosting

Cupcakes are an easy treat to bake, and are fabulous when freshly made. They're easy to whip up in a hurry, too.

25 mins   16–18 mins

SPECIAL EQUIPMENT

electric hand-held mixer

12-hole muffin pan

12 cupcake liners

piping bag and star nozzle (optional)

MAKES 12

7 tbsp butter, softened

⅔ cup granulated sugar

3 large eggs, lightly beaten

1 tsp vanilla extract

1½ cups self-rising flour

1 tsp baking powder

3½ tbsp milk, plus 1 tbsp if needed

FOR THE BUTTERCREAM

1⅔ cups confectioners' sugar

7 tbsp butter, softened

1 tsp vanilla extract

1 Preheat the oven to 350°F (180°C). Place the butter and sugar in a large bowl and use an electric hand-held mixer to cream them together until the mixture is very light and fluffy. Whisk in the eggs and vanilla extract until they are well combined.

2 Sift together the flour and baking powder. Add one-third of the flour to the cake batter and whisk it in well. Add half of the milk and whisk it again, then another one-third of the flour, the rest of the milk, and finally the last one-third of the flour, making sure to whisk well between each addition.

3 Place 12 cupcake liners in a deep 12-hole muffin pan (this will help the cupcakes keep their shape while cooking). Carefully spoon the cake mixture into the liners, filling each two-thirds full.

4 Bake for 16–18 minutes, until lightly colored, firm, and springy to the touch, and a toothpick inserted into the center of a cupcake comes out clean. Do not be tempted to open the oven until at least 15 minutes baking time has passed. Transfer the cupcakes to a wire rack to cool.

5 To make the buttercream, beat the confectioners' sugar, butter, and vanilla until smooth, light, and creamy, adding up to 1 tbsp milk, if needed, for a piping consistency, and transfer it to a piping bag fitted with a star-shaped nozzle (if using).

6 When the cakes are completely cold, they are ready to ice. Ice them by hand using the back of a spoon dipped in warm water to smooth the surface of the frosting, or pipe the buttercream onto the cupcakes.

VARIATION

You can make chocolate cupcakes using the same basic recipe. Simply replace ½ cup of the all-purpose flour in the cakes with cocoa powder. For the buttercream, replace 2 tbsp of the confectioners' sugar with cocoa powder, omit the vanilla, and add 1 tbsp whole milk instead, to make it easy to pipe or spread on the cakes.

PREPARE AHEAD

The cakes can be made 1 day ahead and stored, un-iced, in an airtight container, or frozen for up to 12 weeks. Defrost, then ice on the day they are to be used.

CALORIES: 319kcals/1340kJ

CARBOHYDRATE: 41g
  sugar: 29.5g

FAT: 16g
  saturated: 9g

SALT: 0.6g

FIBER: 0.7g

Red velvet cupcakes with cream cheese icing

These fashionable cupcakes taste as good as they look, with red-toned cake against pale buttery icing.

25 mins   22–25 mins

SPECIAL EQUIPMENT

electric hand-held mixer

18-20 cupcake liners

2 x 12-hole muffin pans

piping bag and star nozzle (optional)

MAKES 18–20

8 tbsp butter, softened

1 cup granulated sugar

2 large eggs, lightly beaten

2 tsp red food coloring

1 tsp vanilla extract

2 cups self-rising flour

¼ cup cocoa powder

¾ cup buttermilk

1 tsp cider vinegar

1 tsp baking soda

FOR THE ICING

¼ cup cream cheese, softened

4 tbsp butter, softened

1⅔ cups confectioners' sugar

1 tsp vanilla extract

1 Preheat the oven to 350°F (180°C). Place the butter and sugar in a large bowl and use an electric hand-held mixer to cream them together until the mixture is very light and fluffy. Whisk in the eggs, food coloring, and vanilla extract until they are well combined.

2 Sift together the flour and cocoa powder. Add one-third of the flour to the cake batter and whisk it in well. Add half of the buttermilk and whisk it again, then another one-third of the flour, the rest of the buttermilk, and the final one-third of the flour, making sure to whisk well between additions.

Mix together the cider vinegar and baking soda and fold quickly into the batter.

3 Place 18–20 cupcake liners in 2 deep 12-hole muffin pans (they will help the cupcakes keep their shape). Spoon the batter into the liners, filling each two-thirds full. Bake for 22–25 minutes, until springy to the touch. Do not open the oven until at least 20 minutes of baking time has passed. Transfer to a wire rack to cool.

4 To make the icing, beat the cream cheese, butter, confectioners' sugar, and vanilla extract until light and creamy and transfer to a piping bag fitted with a star-shaped nozzle (if using).

5 When the cakes are completely cold, they are ready to ice. Ice them by hand using the back of a spoon dipped in warm water to smooth the surface, or pipe the icing onto the cupcakes.

PREPARE AHEAD

The cupcakes can be made up to 1 day ahead and stored, un-iced, in an airtight container. They are best iced on the day they are to be eaten.

HOW TO FREEZE

The un-iced cupcakes can be frozen in an airtight container for up to 12 weeks. Defrost thoroughly before icing.

CALORIES: 228kcals/958kJ

CARBOHYDRATE: 32g
sugar: 23g

FAT: 10g
saturated: 6g

SALT: 0.5g

FIBER: 1g

Chocolate and hazelnut brownies

A classic recipe, these brownies are moist and soft in the center and filled with toasted nuts.

25 mins | 12–15 mins

SPECIAL EQUIPMENT
9 x 12in (23 x 30cm) brownie pan, or similar

MAKES 24

12 tbsp unsalted butter, cut into cubes

10oz (300g) good-quality dark chocolate, broken into pieces

1¼ cups granulated sugar

4 large eggs, lightly beaten

1½ cups all-purpose flour, sifted

3 tbsp cocoa powder, sifted, plus extra for dusting

3½oz (100g) hazelnuts, toasted and chopped

1 Preheat the oven to 400°F (200°C). Line the bottom and sides of a 9 x 12in (23 x 30cm) brownie pan, or similar, with parchment paper. Some should hang over the sides. Place the butter and chocolate in a heatproof bowl over a pan of simmering water. The bowl should not touch the water.

2 Melt the butter and chocolate, stirring until smooth. Remove and let cool. Once the mixture has cooled, mix in the sugar. Now add the eggs, a little at a time, mixing well between additions.

3 Fold in the flour and cocoa until the batter is smooth. Stir in the nuts to distribute them evenly; the batter should be thick.

4 Pour into the prepared pan and spread so the mixture fills the corners. Smooth the top. Bake for 12–15 minutes, or until just firm to the touch but still soft underneath. A skewer inserted should come out coated with a little batter. Remove from the oven.

5 Let the brownies cool completely in the pan to maintain the soft center. Lift the brownie from the pan using the edges of the parchment to get a good grip. Using a long, sharp, or serrated knife, score the surface of the brownie into 24 even pieces.

6 Cut the brownie into 24 pieces, dipping the knife in hot water between cuts and wiping it dry. Sift cocoa powder over the brownies. These will store in an airtight container for up to 3 days.

CALORIES: 243kcals/1021kJ
CARBOHYDRATE: 26g
  sugar: 20g
FAT: 14g
  saturated: 7g
SALT: trace
FIBER: 1g

Sour cherry and chocolate brownies

The sharp flavor and chewy texture of the cherries contrast wonderfully with the rich, dark chocolate.

15 mins | 20–25 mins

SPECIAL EQUIPMENT
9 x 12in (23 x 30cm) brownie pan, or similar

MAKES 16

11 tbsp unsalted butter, cut into cubes

5½oz (150g) good-quality dark chocolate, broken into pieces

1¼ cups llight brown muscovado sugar

3 large eggs, lightly beaten

1 tsp vanilla extract

1¼ cups self-rising flour, sifted

3½oz (100g) dried sour cherries

3½oz (100g) dark chocolate chunks

1 Preheat the oven to 350°F (180°C). Line a 9 x 12in (23 x 30cm) brownie pan, or similar, with parchment paper. Melt the butter and chocolate in a heatproof bowl over simmering water (the bowl should not touch the water). Stir in the sugar and cool slightly.

2 Mix the eggs and vanilla extract into the chocolate mixture. Pour the wet mix into the sifted flour and fold together, being careful not to over-mix. Fold in the sour cherries and chocolate chunks.

3 Pour the brownie mixture into the pan and bake in the center of the oven for 20–25 minutes. It is ready when the edges are firm, but the middle is soft to the touch.

4 Let the brownies cool in the pan for 5 minutes. Remove from the pan and cut into 16 squares, then transfer to a wire rack to cool. These will store in an airtight container for up to 3 days.

VARIATION

To make brownies so soft that they fall apart easily, reduce the cooking time by 5 minutes.

CALORIES: 273kcals/1146kJ
CARBOHYDRATE: 35g
  sugar: 29g
FAT: 13.5g
  saturated: 8g
SALT: 0.3g
FIBER: 1.5g

Layered carrot cake

This rich, heavily iced cake is multi-layered, and makes a really impressive centerpiece at any special occasion.

30 mins   45 mins

SPECIAL EQUIPMENT
2 x 8½in (22cm) springform cake pans
electric hand-held mixer

SERVES 10

5½oz (150g) walnuts

2 cups sunflower or vegetable oil, plus extra for greasing

6 large eggs, lightly beaten

2 tsp vanilla extract

2¼ cups light brown sugar

12oz (350g) finely grated carrots

5½oz (150g) golden raisins

3¾ cups self-rising flour, sifted

½ tsp salt

2 tsp ground cinnamon

2 tsp ground ginger

finely grated zest of 1 large orange

FOR THE ICING

11 tbsp butter, softened

5½oz (150g) cream cheese, softened

4¾ cups confectioners' sugar, sifted

finely grated zest of 2 oranges

2 tsp vanilla extract

1 Preheat the oven to 350°F (180°C). Grease two 8½in (22cm) springform cake pans and line the bottoms with parchment paper. Spread the walnuts on a baking sheet and toast in the oven for about 5 minutes, until lightly browned, watching carefully that they don't burn. Put the nuts into a clean kitchen towel, rub them to get rid of excess skin, then set aside to cool.

2 In a large bowl, whisk together the oil, eggs, vanilla extract, and sugar with an electric hand-held mixer until light, fluffy, and thickened. Put the grated carrot in a clean kitchen towel and squeeze out any excess liquid, then fold it into the cake batter until evenly mixed through.

3 Roughly chop the cooled walnuts and fold them into the mixture with the golden raisins. Finally fold in the flour, salt, spices, and orange zest and mix to combine.

4 Divide the mixture between the pans and bake in the center of the oven for 45 minutes, or until springy to the touch and a skewer inserted into the middle comes out clean from both cakes.

5 Let the cakes cool for 5 minutes in their pans, then turn them to cool completely on a wire rack. Once cool, halve each cake horizontally using a serrated knife to give you 4 layers of cake, keeping the layers an even thickness.

6 To make the icing, cream together the butter, cream cheese, confectioners' sugar, orange zest, and vanilla extract. Sandwich each layer of the cake together with a scant one-fifth of the icing and cover the top and sides of the cake with the remaining icing.

HOW TO FREEZE

The just-cooked, un-iced cakes can be wrapped individually in plastic wrap, sealed with foil, and frozen for up to 12 weeks. Defrost thoroughly before splitting and icing as in steps 5 and 6.

CALORIES: 1285kcals/5389kJ
CARBOHYDRATE: 154g
sugar: 117g
FAT: 68g
saturated: 19g
SALT: 1.2g
FIBER: 4.5g

Cherry and almond cake

The classic combination of flavors in this cake is always popular with guests.

20 mins   1½–1¾ hrs

SPECIAL EQUIPMENT
8in (20cm) deep round springform cake pan

electric hand-held mixer

SERVES 8–10

11 tbsp unsalted butter, softened, plus extra for greasing

⅔ cup granulated sugar

2 large eggs

2 cups self-rising flour, sifted

1 tsp baking powder

1⅓ cups ground almonds

1 tsp vanilla extract or almond extract

⅓ cup whole milk

14oz (400g) pitted cherries

scant 1oz (25g) blanched almonds, chopped

1 Preheat the oven to 350°F (180°C). Grease an 8in (20cm) deep round springform cake pan and line the bottom with parchment paper. Beat the butter and sugar with an electric hand-held mixer until creamy. Beat in the eggs 1 at a time, adding 1 tbsp of flour before the second egg.

2 Mix in the remaining flour, baking powder, ground almonds, vanilla extract, and milk. Mix in half the cherries, then spoon the mixture into the pan and smooth the top. Scatter the remaining cherries and the almonds over the surface.

3 Bake for 1½–1¾ hours, or until golden brown and firm to the touch. A skewer inserted into the cake should come out clean. If the surface of the cake starts to brown before it is fully cooked, cover with foil. When cooked, let cool in the pan for a few minutes, then remove the foil and parchment paper, and transfer to a wire rack to cool completely before serving.

VARIATION
This recipe has classic flavors, but, for a modern twist, use 3½oz (100g) of dried sour cherries instead of fresh.

CALORIES: 409kcals/1719kJ
CARBOHYDRATE: 38g
  sugar: 21g
FAT: 25g
  saturated: 10g
SALT: 0.4g
FIBER: 1.5g

Apple, raisin, and pecan cake

A healthier option, this cake contains only a little fat and is stuffed with fruit and nuts.

25 mins   30-35 mins

SPECIAL EQUIPMENT
9in (23cm) springform cake pan

SERVES 10–12

butter, for greasing

1¾oz (50g) shelled pecan nuts

7oz (200g) apples, peeled, cored, and cut into small cubes

5½oz (150g) brown sugar

9oz (250g) self-rising flour

1 tsp baking powder

2 tsp ground cinnamon

pinch of salt

3½ tbsp sunflower or vegetable oil

3½ tbsp milk, plus extra if necessary

2 large eggs, lightly beaten

1 tsp vanilla extract

1¾oz (50g) golden raisins

whipped cream or confectioners' sugar, to serve (optional)

CALORIES: 198kcals/835kJ
CARBOHYDRATE: 31.5g
  sugar: 17g
FAT: 7g
  saturated: 1g
SALT: 0.4g
FIBER: 1.5g

1 Preheat the oven to 350°F (180°C). Grease a 9in (23cm) springform cake pan and line the bottom with parchment paper. Place the nuts on a baking sheet and toast them in the oven for 5 minutes until golden. Cool and roughly chop.

2 In a large bowl, mix the apples and sugar together. Sift over the flour, baking powder, cinnamon, and salt, and fold them in. In a bowl, whisk together the oil, milk, eggs, and vanilla extract.

3 Pour the milk mixture into the flour mixture and stir until well combined. Fold in the pecans and golden raisins, then pour the batter into the prepared pan.

4 Bake in the center of the oven for 30–35 minutes, until a skewer comes out clean. Let cool for a few minutes in the pan, then turn onto a wire rack. Remove the parchment paper. Serve warm with whipped cream as a dessert, or cooled and dusted with sifted confectioners' sugar.

PREPARE AHEAD
The cake will keep in an airtight container for up to 3 days. The lack of fat means it isn't wise to keep it for longer because it will dry out.

Rosemary focaccia

This is a good-tempered dough that can be left in the fridge to rise overnight. Return to room temperature to bake.

30–35 mins, plus rising and proofing

15–20 mins

SPECIAL EQUIPMENT
15 x 9in (38 x 23cm) Swiss roll pan

SERVES 6–8

1 tbsp dried yeast

3⅓ cups white bread flour, plus extra for dusting

2 tsp salt

leaves from 5–7 rosemary sprigs, two-thirds finely chopped

6 tbsp olive oil, plus extra for greasing

¼ tsp freshly ground black pepper

sea salt flakes

1 Sprinkle the yeast over ¼ cup of warm water. Leave it for 5 minutes, stirring once. In a large bowl, mix the flour with the salt and make a well in the center. Add the chopped rosemary, 4 tbsp of the oil, the yeast mixture, pepper, and 1 cup of warm water.

2 Gradually draw in the flour and work it into the other ingredients to form a smooth dough. It should be soft and sticky, so do not be tempted to add more flour to dry it out. Sprinkle the dough lightly with flour and knead it for 5–7 minutes on a floured work surface.

3 When ready, the dough will be very smooth and elastic. Place in an oiled bowl. Cover with a damp kitchen towel. Let rise in a warm place for 1–1½ hours until doubled in size. Put the dough on a floured work surface and knock out the air. Cover with a dry kitchen towel and let it rest for about 5 minutes.

4 Brush a 15 x 9in (38 x 23cm) Swiss roll pan with oil. Transfer the dough to the pan. With your hands, flatten the dough to fill the pan evenly. Cover with a kitchen towel and let rise in a warm place for 35–45 minutes until it is puffed up.

5 Preheat the oven to 400°F (200°C). Scatter the reserved rosemary leaves on top. With your fingers, poke the dough all over to make deep dimples. Pour the remaining 2 tbsp of oil all over the dough and sprinkle with sea salt flakes. Bake on the top shelf of the oven for 15–20 minutes until browned. Transfer to a wire rack to cool.

VARIATION
For a roast garlic and sage version, omit the rosemary. Instead, add the chopped leaves from 3–5 sage sprigs, and incorporate 5–10 whole roast garlic cloves at the same time, to taste.

CALORIES: 231kcals/978kJ
CARBOHYDRATE: 40g
  sugar: 1g
FAT: 6g
  saturated: 1g
SALT: 1g
FIBER: 2g

Stuffed ciabatta

One of the simplest breads to master, a good ciabatta should be well risen and crusty, with large air pockets.

40 mins, plus proofing   50 mins– 1 hr 5 mins

MAKES 2 LOAVES

2 tsp dried yeast

6 tbsp olive oil, plus extra for greasing

2½ cups white bread flour, plus extra for dusting

1 tsp sea salt

1 red bell pepper, chopped into ½in (1cm) cubes

1 yellow bell pepper, chopped into ½in (1cm) cubes

1 red onion, chopped into ½in(1cm) cubes

1 eggplant, chopped into ½in (1cm) cubes

freshly ground black pepper

2 heaping tbsp pesto

> CALORIES: 1217kcals/5125kJ
> CARBOHYDRATE: 176g
>   sugar: 14g
> FAT: 45g
>   saturated: 5.5g
> SALT: 4g
> FIBER: 16g

1 Dissolve the yeast in 1½ cups of warm water, then add 4 tbsp of the oil. Put the flour and salt in a bowl. Stir in the yeast mixture to form a dough. Knead for 10 minutes, put in an oiled bowl, cover, and leave in a warm place for 2 hours, or until doubled in size.

2 Preheat the oven to 450°F (230°C). Mix the vegetables and remaining oil and season. Bake for 30–40 minutes, until crisp, then let cool.

3 Turn the dough onto a floured surface and knock it back. Form it into two 12 x 8in (30 x 20cm) rectangles. Top each with half the pesto and vegetables, then roll the loaves up like Swiss rolls.

4 Place, seam-side down, on floured baking sheets and tuck the ends under. Cover loosely with plastic wrap and a towel. Leave for 1 hour, or until doubled in size.

5 Preheat the oven again to 450°F (230°C). Spray the loaves with water. Bake for 20–25 minutes until hollow-sounding when tapped. Cool on wire racks.

Southern-style cornbread

This sweetish, rich loaf is traditionally served as an accompaniment for a barbecue, soup, or stew.

10-15 mins   25-35 mins

SPECIAL EQUIPMENT
7in (18cm) loose-bottomed round cake pan or similar-sized flameproof, cast-iron frying pan

SERVES 8

4 tbsp unsalted butter or bacon dripping, melted, and cooled, plus extra for greasing

2 cups fine cornmeal or polenta, (authentically white cornmeal, if you can find it)

2 tsp baking powder

½ tsp fine salt

2 large eggs, lightly beaten

1 cup buttermilk

1 tbsp honey (optional)

> CALORIES: 207kcals/867kJ
> CARBOHYDRATE: 25g
>   sugar: 3g
> FAT: 8g
>   saturated: 4g
> SALT: 0.7g
> FIBER: 1g

1 Preheat the oven to 425°F (220°C). Grease a 7in (18cm) loose-bottomed round cake pan or a similar-sized flameproof, cast-iron frying pan and heat it in the oven. In a bowl, mix the cornmeal, baking powder, and salt. In another bowl, whisk the eggs and buttermilk.

2 Make a well in the cornmeal and stir in the buttermilk mixture. Stir in the butter or bacon dripping, and honey (if using).

3 Remove the cake pan or frying pan from the oven and pour in the mixture. It should sizzle; this is what gives the distinctive crust.

4 Bake in the middle of the oven for 20–25 minutes until it has risen and is browning at the edges. Let cool for 5 minutes before turning out and slicing.

VARIATION

Add 1 red chile, seeded and finely chopped, and ¼ cup finely chopped cilantro with the honey.

Zucchini and feta loaf

This simple, savory loaf is the perfect, piquant accompaniment to a bowl of homemade soup on a cold day.

20 mins   **40–45 mins**

MAKES 1 LOAF

½ cup sunflower or vegetable oil

9oz (250g) zucchini, finely grated

½ tsp salt

1 cup all-purpose flour

½ cup whole wheat flour

1½ tsp baking powder

3 large eggs, lightly beaten

3–4 tbsp whole milk

2 heaping tbsp chopped parsley leaves

3½oz (100g) feta cheese, chopped

1 Preheat the oven to 350°F (180°C). Oil a 1lb (450g) loaf pan and line the bottom with parchment paper. Put the grated zucchini into a colander and toss them in the salt.

2 Sift the flours and baking powder into a large bowl and season well. Whisk the eggs, oil, and milk and mix into the flour.

3 Rinse the zucchini under cold water and press them down well in the colander to remove as much water as possible. Fold the zucchini, parsley, and feta into the loaf mixture.

4 Pour the mixture into the prepared loaf pan and bake in the center of the hot oven for 40–45 minutes, until a skewer inserted into the center comes out clean.

5 Remove the loaf from the oven and turn onto a wire rack. Allow it to cool for at least 10 minutes before cutting into it to serve warm; alternatively, allow it to cool completely before serving. If keeping the loaf for more than 1 day, wrap in plastic wrap and store in the fridge for up to 3 days, or freeze for up to 12 weeks.

CLEVER WITH LEFTOVERS

Although best served warm the same day, this bread is also great toasted, spread with cream cheese, and topped with sliced cucumber and freshly ground black pepper for a quick, healthy lunch.

CALORIES: 1911kcals/7978kJ

CARBOHYDRATE: 145g
sugar: 11g

FAT: 119g
saturated: 30g

SALT: 8g

FIBER: 17g

Zwiebelkuchen

The combination of sour cream and caraway seeds contrast well with the sweet, melting onions in this recipe.

30 mins, plus proving   1 hr–1 hr 5 mins

SPECIAL EQUIPMENT
10 x 13in (26 x 32cm) baking sheet with raised edges

SERVES 8

FOR THE CRUST
4 tsp dried yeast
3 tbsp olive oil, plus extra for greasing
3 cups white bread flour, plus extra for dusting
1 tsp salt

FOR THE FILLING
4 tbsp unsalted butter
2 tbsp olive oil
1lb 5oz (600g) onions, finely sliced
½ tsp caraway seeds
salt and freshly ground black pepper

⅔ cup (5oz) sour cream
⅔ cup (5oz) crème fraîche
3 large eggs, lightly beaten
1 tbsp all-purpose flour
2½oz (75g) thick-cut bacon, chopped

1 To make the crust, dissolve the yeast in 1 cup of warm water. Add the oil. Sift the flour and salt into a large bowl. Make a well and pour in the wet ingredients. Use your hands to form a soft dough. Turn onto a floured work surface and knead for 10 minutes until elastic.

2 Place the dough in an oiled bowl, cover with plastic wrap, and leave in a warm place for 1–2 hours until doubled in size.

3 For the filling, heat the butter and oil in a large, heavy-bottomed saucepan. Put in the onions and caraway seeds, and season. Cover and cook gently for 20 minutes until soft. Remove the lid and cook for 5 minutes until excess liquid evaporates.

4 In a separate bowl, whisk together the sour cream, crème fraîche, eggs, and all-purpose flour and season well. Mix in the cooked onions and set aside to cool.

5 When the dough has risen, turn it onto a floured work surface and knock it back. Lightly oil a 10 x 13in (26 x 32cm) baking sheet with raised edges. Roll the dough out to roughly the size of the sheet and line the sheet with it. Cover with lightly oiled plastic wrap and leave in a warm place for 30 minutes until puffy.

6 Preheat the oven to 400°F (200°C). Gently push down the dough. Spread the filling over and sprinkle the bacon on top.

7 Place on the top rack of the oven and bake for 35–40 minutes until golden. Remove and let cool for 5 minutes before serving warm or cold.

CALORIES: 480kcals/2008kJ
CARBOHYDRATE: 44g
  sugar: 6g
FAT: 29g
  saturated: 13g
SALT: 0.9g
FIBER: 3.5g

Anadama bread

This dark, sweet cornbread originally hails from New England. It is curiously sweet and savory at the same time.

25 mins, plus proving

45–50 mins

SERVES 4

½ cup whole milk

½ cup polenta or fine yellow cornmeal

4 tbsp unsalted butter, softened

½ cup blackstrap molasses

2 tsp dried yeast

2½ cups all-purpose flour, plus extra for dusting

1 tsp salt

vegetable oil, for greasing

1 large egg, lightly beaten, for glazing

CALORIES: 653kcals/2761kJ
CARBOHYDRATE: 111g
   sugar: 19g
FAT: 15g
   saturated: 8g
SALT: 1.2g
FIBER: 5g

1 Heat the milk and ½ cup of water in a small saucepan. Bring to a boil and add the polenta. Cook for 1–2 minutes or until it thickens, then remove from the heat. Stir in the butter until well mixed. Beat in the molasses, then set aside to cool.

2 Dissolve the yeast in ½ cup of warm water and stir well. Sift the flour and salt into a bowl and make a well. Gradually stir in the polenta mixture, then add the yeast mixture to make a soft, sticky dough.

3 Turn the dough onto a lightly floured work surface. Knead for about 10 minutes until soft and elastic. It will remain fairly sticky, but should not stick to your hands. Knead in a little flour if it seems too wet. Put the dough in a lightly oiled bowl, cover loosely with plastic wrap, and let rise in a warm place for up to 2 hours. The dough will not double in size, but should be very soft and pliable when well-risen.

4 Turn the dough onto a lightly floured work surface and gently knock it back. Knead it briefly and shape it into a flattened oval, tucking the sides underneath the center of the dough to get a tight, even shape. Place on a large baking sheet and cover loosely with plastic wrap and a clean kitchen towel. Let it rise in a warm place for about 2 hours. The dough is ready to bake when it is tight and well risen, and a finger gently poked into the dough leaves a dent that springs back quickly.

5 Preheat the oven to 350°F (180°C). Place one oven rack in the middle of the oven and another below it, close to the bottom. Boil a pot of water. Brush the loaf with a little beaten egg and slash the top 2 or 3 times with a sharp knife on a diagonal. Dust the top with flour, if desired, and place it on the middle rack. Place a roasting pan on the bottom rack, then quickly pour the boiling water into it and shut the door.

6 Bake for 45–50 minutes until the crust is nicely darkened and the bottom sounds hollow when tapped. Remove from the oven and let cool on a wire rack. Serve with Emmental or Gruyère cheese, or buttered and topped with ham and mustard.

COOK'S TIP

Slashing the loaf allows the bread to continue rising in the oven, and so does the steam from the pan of boiling water. They also help to give the bread a good crust.

Cornbread

While bread is satisfying to make, it is a lengthy process and can be quite difficult. Cornbread rises with baking powder, not yeast, so is quicker to prepare and easier to produce. Young bakers should start out with easy recipes such as this. Adding corn to the batter is another thing guaranteed to please children and adults alike.

15–20 mins   10 mins, plus cooling

SPECIAL EQUIPMENT

9in (23cm) flameproof cast-iron frying pan or similar-sized loose-bottomed round cake pan

SERVES 8

4 tbsp unsalted butter or bacon dripping, melted and cooled, plus extra for greasing

2 corn cobs, approx. 7oz (200g) weight of kernels

1 cup fine yellow cornmeal or polenta

¾ cup white bread flour

¼ cup granulated sugar

1 tbsp baking powder

1 tsp salt

2 large eggs

1 cup milk

VARIATION

Try adding scraps of fried bacon, scallions, or grilled red bell peppers to the batter. A handful of grated cheese, some fresh herbs, chopped chiles, or even some smoked paprika would also work well.

Cook's tip

Cornbread is delicious eaten when it's still warm, but it doesn't keep well. It is easy to prepare, so try and make it on the day you want to eat it. Any leftovers work really well used as part of a stuffing for a roast chicken.

CALORIES: 272kcals/1143kJ

CARBOHYDRATE: 36g
  sugar: 8g

FAT: 10.5g
  saturated: 5.5g

SALT: 1.1g

FIBER: 2g

1 Preheat the oven to 425°F (220°C) Grease a 9in (23cm) flameproof cast-iron pan, or similar-sized loose-bottomed cake pan, and place it in the oven. Cut away the kernels from the cobs.

2 Sift the cornmeal or polenta, flour, sugar, baking powder, and salt into a bowl. Add the corn and stir until evenly blended. In another bowl, mix together the eggs, butter or dripping, and milk.

3 Pour three-quarters of the milk mixture into the flour mixture and stir until well combined. Add the remaining milk mixture and stir just until blended, with no patches of flour remaining.

4 Carefully take the hot pan out of the oven and pour in the batter, using a spatula to help you get it all into the pan, and working quickly so as not to lose too much heat; the fat in the pan should sizzle.

5 Quickly brush the top with butter or bacon dripping. Be as even as possible so that the surface of the cornbread is protected from the fierce heat of the oven. Bake for 20–25 minutes.

6 When it is ready, the bread should shrink from the sides of the pan and a skewer inserted into the center should emerge clean. Let the cornbread cool slightly. Serve, in wedges, with soup.

Shrimp and vegetable kebabs

Children really like to eat things on sticks, perhaps because it allows them to eat with their fingers. Compiling skewers of their own mean children can add their favorite flavors, and maybe try a few new ones, too. These kebabs are crammed full of healthy vegetables and low-fat protein, and make a fun option at a summer barbecue.

25 mins, plus marinating   15 mins

SPECIAL EQUIPMENT

4 bamboo skewers

rectangular dish that will fit the length of the skewers

SERVES 4

FOR THE MARINADE

juice of 1 lemon

juice of 1 lime

2 tbsp reduced-salt soy sauce

1 garlic clove, crushed or finely chopped

1 tsp light brown sugar

FOR THE KEBABS

½ red bell pepper

½ yellow bell pepper

½ red onion

1 small zucchini

8 cherry tomatoes

5½oz (150g) cooked, shelled, and deveined large shrimp

salad, to serve (optional)

! Use scissors to snip the sharp end off the skewers before eating, to avoid accidents.

Cook's tip

If you are using wooden skewers under a gas grill or on a barbecue they can burn. To avoid this, soak the skewers for at least 30 minutes in cold water before using.

CALORIES: 70kcals/292kJ

CARBOHYDRATE: 7.5g
  sugar: 6.5g

FAT: 0.5g
  saturated: 0.1g

SALT: 1.2g

FIBER: 2g

1 Soak 4 bamboo skewers in water for 30 minutes. Make the marinade by mixing the ingredients together in a glass container. Carefully cut the peppers and red onion into chunks. Slice the zucchini.

2 Thread the vegetables and shrimp onto the skewers, being sure that each kebab gets a piece of everything. Place the kebabs into a rectangular dish long enough to fit them.

3 Pour the marinade over the kebabs, then turn to coat, so that all sides of the kebabs are coated in marinade. Cover, and put the kebabs into the fridge for 1 hour. Turn them over again after 30 minutes.

4 Ask an adult to preheat a broiler to its highest setting, and to broil the kebabs for 15 minutes, turning to cook all sides evenly. Baste the shrimp every 5 minutes with the marinade (discard any leftover marinade).

Granola breakfast bars

Most children love to bake, but eating the results of their efforts may not always be the healthiest thing. Try baking this modern take on an old-fashioned favorite—oatmeal cookies. Granola breakfast bars make a perfect breakfast-on-the-go for hurried teens, or a lunch-box treat for children of all ages.

15 mins   30 mins, plus cooling

SPECIAL EQUIPMENT
12 x 9 x 1½in (30 x 23 x 4cm) baking pan

MAKES 12

8 tbsp butter, plus extra for greasing

½ cup light brown sugar

½ cup corn syrup or honey

3⅓ cups rolled oats

3½oz (100g) raisins

1¾oz (50g) mixed nuts, chopped

VARIATION

This basic recipe can be varied to suit the tastes and ages of your children. Kids can add any combination of dried fruit, nuts, and seeds they like, as long as the overall weight remains the same. A handful of chocolate chips would also be fun.

Cook's tip

A potato masher will help little hands to get the breakfast bars well compressed in the baking pan and evenly spread the mix around before cooking.

CALORIES: 266kcals/1113kJ

CARBOHYDRATE: 36g
  sugar: 21g

FAT: 12g
  saturated: 6g

SALT: 0.17g

FIBER: 2.3g

1 Ask an adult to preheat the oven to 300°F (150°C). Grease your baking pan. Ask an adult to melt the butter, sugar, and corn syrup or honey in a saucepan over low heat.

2 Measure out the rolled oats, raisins, and mixed nuts and place them into a large mixing bowl. Mix in the melted ingredients from the saucepan, using a wooden spoon to combine them evenly.

3 Spread the mixture evenly in a 12 x 9 x 1½in (30 x 23 x 4cm) baking pan, using a potato masher to help compress the mixture well down in the pan. Bake for 20–30 minutes, or until golden brown.

4 When the mixture is baked, let it cool slightly. When cool enough to handle, cut it into 12 squares with a knife, holding the warm pan with a cloth. Take the squares out when they're cold.

Crunchy muffins

Muffins are a good alternative to a whole cake when it comes to baking with children. They are easy to make, and quick to cook. In addition, they come in individual portions, and impatient young cooks do not have to wait until they are cold to fill or ice them. The method for muffins is very forgiving, and allows for a few lumps in the batter.

30-35 mins | 25 mins, plus cooling

SPECIAL EQUIPMENT

12 paper muffin liners

12-hole muffin pan

MAKES 12

1¾ cups all-purpose flour

1 tbsp baking powder

½ tsp salt

½ cup granulated sugar

1 large egg

2 tbsp vegetable oil

1 cup whole milk

4½oz (125g) raspberries

5½oz (150g) white chocolate, finely chopped

3oz (85g) crunchy oat cereal

VARIATION

Frozen raspberries would be fine for this recipe, as long as you thaw them completely. Try using other fresh or frozen fruits, such as strawberries, blueberries, or blackberries. Nuts, dried fruits, or chocolate chips would also taste great!

Cook's tip

The good thing about muffins is that it doesn't matter if the batter is a little lumpy. In fact, an over-whisked batter will result in heavy, dense muffins, so this a perfect recipe to try with young children.

CALORIES: 271kcals/1141kJ

CARBOHYDRATE: 37g
sugar: 21g

FAT: 9g
saturated: 3.5g

SALT: 0.7g

FIBER: 1.5g

1 Ask an adult to preheat the oven to 400°F (200°C). Sift the all-purpose flour, baking powder, and salt into a mixing bowl, tapping the edges to encourage it to slip through. Stir in the sugar.

2 Crack the egg into a glass measuring cup and add the oil. Beat the egg and oil together with a whisk until they are light and fluffy. Add the milk and then whisk the mixture until well combined.

3 Fold the egg mixture into the flour mixture. The mixture will be lumpy but, when you have finished mixing, no flour should be visible in the batter. Now fold in the raspberries and chocolate.

4 Put 12 paper muffin liners into a 12-hole muffin pan and spoon the mixture into them, being sure to divide it equally between the liners. The easiest way is to use two teaspoons.

5 Sprinkle some of the crunchy oat cereal on top of each muffin, dividing it equally between them. Bake the muffins in the center of the hot oven for 25 minutes, or until risen and golden.

6 Remove the muffins from the oven and allow them to cool for 5 minutes in the muffin pan, or until cool enough to handle. Now carefully and gently transfer each one to a wire rack to cool completely.

White chocolate bark

This very easy treat uses dried fruits and nuts to make a snack that is a little more nutritious than most chocolate.

10 mins,
plus cooling

MAKES 14OZ (400G)

10oz (300g) good-quality white chocolate, broken into squares

4½oz (125g) mixed dried fruits and nuts, such as dried cranberries, dried apricots, sliced almonds, or shelled unsalted pistachios

CALORIES:	140kcals/583kJ
CARBOHYDRATE:	12g
sugar:	12g
FAT:	9g
saturated:	4g
SALT:	trace
FIBER:	0.5g

1 Put the white chocolate in a heatproof bowl and melt it gently over a saucepan of simmering water, stirring occasionally. Make sure that the bowl does not touch the water. Be very careful that no water splashes into the chocolate, as this will make it harden.

2 When the chocolate has melted, remove it from the heat and allow it to cool slightly. On a cutting board, cut up your selection of dried fruits and nuts as small as you can. Set aside 2 tbsp of this mixture, then mix the rest into the chocolate.

3 Brush a small baking sheet with water (to help the waxed paper stay in place), and line it with a piece of waced paper, cut to fit. Pour the chocolate mixture onto the paper and spread it out as thinly as you can, using the

back of a damp spoon, making sure there are no gaps. It may not cover the whole pan, but aim for a square measuring 11in (28cm). Scatter the reserved pieces of fruits and nuts over the top and gently press them into the surface with the spoon.

4 Put the chocolate in the fridge for 15 minutes. Now remove the half-set bark and carefully lift it, including the waxed paper, onto a cutting board. Cut the chocolate into squares, leaving it on the paper, then put it back on the pan and return it to the fridge until it hardens. This should take at least 30 minutes. Once it has hardened, break it into squares along the pre-cut lines. These will keep in an airtight container in the fridge for up to 5 days.

VARIATION

For a special, though less nutritious, treat you can use colored sweets and small chocolate treats, instead of the fruits and nuts, for a double chocolate delight.

Chocolate is a great way to introduce nuts into the diet of a child who is otherwise not keen on them. Remember it is vital to check first for nut allergies before offering these to anyone.

Fussy eaters!

Gingerbread men

Making gingerbread men is practically a rite of passage for children. They are quick and easy to make, and the decorating is definitely the most fun a child can have in the kitchen. Get creative with colored icing and even small sweets. This dough is also quite tough, and will withstand several rollings, unlike other cookie doughs.

20 mins | 10–12 mins, plus cooling

SPECIAL EQUIPMENT

4½in (11cm) gingerbread man cutter

piping bag with thin nozzle (optional)

MAKES 16

1¾ cups all-purpose flour, plus extra for dusting

1 tsp baking soda

1½ tsp ground ginger

1½ tsp pumpkin pie spice

7 tbsp unsalted butter, softened and cut into cubes

¾ cup dark brown sugar

¼ cup molasses

1 large egg, lightly beaten

raisins, to decorate

confectioners' sugar, sifted (optional)

PREPARE AHEAD

If you plan to make these with very young children, and want to get to the fun part, prepare the dough ahead of time and chill for up to 2 days, well wrapped in plastic wrap. Bring it back to room temperature before rolling it out.

Cook's tip

For home-made Christmas presents or party bag treats, get your children to make personalised gingerbread men for their guests and wrap them in individual bags, decorated with a pretty ribbon, for a simple gift.

CALORIES: 165kcals/698kJ

CARBOHYDRATE: 26g
  sugar: 13g

FAT: 6g
  saturated: 2.5g

SALT: 0.3g

FIBER: 0.8g

1 Preheat the oven to 375°F (190°C). Sift the flour, baking soda, and spices into a bowl. Rub in the butter with your fingers until it looks like crumbs. Mix in the sugar.

2 Beat the egg into the molasses. Make a well in the flour mixture, pour in the molasses, and bring into a dough. Knead on a floured work surface until smooth. Flour the dough and roll it out to ¼in (5mm) thick.

3 Using a 4½in (11cm) cutter, cut out as many shapes as possible. Transfer to non-stick baking sheets. Mix the scraps of dough, re-roll, and cut out more shapes until all the dough is used.

4 Decorate the men with raisins, giving them eyes, a nose, and buttons down the front. Bake for 10–12 minutes until golden. Transfer carefully to a wire rack with a palette knife to cool completely.

5 If using, mix a little confectioners' sugar in a bowl with enough water to form a thin icing. Transfer the icing into a piping bag with a thin nozzle; placing the bag into a bowl to catch the drips first will help.

6 Decorate the men with the piped icing to resemble clothes, hair, or whatever you prefer; use your imagination (you can also use the icing to stick on other decorations). Let set completely before serving.

Raspberry cream meringues

These pretty little confections are the perfect thing to make for a summer party. If you are entertaining, try getting the kids to prepare them. Meringues are fairly easy to cook (especially small ones), as long as the humidity is not too high where you live. Make sure they are well whisked and cooked long and low and you can't go wrong.

10 mins   1 hr, plus cooling

SPECIAL EQUIPMENT

piping bag with plain nozzle (optional)

MAKES 6–8

4 egg whites, at room temperature (each medium egg white should weigh about 1oz/30g)

about 1 cup granulated sugar (you will need exactly double the weight of sugar to egg whites)

FOR THE FILLING

1¼ cups heavy cream

3½oz (100g) raspberries

1 tbsp confectioners' sugar, sifted

VARIATION

For sweet canapés, pipe smaller meringues and cook for 45 minutes; this makes about 20 filled meringues.

PREPARE AHEAD

The unfilled meringues can be kept in an airtight container for up to 3 days before filling and serving.

Cook's tip

Any crushed soft fruit can be used in the filling, such as strawberries or blueberries. If it seems too liquid once mashed, leave it in a sieve to drip over a bowl for 5 minutes before adding to the cream, to stop the filling from being too runny.

CALORIES: 320kcals/1337kJ

CARBOHYDRATE: 32g
  sugar: 32g

FAT: 8g
  saturated: 4.5g

SALT: trace

FIBER: 0.15g

1 Ask an adult to preheat the oven to around 250°F (130°C). Line a baking sheet with parchment paper. Whisk the egg whites in a metal bowl until they are stiff and form strong peaks.

2 Gradually add half the sugar, 2 tbsp at a time, whisking in between additions. Gently fold the remaining sugar into the egg whites, trying to lose as little air as possible.

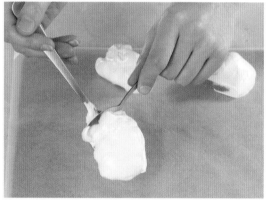

3 Put tablespoons on the baking sheet, leaving 2in (5cm) gaps between; or use a piping bag with a plain nozzle. Bake in the center of the oven for 1 hour, until they lift easily and sound hollow when tapped.

4 Turn off the oven and let the meringues cool inside. Remove to a wire rack until cold. Next, in a bowl, whisk up the heavy cream until billowing and firm, but not stiff.

5 Put the raspberries in a separate bowl and crush them with the back of a fork, so they break up. Then gently fold together the cream and crushed raspberries, and combine with the confectioners' sugar.

6 Spread a little of the raspberry mixture onto the flat bases of half the meringues. Top each with one of the remaining meringue halves and gently press them together to form sandwiches.

Chocolate fudge cake balls

A really great recipe for children. The soft, gooey interior contrasts wonderfully with the crisp casing. Not only do these taste good, but they are also really fun to make. Rolling the balls and dipping them in chocolate is messy, but highly enjoyable. They will make an attractive addition to a children's birthday party.

35 mins   25 mins

SPECIAL EQUIPMENT
electric hand-held mixer

7in (18cm) round cake pan

food processor with blade attachment

MAKES 20–25

7 tbsp unsalted butter, softened, or soft margarine, plus extra for greasing

½ cup granulated sugar

2 large eggs

⅔ cup self-rising flour, sifted

¼ cup cocoa powder, sifted

1 tsp baking powder

1 tbsp milk

5½oz (150g) store-bought chocolate fudge frosting

9oz (250g) dark chocolate coating bark

1¾oz (50g) white chocolate

VARIATION
Try varying these by using a plain vanilla cake and butter icing. Coat them in white chocolate and dip in shredded coconut for some pretty white "snowballs" at Christmas.

Cook's tip
If time is short, or your children very young, packaged or leftover cake can be used, and even store-bought frosting will work here.

CALORIES: 136kcals/570kJ

CARBOHYDRATE: 15g
    sugar: 12g

FAT: 8g
    saturated: 4.5g

SALT: 0.15g

FIBER: 0.5g

1 Ask an adult to preheat the oven to 350°F (180°C). With an electric hand-held mixer, cream the butter and sugar. Beat in the eggs one at a time. Fold in the flour, cocoa, and baking powder. Mix in the milk.

2 Grease a 7in (18cm) round cake pan and line it with parchment paper. Spoon in the batter and bake for 25 minutes until springy to the touch. Get an adult to turn it onto a wire rack to cool completely.

3 Pulse the cake in a food processor fitted with a blade attachment until it looks like breadcrumbs. Add the frosting and blend together to a smooth, uniform mix.

4 Using dry hands, roll the cake mix into balls, each the size of a walnut. Put the balls on a plate, cover, and refrigerate for 3 hours, or freeze for 30 minutes until firm. Line 2 baking sheets with parchment paper.

5 Melt the cake covering according to the package instructions. Using 2 forks, coat the balls in chocolate one at a time. Remove, allowing excess to drip. Transfer the balls to the baking sheets to dry.

6 Ask an adult to melt the white chocolate in a bowl placed over a pan of boiling water. Drizzle it over the balls with a spoon. Let them dry completely before transferring to a serving plate.

About the author

Caroline Bretherton is a busy working mom of two boys and knows the challenges of feeding a growing family only too well. Her love of cooking healthy, fresh food has helped her immensely. Caroline has worked in the food industry for almost 20 years. Her enthusiasm and skills helped her start her own catering company, which soon led to the establishment of an eatery in the heart of London's Notting Hill—Manna Café. Over the years she has worked consistently in television, presenting a wide range of food programs, as well as in print media, contributing to *The Times* as their family food writer. She has already published three books with DK Publishing: *The Kitchen Garden Cookbook*, *Illustrated Step-by-Step Baking*, and *Pies: Sweet and Savory*. Caroline is married and currently living in South Carolina.

The author would like to thank

Peggy Vance, Dawn Henderson, and Scarlett O'Hara at Dorling Kindersley for all their help and encouragement with this massive task. Borra Garson and all at Deborah McKenna for their work on my behalf. Jane Bamforth for her much valued help and recipe contribution and Lucy Bannell for her work as recipe editor. Finally, I would like to thank my family—Luke, Gabriel, and Isaac, whose critical palates and tireless consumption of far too much food helped to shape this book.

DK would like to thank

New photography: Lis Parsons, William Reavell, Stuart West **Photography art direction:** Susan Downing, Geoff Fennell, Lisa Pettibone, Penny Stock **Food styling:** Emma-Jane Frost, Paul Jackman, Jane Lawrie, Rosie Reynolds, Penny Stephens **Prop styling:** Susan Downing, Liz Hippisley, Wei Tang **Photography shoot manager:** Anne Fisher **Design assistance:** Mandy Earey, Kate Fenton, Vanessa Hamilton, Heather Matthews **Editorial assistance:** Priyanka Chatterjee, Christopher Mooney Elizabeth Yeates **Consultant for Babies and Toddlers chapter:** Rosan Meyer **Proofreading:** Claire Cross **Nutritionist:** Fiona Hunter **Indexer:** Liz Cook **Recipe testers:** Jane Bamforth, Ramona Andrews, Anna Burges-Lumsden, Amy Carter, Sue Davie, Francesca Dennis, Hulya Erdal, Georgina Fuggle, Jan Fullwood, Anne Harnan, Richard Harris, Sue Harris, Jo Kerr, Sarah King, Emma Lahaye, Bren Parkins-Knight, Ann Reynolds, Cathy Seward, Rachel Wood, and Amanda Wright.